1998 - 1999

American Business in China

美　商　在　中　國

Includes: -Directory of U.S. Firms Operating in China & Hong Kong
-Hong Kong: A Special Administrative Region
-Exporting to China: Best U.S. Export Prospects
-Marketing, Exhibiting, and Advertising in China
-China's Major Technology Projects till Year 2000
-China's Major Cities for Foreign Investment

Editor: Davisson K. Chang

Resources for US-China Trade

CARAVEL, INC.

23545 Crenshaw Blvd., Suite 101E
Torrance, CA 90505, USA

Tel: 310-325-0100
Fax: 310-325-2583

Published by Caravel, Inc.
23545 Crenshaw Blvd., #101E
Torrance, CA 90505, U.S.A.

ISBN-0-96-44322-9-3: US$93.00

American Business in China: 1st edition published - 1995
2nd edition published - 1998

Printed in the United States of America

The New Frontier in the 21st Century

*When the world's largest developed economy
meets
the world's largest developing economy...*

by Davisson K. Chang

As we approach the end of the century and the millennium, it is a good opportunity to review the role of the United States in the world economy and examine new prospects for the new era. The innovation of technology, development of internet services, breakthroughs in overcoming barriers among trading partners, have all made the entire world a single market place. As the world's largest untapped market, China is extending its industrial revolution and the world braces for a new economic superpower.

Due to the rapid growth of US-China trade in recent years, China has become the fourth largest trading partner of the U.S. by the end of 1996, while it ranked only 24th in 1980. Based on the official statistics from the Department of Commerce, U.S. exports to China in 1996 totaled $11.7 billion, which accounted for only 1.5% of the total U.S. exports, and yet the trade deficit with China was $39.5 billion. What's more, this trade imbalance is worsening as China may soon take the place of Japan and become the No. 1 nation in attributing to the overall U.S. trade deficit.

As China has substantially lowered its import tariff from an average rate of 43.2% in 1992 to the current 17%, exports to China represents a strong growth area for U.S. firms. In fact, the U.S. is the undisputed leader in exports of services to the rest of the world. Nonetheless, the U.S. surplus with China on services was only $2 billion in 1996. This is in sharp contrast to the imbalance with Japan, in which the U.S. surplus on services was a whopping $20 billion, nearly half the $48 billion deficit on merchandises. As China is slowly deregulating its markets in service sectors, one of the biggest areas for potential growth in U.S. exports of services is China. With regard to China's non-tariff measures, the number of products subject to licensing controls has dropped dramatically from 1,247 to only 384 items, and the number is expected to fall even further in the near future.

A "Directory of U.S. Firms Operating in China and Hong Kong" is included in this second edition to facilitate networking among U.S. firms interested in exploring opportunities in China. At least one mailing was sent to the U.S. head office of each company listed in the directory, prior to the publication of this book. The directory was compiled from questionnaires returned by companies themselves, or from other reliable sources. A great deal of time and effort was exhausted in the process of collecting and compiling data listed. While every effort was made to ensure accuracy, information may change even within a short period of time. If errors are found, we will strive to correct them in preparing future editions. If your company is not listed in this edition and would like to be included in the next edition, please contact us.

We have worked diligently to make this publication a useful reference for people interested in doing business with China. Comments are welcome and, best of luck on your ventures in China!

Davisson Chang is the Series Editor for the *American Business in China* and the *Chinese Business in America.* Since 1993, he has been the president of Caravel, Inc., a leading information company specialized in US-China trade. Between 1987 and 1993, he started a new import/export business in New York and successfully sold consumer goods to J.C. Penney, May Co., MACYS, Nordstrom and other mass merchandisers in the U.S. Prior to that, Mr. Chang had worked for multinationals including Bechtel and General Electric. He has an MBA from San Jose State University and an M.S. from University of California, Berkeley. He received his B.S. degree from National Taiwan University in Taipei, Taiwan.

ACKNOWLEDGMENTS

A special note of gratitude is due to the following organizations for
their contributions
and
immeasurable support
during the revision of this publication:

American Embassy, Beijing
American Consulate General, Chengdu
American Consulate General, Guangzhou
American Consulate General, Hong Kong
American Consulate General, Shanghai
American Consulate General, Shenyang
Hong Kong Economic & Trade Office

Contents

Your Financial Bridge Between East and West

East West Bank's strength on both sides of the Pacific provides the expertise our clients need to do business in today's global markets. The Bank's prestigious parent group, Gajah Tunggal, is comprised of over 50 companies in diversified industries in tha Asia Pacific region. East West Bank is among the 5 largest commercial banks headquartered in Southern California.

We specialize in:

- **International Trade Financing** *(Victor Naramura)*
- **Commercial Lending** *(William Chu)*
- **Construction/Real Estate Lending** *(Donald Chow)*
- **Residential Lending** *(Robert Camerota)*

Please Call: 1-888-GO-TO-EWB

1. Profile of the People's Republic of China (PRC)

1.1 Overview

a. PRC is the world's third largest country, next to Russia and Canada.

b. PRC has a population of approximately 1.25 billion people, which constitutes about 22% of the world's population.

c. PRC is divided into 22 provinces, 4 municipalities, 5 autonomous regions and one special administrative region (i.e., Hong Kong). These 32 areas all have equal political status and report directly to the State Council on all matters.

d. PRC has been transforming from a state-controlled economy to market-driven economy in recent years. From 1992 to 1996, the average annual growth rate of PRC's GDP is 12.1% whereas the average growth rate of the developed countries in the same period is merely 2%.

e. From 1992 to 1996, PRC's utilization of accumulated foreign capital is US$200.43 billion. Since 1994, PRC has continuously ranked 2nd in the world in attracting foreign capital, next to the U.S.

1.2 Economy

a. Size of Economy (excluding Hong Kong & Macao)

Year	Total GDP (US$)	Growth	Remarks
1978	$ 25.0 billion		Baseline year for economic reform
1991	372.1 billion		Equal to 10% of Japan's total GDP
1993	562.5 billion	12.7%	
1994	633.3 billion	12.6%	Equal to 9% of total GDP of the U.S.
1995	696.6 billion	10.0%	
1996	818.0 billion		Ranked 7th* in the world
1997	890.8 billion	8.9%	
1998		6% - 8%	Estimated
2025			Equal to the total GDP of the U.S. (Estimated)

* After U.S., Japan, Germany, France, Italy, United Kingdom

b. Foreign Exchange Reserves (excluding Hong Kong & Macao)

Year	Foreign Exchange Reserves (US $)	Remarks
1992	$19.4 billion	
1993	21.2 billion	
1994	51.6 billion	
1995	73.6 billion	
1996	105.0 billion	
1997 (September)	134.1 billion	Ranked 2nd in the world, next to Japan

c. As of to date, PRC maintains the largest state-run economy in the world and yet a large number of PRC's state-owned enterprises are inefficient and over-staffed. It is estimated some of these enterprises support two to three times the number of workers they actually need. In the Fifteenth National Congress of the People's Communist Party held in September 1977, the official ruling party of China decided it would:

1). begin selling ownership of unprofitable state-owned enterprises to private sectors; or,

2). merge unprofitable state-owned enterprises with other enterprises; or,

3). shut down certain unprofitable state-owned enterprises.

1.3 International Trade

a. Size of Foreign Trade

Year	Total Value of Imports (US$ million)	Total Value of Exports (US$ million)
1991	63,791	71,842
1992	80,545	84,940
1993	103,950	91,763
1994	115,693	121,038
1995	132,078	148,770
1996	136,335	153,565
1997	142,360	182,700

b. Major Trading Partners in 1997

Rank	Import From	Export To
1	Japan	Hong Kong
2	Taiwan	Japan
3	U.S.	U.S.
4	Hong Kong	Germany
5	Germany	South Korea
6	South Korea	Russia

c. US-China Trade

Year	Import From the U.S.	Export to the U.S.	Trade Balance
1995	$11.7 billion	$45.6 billion	$33.9 billion
1996	$11.9 billion	$51.4 billion	$39.5 billion
1997 (Jan-June)	$5.8 billion	$27.0 billion	$21.2 billion

1.4 Legal System

China is primarily a civil code country and its legal system is based on codified laws. Case precedents are generally not recognized.

a. Business Law - Formation and operation of business entities in China must be in compliance with general statues in the Civil Code. Foreign enterprises with representative offices in China must be registered under the Provisional Regulations for Handling of Long-Term Representatives of Foreign Enterprises.

For many years, the highly personalized nature of conducting business in China, coupled with a lack of litigating tradition, often make arbitration or other legal remedies impractical when disputes arise. In addition, PRC authorities prefer resolving disputes through informal or personal conciliation. Litigation is usually regarded as a final option. In other words, Chinese enterprises prefer to negotiate first, arbitrate second, and litigate only in extreme situations.

In 1992, the Beijing Conciliation Center (BCC) signed an agreement with the American Arbitration Association (AAA) whereby the BCC and AAA would work together in joint effort to resolve trade and investment disputes between U.S. and Chinese parties.

b. Civil Code - Chinese law is held applicable to civil activities in China, as is Civil Law, which is applicable to foreigners, stateless persons, and citizens unless otherwise specified.

Heart to Heart International

Heart to Heart AIRLIFT to China

Help send a gesture of goodwill to the people of China!

Following its successful Goodwill Medical Airlift to Chengdu and the Sichuan Province in April 1997, Heart to Heart International has received a gracious invitation from the Chinese government to undertake another medical airlift into China's interior, where millions of people face shortages of food and medicine. The airlift will coincide with the Central Government's five-year **"Poverty Alleviation Campaign"** to eliminate these shortages and help people attain a level of sufficiency by 2000.

Heart to Heart is sending a medical airlift in April 1998

• A multimillion-dollar airlift of 30-40 tons of life-saving pharmaceuticals and medical supplies will be sent to hospitals in Chongqing along the Yangtze River in the Three Gorges area.

• Pharmaceutical companies, key corporations, and individuals in numerous countries can help support this humanitarian airlift.

• Heart to Heart is working with the U.S. Embassy, the Chinese Ministry of Health, health care professionals, and numerous caring corporations and individuals to coordinate the shipment.

• FedEx is donating an aircraft and EAS International Ltd. will provide in-land transportation. Heart to Heart seeks to raise $325,000 to cover the cost of procuring the aid.

• A delegation of Heart to Heart staff, business and civic leaders, health care professionals, and others will join the China airlift to distribute supplies and provide accountability.

• Heart to Heart International is a grassroots network which empowers volunteers to mobilize resources and meet needs throughout the world. The organization facilitates projects that alleviate suffering in several areas around the world. *In six short years, Heart to Heart has distributed more than $115 million (U.S. wholesale) in aid — medicines, medical supplies, nutritional products, and other provisions.* Heart to Heart has organized 17 major medical airlifts, responded to disasters with volunteers and supplies, and launched a program to meet the needs of the poor in the United States. More than 98 percent of Heart to Heart contributions goes directly to its relief efforts.

HEART TO HEART INTERNATIONAL

Call Heart to Heart for more information! **001-913-764-5200**

E-Mail: 102223.1246@compuserve.com
Website: www.hearttoheart.org

For more information about helping with the China airlift, please return form to:

**Heart to Heart Intl.
13849 S. Murlen, Suite F
Olathe, KS 66062**

Name _____

Company _____

Address _____

City _____ State _____ Zip _____

Phone (_____) _____

1.5 Foreign Investment

a. Foreign Investment Policy

With a population of 1.2 billion people and double digit annual growth rate, PRC is the most populous country and the largest emerging economy in the world. With sweeping reforms, PRC has transformed its state-run economy into a vital, market-driven economy. In order to attract foreign investment to boost the national economy, PRC has designated a number of regions, such as Special Economic Zones (SEZ) and Open Cities, where foreign investors receive preferential tax treatments. Production and industry have posted major gains, especially in coastal areas where foreign investment and modern production technology have spurred strong economic growth.

Although the preferential tax policy is currently fading out in certain areas, PRC will continue to encourage and promote foreign investment in inland provinces, autonomous regions, and border areas. Foreign investment are particularly encouraged in the following sectors:

- Infrastructures: highways, airports, wharves, etc.

- Key industries: energy, telecommunications, aviation & transportation, etc.

- Service industry: finance, banking, tourism, etc.

- Reform and technological transformation of state-owned enterprises: the portion of such enterprises to the entire businesses has decreased from 77.6% in 1980 to 42.8% in 1995.

b. Current Trend and Regulation Changes in 1996 & 1997

- On October 1, 1997, PRC has lowered the import tariff rate on more than 4,800 products. The average import tariff rate has reduced from 23% to 17% based on this adjustment.

- On April 1, 1996, PRC repealed the tax and tariff exemptions of imports of capital equipment for foreign-investment enterprises (FIEs). However, this regulation change has discouraged foreign investors and caused a sharp decline (approximately 30%-40% decrease) in foreign investment during the first 8 months in 1997 compared to the same period of 1996. Consequently, PRC announced in November, 1997, that the policy of tariff exemptions of imports of capital equipment for FIEs would be reinstated in January, 1998.

- In 1996, the People's Bank of China published its Provisional Management Regulations on the Establishment of Branches of Foreign Banks in China, allowing qualified foreign banks to establish branches in Shanghai, Tianjin, Dalian, and Guangzou.

- PRC has decentralized its control in the process of regulating and approving foreign investment. Now the provincial governments at the coastal areas have the authority to approve projects with investment up to US$30 million, whereas governments of inland provinces and autonomous regions can approve projects with investment up to US$10 million.

- A growing number of "wholly-owned" foreign enterprises are establishing offices in China now; while just a few years ago "joint venture" was the main form of foreign-invested enterprises. In the first 6 months in 1997, there were more newly established wholly-owned foreign enterprises than joint ventures in China for the first time.

- PRC has gradually deregulated its service industry in sectors including insurance, banking, etc.

- PRC has planned on an eight-percent (8%) growth rate for its economy for year 1996-2000. This growth strategy aims not only to balance inflation rate and economic growth, but to concentrate China's financial and material strength on the revival of state-owned enterprises.

- By the end of 1996, the total accumulated U.S. contractual investment in China amounted to $36.85 billion with a direct investment of $15.67 billion. The total foreign contractual investment for the same period was more than $300 billion, with a direct foreign investment of $177.2 billion.

c. Types of Foreign-Invested Enterprise (FIE)

1). Sino-Foreign Joint (Equity) Venture

It takes the form of a limited-liability company with foreign equity ratio greater than or equal to 25% of the total registered capital. The required foreign equity contribution is dependent on the size of the total investment, as illustrated in the following table. Under the equity joint venture, partners shall share profits and losses in proportion to individual equity contributions.

Total Investment (US$)	Required Foreign Equity Participation
Less than $3 million	70%
$3 mil. - $10 million	50%
$10 mil. - $30 million	40%
More than $30 million	33.3%

2). Sino-Foreign Cooperative (Contractual) Joint Venture

In such a venture, a contract is drawn between various parties. Each party shares profits, losses, obligations, and liabilities in accordance with the provisions set forth in the contract. A cooperative joint venture is not subject to the capital contribution requirement as in the case of an equity joint venture.

3). Wholly Foreign-owned Enterprise

Under PRC's law, the entire capital of a wholly foreign-owned enterprise must be contributed by the investor(s). The establishment of a wholly foreign-owned enterprise must be beneficial to the overall development of China's national economy.

4). Representative Office

Foreign representative offices in China are permitted to engage in activities such as liaison work, market research, and execution of contracts. Direct product sales are prohibited through a representative office. A representative office has no tax obligations since no income is generated. A representative office must be formally endorsed by a Chinese entity, which assumes the official responsibility for the foreign enterprise.

5). Branch Office

Effective July 1, 1994, foreign banks, insurance companies, and law firms are permitted to establish branch offices in China. However, the types of business allowed to set up branch offices are under tight scrutiny, because PRC wishes to maintain certain degree of control over an entity with an offshore parent.

d. Foreign Related Land Purchase and Usage

There are four ways for foreign investors to acquire land use rights in China, as outlined below:

- Expropriation of land use rights with compensations;
- Transfer of state-owned land use rights with compensation;
- Land use rights contributed as an investment by a party in a joint venture;
- Leasing of premises and sites.

e. Importation of Machinery and Equipment

- If importation of machinery and equipment is required by a joint venture, the enterprise must apply for import license(s) from the State every six months.

- Import license(s) may be granted when machinery and equipment are contributed as equity investment by foreign investor(s) in a joint venture. For such machinery and equipment, following conditions must be met:

1). They are indispensable for production needs;
2). They can not be manufactured in China, or the cost factor prohibits from domestic production;
3). The price must not be higher than the fair market price of the compatible model(s).

- There is no specific regulations on importation of used machinery and equipment.
- The purchase of office equipment and supplies is not subject to any restrictions.

f. Foreign Investment Laws and Regulations

There are more than 150 laws related to foreign investment, among which the most important are:

- PRC's Law on Sino-Foreign Equity Joint Ventures, and Its Implementing Regulations;
- PRC's Law on Sino-Foreign Cooperative Joint Ventures;
- PRC's Law on Wholly Foreign-owned Enterprises, and Its Implementing Regulations;
- PRC's Income Tax Law on Foreign Invested Enterprises, and Its Implementing Regulations;
- PRC's Accounting Regulations on Foreign Invested Enterprises;
- Regulations on Terms of Operations for Enterprises with Sino-Foreign Investment; Investment
- Regulations on Requirement of Capital Contribution by Parties in Sino-Foreign Joint Ventures;
- Regulations on Requirement of Foreign Equity in Sino-Foreign Joint Ventures;
- Regulations on Promotion of Foreign Investment;
- PRC's Regulations on Labor Management in Sino-Foreign Joint Ventures;
- PRC's Taxation on Import/Export Goods for Foreign Invested Enterprises.

g. Government Agencies Related to Foreign Investment

1). The Ministry of Foreign Trade and Economic Cooperation (MOFTEC)
    - The application for the establishment of a foreign invested enterprise, along with all necessary document, must be first submitted to MOFTEC for review and approval.

2). The State Industry and Commerce Administration Bureau (SICAB)
    - Upon receipt of certificate(s) issued by MOFTEC, a foreign invested enterprise must register with SICAB and apply for appropriate license(s) before the commencement of business.

1.6 Protection of Intellectual Property Rights

Although PRC has made significant progress in its legal system, enforcement of law remains a problem. Under the 1992 US-China Memorandum of Understanding on Intellectual Property Rights (IPR), China has significantly improved its IPR legal regime. In 1995, PRC and U.S. signed a Memorandum of Understanding on IPR enforcement and market access, which calls for bilateral quarterly consultation on IPR protection. On June 17, 1996, a new agreement was made between the U.S. and China stating that, in order to avoid sanctions from the U.S., China will enforce and fulfill its obligations in a timely manner under the 1995 Memorandum. China has promulgated the following laws and regulations:

- Trade Mark Law and Patent Law
- Trade Secret Law (went into effect in October 1993)
- Copyright Law (went into effect in June 1991)
- Regulations on Protection of Computer Software
- Provisions of Implementing International Copyright Treaties
- Regulations on Protection of Agricultural Chemicals and Pharmaceuticals

1.7 Business and Personal Taxation

a. Business Income Tax

In general, foreign invested enterprises must pay a corporate income tax of 33% of earnings. However, depending on the type of business (such as high-tech) and operation span (such as 15-year operation span), enterprises located in the Special Economic Zones (SEZs) and other designated areas may be entitled to preferential tax rates ranging from 10% to 24%. In addition, certain enterprises may be qualified for tax refund if they reinvest the profits into the business.

b. Value Added Tax (VAT), Consumption Tax, and Commercial Tax

These three types of taxes, replacing the previous "consolidated industrial and commercial tax", were imposed on foreign invested enterprises on January 1, 1994. They are summarized as follows:

1). Value Added Tax (VAT) - ranging from 13% to 17%, is imposed on goods and imported items.
2). Consumption Tax - ranging from 3% to 45%, is imposed on consumer goods such as cigarettes.
3). Commercial Tax - ranging from 3% to 20%, is imposed on service companies such as banks.

c. Personal Income Tax

Foreign nationals working in the PRC must pay individual income tax in accordance with "The Individual Tax Law" (amended on October 31, 1993). It should be noted that PRC's personal income tax is based on individual's monthly income, not yearly income, as follows:

Taxable Income = Monthly Income - RMB$4,000 (Foreigner's Tax Exemption Amount)

Taxable Income* (RMB$)	Tax Rate
$500 or less	5%
$501 - $2,000	10%
$2,001 - $5,000	15%
$5,001 - $20,000	20%
$20,001 - $40,000	25%
$40,001 - $60,000	30%
$60,001 - $80,000	35%
$80,001 - $100,000	40%
$100,001 or more	45%

* Taxable income includes wages and salaries, foreign service/hardship allowance, cost of living and automobile allowances, tax reimbursement, bonuses, meals & miscellaneous employee expenses if paid in lump-sum as allowances.

1.8 Autonomous Regions

China has five autonomous regions: Guangxi, Nei Mongol, Ningxia, Xinjiang and Xizang (Tibet). The autonomous regions function exactly like provinces, but are composed primarily of minority nationalities, i.e., those who are not of Han Chinese stock, which constitutes 92% of the total population. The autonomous regions constitutes almost 60% of China's total land area.

1.9 Useful Web Sites for China Trade Information

- HTTP://WWW.CHINA.OR.CN
- HTTP://WWW.TRADECOMPASS.COM/TRADESMART

WE'VE GOT THE SOLUTION TO RELIABLE CHINA SERVICE

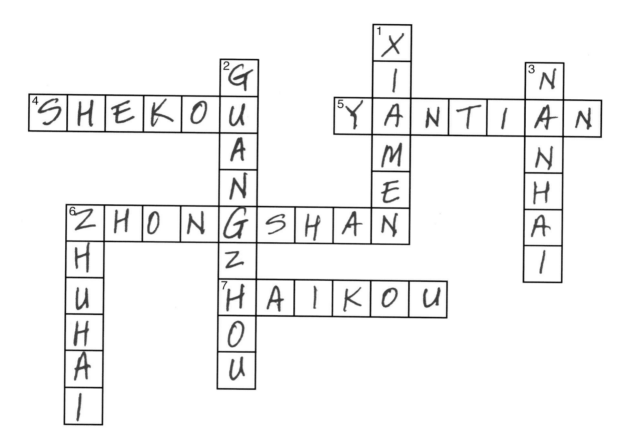

We've filled in the blanks with our comprehensive China service. Hyundai Merchant Marine now offers service from 100 of the most important manufacturing points in China. Starting in 1998, HMM will have a total of 10 weekly Transpacific services for fast transit

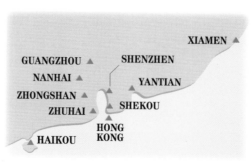

times from every major city in the Far East.

Listed above are just a few of our service points in China. For more information on how our new services are the solution to your transportation needs, please contact your local Hyundai representative today.

HYUNDAI MERCHANT MARINE CO., LTD.

2. Hong Kong - A Special Administrative Region (SAR)

2.1 Overview

a. Political Status

Hong Kong has been a British colony since 1841 until June 30, 1997. In September 1984, the PRC and United Kingdom signed an international treaty - the Joint Declaration on the Question of Hong Kong, calling for China to take back sovereignty over Hong Kong. Based on this Sino-British Joint Declaration, Hong Kong was reverted to PRC effective July 1, 1997, and Hong Kong Special Administrative Region (HKSAR) was established under the State Government of PRC.

b. Territory - Hong Kong consists of 236 islands of varying size, with a total land area of 413 square miles - about one third the size of Rhode Island, the smallest of the 50 United States.

c. Population - Hong Kong has 6.3 million people, of which 98% are ethnic Southern Chinese.

d. Economy - Hong Kong has been transforming from an exotic colonial island into a world-class trade, business, and financial center in the world. Hong Kong maintains one of the most dynamic and richest markets in Asia. During the last 20 years, Hong Kong's GDP has tripled with an average annual growth rate of 7.5%. Current per capita GDP (US$23,000 in 1995) has placed Hong Kong second among nations in Asia, only next to Japan. Hong Kong's current per capita GDP is already ahead of developed countries including United Kingdom, Canada, and Australia.

e. International Trade - In 1996, Hong Kong ranked 8th largest trading economy in the world - its development has been built on a foundation of foreign trade and international investment. During the last 20 years, the international trading revenues has grown more than 44 times in goods and more than 26 times in services.

f. Foreign Exchange Reserves - As of October 1997, Hong Kong's total foreign exchange reserves is US$92 billion, ranked 3rd in the world, next to Japan and China.

2.2 Hong Kong's 1997 Turnover and Current Issues

a. Under the slogan of "One Country, Two Systems:, PRC has promised to allow Hong Kong to become a separate Special Administrative Region within China, retaining its customary political and economic arrangements as a quasi-independent entity for 50 years. Although concerns remain over the return of Hong Kong to Chinese sovereignty, local business interests speak confidently of their annexation of China. In other words, Hong Kong still is and will remain one of the most compelling and challenging places on the globe to conduct business.

b. A growing number of Hong Kong companies have undertaken manufacturing activities in China due to mainland's abundant labor supply and low production cost.

c. The Sino-British Joint Declaration is an international treaty giving rise to rights and obligations under international law, and is registered as such in accordance with Article 102 of the United Nations Charter. In 1990 the National People's Congress of PRC promulgated the Basic Law of the HKSAR which embraces the above policies of China regarding Hong Kong. The Basic Law went into effect on July 1, 1997.

d. Among other things, the Sino-British Joint Declaration provides :

- The HKSAR is entitled to a high degree of autonomy, except in foreign policy and defense matters;

- The current social, economic and legal systems in Hong Kong will remain unchanged. The HKSAR will establish its own economic, trade, monetary and financial policies;

- Private property, ownership of enterprises, right of inheritance and foreign investment will be protected by law;

- The Hong Kong dollar will remain freely convertible and no foreign exchange control policy will be applied;

- The HKSAR will remain its status of a free port, an international financial center and a separate customs territory;

- The HKSAR will operate its finances independently and PRC will not levy taxes on it.

2.3 Legal System

Hong Kong's law is based on Common Law, but with its own unique ordinance and case law. Hong Kong is reforming its business laws and the trend is to improve the climate for foreign investment. However, many rules and regulations that affect foreign invested enterprises are in unpublished government advisories and internal policy statements, rather than in the statues. Foreign business are advised to investigate the status of the legal requirements that may affect particular business activities. For more information, contact the following:

The Law Society of Hong Kong
1403 Swire House
Chater Road, Central, Hong Kong
Tel: (852)-2846-0500 Fax: (852)-2845-0387

2.4 Protection of Intellectual Property

Hong Kong's reputation as a protector and enforcer of intellectual property rights is generally considered as one of the best in the region. The Intellectual Property Department was established in 1990. Since then, it has developed comprehensive laws covering trademarks, trade descriptions, industrial designs, and patents.

Hong Kong has acceded to the following:

- Paris Convention for the Protection of Industrial Property;
- Berne International Copyright Convention;
- Geneva and Paris Universal Copyright Conventions.

2.5 Hong Kong's Role in US-China Trade

Hong Kong's strategic location makes it the gateway to China. At least 45% of China's exports and 30% of its imports pass through Hong Kong. For U.S. firms, Hong Kong's unparalleled access to the Chinese mainland provides a unique gateway to the world's largest emerging market - China. This is well demonstrated by the huge increase in US-China trade in recent years.

There are approximately 38,000 U.S. citizens currently (in 1997) residing in Hong Kong and they represent one of the most significant foreign presence. In addition, 12 States - California, Hawaii. Illinois, Iowa, Maryland, Michigan, Mississippi, New York, North Carolina, Ohio, Rhode Island, and Wisconsin, have established representative offices in Hong Kong.

2.6 Hong Kong's Trade Organizations in the U.S.

a. Hong Kong Trade Development Council (HKTDC)

HKTDC is a quasi-official trade organization which offers a multitude of business services designed to help U.S. firms enter the China/Hong Kong market. In addition to providing comprehensive market intelligence, it also assists business in searching trade partners and identifying distribution channels. American companies interested in doing business with China/Hong Kong are encouraged to make use of the Council's extensive market information. For more information, contact;

1). Hong Kong Trade Development Council
219 E. 46th St.
New York, NY 10017
Tel: 212-838-8688 Fax: 212-838-8941

2). Hong Kong Trade Development Council
350 S. Figueroa St., #282
Los Angeles, CA 90071
Tel: 213-622-3194 Fax: 213-613-1490

b. Hong Kong Economic & Trade Office (HKETO)

HKETO is Hong Kong Government's official representative office in the U.S. It acts as a source of information and its main function is to promote Hong Kong's economic and trade policies in the U.S. For more information, contact:

1). Hong Kong Economic & Trade Office
680 Fifth Ave., 22/F
New York, NY 10019
Tel: 212-265-8888 Fax: 212-541-7321

2). Hong Kong Economic & Trade Office
130 Montgomery St.
San Francisco, CA 94104
Tel: 415-835-9300 Fax: 415-421-0646

2.7 Hong Kong's Government Agencies Related to Foreign Investment

a. The Hong Kong Government's Industry Department promotes foreign investment in Hong Kong, and it offers valuable information on potential joint venture partners, suppliers, rental costs, labor statistics, and other parameters related to foreign investment. For more information, contact:

Industry Department
14/F, Ocean Centre
5 Canton Road, Kowloon, Hong Kong
Tel: (852)-2737-2573 Fax: (852)-2730-4633

b. The Trade Department regulates Hong Kong's trade policy as well as import/export licensing requirements. Its functions include administering quotas and issuing certificates of Hong Kong origin for goods manufactured locally. For more information, contact:

Trade Department
700 Nathan Road, Kowloon, Hong Kong
Tel: (852)-2789-7555 Fax: (852)-2789-2491

c. Foreign business are advised to obtain a copy of the Companies Ordinance from the Hong Kong government printing office as follows:

Information Services Department
Beaconsfield House
4 Queen's Road, Central, Hong Kong
Tel: (852)-2842-8777 Fax: (852)-2845-9078

2.8 Advantages of Using Hong Kong as a Gateway to China

In 1997, there were more than 1,000 U.S. firms registered in Hong Kong and more than 25% of the U.S. investment in Asia Pacific (excluding Japan, New Zealand and Australia) was in Hong Kong. U.S. investment in Hong Kong was valued at $14 billion in 1997 dollars. The advantages of setting up an office in Hong Kong are outlined below:

- There is no discrimination against overseas investors, or special conditions attached to foreign investment; in addition, there are no limits to the percentage of foreign participation in a business either in terms of ownership or employees;

- Government policies are pro-business and are based upon a philosophy of minimum interference with market forces; there is no foreign exchange control or restriction on remittance of capital and profits overseas;

- Corporate income tax rate is 16.5% - an initial 60% of corporate income tax is allowed for capital depreciation on plant and machinery, and losses can be carried forward indefinitely;

- Hong Kong is a free port - controls on imports/exports and re-exports are determined only by health, safety, and security considerations;

- Hong Kong is strategically located at the crossroads of Asia and serves as a bridge between China the rest of the world;

- Hong Kong has a fine natural harbor and world's largest container port in terms of container throughput, its airport is the second busiest in the world in terms of air-freight tonnage handles; in addition, its communication infrastructure is modern, reliable, and affordable;

- Hong Kong is a reputable international financial center which offers banking services of the highest standard; its government maintains prudent fiscal policies whereas the currency is backed by substantial foreign exchange reserves and is linked to the US dollar;

- Hong Kong's population is upwardly mobile with a good supply of high-quality professionals; the manufacturing sector is well-developed and supported by a network of industries, technical services, and institutions; its labor force is intelligent, hard-working, versatile, and flexible. In addition, industrial relations are excellent and productivity is high.

2.9 Establishing an Office in Hong Kong

a. Registration of a New Business

Enterprises and individuals must register with the Business Registration Office within one month of the commencement of the new business. The annual registration fee and tax is HK$2,250. Forms for application may be obtained in person or by mail, free of charge, from the following:

Business Registration Office
Inland Revenue Department
1/ Revenue Tower
5 Gloucester Road, Wanchai, Hong Kong
Tel: (852)-2594-0888 Fax: (852)-2802-7202

There are four different application forms for different types of business, as follows:

1). Form 1(a) - for business conducted by an individual (similar to sole-proprietorship in the U.S.);
2). Form 1(b) - for business conducted by a body corporate (similar to corporation in the U.S.);
3). Form 1(c) - for business conducted by a partnership or by other body unincorporated;
4). Form 1(d) - for branch office(s).

For registering a business conducted by a body corporate, two photocopies of the certificate of incorporation should be forwarded with Form 1(b); for sole proprietorship or partnership, a photocopy of the Hong Kong Identity Card and/or passport of the proprietor/partners should be submitted with appropriate application form(s).

b. Registration as a Branch Office of a Foreign Company with Limited Liabilities

In the process of registering a branch with the Companies Registry, the parent company must submit its articles of incorporation as well as information of directors and the name of at least one official contact person in Hong Kong. For more information, contact the following:

Registrar General's Department (Companies Registry)
Queensway Government Offices
13/F & 14/F, No. 66 Queensway, Central, Hong Kong
Tel: (852)-2867-2600/2604 Fax: (852)-2596-0585

c. Formation of a Subsidiary Company with Limited Liabilities

For process and requirements, contact the following:

Registrar General's Offices
Queensway Government Offices
13/F & 14/F, No. 66 Queensway, Central, Hong Kong
Tel: (852)-2867-2587 Fax: (852)-2596-0585

d. Establishment of a Joint Venture or Acquisition of an Existing Business

For details, contact: Hong Kong Economic & Trade Office
680 Fifth Avenue, 22nd Floor
New York, NY 10019
Tel: 212-265-8888 Fax: 212-541-7321

e. Registration for Factories

All Hong Kong factories whose products require Certificate of Origin must register with the Trade Department. The annual registration fee is HK$2,575 and the renewal of registration takes place on August 1 each year. For more information on factory registration, contact:

Factory Registration Section
Certification Branch, Trade Department
3/F Trade Department Tower
700 Nathan Road, Kowloon, Hong Kong
Tel: (852)-2398-5531/5532 Fax: (852)-2789-2491

f. Requirements of Reporting Change of Particulars in a Business

A business must report to the Business Registration Office of any change in the particulars, such as business name or number of partners, as stated on the application form for registration. Failure to do so may result in prosecution.

g. The Securities and Futures Commission (SFC) oversees the Hong Kong Stock Exchange and regulates the promotion of investment outside Hong Kong. Thus, enterprises or individuals in Hong Kong involved in promoting commercial real estate or other types of investment outside Hong Kong may be required to have SFC clearance. For more information, contact the following:

Securities and Futures Commission (SFC)
38/F, Tower II, Exchange Square
8 Connaught Place, Central, Hong Kong
Tel: (852)-2840-9222 Fax: (852)-2845-9553

h. The American Chamber of Commerce in Hong Kong is the largest American Chamber outside North America. The Chamber's reference and instructional guides include "Living in Hong Kong", "Doing Business in Today's Hong Kong" and other industry-specific publications. The Chamber consists of 23 committees with 2,800 members. Membership is not limited to American companies. For more information, contact:

American Chamber of Commerce
1030 Swire House
6 Chater Road, Central, Hong Kong
Tel: (852)-2526-0165 Fax: (852)-2810-1289

2.10 Exhibiting in Hong Kong Trade Fairs

a. Trade Show Listings

Hong Kong hosts a wide range of trade shows and expositions in various industries. Hong Kong Trade Development Council (HKTDC) is the best source of information on trade fairs in Hong Kong. HKTDC publishes "Business Calendar: Trade Exhibitions & Conference in Hong Kong" quarterly in January, March, June, and September. For more information, contact:

Hong Kong Trade Development Council (HKTDC)
38/F, Convention Plaza
1 Harbour Road, Wanchai, Hong Kong
Tel: (852)-2584-4333 Fax: (852)-2824-0249

b. ATA Carnets

ATA stands for "Admission Temporaire - Temporary Admission". Hong Kong is a signatory to the ATA Carnet Convention, which enables one to bring several different products into the territory with a single document (carnet). The carnet allows for expeditious and duty-free entry of articles that are intended for display at trade fairs, exhibitions, seminars, and similar events. Such goods may remain in Hong Kong for up to 12 months. For more information or to apply for an ATA carnet, contact the following:

1). US Council of the ICC
Tel: 212-354-4480 Fax: 212-944-0012

2). General Chamber of Commerce
22/F, United Square
95 Queensway, Hong Kong
Tel: (852)-2527-9843 Fax: (852)-2527-9843

2.11 Adverse Factors to be Considered by Foreign Investors

Although Hong Kong has many advantages to attract foreign investment, it is advised to take the following factors into consideration before embarking any activities:

a. High Rental Expenses

In 1997, rents for prime quality commercial premises are estimated at US$70-$110 per square foot per annum, which is among the most expensive in the world. Average commercial space is available at approximately US$50-$70 per square foot. Office accommodation is currently in good supply. Two to three year leases are standard. Management/service charges are an 15%-20% extra.

b. High Staff Costs

The 1996 average annual wage for various non-production workers in the wholesale, retail, import and export trade, restaurant and hotel sector was US$15,000. Average annual salaries, including fringe benefits, for managerial and professional employees are over US$40,000.

c. High Staff Turnover

A survey was conducted by Hong Kong Industrial Department to assess foreign companies' views on Hong Kong's role as regional headquarters/office. In the survey, 36% of the respondents said that high staff turnover was a major problem.

d. Deteriorated Financial Climate

Since August 1997, the financial crisis in Thailand has caused a domino effect in the rest of Asia, including Hong Kong. On October 28, 1997, the Hong Kong Hang Seng Stock Index staged a record drop of 13.7%, which subsequently led a worldwide stock decline, including a nose-dive of Dow Jones (a drop of 554.26, or 7.18%, in one day). Although the Hang Seng index surged dramatically (18.8%) the next day, the entire stock market had lost 45% of its value from the 1997 high (16,673) to 9,200 by mid-January, 1998. Despite Hong Kong Government's vigorous effort to prevent Hong Kong dollar from deflating, the high interest rate will inevitably slow down the local economy which may in turn undermine the real estate market. In addition, the currency deflation in neighboring countries may effect an increase of operating costs in Hong Kong, another factor which may deteriorate Hong Kong's position in attracting foreign investment.

3. China's Major Cities for Foreign Investment

3.1 Municipalities Directly under the Central Government

a. The Beijing Municipality

Beijing is the capital of the People's Republic of China. It is China's largest industrial and financial center. It is also the country's science, education, and cultural center. With a population of 11 million people, Beijing is divided into 10 districts and 8 counties. By the end of 1996, there were more than 9,000 foreign investment enterprises in Beijing with a contract value amounting to US$20 billion and a direct foreign investment totaling US$11 billion.

Following industries are among the most promising for foreign investment in Beijing:

1). Urban infrastructures - including local expressway, urban light rail transportation system, water and garbage treatment facilities, and thermal power plants;

2). Agricultural industry - including the technology transfer of upkeep of fresh vegetables, fruits, and meats, as well as the know-how of producing quality farm products;

3). Auto industry - including technology transfer of new techniques in manufacturing vehicle components and parts;

4). Electronic industry - including technology transfer of new techniques in manufacturing electronic components and precision instruments, as well as the introduction of new materials in photoelectrons and semiconductor fields;

5). Electro-mechanical industry - including the latest techniques in manufacturing laser equipment and digital-controlled mechanical tools;

6). Textile industry - including the know-how of producing high-grade chemical fiber, oil agent, and special textile materials for industrial use;

7). Chemical industry - including technology transfer of recycling waste materials;

8). Medical industry - including the application of bio-engineering technologies;

9). Service industry - including the promotion of fast food, tourism, and financial sectors.

For more information on foreign investment issues in Beijing, contact the following:

- Beijing Municipal Foreign Economic Relations & Trade Commission
  190 Chaoyangmenwai Dajie
  Dongcheng District, Beijing 100010
  Tel: (86-10)-6513-5946; 6523-6688; 6524-8780
  Fax: (86-10)-6513-0181

- CCPIT Beijing (China Council for Promotion of International Trade - Beijing Sub-council)
  4/F Erduan, Zhonglou, Hualong Jie
  Nanheyan, Dongcheng District, Beijing 100006
  Tel: (86-10)-6512-5175
  Fax: (86-10)-6512-5165; 6512-5183

b. The Chongqing Municipality

On March 14, 1997, Chongqing became a municipality directly under the Central Government. With a population of 31 million people covering an area of 32,000 square miles (approximately half the size of Washington State), it is the largest city in the world. A historic and beautiful mountain city located in China's southwest region, Chongqing is the hub of communications, transportation and freight distribution. In addition, Chongqing has a modern airport and is the only major city in China that has surplus energy. It is also rich in natural resources including coal, natural gas, iron ore, fire clay, strontium, dolomite, rock salt.

Chongqing is a major scientific and technological center in China. It has 20 universities and more than 400 institutes with 400,000 engineers and technical professionals holding academic degrees. In addition, with an annual turnover of 10 million tons, Chongqing is the largest port in the upper reaches of the Yangtze River. After the completion of the Three Gorges Dam, its capacity can be upgraded for boats of 10,000 tons.

In order to develop the local economy , Chongqing has established a number of policies with preferential tax treatments to encourage foreign investment. These policies are similar to the ones promoted in the Special Economic Zones (SEZs) and coastal cities, but more comprehensive in scope. For more information on foreign investment issues in Chongqing, contact the following:

- Chongqing Foreign Economic & Relation Trade Commission
  65 Jianxin North Road, Chongqing 630020
  Tel: (86-23)-6785-3525, 6785-8011 Fax:(86-23)-6785-3458

- CCPIT Chongqing
  4/F, Unit 5, Block B, Jialing Building
  Jianbei, Sancun, Jianbei District, Chongqing 630020
  Tel: (86-23)-6787-0878, 6786-2239 Fax: (86-23)-6787-0818

c. The Shanghai Municipality

With a population of 14 million people and a area of 2,500 square miles , Shanghai is the largest commercial city in China. Shanghai has a well-developed infrastructure system and Shanghai Harbor is one of the ten biggest ports in the world. Shanghai Securities Exchange and Shanghai Foreign Exchange Swapping Center were established just a few years ago with the goal of making Shanghai as one of the most important financial centers in Asia.

The area being developed the fastest in Shanghai is the New District of Pudong - a triangular area of 200 square miles with a population of 1.5 million people. Enterprises in the New District of Pudong are allowed to set up establishments including financial institutions, department stores, insurance companies, and other service-oriented business. In addition, they are entitled to most of the preferential benefits offered in the Special Economic Zones (SEZs). For more information on investment issues in Shanghai, contact the following:

- Shanghai Foreign Economic Relations and Trade Commission
  55 Lou Shan Guan Road, Shanghai 200335
  Tel: (86-21)-6275-2200 Fax: (86-21)-6275-1778

- CCPIT Shanghai
  14/F New Town Mansion
  55 Lou Shan Guan Road, Shanghai 200335
  Tel: (86-21)-6275-6778 Fax: (86-21)-6275-6364

d. The Tianjin Municipality

With a population of 9 million people, Tianjin has a total area of 4,400 square miles with 800 square miles of offshore fishing zone. Tianjin is rich in natural resources including petroleum, natural gas, coal, raw silk, tungsten, limestone, boron, dolomite, and pottery clay.

Tianjin has a long history of industrial development. As a result, Tianjin is now one of the major industrial bases in coastal China characterized by a comprehensive industrial network consisting of the following industries: textiles, machinery, maritime chemicals, petrochemicals, light industry, electronics, and consumer electronics. Being the second largest port in China (after Shanghai), Tianjin is also a major distribution center in Northern China. The Port of Tianjin has 61 berths for passengers and goods, 7 of which are container berths. In addition, upon the completion of its airport renovation project, Tianjin will have the largest air cargo center in China.

With more than 1,000 financial institutions, Tianjin is the largest financial center in Northern China. In addition, with an annual total import and export value exceeding US$10 billion, it remains the largest international trading port city in Northern China. The city is well-endowed with with an underground metro system, three rail stations, and an airport with direct flights to Hong Kong and Beijing.

Foreign investment is particularly welcomed and encouraged in the following sectors:

1). Infrastructures including power plants, railways, ports and wharves;
2). Key industries including electronics, machinery, automobiles and parts, chemicals, etc.;
3). Service industry including finance, real estate, etc.

There are three special open zones for foreign investment in Tianjin: (1) Tianjin Economic & Technological Development Area (TEDA); (2) Tianjin New Technology Industrial Park; (3) Free Trade Areas of the port of Tianjin.

For more information on foreign investment issues in Tianjin, contact the following:

- Tianjin Commission of Foreign Economic Relations and Trade
  80 Qufu Dao, Tianjin 300042
  Tel: (86-22)-2331-6143; 2331-4828; 2331-2698
  Fax: (86-2)-2331-5231

- CCPIT Tianjin
  International Trade Building
  84 Jianshe Road, Hepingqu, Tianjin 300042
  Tel: (86-22)-2330-1333; 2330-1367; 2330-1371
  Fax: (86-22)-2330-1344

3.2 Provincial Cities and Cities under the Jurisdiction of Autonomous Regions

a. Beihai

Beihai is located in the southern tip of Guangxi Zhuang Autonomous Region. It has a total area of 1,300 square miles and a population of 1.3 million people. Beihai is rich in mineral resources, aquatic products, agricultural and by-products. Beihai Port has 13 berths with convenient transport facilities to Hainan Province and neighboring cities.

Beihai's major industries include mechanical, electrical, metallurgy, petrochemicals, textile, food, paper & pulp, and light industry. It has 69 research institutions with 16,000 professionals. Foreign investment in Beihai is encouraged in the following areas:

- Infrastructures; including highway, bridge, and telecommunications;
- Export-oriented industries;
- Projects involving technology-transfer;
- Energy-saving technologies;
- Processing of raw materials.

For more information in foreign investment issues in Beihai, contact the following:

- Foreign Trade & Economic Dept. of Guangxi Zhuang Autonomous Region
  137 Qixing Road, Nanning, Guangxi 530022
  Tel: (86-771)-280-0676 ext. 2790 Fax: (86-771)-585-1581

- CCPIT Guangxi
  3 Dongge Road, Nanning, Guangxi 530022
  Tel: (86-771)-282-0671 Fax: (86-771)-282-5728

b. Dalian

Located at the southern end of Liaodong peninsula, Dalian is a major industrial city in the Province of Liaoning. There are 5 ports in Dalian with a total of 59 berths, 32 of which can handle ships over 10,000 tons. An additional 80-100 berths are planned for the long-term development with an annual turnover of 60-80 million tons. With a population of 5.5 million people, Dalian's most important industrial sectors include machinery, petrochemical products, textiles, shipbuilding, locomotives, and metallurgical industries. Dalian is attracting foreign investment in the following industries:

- Infrastructure including port, energy, telecommunications;
- Electronics and instruments;
- Processing facilities for imported materials and parts;
- Breeding and processing of various types of sea products;
- Development of non-metallic minerals and products for export.

For more information on foreign investment issues in Dalian, contact the following:

- CCPIT Dalian
  Wanda Building, 18 Hongda Road, Dalian 116001
  Tel: (86-411)-281-5736, 280-8040 Fax: (86-411)-280-6905

c. Fuzhou

Situated in the lower reaches of the Minjiang River in eastern part of Fujian Province, Fuzhou has a total area of 4,700 square miles and a population of 5.5 million people. Rich in natural resources, Fuzhou is known as "a land of fish and rice" as well as "a place of flowers and fruits".

Fuzhou faces Taiwan across the Taiwan Strait, with the closet point of only 68 nautical miles. A direct flight from Fuzhou to Taipei would only take 25 minutes. As one of the most important coastal cities of China, Fuzhou serves as a bridge linking China and Southeast Asia.

Foreign investment in Fuzhou is encouraged in the following areas:

- Infrastructures: including highway, bridge, port, and telecommunications;
- Projects involving technology transfer, such as electronics and metallurgy;
- Processing of raw materials, chemicals, food, etc.;
- Industries including textile, pharmaceutical, building materials, etc.

For more information on foreign investment issues in Fuzhou contact the following:

- Fuzhou Committee of Foreign Economic Relations & Trade
  92 Wushan Road, Fuzhou, Fujian 350001
  Tel: (86-591)-335-5308 Fax: (86-591)-335-7232

- CCPIT Fujian
  20/F Pingdong Office Building
  128 Hualin Road, Fuzhou, Fujian 350003
  Tel: (86-591)-784-1878, 784-2084 Fax: (86-591)-784-2827

d. Guangzhou

Located in the lower reaches of the Pearl River in Guangdong Province, Guangzhou has a total area of 2,900 square miles and a population of 6.5 million people. Guangzhou is strategically situated at the northern tip of the Pearl River Delta, with the South China Sea to its south and Hong Kong and Macao as its neighbors.

Guangzhou Port has 700 berths, of which more than 20 are deep-water ones with capacity of 10,000 tons. Guangzhou is also a major railway hub in south China, with direct lines to Hong Kong and the rest of China. Guangzhou has the third largest international airport in China.

Guangzhou not only has a very strong light industry, its heavy industry is also well-developed. In addition, it is a major financial center in south China. With more than 400 research institutions and many educational establishments, Guangzhou provides a good supply of professional and technical talents. For more information on foreign investment issues in Guangzhou, contact the following:

- Guangzhou International Economic & Trade Plaza
  158 Dongfeng West Road, Guangzhou, Guangdong 510170
  Tel: (86-20)-8486-6479 Fax: (86-20)-8187-7879

- CCPIT Guangzhou
  305 Dongfeng Zhong Road, Guangzhou, Guangdong 510031
  Tel: (86-20)-8333-0860, 8333-2756 Fax: (86-20)-8334-3984

e. Hainan

Situated between the South China Sea and the Vietnam Bay, Hainan, became a full-fledged province in 1988. With a total land area of 13,300 square miles, Hainan is the second largest island in China.

Hainan has 17 ports with 59 berths. Its annual turnover is over 10 million tons. It has a cross-island expressway with a total length of 8,000 miles. It also has an international airport.

Hainan is rich in tropical resources including coconut, rubber, pepper, coffee, etc. It is also rich in minerals and tropical fruits. In addition, it has the capacity of generating more than 1,650 billion kilowatts of electricity per year.

CHINA DAILY

* China's only international English language newspaper - the world's most widely quoted Chinese newspaper today.

* Expert analysis of all the leading events in China trade, finance and law. Even more comprehensive coverage of business issue in weekly business supplement.

* High quality features on Chinese culture and arts, and lively portraits of contemporary Chinese life.

For more information on foreign investment issues in Hainan, contact the following:

- CCPIT Hainan
  International Trade Center, Longkun Road, Haikou, Hainan 570005
  Tel: (86-898)-677-7401, 677-7402 Fax: (86-898)-675-0030

f. Nanjing

Nanjing is located at the lower reaches of the Changjiang (Yangtze) River in the Province of Jiangsu. With a population of 5.5 million people, it has a tropical monsoon climate with four seasons. Nanjing port is accessible to both river and sea traffic. The harbor is 240 miles away from the sea with 64 berths, of which 16 are capable of handling 10,000-ton vessels.

Nanjing is encouraging foreign investment in the following areas:

- Infrastructures: subway, bridges and roads;
- Agriculture, forestry, animal husbandry and fishery;
- Industries including electronics, communications, automobile and parts, machine tools, building materials, pharmaceuticals, energy-saving and textile products.

For more information, contact the following:

- Commission of the Foreign Economic Relations & Trade, Jiangsu
  29 Beijing East Road, Nanjing, Jiangsu 210008
  Tel: (86-25)-771-0312 Fax: (86-25)-771-2072

- CCPIT Nanjing
  10 Hongwu North Road, Nanjing, Jiangsu 210005
  Tel: (86-25)-452-0465 Fax: (86-25)-440-1714

g. Nantong

Located at the northern bank of the entrance of Yangtze River in Jiangsu Province, Nantong faces Shanghai which is located across the River. Nantong has a population of 8 million people, of which 80% is involved in agricultural production.

There are 25 berths at the Port of Nantong, 8 of which can handle ships over 10,000 tons. Nantong is also known as the Textile City. The total volume of rotating-arm NC universal milling machines accounts for more than 90% of China's total export of milling machines. Other export industries include machinery, electronics, chemical, medicine, building materials and shipbuilding.

Nantong has a medium-size airport and is the first city in China equipped with a modern digital telecommunication network. It is also rich in water and electricity resources. For more information in foreign investment issues in Nantong, contact the following:

- CCPIT Jiangsu
  29 Beijing East Road, Nanjing, Jiangsu 210008
  Tel: (86-25)-771-3560 Fax: (86-25)-771-3048

h. Ningbo

Situated in the coast of East China Sea, Ningbo is the political, commercial, and cultural center in the eastern part of Zhejiang Province. It has a total area of 3,700 square miles and a population of 5.2 million people.

With an annual turnover of more than 50 million tons, the Port of Ningbo has 45 berths with capacity ranging from 500 tons to 150,000 tons. Ningbo is one of the major cities in China for production of grain, cotton, oils, and aquatic products. In addition, its industrial base is strong.

For more information on foreign investment issues in Ningbo, contact the following:

- Ningbo Municipal Commission for Foreign Trade & Economic Cooperation
  190 Lingqiao Road, Ningbo, Zhejiang 315000
  Tel: (87-574)-732-8188, 731-0380 Fax: (86-574)-732-8288

- CCPIT Ningbo
  15/F Sino-Trans Mansion
  69 Jiefang South Road, Ningbo, Zhejiang 315010
  Tel: (86-574)-730-2459, 729-3835 Fax: (86-574)-729-2595

i. Qingdao

Located at the southwestern tip of the Province of Shandong, Qingdao has the fourth largest port in China. It has 10 wharves with a total of 63 berths, 16 of which can handle ships of 10,000 tons. It has 10 wharves with a total of 63 berths, 16 of which can handle 10,000-ton vessels. Oingdao also has an international airport called Qingdao Liuting Airport which offers more than 20 domestic flights to major cities in China.

With a population of 7 million, the majority of Qingdao's foreign trade encompasses the sale of textiles, silk, light industrial products, machinery and electronics. Qingdao in rich in natural resources including and is an important production base in China for grains, cotton, oils, fruits, natural silk, poultry and animals, fishing, salt, and aquatic products. Qingdao is currently attracting foreign investment in the following areas:

- Infrastructure: ports, highway, telecommunications;
- Marine engineering: polyploid breeding technology of fish, shrimp, and shellfish; application of satellite remote-sensing technology in forecasting fish farm and physical detection; oceanic meters instruments;
- Bio-engineering: new varieties of wheat;
- Chemical and material science: new structural and energy-saving materials;
- Hi-tech products including computers and micro-electronics.

For more information on foreign investment issues in Qingdao, contact the following:

- Shandong Foreign Economic Relations & Trade Commission
  11 Nanhai Road, Qingdao, Shandong 266003
  Tel: (86-532)-287-0011, 287-0493 Fax: (86-532)-287-0786

- CCPIT Qingdao
  58 Zhanshan Dalu, Qingdao, Shandong 266071
  Tel: (86-532)-386-8797, 387-2381 Fax: (86-532)-387-2566

j. Shenzhen

Located in the southern tip of Guangdong Province, Shenzhen is only 20 miles away from Hong Kong. Connected by mountains and separated by a river, Shenzhen and Hong Kong serve as two sister cities dependent upon each other for growth and development.

US $58

1997 - 1998
Chinese Business in America
華 商 在 美 國

包括 — 全美華人進出口商名錄（含中資、港資及台資企業）
　　 — 如何在美國成立公司行號及應注意事項
　　 — 如何在美國開發市場及尋找貨源

Includes — Directory of Chinese Importers/Exporters in the U.S.
— How to Establish a New Business in the U.S.
— Marketing & Sourcing in the U.S.

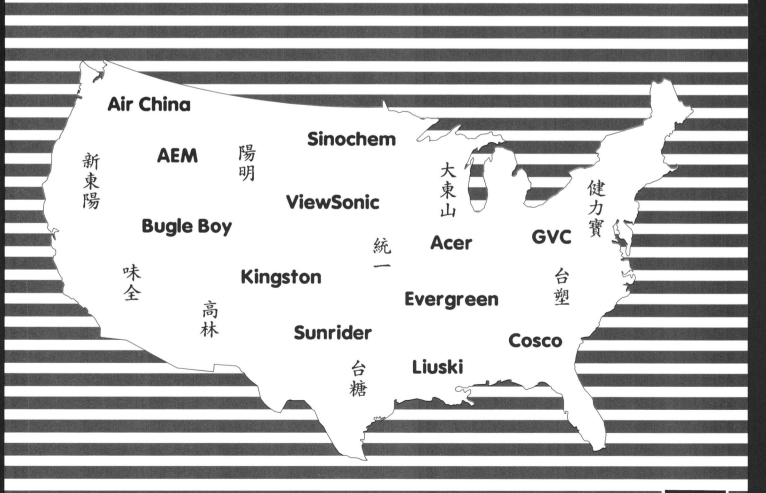

Published by Caravel, Inc., Torrance, California, USA　　　ISBN-0-9644322-1-8

A Landmark Publication Published First Time in the U.S. !

An indispensible reference for import/export firms, overseas suppliers, wholesalers, retailers, freight forwarders, air cargo companies, shipping lines, banks, libraries, marketing firms, etc.

Contains information of 2,800 major firms owned by Chinese or Chinese Americans in the U.S. Listings include company's name, address, tel & fax numbers, contact person, products, etc. Each company was contacted by phone during July and December, 1996, for verification of data listed.

《第一部由中美資訊專家編著·中英雙語實用貿易工具書》

本名録之資料蒐集費時三年，共編入華資企業**2,800**家**(**含加州**1,700**家、紐約州**350**家**)**。企業資料包括公司名稱、地址、電話、傳真、負責人姓名、進出口或製造之主要產品等。每家公司均於**1996**年**7**月至**12**月間以電話聯絡，以查核資料之時效及正確性。

價格：每本美金 **$58.00 (** 加州居民請另加**8.25%**稅金**)**
運費：美國境內每本美金 **$6.95**；美國境外每本美金 **$25.00(** 空郵**)**
Price: US $58.00 per copy(California resident please add 8.25% sales tax)
S & H charges: US $6.95 per copy(domestic); US $25.00 per copy (overseas)

Shenzhen has a total area of 800 square miles, twice the size of Hong Kong. However, with the Dapeng Bay to its east, the rich Pearl River Delta to its west, the New Territory of Hong Kong to its south, and Dongguan and Huizhou to its north, Shenzhen has a huge potential for growth and future development.

Between 1980 and 1991, Shenzhen allocated a total of US$3.5 billion, 25% of which was foreign investment, for infrastructure development. By the end of 1991, Shenzhen had constructed nine industrial parks, 8 harbors, 5 ports, an airport, a helicopter field, and a municipal highway of 180 miles in length. In addition, Shenzhen had installed modern telecommunication network and power generating facilities with an annual supply of over 4 billion kilowatts of electricity.

For more information on foreign investment issues in Shenzhen, contact the following:

- CCPIT Shenzhen
  10/F Jinye Building
  52 Dongmen South Road, Shenzhen, Guangdong 518002
  Tel: (86-755)-228-7791, 223-0333 Fax: (86-755)-222-8673

k. Wenzhou

Situated in the middle section of China's coast, Wenzhou is the economic, cultural, and distribution center in the southern part of Zhejiang Province. Wenzhou has a total area of 4,600 square miles and a population of 7 million people. As one of major ports in China, Wenzhou Port is well-known for its excellent geographic location - it is 320 nautical miles from Shanghai to its north, 564 nautical miles from Hong Kong to its south, and 206 nautical miles from Keelong Port of Taiwan to its east. It has 33 berths, one of which can handle ships of 20,000 tons.

Wenzhou is rich in mineral resources with vast oil and gas reserves under the continental shelf of the East China Sea. For more information on foreign investment issues in Wenzhou, contact:

- Wenzhou Commission for Foreign Economic Relations & Trade
  8 Liming West Road, Wenzhou, Zhejiang 325003
  Tel: (86-577)-833-4777, 833-9576 Fax: (86-577)-833-9575

l. Xiamen

Located in the southeast of Fujian Province, Xiamen is facing Taiwan across the Taiwan Strait. It has a total area of 600 square miles and a population of 1.2 million people. Xiamen is one of the three major fishing grounds in China and is rich in maritime products including oyster, clams, scallop, etc. In addition, mineral resources, such as kaolin earth and granite, are abundant.

For more information on foreign investment issues in Xiamen contact the following;

- CCPIT Xiamen
  11/F Information Building, Huli, Xiamen, Fujian 361006
  Tel: (86-592)-602-1772, 602-2026 Fax: (86-592)-602-2377

m. Zhanjiang

Zhanjiang is located in the southwest of Guangdong Province - a crossway between Guangdong, Hainan Island, and Guangxi Zhuang Autonomous Region. It has a total area of 4,900 square miles and a population of 5.5 million people.

As one of the 10 major ports in China, Zhanjiang Port is a natural deep-water port with shipping connections to 80 countries in the world. Its also has convenient land and air transport facilities. Zhanjiang is rich in natural resources including minerals, agricultural , and maritime products.

It contains huge reserves of petroleum and natural gas in the continental shelf west of South China Sea. Zhanjiang's main industry is food-oriented, with sugar as the major product. Other industries include processing of cotton clothes, electronics, chemicals, building materials, and tobacco.

Foreign investment in Zhanjiang is encouraged in the following areas:

- Infrastructures: including energy, communications, and transportation projects;
- Construction of export-oriented facilities;
- Key industries: including automobiles, electronics and machinery;
- Processing of value-added agricultural and by-products.

For more information on foreign investment issues in Zhanjiang, contact the following:

- Zhanjiang Foreign Economic Relations & Trade Committee
  West Gate, 31 Nanfang Road, Chikan, Zhanjiang, Guangdong 524038
  Tel: (86-759)-331-4774, 333-8893 Fax: (86-759)-333-7601

3.3 Special Economic Zones (SEZs)

There are 5 SEZs in China: Hainan, Shantou, Shenzhen, Xiamen and Zhuhai. Foreign invested enterprises (FIEs) in the SEZs are entitled to the following preferential treatments:

a. In general, FIEs are eligible for a reduced corporate income tax rate of 15% (regular rate is 33%) and lower land usage fees. In addition, certain types of enterprises may be exempt from the VAT and Commercial Taxes.

b. Established enterprises with long term (10-year or more) history may be tax-free for the first two profitable years in operation and the corporate income tax may be reduced in half for the next three years. Hi-tech enterprises may be eligible for this reduced income tax for three more years.

c. An export-oriented enterprises with total export revenue greater than 70% of its yearly production value in any year is eligible for a flat income tax rate of 10% for that year.

3.4 Open Cities

In May 1984, China first designated the following 14 coastal port cities as "Open Cities":
- Beihai, Dalian, Fuzhou, Guangzhou, Lianyungang, Nantong, Ningbo, Qianhuandao, Qingdao, Shanghai, Tianjin, Wenzhou, Yantai (including Weihai), and Zhanjiang.

In 1992, China further approved the following cities as "Open Cities":

a. Along the Yangtze River: Chongqing, Huangshi, Jiujiang, Wuhan, Wuhu, and Yueyang;
b. Provincial cities in border areas: Changchun, Harbin, Huhehot, Kunming, Nanning, Shijiazhuang, and Wulumuqi;
c. Provincial cities in inland areas: Changsha, Chengdu, Guiyang, Hefei, Lanzhou, Nanchang, Taiyuan, Xi'an, Xining, Yinchuan, and Zhengzhou.

In addition, the following 13 cities in border areas were also authorized the status of "Open Cities":

- Bole Municipality, Dongxing Town, Erlianhaote Municipality, Heihe Municipality, Hekou County, Huichun Municipality, Manzhouli Municipality, Pingxiang Municipality, Ruili County, Suifenhe Municipality, Tacheng Municipality, Wanding Municipality, and Yining Municipality.

Foreign invested enterprises (FIEs) in Open Cities may enjoy the following benefits:

a. In general, FIEs are eligible for a flat corporate income tax rate of 24% (regular tax rate is 33%). In addition, certain types of enterprises may be exempt from the VAT and Commercial Taxes.

b. Enterprises may be eligible for a reduced tax rate of 15% if the following conditions are met:

1). the project is technology-oriented and involves the transfer of know-how;
2). the project involves construction of ports and wharves;
3). the project involves establishment of financial institutions with investment of US$10 million or more, and the financial institution will operate for a minimum of 10 years;
4). the investment of the project is US$30 million or more.

c. An export-oriented enterprises with total export revenue greater than 70% of its yearly production value in any year is eligible for a reduced tax rate of 12% for that year.

d. Enterprise with long-term (10-year or more) operation history may be tax-free for the first two profitable years in its operation and the corporate income tax may be reduced in half for the next three years. Hugh-tech enterprises may be eligible for this reduced income tax for three more years.

3.5 Economic and Technological Development Zones (ETDZs)

Since 1984, China has designated the following ETDZs:

- Caohejing,	Changchun,	Chongqing,
Dalian,	Dayawan,	Fuzhou,
Guangzhou,	Hangzhou,	Harbin,
Hongqiao,	Kunshan,	Lianyungang,
Minhang,	Nansha,	Nantong,
Ningbo,	Qinhuangdao,	Qingdao,
Rongqiao,	Shenyang,	Tianjin,
Weihei,	Wenzhou,	Wuhan,
Wuhu,	Xiaoshan,	Yantai,
Yingkou,	Zhanjiang,	Zhangzhou

Foreign invested enterprises (FIEs) located in the ETDZs are eligible for the following benefits:

a. In general, enterprises are eligible for a reduced corporate income tax rate of 15% (regular tax rate is 33%). Certain types of enterprises may be exempt from the VAT and Commercial Taxes.

b. Enterprises with long-term (10-year or more) operation history may be tax-free for the first two profitable years in operation and the corporate income tax may be reduced in half for the next three years. High-tech enterprises may be eligible for this reduced income tax for three more years.

c. An export-oriented enterprises with total export revenue greater than 70% of its yearly production value in any year is eligible for a flat income tax rate of 10% for that year.

3.6 Coastal Open Economic Zones (COEZs)

Since 1985, China has established COEZs in the following areas:

- Liaodong Peninsular;
- Pearl River Delta;
- Shandong Peninsular;
- Triangle Area (i.e., Quanzhou, Xiamen and Zhangzhou);
- Yangtze River Delta

Foreign invested enterprises (FIEs) in the COEZs may be entitled the following:

a. In general, FIEs are eligible for a reduced corporate income tax rate of 24% (regular tax rate is 33%). Certain types of enterprises may be exempt from the VAT and Commercial Taxes.

b. Enterprises may be eligible for a reduced tax rate of 15% if the following conditions are met:

   1). the project is technology-oriented and involves the transfer of know-how;
   2). the project involves infrastructure development such as energy, transportation, port construction;
   3). the investment of the project is US$30 million or more.

c. An export-oriented enterprise with total export revenue greater than 70% of its yearly production value in any year is eligible for a flat income tax rate of 12% for that year.

d. Enterprises with long-term (10-year or more) operation history may be tax-free for the first two profitable years in operation and the corporate income tax may be reduced in half for the next three years. High-tech enterprises may be eligible this reduced income tax rate for three more years.

3.7 National Development Zones (NDZs)

In order to develop the field of advanced technology and technology-sensitive industries, the State Science and Technology Commission of PRC has designated 52 NDZs, as follows:

- Anshan, Baoding, Baoji, Baotou, Beijing, Changchun, Changsha, Changzhou, Chengdu, Chongqing, Dalian, Daqing, Foshan, Fuzhou, Guangzhou, Guilin, Guiyang, Hainan, Hangzhou, Harbin, Hefei, Huizhou, Jilin, Kunming, Lanzhou, Luoyang, Mianyang, Nanchang, Nanjing, Nanning, Qingdao, Shanghai, Shenzhen, Shenyang, Shijiazhuang, Suzhou, Taiyuan, Tianjin, Weifang, Weihai, Wuhan, Wulumuqi, Wuxi, Wuzhou, Xiamen, Xiangfan, Xi'an, Zhengzhou, Zhongshan, Zhuhai, Zibo.

Foreign invested enterprises (FIEs) located in the NDZs are entitled to the following benefits:

a. In general, FIEs are eligible for a reduced corporate income tax rate of 15% (regular tax rate is 33%);

b. An export-oriented enterprise with total export revenue greater than 70% of its yearly production value in any year may be eligible for a flat income tax rate of 10% for that year;

c. New enterprises may be eligible for tax exemption for the first two years in operation. Enterprises with long-term history (10-year or more) may be tax-free for the first two profitable years in operation.

3.8 Free Trade Areas (FTAs)

Since 1990, PRC has designated the following 14 FTAs to facilitate export operation:

- Dalian, Futian (Shenzhen), Fuzhou, Guangzhou, Hainan, Ningbo, Qingdao, Shantou, Shatoujiao (Shenzhen), Tianjin, Waigaoqiao (Shanghai), Xiamen, Zhangjiagang, Zhuhai.

Enterprises located in FTAs are allowed to establish their own operations in areas of management and import/export procedures with minimum government interference. In addition, following items may be exempt from the VAT and Commercial Taxes, as well as the requirements of import and export licenses:

a. Machines, equipment, raw materials, and supplies imported for the purpose of infrastructure development within FTAs;

b. Raw materials, components, and packaging supplies imported for the production of goods to be exported;

c. Transshipping goods stored temporarily in FTAs.

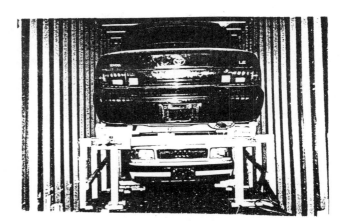

4. Exporting to China: Best U. S. Export Prospects

4.1 Introduction

China began to open its door to the outside world in the 1980s. However, it was not until 1992 when China decided to transform from state-run economy to a sophisticated, market-driven industrial economy based on imports of technology and export-oriented production. In October 1992, China reformed its import regime significantly. As a result, China currently operates a complex system of market and administrative controls which regulates access of foreign firms into the China market.

Whereas in the past only a few designated foreign trade corporations (FTCs) were allowed to import goods and services, now more and more factories and enterprises are authorized to engage directly in import/export trading. In general, enterprises other than FTCs or FIEs must obtain the following first before the commencement of international transactions:

a. MOFTEC-authorized approval from the local foreign trade bureau;
b. A license form the local bureau of industry and commerce.

4.2 Current Status of US-China Trade

In 1996, the U.S. imports from China amounted to $51.2 billion, while the exports to China valued at $11.7 billion. The $39.5 billion trade deficit has placed China the No. 2 nation (after Japan's $48 billion) attributing to the U.S. trade deficit, which totaled $165.1 billion in 1996, an 11.4% increase from 1995. Although the Chinese government has challenged the accuracy of the $39.5 billion figure, on the basis of overcounting American imports passing through Hong Kong, the trade imbalance is worsening - the U.S. trade deficit with China in the first 9 months of 1997 was already $48.7 billion.

4.3 PRC's Regulatory Authorities on Imports

a. The Ministry of Foreign Trade and Economic Cooperation (MOFTEC) is the central government agency which formulates and administers China's foreign trade policy. MOFTEC develops an annual import plan specifying items to be imported and issues the necessary import license. However, only about 20% of total imports are now specifically planned each year, which involve primarily raw materials such as cotton, grain, fertilizer, and iron ore.

b. Each province and municipality operates an individual foreign trade system, which includes a foreign trade bureau, FTCs, and investment and trust corporations. Foreign exporters wishing to do business may contact the local FTC, which coordinates and overseas local branches of national foreign trade organizations.

c. All foreign invested enterprises (FIEs) are authorized to engage directly in international trade. In addition, most imports by joint ventures are eligible for duty reduction or exemption.

4.4 PRC's Import Policy & Procedures

China administers a complex system of non-tariff trade barriers, including import licenses required for restricted imports, as well as individual quotas on imports of machinery, electronic products and general goods such as grain, fertilizer, textiles and chemicals.

a. Import License:

1). Products require import licenses include certain types of consumer goods, raw materials and production equipment. Issuance of an import license typically requires approval from several government agencies including local government authorities. Effective January 1, 1994, importing of the following 43 kinds of commodity required import license:

- Scrap ships, natural rubber, timber, plywood, wood, chemical-fiber, monomer, ABS resin, synthetic glue, sodium cyanide, carbonic acid drinks, automobile and parts, autocrane, OE-spinner, electronic microscope, electronic color scanner, X-ray topography scanner, computer, magnetic tape recording machines, video recorder (player), copier, air conditioner, agricultural chemicals, tobacco products, cigarette filter, cellulose acetate, automobile tire, civilian blasting equipment, chemical fiber cloth, chemical-fiber clothes, refrigerator, washing machine, tape recorder, TV set, motorcycle and parts, camera, camera body and watch.

2). The following items may be imported only with central government approval:

- Grain, sugar, steel, fertilizers, oil, timber, polyester fibers, tobacco, cotton, and pesticides.

3). The following items are tightly controlled; importing these items may require as many as 15 clearance from various government agencies, depending upon the locality:

- Wool, Wood Pulp, Plywood, hard & corrugated paper, chemicals, scrap ships, and TV tubes.

4). Certain designated important and sensitive commodities are required to secure certificate(s) of registration prior to importation. The certificate is valid for six months. In addition, following items are prohibited from being imported into China:

- Used garments, diseased animals, garbage, poisons, narcotic drugs, plants;
- Weapons, ammunition, explosives, radio receivers and transmitters;
- Manuscripts, films, printed and recorded materials detrimental to Chinese interests.

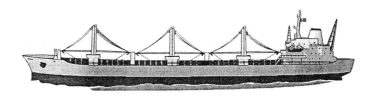
b. Import Quota:

China administers import quota on commodities which, if imported excessively, may threaten its domestic industries and overall economic development. China exercises two types of import quota: type I applies to machinery & electronic equipment while type II covers general goods.

1). Type I import quota covers the following 18 kinds of machinery & electronic equipment:

- Vehicles other than railway or transway rolling-stock;
- Motor chassis, engines, drive-axles & bodies;
- Motorcycles, engines & frames;
- Color TV tubes;
- Electronic components & accessories;
- Recorders and transport mechanisms;
- Refrigerators and compressors;
- Washing machines;
- Video recording apparatus and parts;
- Camera and parts;
- Air conditioners and compressors;
- Copiers;
- Audio/Video devices;
- Crane lorries and chassis;
- Topography scanners;
- Electric microscopes;
- Rotor spinning machines;
- Color scanners

In order to import any of the above products into China, importers must first obtain import quota certificates from the state government before import license can be issued.

2). There are 24 categories of general goods which are under import quota requirement, as follows:

- Petroleum oil, oil products, wool, polyester fiber, acrylic fiber, polyester products, plywood, rubber (natural & synthetic), automobile tires, sodium cyanide, sugar, ABS resin, agricultural chemicals, chemical fertilizer, cellulose acetate, grain, cotton, vegetable oil, alcoholic drink, soda drink, color sensitized materials, chemical fiber clothes, tobacco products.

Local foreign trade bureaus are responsible for the administration and coordination of import quota for general goods in their respective regions.

c. Tariff

China Maintains two kinds of tariffs: MFN and general. MFN rates apply to imports originating from countries and regions with which China has concluded reciprocal tariff agreements whereas general rates apply to countries otherwise. Official tariff rates can range from 3% on imports beneficial for China's economic development to 250% on imports detrimental to China's domestic industries.

China adopted the Harmonized Commodity Description and Coding System on January 1, 1992 and joined the International Convention on the Harmonized Commodity Description and Coding System the same year. There are 21 sections, 97 chapters and 6550 tariff headings in the Customs Import and Export Tariff of the People's Republic of China. Since 1992, China has effected four (4) significant tariff reductions, as illustrated below: (As of 1997, the average tariff rate for developed countries is 4.7%)

Date	Average Tariff Rate	Number (%) of Headings Affected
Jan. 1992	43.2%	
Dec. 1992	35.9%	2,898 (44%)
Dec. 1993	27.1%	3,371 (51%)
Apr. 1996	23.0%	4,900 (75%)
Oct. 1997*	17.0%	4,800 (73%)
Year 2000	15.0% (estimated)	

* The total imports of China in October, 1997 increased 17%, compared with the same month in 1996, due to the tariff reduction. It was 14.8% more than the total imports of September, 1997.

4.5. U.S. Export Regulations

The export of goods and services from the U.S. to other countries is regulated by the Bureau of Export Administration (BXA) of the United States Department of Commerce. Two types of export licenses are available, depending on the type of exporting goods or services, as described below:

a. General License:

The general license is automatically granted by the U.S. government to U.S. exporters (i.e., exporters are not required to file any application for such licenses) for a wide range of product categories. The exporter must complete a Shipper's Export Declaration (SED) if the total value of the shipment is more than US$2,500.

DART EXPRESS GROUP

SINCE 1970

Dart Express is committed to the effective service and efficient transportation of goods worldwide. Our staff has the knowledge and ability to facilitate and promote international trade. With stations and agents in most major gateway cities of the world, we are able to meet the increasing demands and needs of importers and exporters worldwide. Dart Express Group offers the following services:

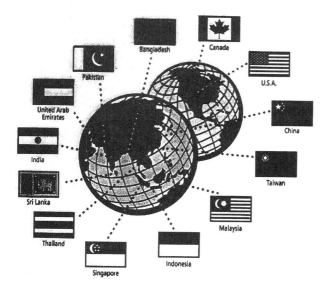

Worldwide Air/Ocean Freight Services
Ground Transportation
International Documentation
Crating and Handling
Export Declaration
Banking/Letter of Credit/Bank Presentation
Certificate of Origin
Warehousing/Distribution
Import Transaction
US Customs Clearance (Advanced ABI Systems
Cargoes Consolidation

Dart Express (LAX) Inc.
821 W. Arbor Vitae Street
Inglewood, Ca. 90301

Tel: 310-649-3641 Fax: 213-776-6132
www.dartexpress.com

LION INTERNATIONAL TRADING LLC

獅 子 城 國 際 貿 易 公 司

2296 Quimby Road
San Jose, CA 95122
USA

Phone: (408) 238-4896
Fax: (408) 274-4932
E-Mail: JZOOM@PACBELL.NET

* Factory-Direct Importer of Quality Granites
* Large Inventory
* Variety Selection
* Local Warehouse
* Quality Products

Contact: Stanley K. Woo

吳 開 山

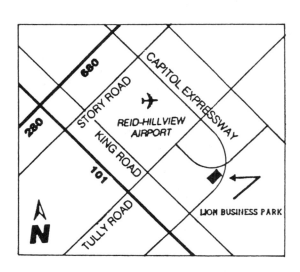

b. Individual Validated License (IVL):

The IVL is a specific grant of authority from the U.S. government to a particular exporter for exporting a specified quantity of a product to a destination. In general, an IVL is required for products such as weapons and hi-tech merchandises which may be used against the U.S. or its allies, or for commodities in short supply in the U.S. If an IVL is required, the exporter must prepare a form BXA-622P "Application for Export License" and submit it to the BXA. If the application is approved, a Validated Export License (VEL) with an authorization number will be issued to the applicant. All goods exported under an IVL must be accompanied by an Shipper's Export Declaration (SED).

For more information of U.S. regulations on exports to China, contact the following:

- Bureau of Export Administration (BXA)
 U.S. Department of Commerce
 14th St. and Constitution Ave. NW.
 Washington, DC 20230
 Tel: 202-482-2721 Fax: 202-482-2387

- Office of China, Hong Kong and Taiwan
 U. S. Department of Commerce
 Room 2317, 14th & Constitution Ave. NW.
 Washington, DC 20230
 Tel: 202-482-4681 Fax: 202-482-15

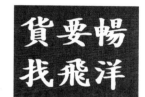

4.6 Best U.S. Export Prospects (Value unit: US$ million)

Commodity	Total Value of Imports in 1995	Total Value of Imports in 1994
Aircraft	1,053.1	3,239.0
Aircraft parts	217.4	162.1
Auto spare parts	749.9	508.5
Cellulose acetates	15.9	47.1
Cereals	3,728.8	1,314.2
Chemical fertilizer	3,722.1	1,923.3
Crude oil	2,356.4	1,573.4
Electric motors, generators and parts	746.7	728.3
Electronic computer and its parts	2,399.1	1,743.2
Flours and meals of fish	327.3	273.4
Generating sets	685.9	320.9
Iron ores	1,226.9	1,025.7
Machine tools	2,200.8	2,075.1
Natural rubber	422.5	331.1
Paper	1,722.1	1,540.7
Paper products	744.0	602.2
Paper pulp	14.2	8.9
Petroleum products	2,065.5	1,957.6
Pharmaceuticals	254.5	212.8
Plastic articles	743.2	639.2
Plywood	773.5	818.1
Polyethylene	1,444.6	877.4
Polypropylene	813.1	527.9
Polystyrene	909.8	762.2
Polyvinyl chloride	473.9	368.2
Printing machines	635.4	654.1
Rubber/plastic making machines	1,347.4	1,516.9
Sewing machine	324.5	396.2
Synthetic rubber	326.3	248.0
Telecommunication equipment	2,248.1	2,240.9
Textile machines	2,553.1	2,613.7
Timber	225.6	211.4
Vehicles	1,536.2	3,467.5
Vegetable oil	2,426.5	1,736.1
Wood pulp	657.9	392.0

Other top-selling commodities for U.S. exporters include the following:

- Oil/gas field machinery and services
- Mining industry equipment
- Airport and ground support equipment
- Agricultural machinery
- Chemical production machinery
- Laboratory scientific instruments
- Plastics production machinery
- Food processing and packaging machinery
- Packaging machinery and equipment
- Computer software
- Medical equipment
- Electronics production and test equipment
- Construction equipment
- Pumps, calves and compressors
- Architectural, construction and engineering services

4.7 Valuation and Customs Clearance of Shipments to China

Duties of import shipments are generally assessed by Chinese custom officials on the basis of the CIF value of the shipment, which includes the normal wholesale price in the country of origin, freight, packing charges, insurance, export duties, and commissions. Except for shipments under bond, customs clearance and payment of duty must be accomplished within three months of importation. Goods imported into China on a temporary basis (e.g. samples for exhibiting in trade fairs) must be reexported within six months.

1998/99 China Trade Publications
Keep up with China's rapid changes...
~ Your keys to success in China

P1

P3

P2

P5

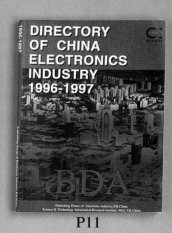

P6

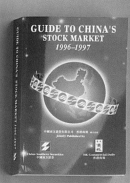

P4

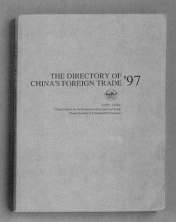

P7

P8

P9

P10

P11

P12

CARAVEL, INC.
23545 Crenshaw Blvd., #101E, Torrance, CA 90505
Tel: 310-325-0100 • Fax: 310-325-2583

Notes: 1. Delivery via UPS in 2-4 weeks upon receipt of confirmed order.
2. Please pass this brochure to anyone who may be interested in above products.

ITEM	TITLE / DESCRIPTION	PRICE*
P1	1998/99 中國大陸百萬家企業總覽 － 內含182萬家中國大陸企業詳細資料。包括企業名稱，地址，電話，傳真，負責人姓名，年營業金額及主要產品等。可按產品或名稱等尋找所需資料並可自行列印mailing label或報表。必須在中文視窗3.1或95環境中使用。使用英文windows3.1或95者須與其它中文軟體(如雙橋、理想)合用。此CD-ROM需PC386 or better, 4MB RAM &12MB hard disk.	$99.00
P2	*The Passage to China* - A self-learning multimedia CD-ROM on doing business in China. It offers insightful analysis of the business culture and guidelines on protocols for various business contexts. Also includes *Travel Tips* and *Essential Expressions*. Published 1997. Needs PC486, Windows 3.1 or higher.	$99.00
P3	1997/98中國大陸十萬家企業資訊總覽 － 根據中國國家統計局提供之資料編印，全套分三大冊，共三千餘頁。資料包括企業名稱、地址、電話、傳真、產品、負責人姓名、員工人數、經濟類型(國有、個體、外資、股份)等。含十萬家企業，行業共分七大類715小類。精裝本。1997出版。	$395.00
P4	大陸地區臺商協會會員名錄 － 含廣州、上海、重慶等35個臺商協會之5,500餘家台商資料。內容包括會員廠商名稱、地址、電話、傳真、負責人姓名及主要產品等。附贈電腦資料磁碟片。	$99.00
P5	1998 Fairs & Exhibitions China 中國博覽會和展覽會 - Bilingual. Published by CCPIT in 1997. contains information on 260+ fairs & exhibitions in 19 cities of China. Includes name of exhibition, date, organizer's phone & fax #, frequency, number of exhibitors & attendees, etc. 中英對照。	$99.00
P6	1997/98 China Business Register 中國工商企業機構總覽 － Contains information on 23,000 enterprises, including annual sales & type of ownership. Search by SIC or products. Bilingual. 中英對照。	$189.00
P7	1998 China Phone Book & Business Directory 中國電話簿 － Includes 19,000 listings of major organizations in China with fax numbes. Updated in January and July of each year. 中英對照。	$115.00
P8	1997 Directory of China's Foreign Trade - Published 1997 by CCPIT. Covers 9,000 China's major international trading enterprises including import/export companies. Products is divided into 16 categories.	$185.00
P9	1997/98 Almanac of China's Foreign Economic Relations & Trade - Covers China's economic and trade policies, foreign investment laws & regulations, import/export statistics, etc. Published annually.	$195.00
P10	1997/98 CBU Directory of Chinese Vehicle, Component and Parts Manufacturers - Lists more than 4,800 companies arranged alphabetically by province and city. Information includes company's name, phone & fax #, products, sales, executive's name, year of establishment and type of ownership.	$495.00
P11	1997/98 Directory of China Electronics Industry - Contains 1,000 major companies arranged by province and city alphabetically. Includes company's name, address, sales, executive's name, capital, etc.	$195.00
P12	1996/97 Guide to China's Stock Market - The only English-language guide to China's burgeoning stock market. It contains comprehensive information on the 529 A shares and B shares now trading on the Shenzhen and Shanghai stock exchanges. Also includes: company profile & scope of business; tips on investment & risk analysis; financial data including P/E ratios & net assets; movement charts; etc.	$195.00

*California residents please add 8.25% sales tax   S&H charges: $6.95 per order

---

ORDER FORM   ____ Invoice Me

A check / money order of $_____ is enclosed for items # _____

Name of company: _____

Address: _____ Tel: _____

City: _____ State: _____ Zip: _____ Fax: _____

Name: _____ Title: _____

5. Marketing, Advertising, and Exhibiting in China

5.1 Marketing in China

Due to the vast geographic areas and distinctive demographics in different parts of the PRC, when marketing a product, its is important to conduct a market research first. In addition, foreign companies are not permitted to directly engage in trade in China, other than direct marketing of goods they have manufactured in China. In other words, although foreign companies are allowed to set up representative offices in China to promote their products or services, they are prohibited from engaging in direct profit making activities. Accordingly, U.S. firms need to use a domestic Chinese agent or distributor for importation of their goods and selling them within China. Only companies that have been authorized by the state government to engage in import/export are permitted to sign import and export trade contracts.

As the number of enterprises obtaining import/export rights soars while the number of products subject to regulations drops, foreign companies in China are finding more opportunities to establish contacts with potential customers. However, determining which Chinese enterprises to deal with can be a challenging task. Any American firm seeking to appoint a Chinese enterprise as sales agent or distributor should inspect the English translation of the business license and make certain the local enterprise is officially authorized to engage in business. In addition, the Chinese term for "agent" and "representative" are often used interchangeably. Therefore, American companies should clearly define the terms and obligations in the contract.

There are a number of channels to approach the Chinese market, as illustrated below:

a. Establish a representative office

   A local representative office allows a foreign company to gain a competitive edge in prompt service, long-term commitment, and immediate customer response. The drawback of a representative office is it is not allowed to engage in any transactions but image building.

b. Exhibit at trade fairs

   Exhibiting in trade shows allows vendors to have direct contacts with buyers. In addition, on-site demonstration may increase product awareness and generate more sales.

c. Contract a local agent or distributor in China

   While this approach may eliminate the time and effort for establishing a new marketing network, it may increase the selling price due to the middleman costs. Besides, it is difficult to obtain feedback from end-users and marketing is limited by agent's performance.

d. Negotiate a joint venture with a local Chinese company

   When negotiating a joint venture in China, following factors should be taken into consideration:

   -Location of the joint venture: What are the advantages and disadvantages of coast cities vs. others?
   -Type of joint venture: An equity or cooperative joint venture? Any tax incentives?
   -Selection of Chinese partner: Who are the real decision makers on the Chinese side?
   -Letters of intents, feasibility studies, and other preliminary agreements: What should be included?
   -Protection of intellectual property: What are the legal protections available? Enforcement?
   -Land purchase and usage issues: How to acquire land use rights in China? Any restrictions?

BERKELEY MARKETING RESEARCH, LTD.

Greater China Region

Taiwan Beijing Shanghai Guangzhou Chengdu

- **QUALITATIVE**

  - Focused Group Discussion
  - In-depth Interview

- **QUANTITATIVE**

  - Door-to-door
  - Central Location Test
  - Telephone Interview
  - Mail Survey

- **SALES PROMOTION**

  - Sampling
  - Tasting

Taiwan Office (Taipei)

Contact: Jessie Cheng

Tel: (886-2)-2578-1717
Fax: (886-2)-2578-8599

China Office (Beijing)

Contact: Linda Yang

Tel: (86-10)-6424-1538
Fax: (86-10)-6424-1542

5.2 Market Segmentation

On the surface, China offers a vast market to foreign companies selling products and services. In reality, China is divided into many regional markets, each with its own demographics. For example, due to the economic reform, coastal areas have enjoyed fast economic growth and created a pool of affluent consumers. On the other hand, most population in inland and border areas are still living at the poverty level. Therefore, it is impractical to market a product at a national level since living standards vary widely throughout the country.

It is strongly recommended that a market survey be conducted before penetrating a regional market. In addition, distribution is another factor which should be taken into serious consideration. Although establishing direct market access by operating distributorships or retail outlets may eliminate the middlemen and keep prices competitive, the high setup and maintenance cost may offset the benefits.

5.3 Advertising in China

The communications media and advertising industries in China have expanded dramatically in the past decade. Despite the rapid growth in recent years, advertising in China remains underdeveloped and the level of advertising expenditures remains low compared with developed countries.

China's economic growth in recent years has brought with it a huge increase in the number and variety of media available to advertisers. Virtually all the advertising options available in the West now exist in China. The current advertising law was passed in October 1994 and came into effect on February 1, 1995. The law stresses truthfulness, fairness and honesty, and forbids disparagement of other products. There are also special regulations for pharmaceuticals, medical products, cosmetics, food and agro-chemicals. Tobacco and liquor advertising has been banned from all media except outdoor. In addition, the words "best", "top', and "only" are not allowed to appear on advertisements.

Currently, advertisers can employ ad agencies to design and produce their ads or commercials. However, planning an advertising strategy to reach China's burgeoning consumer market can be a dizzying task and dealing with Chinese media can be tiresome since it is very much a seller's market. In spite of rate hikes and new TV stations and newspapers, demand is still much greater than supply. Traditional media such as state-run television and newspapers now accept advertisements from both Chinese and foreign companies.

Television is believed to be the most cost-effective method for introducing new products in China due to the fact that an advertisement on television during the evening news will typically reach as many as 600 million viewers. Foreign companies advertise in China mostly on television since it can reach 90% of China's urban population. Regional television advertisements are also cost-effective in penetrating certain markets. For example, in northern China, women prefer oil-based moisturizers due to the dry weather while in southern China, women don't like moisturizers to be too oily due to the humid climate.

Foreign companies operating in China usually employ international advertising agencies for their advertising needs. Many international agencies now have either representative offices or joint ventures in China. When planning an advertisement strategy, it is important to select an agency with strong connections with local media, as this may affect not only the rates and service, but also the desired location and viewing time. It is not unusual that many media in China don't have proper rate cards with details and agencies with good connections often get better deals than others.

5.4 Exhibiting in China

The number of trade fairs in China has increased dramatically in recent years. More than 200 international exhibitions per year are now held in China. Though costs for participating trade shows in China are high, it can be an effective way to reach end users and to demonstrate new products.

China has signed treaties granting it membership into the ATA Carnet System and items imported into China for exhibitions and trade shows are exempt from customs duties if they are reexported within three months.

a. The Chinese Export Commodities Fair

Since 1957, the Chinese Export Commodities Fair, formerly known as the Canton Trade Fair, has been running twice a year (in April and October) in Guangzhou, Guangdong Province. The show is devoted primarily to the promotion of Chinese export commodities, particularly in light industrial products as well as arts and crafts. The event is held at the China Foreign Trade Center, 117 Liu Hua Road, Guangzhou, and is organized by the China Foreign Trade Center Group. Invitation is required to attend the fair. Participants must turn in the invitation in Guangzhou to exchange for admission ticket into the fair. For information on obtaining invitation and other details, contact:

1). China Chamber of International Commerce
1 Fuxingmenwai Dajie, Beijing 100860
Tel: (86-10)-6801-1320 Fax: (86-10)-6801-1370

2). US China Travel Service
212 Sutter Street, 2/F, San Francisco, CA 94108
Tel: (415)-398-6627 Fax: (415)-398-6669

b. Source for Comprehensive China Trade Show Listings

"Fairs & Exhibitions China" - a bilingual, annual publication by China Council for the Promotion of International Trade in Beijing. It lists more than 260 fairs and exhibitions in 19 major cities in China. Information includes show date, location, frequency, organizer's phone and fax numbers. U.S. distributor: Caravel, Inc. Tel: 310-325-0100 Fax: 310-325-2583

6. China's Major Technology Projects from Year 1993 - 2000

6.1 Agriculture

No.	Project	Description
1	Agricultural Development in Henan Province	Upgrading of 111,000 acres of low-yield farmland along the Yellow River and expanding irrigation area to 60,000 acres
2	Agricultural Development in Sichuan Province	Upgrading of Wudu-Shengzhong irrigation facilities which covers an irrigation area of 60,000 acres of farmland
3	Agricultural Irrigation Works of the Basins of the Yellow River, Huaihe River and Haihe River	Building grain production facilities and improving irrigation systems in the following Provinces: Jiangsu, Shandong and Anhui
4	Irrigation Works at Uygur Autonomous Region in Southern Xinjiang	Cultivation of 30,000 acres of uninhabited area and upgrading of 45,000 acres of low-yield farmland
5	Tongyuhe River Project in Northern Jiangsu	Project covers 46,000 acres of irrigation area of farmland with a river course of 150 miles in length
6	Development of Agricultural Irrigation Works in Hunan	Agricultural development with enhancement of water conservation facilities in Lake Dongting area
7	Development of Agricultural Irrigation Works in Hubei	Agricultural development in Jianghan Plain; enhancement of water conservation facilities; promotion of afforestation
8	Agricultural Development in Jilin Province and Changchun City	Agricultural plantation with modern processing of animal and agricultural by-products in Baicheng and Changchun
9	Agricultural Development in Liaohe Plain, Liaoning Province	Agricultural plantation with modern processing of aquatic agricultural by-products
10	Promulgation of Agricultural Technology and Related Services	Promotion of new techniques on breeding of seeds as well as livestock
11	Plantation of Tropical Crops in Guangdong Province	Cultivation and processing of tropical crops including gum-trees and sugarcane
12	Cultivation of Seafood Varieties in Bohai Bay	Farming and processing of value-added products
13	Agricultural Development in Hainan	Plantation and processing of agricultural products
14	Agricultural Development in West Henan	Plantation and processing of fruit products; breeding and processing of livestock products
15	Agricultural Development in Fujian	Plantation and processing of agricultural products
16	Flood Protection at Lake Taihu	Comprehensive management of flood protection and drainage
17	National Afforestation Project, Phase II	Plantation of over 1.2 million acres of windbreak forests

18	Development of Animal Feeds Industry	Building facilities for production and storage of forage additives and animal feeds
19	Development of Grain Distribution Network	Constructing grain storage facilities; building transportation network to facilitate and expedite grain distribution
20	Red Soil Rehabilitation, Phase II	Agricultural cultivation in five provinces of South China; comprehensive study/management of red soil transformation
21	Transformation of Loess Plateau	Comprehensive project management for alleviating soil erosion in middle reaches of the Yellow River
22	Plantation of Seeds, Phase II	Search ways to grow seeds in better environment affected by soil, water and temperature
23	Development along the West Bank of the Yellow River in Gansu Province	In-depth agricultural cultivation across the Shule River Valley
24	Agricultural Development in South-West China	Agricultural cultivation in Provinces of Guizhou, Yunnan and Guangxi Autonomous Region

6.2 Building Materials

No.	Project	Description
1	Ningbo Cement Grinding Mill	Building facilities to produce 690,000 tons of No. 525 Portland cement per year
2	Renovation of Nanjing China Cement Plant	Building a new dry kiln to produce 2,000 tons of cement per day
3	Kaolin Project in Zhanjiang, Guangdong Province	Increasing the production capacity by 100,000 tons per year
4	Wulan Cement Plant at Nei Mongol Autonomous Region	Building facilities to produce 700,000 tons of cement per year
5	Hebi Cement Plant in Henan	Building facilities to produce 600,000 tons of cement per year
6	Yaohua Glass Plant at Qinhuangdao in Hebei Province	Expanding floating glass production line

6.3 Chemical Products

No.	Project	Description
1	Wengfu Phosphate Fertilizer Factory in Guizhou Province	Building facilities to produce 80,000 tons of double superphosphate per year
2	Yanshan Di-Phenol Complex	Building facilities to produce 30,000 tons of Di-phenol per year
3	Environmental Protection and Chemical Plant Renovation at Southern Jiangsu	Project covers sewerage treatment and renovation of chemical plant, in order to improve environmental protection

4	Kaifeng Carbon Steel Factory in Henan	Building facilities to produce 30,000 tons of high grade graphite electrode per year
5	Honghe Chemical Plant in Sichuan Province	Increasing caustic soda production capacity from 50,000 tons per year to 70,000 tons per year
6	Xuanghua Chemical Fertilizer Factory in Hebei Province	Building facilities to produce 240,000 tons of Di-ammonium hydrogen phosphate and 400,000 tons of sulfuric acid yearly
7	Jilin Chemical Fertilizer Factory	Building facilities to produce 300,000 tons of ammonia and 520,000 tons of urea per year
8	Haiyang Audio-Video Co. in Shantou, Guangdong Province	Building facilities to produce 40,000 tons of polyester slice per year
9	Yunnan Chemical Plant	Increasing production capacity of caustic soda by 50,000 tons
10	Dagu Chemical Plant in Tianjin	Building facilities to produce 80,000 tons of PVC per year
11	Nanhua (Grouping) Chemical Corporation in Nanjing	Building facilities to produce 300,000 tons of ammonia and 520,000 tons of urea per year
12	Beijing United Chemical Corp.	Building facilities to produce 40,000 tons of EVA resin yearly
13	Pingdingshan Nylon-66 Salt Project in Henan Province	Building facilities to produce 300,000 tons of Nylon-66 Salt per year
14	Nanning Titanium Dioxide Plant in Guangxi Zhuang Autonomous Region	Building facilities to produce 15,000 tons of titanium dioxide per year
15	Maluping Phosphate Mine at Kaiyang, Guizhou Province	Importing modern mining equipment to increase the production capacity to 1 million tons per year
16	Ion-membrane Project at Nantong, Jiangsu Province	Building facilities to produce 180,000 square feet of ion-membrane per year
17	Chuandong Salt Chemical Co. in Sichuan Province	Building facilities to produce 180,000 square feet of ion-membrane per year

6.4 Civil Aviation

No.	Project	Description
1	Xiamen Airport, Phase II	Acquisition of equipment, instruments, and materials
2	Refining of Civil Aviation System	Upgrading of navigation control & meteorological systems
3	Jingdezhen and Ganzhou Airports in Jiangxi Province	Airport extension to facilitate takeoff and landing of MD-82 and Boeing 737 aircraft
4	Lukou Civic Airport in Nanjing	Acquisition of modern navigation systems
5	Zhengzhou Airport in Henan Province	Acquisition of modern navigation systems

| 6 | Beijing Capital Airport Project | Building a new terminal complex with a floor area of 1.1 million square feet and related infrastructures |

6.5 Coal

No.	Project	Description
1	Houjitu Pit at Shengfu Coal Mine in Dongsheng Mining Area	Building facilities and related infrastructures to produce 5 million tons of raw coal per year
2	Jining No. 2 Coal Mine in Yanzhou Mining Area, Shandong Province	Building facilities and related infrastructures to produce 4 million tons of raw coal per year
3	Jining No. 3 Coal Mine in Yanzhou Mining Area, Shandong Province	Building facilities and related infrastructures to produce 5 million tons of raw coal per year
4	Xuchang Coal Mine in Yanzhou Mining Area, Shandong Province	Building facilities and related infrastructures to produce 5 million tons of raw coal per year
5	Daizhuang Coal Mine in Yanzhou Mining Area, Shandong Province	Building facilities and related infrastructures to produce 1.5 million tons of raw coal per year
6	Fucun Coal Mine in Tengnan Mining Area, Shandong Province	Building facilities and related infrastructures to produce 3 million tons of raw coal per year
7	Anjialing Opencut Coal Mine in Pingshuo Mining Area, Shaanxi	Building facilities and related infrastructures to produce 15 million tons of raw coal per year
8	Chensilou Coal Mine in Yongcheng Mining Area, Henan Province	Building facilities and related infrastructures to produce 2.4 million tons of raw coal per year
9	Cheji Coal Mine in Yongcheng Mining Area, Henan Province	Building facilities and related infrastructures to produce 1.8 million tons of raw coal per year

6.6 Electronics

No.	Project	Description
1	Overall Development of Electronics Industry	Introducing latest technologies in the industry; encouraging technology transfer; acquisition of modern equipment

6.7 Energy

No.	Project	Description
1	Jiujiang Power Plant in Jiangxi Province, Phase III	Installing unit(s) to generate 2x300,000 kw of electricity
2	Sanhe Power Station in Beijing	Installing unit(s) to generate 2x350,000 kw of electricity
3	E-zhou Power Plant in Hubei Province	Installing unit(s) to generate 2x300,000 kw of electricity
4	Wangpuzhou Hydropower Station in Hubei Province	Installing unit(s) to generate 4x275,000 kw of electricity

5	Xiaolangdi Key Water Control Project in Henan Province	Reservoir capacity to be 110 billion cubic feet and generating capacity to be 1,560,000 kw after project
6	Dagi Power Plant in Nei Mongol Autonomous Region	Acquisition of key equipment to generate 2x300,000 kw of electricity
7	Ertan Hydropower Station in Sichuan Province	Installing unit(s) to generate 6x550,000 kw of electricity
8	Tianshenqiao Chain Hydropower Stations	Project includes installation of generating units, transmission line and transformers; new capacity to be 4x300,000 kw
9	Hejin Power Plant in Shaanxi Province	Installing unit(s) to generate 2x300,000 kw of electricity
10	Guangdong Power Station, Phase II	Installing unit(s) to generate 4x300,000 kw of electricity
11	Qitaihe Power Plant in Heilongjiang	Installing unit(s) to generate 2x300,000 kw of electricity
12	Hongjiadu Hydropower Station in Guizhou Province	Installing unit(s) to generate 3x180,000 kw of electricity
13	Mianhuatan Hydropower Station in Fujian Province	Installing unit(s) to generate 4x150,000 kw of electricity
14	Shanghai Natural Gas Development Project near East China Sea	Developing Pinghu Gas Field; Erecting gas pipeline and establishing distribution network in urban areas
15	Lingjintan Hydropower Station in Hunan Province	Installing unit(s) to generate 8x30,000 kw of electricity
16	Longtan Hydropower Station in Guangxi Zhuang Autonomous Region	Installing unit(s) to generate 7x600,000 kw of electricity
17	Yangzhou Power Plant in Jiangsu	Installing unit(s) to generate 2x600,000 kw of electricity
18	Beilunggang Power Plant in Zhejiang Province	Project includes renovation of major transmission network; installing unit(s) to generate 2x600,000 kw of electricity
19	Tuoketuo Power Plant in Nei Mongol Autonomous Region	Installing unit(s) to generate 2x600,000 kw of electricity
20	Dalian Power Plant, Phase II	Installing unit(s) to generate 2x350,000 kw of electricity
21	Qinshan Nuclear Power Plant, Phase II	Acquisition of key equipment for 2x600,000 kw power units

6.8 Environmental Protection

No.	Project	Description
1	Environmental Protection Project in Chengde and Tangshan Cities	Utilizing innovative technologies in industrial productions to minimize pollution caused by waste water, slag and gas
2	Dalian Water Supply Project	Building facilities to increase water supplying capacity in Biluhe River to 1.2 million tons per day

| 3 | Environmental Protection at Major Ports in China | Upgrading of environment protection facilities at ports with the aid of Global Environment Protection Fund |

6.9 Forestry/Paper Industry

No.	Project	Description
1	Wuchagou Forest Bureau of Xing-An Prefecture, Nei Mongol	Building facilities to produce 405,000 cubic feet of particle board per year
2	Yibin Wood Processing Plant in Sichuan Province	Building facilities to produce 270,000 cubic feet of MDF per year
3	Eucalyptus Pulp and Paper Making Mill in Leizhou City, Guangdong	Building facilities to produce 50,000 tons of pulp per year; project calls for high grade paper production
4	Simao Paper Mill in Yunnan Province	Building facilities to produce 50,000 tons of wooden paste for bleaching powder per year
5	Qingzhou Paper Mill in Fujian Province	Acquisition of bleaching equipment for paper production
6	Yuzhou Paper Mill in Chongqing	Building facilities to produce 20,000 tons of bamboo paste and 15,000 tons of paper per year
7	Jinggangshan Pulp Mill in Jiangxi	Acquisition of modern equipment and latest technologies

| 8 | Nanning Paper Mill | Building facilities to produce 100,000 tons of chemical wood pulp for bleaching powder per year |

6.10 Machinery

No.	Project	Description
1	Machinery Industry in Tianjin	Industrial innovation in the fields of lathes, vehicle parts, electronic components and engineering machinery
2	Machinery Industry in Shenyang, Liaoning Province	Renovation of factories manufacturing lathes; Development of numerical-controlled machines and digital instruments

6.11 Metallurgy

No.	Project	Description
1	Baoshan Iron and Steel Works, Phase III	Installing a power station and facilities to generate 350,000 kw of electricity and increasing production of steel by 3 million tons per year
2	Baoshan Iron and Steel Works, Phase Ii	Modernization of hot rolling mill to improve performance
3	Taiyuan Iron and Steel Company	Building a continuous slab caster, a secondary metallurgy systems, and vacuum treatment facilities
4	Benxi Iron and Steel Company	Building a continuous slab caster and auxiliary facilities
5	Baotou Iron and Steel Company	Building facilities for hot metal pre-treatment and quench post-processing

6.12 Meteorology

No.	Project	Description
1	State Bureau of Meteorology	Development of multi-purpose meteorological satellite

6.13 Nonferrous Metals

No.	Project	Description
1	Zhongzhou Aluminum Plant in Henan Province	Erection of an Alumina Calciner
2	Zhuzhou Hard Alloy Plant	Building facilities to produce an additional 500 tons of hard alloy per year
3	Shanghai Smelter	Acquisition of modern equipment to upgrade the copper foil production line, and to increase the production capacity of copper foil to 1,000 tons per year

6.14 Railway

No.	Project	Description
1	Railway Construction of the 7th Lot	Project includes 591 miles of railway electrification from Harbin to Dalian, and 665 miles from Wuhan to Guangzhou
2	Zhangping-Quanzhou-Xiaocuo Railway Construction, Fujian Province	Erection of 61 miles of railway from Zhangping to Quanzhou; erection of 36 miles of railway from Quanzhou to Xiaocuo
3	Railway Construction of the 6th Lot	Project includes 1089 miles of railway electrification (from Beijing to Zhengzhou and from Chengdu to Kunming); also modernization of railway communication and signal systems
4	Xian-Ankang Railway Construction	Erection of 171 miles of railway with transportation capacity of 20 millions tons per year
5	Erection of a railway connecting Shuoxian and Huanghua Harbor	Project includes construction of 3 berths at the Huanghua Harbor, as well as erection of a railway of 366 miles
6	Erection of a railway connecting Zhejiang and Jianxi Provinces	Erection of a dual-line railway of 586 miles, to increase the transportation capacity by 10 million tons per year
7	Construction of Xuzhou Railway Hub	Hub construction and infrastructure development
8	Guangzhou-Meixian-Shantou Railway Construction, Guangdong Province	Erection of 267 miles of local railway
9	Railway Construction from Hefei to Jiujiang	Erection of 188 miles of first class railway with transportation capacity of 16 million tons per year
10	Railway Construction from Nanning to Kunming	Erection of 544 miles of railway with transportation capacity of 10 million tons per year
11	Railway Construction from Henshui to Shangqiu	Erection of 248 miles of railway with transportation capacity of 16 million tons per year
12	Railway Construction from Beijing to Kowloon, Hong Kong	Erection of railway and signaling systems in Jiangxi Province
13	Railway Construction from Guangzhou to Zhuhai	Erection of 92 miles of railway from Guangzhou to Zhuhai

6.15 Transportation (Excluding Railway)

No.	Project	Description
1	Special Coal Quay at Qinhuangdao, Hebei Province	Construction of 3 deep water berths which can handle 30 million tons per year
2	Dayaowan Port Area at Dalian Harbor, Phase I	Construction of the remaining 6 berths with handling capacity of 3.1 million tons per year

3	Rizhao Harbor Project in Shandong Province, Phase II	Construction of five deep water berths with handling capacity of 2 million tons per year
4	Dadong Port Expansion Project at Dadong Harbor, Liaoning Province	Construction of 3 berths to facilitate 10,000-ton vessels, with handling capacity of 950,000 tons per year
5	Yinkou Port, Liaoning Province	Acquisition of port loading/unloading equipment
6	Yantai Harbor in Shandong Province, Phase II	Construction of 6 berths at Xigangchi Port with handling capacity of 3.4 million tons per year
7	Shanghai Harbor Expansion	Construction of two berths at Luojing Port for 25,000-ton coal vessels; Phase I construction of Waigaoqiao Port
8	Shuji Wharf at Qinhuangdao Harbor, Hebei Province	Construction of 7 berths with handling capacity of 3 million tons per year
9	Xugou Port at Lianyungang Harbor, Jiangxu Province	Construction of 6 berths with handling capacity of 2.1 million tons per year
10	Inland Water Transportation	Management of water transportation in the following areas: Xiangjiang River in Hunan Province, Xijiang River in Guangxi Zhuang Autonomous Region, water channel from Beijing to Hangzhou in Zhejiang Province

6.16 Telecommunications

No.	Project	Description
1	Installation of Digital Telephone Exchangers for 9 Provinces & Cities	Importation of digital exchangers with 760,000 lines (125,000 lines for Tianjin and Guangdong each; 120,000 lines for Shanghai and Jiangxu each; 60,000 lines for Harbin, Xian and Zhejiang each; 50,000 lines for Fujian and 40,000 lines for Changchun) including 31,000 long distance lines
2	Infrastructure development for Qingdao and Huangdao Island	Acquisition of digital exchanger with 80,000 lines; construction of 53 miles of first class highway; building sewerage treatment facilities with processing capacity of 35,000 tons per year
3	Telecommunication network in Helongjiang, Hunan, Fujian, Jiangxu Provinces and Chongqing	Installation of digital exchanger with 2 million lines
4	Bureau of Telecommunications Administration, Beijing	Project includes upgrading and expansion of current digital exchanger systems
5	Development of Optical Fiber Communications	Project includes installation of trunk optical fiber lines in the following areas: Beijing-Wuhan-Guangzhou; Beijing-Taiyuan-Xian; Beijing-Hohhot-Yinchuan-Lianzhou; Fuzhou-Guiyang-Chengdu

6.17 Contact Information

For more information regarding above projects, please contact the following;

Ministry of Foreign Trade & Economic Cooperation
2 Dong Chang An Street, Dong Cheng District
Beijing 100732, People's Republic of China

Tel: 6519-8114, 6519-8322, 6519-8804
Fax: 6512-9568, 6519-8904

PROFIT

FROM THE

P**O**WER

OF

MOL

Land, Sea and Air Transport ● 123 Years of Continuous Service ● $6.2 Billion (US) in Consolidated Revenue ● Diverse Fleet of 354 Vessels (19.82 Million dwt.) Specializing in Container, Automobile, Bulk Commodities, Passenger and LNG Projects ● Global Service Covering All Hemispheres (Over 100 Countries, Over 200 Ports and Over 2,500 Voyages) ● 23 Warehouse and Physical Distribution Centers Located in Asia, Europe and North America for Transparent Supply Chain Management ● 550 Offices Worldwide ● Nine Technologically-Advanced Container Terminals Located in Japan, Asia and North America

MOL

Atlanta 404/763-0111 ● Chicago 312/683-7300 ● Long Beach 562/983-6200 ● Jersey City 201/200-5200 ● Seattle 206/464-3930

China Southern Airlines

The Gateway to China

As the largest domestic airline in China, now we provide non-stop service between Los Angeles and Guangzhou (Canton) with Boeing 777. By flying China Southern Airlines, you will find it the most **convenient** way to reach major cities in **China and Southeast Asia.**

Los Angeles to Guangzhou (Canton)

Non-stop flights with the most modern and comfortable *deluxe* Boeing 777

It is always our pleasure to serve you!

For more information, please call:

1-888-338-8988

CHINA SOUTHERN AIRLINES

1998 - 1999

Directory of U.S. Firms Operating in China & Hong Kong

Province	City	Area Code	Number of Listing	Page No.
- - - - -	*BEIJING*	10	459	69
- - - - -	*CHONGQING*	23	7	120
FUJIAN	Fuzhou	591	5	121
FUJIAN	Xiamen	592	13	121
GUANGDONG	Dongguan	769	3	123
GUANGDONG	Foshan	757	2	123
GUANGDONG	Guangzhou	20	188	124
GUANGDONG	Shenzhen	755	45	145
HEILONGJIANG	Harbin	451	4	150
- - - - -	*HONG KONG*	852	618	151
JIANGSU	Nanjing	25	7	224
JIANGSU	Wuxi	510	2	224
LIAONING	Dalian	411	18	225
LIAONING	Shenyang	24	27	227
- - - - -	*SHANGHAI*	21	355	231
SICHUAN	Chengdu	28	63	271
- - - - -	*TIANJIN*	22	18	278
- - - - -	*Other Cities*	- -	6	280

Total number of listng: 1,840

FREE LISTING!

The new (2000/2001) edition of **"American Business in China" (ABC)** will be published in January, 2000. U.S. firms with representation(s) in China and Hong Kong are eligible to be listed free of charge (up to 3 locations). Please provide us with the following information of your company for accurate listing.

U. S. Head Office

Name of comapny: _____

Address: _____

City: _____ State: _____ Zip Code: _____

Tel #:_____ Fax #: _____

Name of person in charge of China or Asia/Pacific operations: _____

China / Hong Kong Office*

Name of company: _____

Address: _____

_____

Tel #: _____ Fax #: _____

Name of contact person: _____

Nature of business: _____

* Please use additional sheet(s) if you have more than one office in China & Hong Kong.

Please check the following if appropriate:

_____ We are interested in advertsing in **"American Business in China" (ABC)**, please send us a media kit with detailed information.

_____ Please send us a free brochure with order form of **"American Business in China" (ABC)** when the new edition is published.

Please mail or fax this form to:

CARAVEL, INC.
2508 West 225th Place
Torrance, CA 90505 USA

Tel: 310-325-0100
310-325-0331
Fax: 310-325-2583

China Office	Product/Service	U.S. Head Office
3Com Corp. #1656/60 New Century Hotel Office Tower Beijing 100046 T: 6849-2568 F: 6849-2789 General Manager	Communication Servers Network Mgmt Software Local Area Networks	3Com Corp. 5400 Bayfront Plaza Santa Clara, CA 95052 T: 408-764-5000 F: 408-764-5001 Matthew Kapp
3M China Limited 11/F, CATIC Plaza, 18 Beichen Rd. E. Chaoyang District, Beijing 100101 T: 6494-3336 F: 6494-0668 Kalleen Li	Chemical Products Medical Equipments Automotive Products Office Products Consumer Goods	**3M Company** 3M Center Bldg., Bldg 220-14E-02 Saint Paul, MN 55144-1000 T: 612-737-0702 F: 612-733-2095 Tony Gastaldo
A & W Restaurant of Beijing Rm. 201, Silver Bridge Hotel 44 Center Rd. N., Beijing 100088 T: 6201-8877 F: 6206-3181 Frank Miu	Food & Entertainment Franchised Business	A & W Restaurants, Inc. 17197 N. Laurel Park Dr., #500 Livonia, MI 48152 T: 313-462-0029 F: 313-462-2091 Patty Piotrowski
A C Nielsen SRG China 9/F Keying Bldg, 74 Xinjiekou Beidajie, Xincheng Dist., Beijing 100035 T: 6618-9874 F: 6618-9931 General Manager	Market Research	A C Nielsen 177 Broad St. Stamford, CT 06901 T: 203-961-3300 F: 203-961-3170 Nicholas Trivisonno
A. T. Kearney Inc. China World Trade Center #1428/30 1 Jianguomenwai Dajie, Beijing 100004 T: 6505-4627 F: 6505-5009 Richard Miskewicz	Management Consultants	A T Kearney Inc. 222 West Adams St., #2500 Chicago, IL 60606 T: 312-648-0111 F: 312-223-6200 William J Best
ABB China Ltd. South Tower, Rainbow Plaza 14 N. Dongsanhuan Rd., Beijing 100026 T: 6596-6688 F: 6595-5048 Yan Chen	Industrial Automation Power	**ABB** 1515 Broad St. Bloomfield, NJ 07003-3096 T: 201-893-2416 F: 201-893-3150 Y J Chen
ABB Lummus Overseas Corp. Rm. 801, SCITE Tower 22 Jianguomenwai Dajie, Beijing 100004 T: 6513-1169 F: 6512-6860 Jun-Yan Chen	Petrochemical Refining Chemicals Petroleum Products	ABB Lummus Global Inc. 1515 Broad St. Bloomfield, NJ 07003 T: 201-893-1515 F: 201-893-2000 Y J Chen
Abbott International Rm. 3411, Jing Guang Center Beijing 100020 T: 6501-5201/02 F: 6501-3058 Raymond Wong	Pharmaceutical	Abbott Laboratories 100 Abbott Park Rd. Abbot Park, IL 60064 T: 847-937-6100 F: 847-937-1511 Robert Parkinson
Accuracy Language Services Wanquan Zhuang Yuan #861 Zhixi Dong Lu, Beijing 100083 T: 6232-4499 x336861 F: 6231-1372 Paul E. McArthur	Language Services	

- - - - - T: Telephone # - - - - - F: Fax # - - - - - Beijing Area Code: (86)10 - - - - -

China Office	Product/Service	U.S. Head Office
Actava World Trade Corp. Guang Ming Bldg., #1405-6 Liangmaqiao Rd., Beijing 100016 T: 6467-7699/7899 F: 6467-7662 Evan Wonacott	Light Industry Sporting Goods	American Camper 14760 Santa Fe Trail Dr. Lenexa, KS 66215-2001 T: 913-492-3200 F: 913-492-1367 Peter Boyle
AES China Generating Co. 3/F Jing Qiao Bldg. A1 Jianguomenwai Dajie, Beijing 100020 T: 6508-9619 F: 6508-9628 Paul Hanrahan; Kerry Yeager	Power	AES Corp. 1001 19th St. N. Arlington, VA 22209 T: 703-522-1315 F: 703-528-4510 Thomas A. Tribone
AETNA International, Inc. Rm. 3043, Jinlun Hotel Beijing Toronto 3 Jianguomenwai Dajie, Beijing 100020 T: 6500-2266 x3043 F: 6500-2022 x 3043 Ka Ning	Insurance	AETNA International 151 Farmington Ave. Hartford, CT 06156 T: 860-273-0123 F: 860-275-2677 Frederick C Copeland, Jr.
Alcoa Asia Ltd. Lufthansa Center #C816 50 Liangmaqiao Rd., Beijing 100016 T: 6463-8034/35 F: 6463-8032 Joseph Stasiuk	Aluminum Industry	Aluminum Co of America (Alcoa) Alcoa Bldg., 425 Sixth Ave. Pittsburgh, PA 15219-1850 T: 412-553-4545 F: 412-553-4585 Robert F. Slagle
Alcon China 220 Zhongfa Building No. 12 Jiu Xian Qiao Road, Beijing 100016 T: 6437-0257 F: 6437-0258 Claire Lee	Ophthalmic Instrument Pharmaceutical	Alcon Laboratories, Inc. 6201 S. Freeway Ft. Worth, TX 76134 T: 817-293-0450 F: 817-568-6200 Fred W. Aebi
Allen Telecom Group Inc. CITIC Building #11-04 19 Jianguomenwai Dajie, Beijing 100004 T: 6508-3088 F: 6508-3066 Harry Li	Telecommunications	Allen Telecom, Inc. 25101 Chagrin Blvd., #350 Beachwood, OH 44122-5619 T: 216-765-5800 F: 216-765-0410 Peter de Villers
Allen-Bradley Beijing-Toronto Hotel #4047 Beijing 100020 T: 6500-2266 x 4047 F: 6500-2266 x 4038 Carl A. Cozine	Industrial Automation Controls	Allen-Bradley Co. 1201 S. Second St., PO Box 2086 Milwaukke, WI 53201 T: 414-382-2000 F: 414-382-4444 Richard E. Shelton
Allergan Northern China Office Yinghang Building 5/F, 1 Beinhe Road, Hepingli Dongjie, Beijing 100013 T: 6837-2959 F: 6837-2967 Zheng Zhong	Eye Care Pharmaceutical	Allergan Pharmaceutical Int'l Inc. 2525 DuPont Dr., PO Box 19534 Irvine, CA 92612 T: 714-752-4500 F: 714-752-4359 Jacqueline J. Schiavo
Allied Pickfords China No. 9 Ri Tan Dong Lu, Room B02 Beijing 100020 T: 6595-8759/60 F: 6595-8764 Oscar Lau	Moving Service	Allied International 215 W. Diehl Rd. Naperville, IL 60563 T: 630-717-3500 F: 630-717-3496 Mike Cosnett / Dave Buth

China Office	Product/Service	U.S. Head Office
Allied Signal China Inc. A1-514 Lido Commercial Center Jiangtai Rd., Beijing 100004 T: 6437-6763 F: 6437-6616 Francis Yuen	Avionics/Aerospace Trading	Allied Signal International, Inc. 101 Columbia Road, P O Box 2245 Morristown, NJ 07962 T: 201-455-2000 F: 201-455-4807 Paul R. Schindler
Alpha Yunnan Tin Solder Co., Ltd. No. 5, Jiu Xian Qiao Bei Rd. Dashanzi, Beijing 100015 T: 6437-4957 F: 6437-4969 Ernest Ho / Sara Zhou	Metal Products	Alpha Metals Inc. 600 Route 440 Jersey City, NJ 07304 T: 201-434-6778 F: 201-434-2307 David B. Zerfoss
Altman Companies International Club #214 21 Jianguomenwai Dajie, Beijing 100020 T: 6512-9809 F: 6532-3887 Donald R. Altman; Zhao Junli	Trading Consulting	Altman, Inc. P. O. Box 54 Purdys, NY 10578 T: 914-277-8016 F: 914-277-3556 Donald Altman
Alumax International 3518 CWTC Tower 1 Jianguomenwai Dajie, Beijing 100004 T: 6505-5305 F: 6505-5306 Marc R. Pomerleau	Aluminum Products	Alumax Inc. 5655 Peachtree Pkwy. Norcross, GA 30092 T: 770-246-6600 F: 770-246-6691 Thomas Hagley

China Office	Product/Service	U.S. Head Office

AMD Beijing Office
Rm.558, Office Bldg., Hong Kong Macau Ctr. Computers
Dongsishitiao Lijiaqiao, Beijing 100027
T: 6501-1566 F: 6501-3815
General Manager

Advanced Micro Devices, Inc.
One AMD Pl.
Sunnyvale, CA 94085
T: 408-732-2400 F: 408-749-3127
Gerald A. Lynch

Amer-China Partners Ltd.
Xinqiao Hotel #560, 561, 562
Beijing 100004
T: 6513-3366 x 560 F: 6513-3516
Zhihai Zhai

Home Healthcare
Health Food
Marketing Research
Consulting
Headhunting

Amer-China Partners Ltd.
620 North Third Ave.
St. Charles, IL 60174
T: 708-513-5765 F: 708-513-5338
George C Bergland

American Airlines
A15 Guang Hua Rd, Ritan Office Bldg.
Suite 2168, Chao Yang Dist, Beijing 100020
T: 6595-7559 F: 6595-7560
Matthew F Chen

Airline

American Airlines Inc.
4333 Amon Carter Blvd.
Fort Worth, TX 76155
T: 817-963-1234 F: 817-967-3816
Hans Mirka

American Appraisal Ltd.
Beijing Asia Hotel #1913
8 Xinzhong Xi Jie, Beijing 100027
T: 6500-7788 F: 6500-7515
K K Ip

Asset Valuation

American Appraisal Associates
411 East Wisconsin Ave.
Milwaukee, WI 53202
T: 414-225-2005 F: 414-271-1041
George H. Liu

American Asian Art Foundation
Rm. 1001-1005, Jingheng Guesthouse
Laogucheng Dajie, Shi Jing Shan Dist. Beijing
T: 6883-3035 F: 6884-5571
Yu Renxun

Art Foundation

American Chamber of Commerce (AMCHAM) Trade Organization
Great Wall Sheraton Hotel #444
Beijing 100026
T: 6500-5566 x2271 F: 6501-8273
Jane Drake

China Phone Book & Business Directory

With a circulation of 15,000 copies in over 46 countries around the world, it includes 19,000 listings of major organizations in China. Also include fax numbers. Bilingual.

Caravel, Inc.
Tel: 310-325-0100
Fax: 310-325-2583

American Express Int'l, Inc.
2313 CWTC Tower
1 Jianguomenwai Dajie, Beijing 100004
T: 6505-2838 F: 6505-4626
Jean Young

Banking

American Express Co.
200 Vessey St.
New York, NY 10285
T: 212-640-2000 F: 212-619-8802
David Beeman

American Express
2101 CWTC Tower
1 Jianguomenwai Dajie, Beijing 100004
T: 6505-2228 x 2702 F: 6505-2818
Yu-Jin Xi

Travel-related Service

American Express Co.
200 Vessey St.
New York, NY 10285
T: 212-640-2000 F: 212-619-8802
Stephen Friedman / John Sutphen

American International Group
Jing Guang Center #3407
Beijing 100020
T: 6501-2889 F: 6501-2878
Lai Xiang Lin

Insurance

American International Group
70 Pine Street
New York, N 10270
T: 212-770-7000 F: 212-770-7821
Evan Greenberg / Martin J. Sullivan

China Office	Product/Service	U.S. Head Office

American President Line
3 Technical Club, 15 Guanghuali
Chaoyang Dist., Beijing 100020
T: 6591-3177/78 F: 6591-3179
Chang Zong Qing

Shipping Line

APL Ltd.
1111 Broadway
Oakland, CA 94607
T: 510-272-8000 F: 510-272-7941
Keith Mackie

American Soybean Association
1323 CWTC Tower
1 Jianguomenwai Dajie, Beijing 100004
T: 6505-1830/31 F: 6505-2201
Phillip Laney

Market Development

American Soybean Association
12125 Woodcrest Ever Dr., #100
St. Louis, MO 63141
T: 314-576-1770 F: 314-576-2786
Steve Censky

Amgen Greater China Ltd.
Rm 1702-04, Block A, Lucky Tower
3 North Dongsanhuan Rd., Beijing 100027
T: 6467-9225/9228 F: 6467-9233
Rick Woo

Pharmaceuticals

Amgen Inc.
Amgen Center, 1840 DeHavilland Dr.
Thousand Oaks, CA 91230
T: 805-447-1000 F: 805-447-1010
Daryl D. Hill

AMOCO Orient Co.
Jing Guang Center #3303/05
Beijing 100020
T: 6501-4580 F: 6501-4581
C. Patrick Chu

Oil & Petrochemical

AMOCO Chemical Corp.
200 E. Randolph Dr.
Chicago, IL 60601
T: 312-856-2777 F: 312-856-3800
Enrique J. Sosa

AMOCO Orient Petroleum Co.
rm. 705 Lido Bldg.
Jichang Rd., Beijing 100004
T: 6436-7381 F: 6436-7382
William Hudson

Exploration
Oil & Gas
Petroleum Equipment

AMOCO Chemical Corp.
200 E. Randolph Dr.
Chicago, IL 60601
T: 312-856-2777 F: 312-856-3800
Enrique J. Sosa

AMOCO Oriental Oil Co.
Jing Guang Center 2506
Beijing 100020
T: 6501-2031 F: 6501-2024
Anna Catalano

Refining

AMOCO Chemical Corp.
200 E. Randolph Dr.
Chicago, IL 60601
T: 312-856-2777 F: 312-856-3800
Enrique J. Sosa

AMT
SAS Hotel #310/312
Beisanhuandonglu, Beijing 100028
T: 6467-2924 F: 6467-7830
Kaijiang Ma; Li Xingbin

Association for
Manufacturing Technology

AMTEX Inc.
B19, Beisanhuan Middle Road
Beijing 100029
T: 6204-3924/25 F: 6204-3929
Judy Wu

Medical Supply

AN-TAI Corp. (N.Y.)
10/F, Pana Tower,
No. 36 Haidian Rd., Beijing 100086
T: 6262-9068/9070 F: 6256-5668
Qing-Yuan Deng

Computer Work Station

- - - - - T: Telephone # - - - - - F: Fax # - - - - - Beijing Area Code: (86)10 - - - - -

China Office	Product/Service	U.S. Head Office
Analog Devices 59A Fuxing Rd. Haidian Dist., Beijing 100854 T: 6837-3894 F: 6838-5621 Fan Hu	Medical Electronic Equipment Scientific Instruments Signal Processing Equipment Imaging Equipment	Analog Devices Inc. One Technology Way Norwood, MA 02062 T: 617-329-4700 F: 617-326-8703 Rob Marshall
Aon Corp. 1803 China Travel Service Tower 2 Beisanhuandong Rd., Beijing 100028 T: 6462-2288 F: 6460-3169 David L. Liu	Insurance	Aon Corp. 123 N. Wacker Dr. Chicago, IL 60606 T: 312-701-4592 F: 312-701-4359 Philip Gawthorpe
Apple Computer No. 6 Fuxingmenwai Dajie, 12/F Everbright Bldg, Beijing 100045 T: 6856-3330 F: 6856-1169 Vincent Tai	Computers	Apple Computer Inc. 1 Infinite Loop Cupertino, CA 95014 T: 408-996-1010 F: 408-974-2113 Dave Manovich
ARCO Chemical China Ltd. 15/F Consultec Blvd., Guanghua Rd. Jianguomenwai, Beijing 100020 T: 6505-5888 F: 6505-0647 Jim Weeks; Simon Feng	Chemical Petroleum	**Atlantic Richfield Co.** 515 S. Flower St. Los Angeles, CA 90071 T: 213-486-3511 F: 213-486-1544 Walter A. Coyne
Arthur Andersen Huaqiang CPA China World Tower #1118 Beijing 100004 T: 6505-3333 F: 6505-1828 Clyde Dickey	Accounting Consulting	**Arthur Andersen & Co.** 69 W. Washington St. Chicago, IL 60602 T: 312-580-0069 F: 312-507-6748 Richard Measelle
Aseptico, Inc. 107 Bei Wei Lou of the Rainbow Hotel 11 Xi Jing Rd, Xuan Wu Dist, Beijing 100050 T: 6315-2835 F: 6315-2835 Peter Xiao	Medical & Dental Eqmt	Aseptico Inc. P. O. Box 3209 Kirkland, WA 98083 T: 206-487-3157 F: 206-487-2608 Peter Xiao
Ashland Inc. 416A Business Bldg. Holiday Inn Lido Jichang Rd., Beijing 100004 T: 6437-6620 F: 6437-6623 Jiang Fu	Petroleum	Ashland Inc. 1000 Ashland Dr. Russel, KY 41169 T: 606-329-3333 F: 606-329-3922 Stuart Davidson / Stanford Lampe
Asia System Media (ASM Group) Xizhimen Nan Dajie No. 16, 2/F, Beijing 100035 T: 6616-3776/3768 F: 6616-3772 Dr. Albert S. Lai	Information Internet Consulting	Asia System Media Inc. 9550 Flair Dr., #200 El Monte, CA 91731 T: 626-582-1068 F: 626-582-1069 Tsung Chin Wu
AST Research Inc. Friendship Hotel 3 Baishiqiao Rd., Beijing 100873 T: 6849-8318 F: 6849-8319 S. M. Chen	Computers	AST Research Inc. 16215 Alton Parkway Irvine, CA 92619 T: 714-727-4141 F: 714-727-8584 Hoon Choo / Scott Bower

China Office	Product/Service	U.S. Head Office
AT&T China Inc. 8/F, CVIK Palace 22 Jianguomenwai Dajie, Beijing 100004 T: 6515-0808 F: 6522-7785 Bill Warwick; Hanh Tu; Kuang Chow	Telecommunications	AT&T International 295 N. Maple Ave., Rm. I-14 Basking Ridge, NJ 07920 T: 248-262-6646 F: 248-952-5095 Elizabeth Mallek
ATC International Inc. Lido Center, Blk A-2, #405 Beijing 100004 T: 6437-6663 F: 6437-6904 Paul W. Speltz	Petroleum Aviation Automotive Pharmaceuticals	ATC International Inc. 1776 Yorktown, #340 Houston, TX 77056 T: 713-622-3047 F: 713-622-1864 Bruce Bentley
Autodesk Fareast Ltd. Suite 1892, Pana Tower 128 Haidian Rd., Beijing 100086 T: 6264-9581 F: 6264-9584 Jack Gao; Li Xiaoming	CAD/CAM Software	Autodesk, Inc. 111 McInnis Parkway San Rafael, CA 94903 T: 415-507-5000 F: 415-507-5100 Tom Norring
B&J Industrial Supply Co. Towercrest, Suite 222 3 Mai Zi Dian West Rd., Beijing 100016 T: 6467-2656 F: 6467-2657 Bill Burkland	Industrial Supplies	B&J Industrial Supply 5601 First Ave. S. Seattle, WA 98108 T: 206-762-4430 F: 206-762-5329 Bill Burkland
Babcock & Wilcock Beijing Rm. 168 Jianguo Hotel 5 Jianquomenwai Dajie, Beijing 100020 T: 6591-8480 F: 6591-8479 Geo Karakis	Power Generation Boilers	Babcock & Wilcox Int'l Inc. 120 S. Van Buren Ave. Barberton, OH 44203 T: 216-753-4511 F: 216-860-1886 P. P. Koenderman / R. J. Batyko
Bailey Beijing Controls 41 Gulou West Street Beijing 100020 T: 6401-0671 F: 6401-1643 Wayne Wortman	Process Controls	Bailey Controls Co. 29801 Enclid Ave. Wickliffe, OH 44092 T: 216-585-8500 F: 216-943-4609 R. P. Browngardt
Bain & Co. China, Inc. Jing Guang Center #819 Beijing 100020 T: 6501-3388 F: 6501-4592 Rick Yan	Market Survey & Research	Bain & Co., Inc. 2 Copley Place Boston, MA 02116 T: 617-572-2000 F: 617-572-2427 Sue Blake
Baird Corp. Rm. 4H Guo Men Bldg. No. 1 Zuo Jia Zhuang, Beijing 100028 T: 6460-6843 F: 6460-6849 Jean Jones	Analytical Instrumentation	Baird Corp. 27 Forge Pkwy. Franklin, MA 02038 T: 508-520-1880 F: 508-541-6938 A. I. Priede
Baker & McKenzie 2526 China World Tower 1 Jianquomenwai Dajie, Beijing 100004 T: 6505-0591/92 F: 6505-2309 John W. Sullivan; John Eichelberger	Law	Baker & McKenzie 1 Prudential Plaza 130 E. Randolph Dr. Chicago, IL 60601 T: 312-861-8800 F: 312-861-8823 Teresa A Townsend / Jennifer Flynn

China Office	**Product/Service**	**U.S. Head Office**
Baker Hughes, Inc. Suite 1001, Consultec Bldg. B12 Beijing 100020 T: 6505-2501 F: 6505-2831/32/33 Ellen Zhang	Petroleum Equipment Mining Equipment Waste Water Treatment Eq. Process Equipment	Baker Hughes Inc. 3900 Essex Ln., #1200 Houston, TX 77027 T: 713-439-8600 F: 713-439-8261 R. Pat Herbert / Andy Szescila
Baldwin Printing Control Equipment Co. Rm. 115, Juyuan Office Bldg., 33 Juer Alley Jiaodaokou Nan Dajie, Beijing 100009 T: 6407-0593/94 F: 6407-0593 Ben Liang	Printing Equipment	Baldwin Technology Corp. 65 Rowayton Ave. Rowayton, CT 06853 T: 203-838-7470 F: 203-852-7040 Akira Hara
Bandag, Inc. 708 Beijing Silver Tower 2 Dongsanhuan N. Rd., Beijing 100027 T: 6410-6301 F: 6410-6299 K. K. Lim	Tires	**Bandag, Inc.** 2505 North Highway 61 Muscatine, IA 52761 T: 319-262-1400 F: 319-262-1426 Hong Yan Henry Li / Gerald Borenstein
Bank of America NT & SA World Trade Tower Room 2609 Beijing 100004 T: 6505-3508 F: 6505-3509 Tony Cheng; Ben Cheng	Banking	BankAmerica Corp. 315 Montgomery St., M/S-10540 San Francisco, CA 94010 T: 415-622-2507 F: 415-622-5719 John Mauney
Bank of Boston 10-D, CITIC Building 19 Jianguomenwai Dajie, Beijing 100004 T: 6593-1850 F: 6593-1851 Katherine Sun	Banking	Bank Boston Corp. 100 Federal St. Boston, MA 02110 T: 617-434-2200 Clark W. Miller
Bank of New York Rm. 220 Landmark Tower 8 Dongsanhuanbei Rd., Beijing 100004 T: 6506-6548 F: 6506-6943 General Manager	Banking	Bank of New York 48 Wall St. New York, NY 10286 T: 212-495-3007 F: 212-495-2413 Thomas A. Renyi
Bankers Trust Company Suite 125, Lufthansa Center Offices 50 Liangmaqiao Rd., Beijing 100016 T: 6463-8038 F: 6463-8037 Qian Heng	Banking	Bankers Trust Co. 280 Park Avenue New York, NY 10017 T: 212-454-3047 F: 212-454-3110 Karen Horn
Banyan Systems Rm. 1060A, New Century Hotel Beijing T: 6849-2668 F: 6849-2667 Homuel Yick	LAN Software	Banyan Systems, Inc. 115 & 120 Flanders Rd. Westboro, MA 01581 T: 508-898-1000 F: 508-898-1755 W. Fitzsimmons / Ann Reilly
Bard International 9/F Swiss Hotel Dong Sisitiao, Beijing T: 6501-4225 General Manager	Health Care Products	C R Bard Inc. 730 Central Ave. Murray Hill, NJ 07974 T: 908-277-8000 F: 908-277-8240 Louis G. Salgueiro

China Office	Product/Service	U.S. Head Office
Baskin-Robbins & Dunkin Donuts 1802 Capital Mansion 6 Xin Yuan S. Rd., Beijing 10004 T: 6465-4342 F: 6465-4325 Greg Combs	Ice Cream	Allied Domecq Retailing Int'l 31 Baskin-Robbins Place Glendale, CA 91201 T: 818-956-0031 F: 818-240-7953 Paul Fischer
Bausch & Lomb Eyecare Co. No. 37 Xingfu Ave. Chongwen Dist., Beijing 100061 T: 6712-7181 F: 6711-1601 Eddie Wong	Healthcare and Optics	Bausch & Lomb Inc. One Bausch & Lomb Place Rochester, NY 14604 T: 716-338-6000 F: 716-338-6007 Alexander E. Izzard
Baxter Healthcare Ltd. China World Tower #2401 Beijing 100004 T: 6505-0557/58 F: 6505-0556 Javier Henao	Medical Equipment Microorganism Cultures	Baxter International Inc. One Baxter Parkway Deerfield, IL 60015 T: 847-948-2000 F: 847-948-2887 John F. Gaither, Jr.
BBDO/CNUAC Advertsing Co. Capital Mansion 23/F Beijing 100027 T: 6466-3318 F: 6466-2311 Victor Chan	Advertsing	BBDO Worldwide 1285 Avenue of the Americas New York, NY 10019 T: 212-459-5000 Philippe Krakowsky
Bear Stearns Ltd. China World Tower #923 Beijing 100004 T: 6505-5101/03 F: 6505-5203 Yucheng Ding	Investment Banking	Bear Stearns & Co., Inc. 245 Park Ave. New York, NY 10167 T: 212-272-2000 F: 212-272-5143 Michael Conway
Bechtel China Inc. Rm. 501 Parkview Center 2 Jiangtai Rd., Beijing 100016 T: 6437-6669 F: 6437-6455 Charles Harper	Civil Engineering Construction Contracting Power, Industrial, Metals Finance & Investment Project Management	Bechtel Group Inc. 50 Beale St. San Francisco, CA 94105 T: 415-768-1234 F: 415-768-2154 Riley P Bechtel
Becker ^ Poliakoff Suite 61824 Friendship Hotel 3 Baishiqiao Rd., Beijing 100873 T: 6849-8685 F: 6849-8779 General Manager	Law	Becker ^ Poliakoff & Streitfeld 33 N. Garden Ave., #960 Clearwater, FL 34615 T: 813-443-3781 F: 813-443-4079 Robert Tankel
Beckman Instruments Inc. China World Tower #1006-1007 Beijing 100004 T: 6505-1241/42 F: 6505-1243 Siu Fan; Wei Zhang (Ms.)	Chemical Instruments Medical Instruments	Beckman Instruments Inc. 2500 Harbor Blvd. Fullerton, CA 92634 T: 714-871-4848 F: 714-773-8898 Barbara Keeler
Becton Dicknson Asia, Ltd. Unit 1001/02, 10/F, Tower A, Kelung Bldg. 12 Guanghau Rd., Beijing 100020 T: 6593-3072/77 F: 6593-3070 Philip Lee	Pharmaceuticals	Becton Dickinson & Co. 1 Becton Dr. Franklin Lakes, NJ 07417 T: 201-847-6800 F: 201-847-6475 Mark Throdahl / Kenneth Weisshaar

China Office	Product/Service	U.S. Head Office
Beijing Bama Food Processing Co., Ltd. Nanjiao Nogchago Jiu Gong Bei, Beijing T: 6796-2555 F: 6799-6092 Lim Joohoe	Food Manufacturing Supplier to McDonald's	Bama Pie Ltd. P. O. Box 4829 Tulsa, OK 74159 T: 918-592-0778 F: 918-592-7498 Karen Kiely
Beijing Crown Can Company Ltd. #301 Movenpick Hotel P. O. Box 6913, Beijing 100621 T: 6456-1277 F: 6456-1276 General Manager	Packaging	Crown Cork & Seal Co., Inc. PO Box 63290, 9300 Ashton Rd. Philadelphia, PA 19136 T: 215-698-5100 F: 215-698-5201 William Voss
Beijing DDB Needham Advertising Co. A-12 Yabao Rd. Chaoyang Dist, Beijing 100020 T: 6591-3565 F: 6591-1797 David Chadima	Advertising	DDB Needham Worldwide Inc. 437 Madison Ave. New York, NY 10022 T: 212-415-2000 F: 212-415-3562 Bernard Brochard
Beijing Eastern Rohm & Haas Co. Suite C-514, Beijing Lufthansa Center 50 Liangmaqiao Rd., Beijing 100016 T: 6467-0440 F: 6467-0441 H. John Eyman	Chemical Products	Rohm & Haas Co. 100 Independence Mall West Philadelphia, PA 19106 T: 215-592-3000 F: 215-592-3377 Rajiv L. Gupta
Beijing ELF Atochem Polystab Co. Ltd. 61 Songzhuang Rd. Fengtai Dist., Beijing 100078 T: 6761-0979 F: 6761-1354 General Manager	Plastic Products	ELF Atochem North America Inc. 2000 Market St. Philadelphia, PA 19103 T: 215-419-7000 Tom Stocker
Beijing Eveready Battery Co., Ltd. 23 Nansanhuan Donglu 6/F Beijing 100078 T: 6763-2939 F: 6762-1862 Sunny Hui	Battery Products	Eveready Battery Co., Inc. 801 Chouteau Ave. St. Louis, MO 63102 T: 314-982-2000 F: 314-982-2320 D. P. Hatfield / W. M. Klein
Beijing Great Wall Hotel Co. Liangma Qiao Chaoyang Dist., Beijing T: 6500-5566 F: 6500-1938 Jasmina Janik	Real Estate Developer Travel & Tourism	E-S Pacific Development Co. 651 Gateway Blvd., #800 S. San Francisco, CA 94080 T: 650-877-0780 F: 650-742-0828 C B Sung
Beijing Huimeng Int'l Business Consultants 15 Fuxing Road Beijing 100038 T: 6852-4501 F: 6852-4483 Wei-ping Zhang	Information Services Advertising Services	**Link China Inc. /WTDB, Inc.** 246 30th St., Suite 101 Oakland, CA 94611 T: 510-628-0500 F: 510-628-0400 Carl W. Gustafson
Beijing Jeep Co., Ltd. Shuang Jing, Chaoyang Dist., Beijing 100022 T: 6771-1366/1369 F: 6771-1363 Franc Krebs; William Pfau	Chrysler Automotive	Chrysler Corp. 1000 Chrysler Drive Auburn Hill, MI 48326 T: 810-576-5741 Joseph E. Cappy / P. J. Trimmer

China Office	Product/Service	U.S. Head Office
Beijing KFC Company No. 50 Dajue Alley Xicheng Dist., Beijing 100035 T: 6617-2072/75 F: 6617-7127 Jacob Tsui	Fast Food Franchised Business	KFC Corp. P. O. Box 32070 Louisville, KY 40232 T: 502-456-8300 F: 502-456-8306 Donald Parkinson / Jean Litterst
Beijing Kraft Food Corp. Deshengmenwai, Xisanqi Beijing 100085 T: 6291-2266 F: 6291-3945 K. K. Li	Food	Kraft General Foods Int'l Inc. 800 Westchester Avenue Rye Brook, NY 10573 T: 914-335-2500 F: 914-335-1522 James King / James Ko
Beijing Luhuan Super Nu-Life Products Co. No. 22 Dong Jia Li Haidian Dist., Beijing T: 6254-9043/48 F: 6254-9054 General Manager	Health Food Products	Super Nu-Life Products, Inc. 9922 Tabor Place Santa Fe Springs, CA 90670 T: 213-888-9900 F: 310-941-6223 Lucy Lu
Beijing Otis Elevator Co. Ltd. 5 Bei Bin He Rd., Xibian Men Fuxingmenwai, Beijing 100045 T: 6301-1126 F: 6301-7887 Zi Ning	Elevators & Escalators	Otis Elevators Co. 10 Farm Springs Farmington, CT 06032 T: 860-676-6000 F: 860-676-6970 Steve Page
Beijing Praxair Inc. Dajiaoting, Chaoyang Dist. Beijing 100022 T: 6771-6715 F: 6771-4768 Mike Troy	Industrial Gases	Praxair Inc. 39 Old Ridgebury Rd. Danbury, CT 06817 T: 203-837-2000 F: 203-837-2505 Jose L. Travassos
Beijing Simplot Food Process Co. Red Star Frozen Plant Yard, Fengtai Nanyuan North Bridge, Beijing 100076 T: 6709-2189 F: 6709-1150 Kent Plasisted	Food	Simplot Co., J. R. 999 Main St., #1300, P. O. Box 27 Boise, ID 83707 T: 208-336-2110 F: 208-389-7515 Fred Zerza / Kent Ernest
Beijing Trade Exchange Friendship Hotel #65311 Beijing 100873 T: 6849-8105 F: 6842-5510 Lu Feng	Trading	Beijing Trade Exchange Inc. 701 E St. SE Washington, DC 20003 T: 202-546-5534 F: 202-543-2488 John Canellakis
Beijing Warner Gear Co., Ltd. 2 Dingfuzhuang Xili Chaoyang Dist., Beijing 100024 T: 6576-5459 F: 6576-3925 Ricky Wong	Tools Automotive Components	Borg-Warner Automotive Inc. 200 S. Michigan Ave. Chicago, IL 60604 T: 312-322-8500 F: 312-322-8398 Donald Transcht / Christopher Gebelein
Beijing YiYi Ecology and Enviro. Engr. Co. B9 Zirong Zian Lane Liubukou, Beijing 100041 T: 6615-7754 F: 6615-7741 Ketu Li	Consulting Environmental Scientific Engineering	Ecology and Environment Inc. 368 Pleasant View Dr. East Amherst, NY 14086 T: 716-684-8060 F: 716-684-0844 Ronald Skare

- - - - - T: Telephone # - - - - - F: Fax # - - - - - Beijing Area Code: (86)10 - - - - -

China Office	**Product/Service**	**U.S. Head Office**
Beijing-Oakland Waterproof Materials Co. A-1 Jiu Jing Zhuang Rd. Feng Tai Dist., Beijing T: 6709-1831 F: 6709-1960 General Manager	Construction Materials Sealing Materials Construction Asphalt	BITIC of California 1411 Harbor Bay Pkwy., #2008 Alameda, CA 94502 T: 510-748-6120 F: 510-748-6129 General Manager
Bell South 5123 Beijing Lufthansa Center Beijing 100016 T: 6465-1685 F: 6465-1686 Buddy Neal; Ken Hood	Telecommunications	Bellsouth International 1155 Peachtree St. NE, #2001 Atlanta, GA 30309-3610 T: 404-249-2000 F: 404-249-2866 Charles C Miller, III
Bentley Nevada Corp. 3/F, Richland Court 199 Chaoyangmenneo, Beijing 100010 T: 6407-9594/96/97 F: 6407-9593 Yang Xiaodong	Rotation Monitoring System	Bentley Nevada Corp. P. O. Box 157, 1617 Water St. Minden, NV 89423 T: 702-782-3611 F: 702-782-9253 Stevens Riggs
Bessemer Asia Ltd. Rm. 701 Beijing Tower 10 Dongchangan Jie, Beijing 100006 T: 6522-6940 F: 6522-6997 General Manager	Investment Advisors	Bessmer Group, Inc. 630 Fifth Avenue New York, NY 10111 T: 212-708-9100 F: 212-265-5826 Timothy Morris / Paul Baneroft III
Bio-Rad Labs 14 Zhichun Rd. Haidian Dist., Beijing 100088 T: 6205-1850/51 F: 6205-1876 David Schwartz	Bio-Chemistry Lab Equipment Clinical Diagnostics Analytical Instruments	Bio-Rad Laboratories Inc. 1000 Alfred Nobel Dr. Hercules, CA 94547 T: 510-724-7000 F: 510-724-3167 Warren R. Howell
Black & Veatch International Rm. 1501/02 Scriven Tower 24 Jianguomenwai Dajie, Beijing 100022 T: 6515-9866 F: 6515-9119 Frederick Q. Yang	Engineering Service	Black & Veatch International 8400 Ward Pkwy., PO Box 8405 Kansas City, MO 64114 T: 913-458-2000 F: 913-458-7677 Ronald E. Zitterkopf
Black Clawson #515 Tower A, Beijing Kelun Bldg. 12 Guanghua Lu, Beijing 100020 T: 6593-3011/12 F: 6593-2268 Isabelle Zhaong; Andrew Gan	Paper Packaging	Black Clawson Co. 405 Lexington Ave., 61/F New York, NY 10174 T: 212-916-8000 F: 212-916-8057 Carl C. Landegger
Bloomberg Co. 7-2-123 Jianguomenwai Dajie Diplomatic Apt., Beijing 100600 T: 6532-4492 F: 6532-4492 Peter Hannam	Financial Services	Bloomberg Financial Markets 499 Park Ave. New York, NY 10022 T: 212-318-2000 F: 212-893-5999 Ted Merz
Boeing China, Inc. 2/F Block A, Beijing Cofco Plaza 8 Jian Nei Dajie, Beijing 100005 T: 6526-4010 F: 6526-4033/34 Michael Zimmerman	Aviation	**The Boeing Company** 7755 E. Marginal Way South Seattle, WA 98108 T: 206-655-7300 F: 206-544-2791 Raymond J. Waldmann

China Office	**Product/Service**	**U.S. Head Office**
Bombardier Inc. 2174 Dongzhimen Int'l Apartment 35 Dongzhimenwai Dajie, Beijing 100027 T: 6467-8061 F: 6467-7929 Lester Ingram	Aviation Services	Bombardier Inc. 1 Bradley Int'l Airport Windsor Locks, CT 06096 T: 860-627-9491 F: 860-292-7350 Doug Moffatt
Brighton Information Technology Ritan Office Bldg. 15A Guanghua Rd., Beijing 100020 T: 6595-7553 F: 6595-7150 General Manager	Computer Products Software	Brighton Industries Corp. 6 Pearl Ct. Allendale, NJ 07401 T: 201-818-2889 F: 201-818-0983 K. Kung
Brown & Root International, Inc. #303, 3/F, Bldg. A-2 Lido Center, Beijing 100004 T: 6437-6662 F: 6437-6331 Hua An Liu	Engineering Construction	Brown & Root Inc. 4100 Clinton Dr. Houston, TX 77001 T: 713-676-3011 F: 713-676-4109 R M Bunker
Brunswick China Ltd. Room 207 & 209, Towercrest Int'l Plaza 3 Maizidian Xilu, Beijing 100016 T: 6467-4322/23 F: 6467-4325 Diana Jiang Jing	Bowling Equipment	Brunswick Corp. One N. Field Ct. Lake Forest, IL 60045 T: 847-735-4700 F: 847-735-4765 Jerry Perkins
Bucyrus China 8/F, Office Tower 2, Henderson Center 18 Jianguomennei Dajie, Beijing 100005 T: 6518-3110 F: 6517-1532 Yang Li Xing	Mining Equipment Blast Hole Drills Mining Shovels & Draglines	Bucyrus International Inc. 1100 Milwaukee Ave., PO Box 500 South Milwaukee, WI 53172 T: 414-768-4000 F: 414-768-4474 Timothy Sullivan / Jim Rosso
Burlington Air Express Room 1004 Liangmaqiao Rd., Beijing 100016 T: 6435-0202/0030 F: 6462-0247 Irene Thalamy	Express Mail Freight Forwarding	**Burlington Air Express** 2005 W. 14th St., Suite 130 Tempe, AZ 85281 T: 602-966-5094 F: 602-921-8111 Larry Manrose
Burson-Marsteller Beijing 2/F Golden Bridge Plaza 1A Jianguomenwai Dajie, Beijing 100020 T: 6507-9278/9289 F: 6507-9249 Curtis Chin	Public Relations	Burson-Marsteller 230 Park Ave South New York, NY 10003-1566 T: 212-614-4000 F: 212-614-4262 Thomas D. Bell, Jr.
C. Melchers GmbH & Co. Rm. 503/04 Beijing Tower 10 Dongchangan Jie, Beijing 100006 T: 6512-3355/56 F: 6512-3505 Ron Glotzer	Machinery Tools	C. Melchers America 55 New Montgomery St., #888 San Francisco, CA 94105 T: 415-974-6210 F: 415-974-1640 Hellmuth Starnitzky
Calcomp Graphic Peripherals (China) Ltd. New Century Hotel #808 6 Shodu Tiyuguan Rd., Beijing 100046 T: 6849-2127/28 F: 6849-2125 Don Lightfoot	Graphics Equipment	Calcomp Inc. 2411 W. La Palma Ave. Anaheim, CA 92803 T: 714-821-2000 F: 714-821-2832 Winfried Rohloff / Donald Lightfoot

China Office	Product/Service	U.S. Head Office
Califas Beijing Office Lianhua Office Bldg., #6090 26 Dongsi Xi Jie, Beijing 100020 T: 6525-3316 F: 6513-8308 I-Wan Chen; Xiaohong Wu	Pharmaceuticals	Califas Ltd. 33812 Valley Rd. San Juan Capistrano, CA 92675 T: 714-248-9813 F: 714-248-9813 David Mozingo
Caltex Oil Corp. Rm. 3612 Jin Guang Center Huajialou, Beijing 100020 T: 6501-5158 F: 6501-5254 John Brandenburg	Petroleum Products	Caltex Petroleum Corp. 125 E. John Carpenter Freeway Irving, TX 75602 T: 972-830-1000 F: 972-830-3034 H. S. Nichols
Cargill Trading Ltd. Suite 2105 & 2106 Capital Mansion 6 Xingyuan Nanlu, Beijing 100004 T: 6466-8191 F: 6466-8167 John L. Holden	Agriculture Machinery	Cargill Corp. 15407 McGinty Rd. Minnetonka, MN 55391 T: 612-742-6000 F: 612-742-2185 Don Huber
Carrier Transicold Rm. 1602A, CITIC Bldg. 19 Jianguomenwai Dajie, Beijing 100004 T: 6512-7546 F: 6500-4921 Wen Chen	Air Condition	Carrier International Carrier Pkwy., P. O. Box 4808 Syracuse, NY 13221 T: 315-432-3352 F: 315-432-7216 Robert Fiesinger
Caterpillar China Ltd. New Century Hotel Office Tower #1555 Beijing 100044 T: 6849-2189 F: 6849-2193 J. R. Creamer; H. Y. Shen	Construction Machinery Generator Sets Engines Gas Turbines	Caterpillar Inc. 100 NE Adams St. Peoria, IL 61629 T: 309-675-1000 F: 309-675-1717 Siegfried R. Ramseyer
Cathay Northwest, Inc. 8th Floor, Bldg. D, Fuhua Mansion 8, Chaoyangmen North St., Beijing 100027 T: 6554-1095 thru 99 F: 6554-1094 Rebecca Zhang	Textile Materials Trading	Cathay Northwest Inc. 626 13th Ave. East #M Seattle, WA 98102 T: 206-329-1201 F: 206-325-3039 Max Lu
Celite China Rm. 308 Towercrest Plaza 3 Mai Zi Dian West Rd., Beijing 100016 T: 6467-2675 F: 6467-2670 Jurgen Getermann	Diatomaceous Earth Diatomite	Celite Corp. c/o World Minerals Inc. 130 Castilian Dr. Santa Barbara, CA 93117 T: 805-562-0200 F: 805-562-0298 Jurgen Getermann
Chase Manhattan Bank SCITE Tower #509 Beijing 100004 T: 6512-3457 F: 6512-3693 Christian Murck	Banking	Chase Manhattan Corp. 270 Park Ave., #220 New York, NY 10017 T: 212-270-6000 F: 212-270-2613 Donald H. Layton
Chelbi Engineering Consultants Inc. Ding 28 Guozijian St. An Nei Dist., Beijing 100007 T: 6403-1154 F: 6403-1605 Lee Ahlstrom	Enginering Consultancy	Louis Berger International, Inc. 100 Halsted St. East Orange, NJ 07019 T: 201-678-1960 F: 201-672-4284 Lee Ahlstrom

China Office	Product/Service	U.S. Head Office
Chemical Bank SCITE Tower #1812 22 Jianguomenwai Dajie, Beijing 100004 T: 6512-3722/3700 F: 6512-3771 Hua Qing Cheng	Banking	Chase Manhattan Corp. 270 Park Ave. New York, NY 10017 T: 212-270-6000 F: 212-270-2613 Donald H. Layton
Chemtex International Inc. 22-02 Liangma Bldg. Dongsanhuanbeilu, Beijing 100004 T: 6501-1963 F: 6501-1964 Brent Carlson	Textile Construction	Chemtex International Inc. 560 Lexington Avenue New York, NY 10022 T: 212-752-5220 F: 212-752-0872 Nitoshi Kono
Cherry Lane Inc. Suite 540, Grand Hotel Wangfujing, Beijing 100006 T: 6522-4046 F: 6522-4047 Michael Primont	Entertainment Publishing Concerts & Trade	Cherry Lane Music Co. 10 Midland Avenue Port Chester, NY 10573 T: 914-935-5200 F: 914-937-0614 Peter Primont
Chesterton Petty Ltd. Rm. 814 Jing Guang Center Hu Jia Lou, Beijing 100020 T: 6501-8888 x 814 F: 6501-3067 General Manager	Real Estate	Chesterton Bagel Int'l Inc. 747 Third Ave., 37/F New York, NY 10017 T: 212-838-6888 F: 212-838-0060 Nick Renny
Chevron Overseas Petroleum Ltd. Jing Guang Center #3012 Beijing 100020 T: 6501-9611/3013 F: 6501-9337 Ross A Deegan; Helen Yan	Petroleum	Chevron Corp. 575 Market St. San Francisco, CA 94104 T: 415-894-7700 F: 415-894-6817 Greg J. Matiuk
China Advocates Beijing Petroleum Institute Beijing 100083 T: 6201-0066 x 2907 Jia Xiao Xiong	Culture & Education Tours	China Advocates 1635 Irving St. San Francisco, CA 94122 T: 415-665-4505 F: 415-753-0412 Howard Dewar
China Brown & Root Marine Engineering 10 Yuetan Beixiaojie Beijing T: 6831-5584 F: 6831-5564 General Manager	Engineering	Brown & Root Inc. 4100 Clinton Dr. Houston, TX 77001 T: 713-676-3011 F: 713-676-4109 R M Bunker
China Business Associates Liangjiayuan #10 Jianguomenwai Dajie, Beijing 100022 T: 6506-2990/94 F: 6506-2995 Raja Magasweran; Peter Hoffman	Trading	China Business Associates 760 Harrison St. San Francisco, CA 94107 T: 415-543-2227 F: 415-543-3739 Alex Gold
China Business Update / Gnix Transpacific Co. 18 Beichengdong lu, Suite 1005 Chaoyang Dist, Beijing 100101 T: 6494-1450 F: 6494-1451 Yan Xing	Automotive Publications Consulting Services	China Business Update/Gnix Transpacif 44 South Mt. Holyoke Dr, PO Box 1368 Amherst, MA 01004-1368 T: 413-253-5477 F: 413-253-2775 Wayne W. J. Xing

China Office	Product/Service	U.S. Head Office
China Computer World Publishing Co. 3/F, 16 Cui Wei Zhong Li Wanshou Rd., Beijing 100036 T: 6825-9401 F: 6825-9409 Tang Baoxing	Computers Information Technology Publishers of Computer World Show Organizer	Int'l Data Group (IDG) 15/F One Exeter Plaza Boston, MA 02116 T: 617-534-1200 F: 617-859-8642 Chris McAndrews
The Christian Science Monitor 7-2-133 Jianguomenwai Dajie Beijing T: 6532-3125 F: 6532-3125 Kevin Platt	Newspaper Media	The Christian Science Publishing 1 Norway St. Boston, MA 02115 T: 617-450-2410 Clayton Jones
Chrysler International Jing Guang Center #2603/04/05 Beijing 100020 T: 6501-2894 F: 6501-4595 Ping Lee; Edmund Chu; Larry Burger	Automotive Products	Chryster Corp. 1000 Chrysler Drive Auburn Hill, MI 48326 T: 810-576-5741 Joseph E. Cappy / P. J. Trimmer
Chubb Group of Companies Great Wall Sherton Hotel #350/52 Beijing 100026 T: 6591-7876 F: 6508-5554 Ian Lancaster	Insurance	**The Chubb Corp.** 15 Mountain View Rd. Warren, NJ 07059 T: 908-903-2000 F: 908-903-2003 Robert M Lynyak
Ciba Corning Rm. 325-328 South Building Cuiwei Hotel, Beijing 100036 T: 6825-3435/36; F: 6825-9522 Yang Li Xie	Therapeutics & Vaccines Diagnostics & Ophthalmics	Chiron Corp. 4560 Horton St. Emeryville, CA 94608 T: 510-601-2412 F: 510-655-9910 Rajen K. Dalal
Ciba-Geigy (China) Ltd. Rm. 3312 Jin Guang Center Hujialou, Beijing 100020 T: 6501-2811/16 F: 6501-2822 General Manager	Chemicals Pharmaceuticals	Geneva Pharmaceuticals 2655 W. Midway Blvd. Bloomfield, CO 80038 T: 303-466-2400 F: 303-466-6378 Jerry McIntyre
CIGNA Beijing Office Suite A, China Travel Service Tower 2 Beisanhuandonglu, Beijing 100028 T: 6461-3038 F: 6461-3037 Wm. Patrick Ganley	Insurance	CIGNA Corp. One Liberty Place, 1650 Market St. Philadelphia, PA 19192 T: 215-761-1000 F: 215-761-5505 B. Kingsley Schubert / Ed Loughman
Cincinnati Milacron Int'l Rm. 368/70 Duli Dynasty Office Center 6 E. Beisanhuan Rd., Beijing 100028 T: 6461-9544/9565 F: 6461-9510 Tony Tan; Xin Hong	Machine Tools	Cincinnati Milacron, Inc. 4701 Marburg Ave. Cincinnati, OH 45209 T: 513-841-8100F: 513-841-8550 D. Michael Clabaugh / Wanli Chuang
Citibank N.A. 16/F Bright China Chang An Bldg. 7 Jianguomenwai Dajie, Beijing 100005 T: 6500-4425 F: 6512-7930 William To	Banking	Citicorp 399 Park Ave. New York, NY 10043 T: 212-559-1000 F: 212-559-5138 Robert Martinsen / Peter Schuring

China Office	Product/Service	U.S. Head Office
CNG Beijing Rep Office 815 Hua-pu Int'l Plaza 19 Chao Wai Ave., Beijing 100020 T: 6599-2712 F: 6599-2711 Tiean Huang	Pulp & Paper Sales	Central National-Gottesman Inc. 3 Manhattanville Rd. Purchase, NY 10577 T: 914-696-9000 F: 914-696-1066 Kenneth L. Wallach
Coherent 517, Tower 2, Bright China Chang An Bldg. 7 Jianguomenwai Dajie, Beijing 100005 T: 6510-2620 Zhu Huimin	Medical	Coherent, Inc. 5100 Patrick Henry Dr. Santa Clara, CA 95054 T: 408-764-4129 F: 408-970-9998 Edwina DeRousse
Cometals China Inc. Beijing Exhibition Center Hotel West Wing #209-#211, Beijing 100044 T: 6831-6633 x 5209 F: 6832-8110 Heidi Schumacher; Peter Deneen	Metals Chemicals Minerals	Commercial Metals Co. 7800 Stemmons Fwy. Dallas, TX 75221 T: 214-689-4300 F: 214-689-4320 Murray R. McClear
Compaq Computer Beijing Bldg. 11 Xiyuan Hotel 1 Sanlihe d., Beijing 100044 T: 6831-6738/39 F: 6834-6711 T. C. Hsi	Computers	Compaq Computer Corp. 20555 State Highway 249 Houston, TX 77070 T: 281-370-0670 F: 281-514-1740 Michael Heil
Compression Labs Inc. (CLI) 20/F, Everbright Bldg. 6 Fuxingmenwai Dajie, Beijing 100045 T: 6856-1026 thru 30 F: 6856-1018 Raymond Hsu	Video Communications Eqmt	Compression Labs, Inc. 350 E. Plumeria San Jose, CA 95134 T: 408-435-3000 F: 408-922-5429 Ted Augustine
Computer Associates Int'l Rm. 2307 Capital Mansion No. 6 Xin Yuan Nan Lu, Beijing 100004 T: 6466-1136 F: 6466-1135 General Manager	Software	Computer Associates Int'l Inc. 1 Computer Associates Plaza Islandia, NY 11788-7000 T: 516-342-2811 F: 516-342-4864 Kurt Seibert
Computerland No. 1 Wenxing St. Xi Zhi Men, Beijing 100044 T: 6832-1279 F: 6835-0777 Elaine Lim; Dennis Li	Computers	Synnex Corp. 3797 Spinnaker Ct. Fremont, CA 94538 T: 510-668-8200 F: 510-440-3763 C K Cheng
Computervision Technology Corp. Exhibition Center Hotel 8/F 135 Xi Zhi MenWai, Beijing 100044 T: 6834-7826 F: 6834-6604 Hanson Suen	CAD/CAM Software	Computervision Corp. 100 Crosby Dr. MS21-17 Bedford, MA 01730 T: 617-275-1800 F: 617-275-2670 Richard Moore
Concord Resources Ltd. Jing Guang Center #2506 Hujialou, Beijing 100020 T: 6501-5270 F: 6501-5277 Michael D. Laske	Misc. Business Services	Concord Services Inc. 1515 Arapahoe St., #1000 3 Park Central, Denver, CO 80202 T: 303-899-4400 F: 303-899-4580 Kelly Jorgenson

China Office	Product/Service	U.S. Head Office
Consarc Corporation 1616 Jin Chao World Jing Pin Bldg. 10 Chao Wai Dajie, Beijing 100020 T: 6599-5189/90 F: 6599-5181 Ruan Ning Yu	Vacuum Furnaces	Consarc Corp. 100 Indel Ave. Rancocas, NJ 08073 T: 609-267-8000 F: 609-267-1366 G. Robert Mumau
Conti Feed Additives (Beijing) Ltd. 6/F, Ceroil Food Xing Da Bldg. 19B, Minwang, Beijing 100013 T: 6427-2288 F: 6427-6067 Tony Wen	Feed Additives Technical Services	Continental Grain Co. 277 Park Avenue, 50/F New York, NY 10172 T: 212-207-5100 F: 212-207-5181 Thomas Coyle / Peter Schroeder
Continental Insurance Room 518 Century Hotel Beijing 100016 T: 6466-3311 x 518 F: 6466-4812 x 518 Oliver Shilling	Insurance	Continental Insurance 180 Maiden Lane New York, NY 10038 T: 212-440-3000 F: 212-440-7130 John H Bretherick, Jr.
Control Data China Inc. SCITE Tower #1701-06 Beijing 100004 T: 6512/5686 F: 6512-4069 Jocelyn Wang	Computers	Control Data Systems, Inc. 4201 Lexington Avenue Arden Hills, MN 55126 T: 612-482-2100 F: 612-482-2000 Arnold Rutgers
Coopers & Lybrand 12/F, Block C, Fu Hua Mansion Dongcheng Dist., Beijing 100027 T: 6554-2288 F: 6554-1612/13 May Huang	Accounting Consulting	Coopers & Lybrand 1530 Wilson Blvd. Arlington, VA 22209-2447 T: 703-908-1500 F: 703-908-1695 Bob Rourke
Coudert Brothers Jing Guang Center #2708-09 Beijing 100020 T: 6501-2851/53 F: 6501-2856 Bruce Schulberg; Jingzhou Tao; Ning Zhu	Law	Coudert Brothers 1114 Avenue of the Americas New York, NY 10036 T: 212-626-4400 F: 212-626-4120 Robert Hornick
Coulter Electronics Rm. 1005, Bldg. R, Huiyuan Apartment 8 Anlilu, Andingmenwai, Beijing 100101 T: 6499-3040 F: 6499-3542 Guo Feng	Electronics	Coulter Electronics 11800 S W 147th Ave., PO Box 169015 Miami, FL 33116-9015 T: 305-380-3800 F: 305-380-8312 Mike Crochu / James Schepp
CPC Foods Co. Ltd. Beijing 234 Nanding Rd., Yongdingmenwai Fengtai Dist., Beijing 100075 T: 6721-9050 F: 6721-3170 Jeffrey P. Reed; Charles Hooi	Food Products	CPC International Inc. Int'l Plaza, P. O. Box 8000 Englewwod Cliffs, NJ 07632 T: 201-894-4000 F: 201-541-5304 Robert J. Gillespie
Cray Asia/Pacific Beijing Rep. Office 7/F, Sinochem Bldg. No. A2, Fuxingmenwai, Beijing 100046 T: 6856-2233 F: 6856-8299 Mac Townsend; Han Chen	Computers	Cray Research, Inc. 655-A Lone Oak Dr. Eagan, MN 55121 T: 612-452-6650 F: 612-683-7198 Karl M. Freund

- - - - - T: Telephone # - - - - - F: Fax # - - - - - Beijing Area Code: (86)10 - - - - -

China Office	Product/Service	U.S. Head Office
Crown Worldwide (China) Ltd. Rm. 1104, CITIC Bldg. 19 Jianguomenwai Dajie, Beijing 100004 T: 6500-7480 F: 6500-7487 Anita Staff	Freight Forwarding	Crown Pacific 5252 Argosy Dr. Huntington Beach, CA 92649 T: 714-898-0955 F: 714-898-5640 James Thompson
CS First Boston 34/F Silver Tower 2 Dong Sanhuanbei Rd., Beijing 100027 T: 6410-6611 F: 6410-6133 General Manager	Investment Banking	Credit Suisse First Boston Inc. 11 Madison Ave. New York, NY 10010 T: 212-325-2000 F: 212-325-6665 Stephen E. Stonefield
Cummins Corp. China World Tower #917 Beijing 100004 T: 6505-1658/59 F: 6505-4211 Francis Chu	Diesel Engines	Cummins Engine Co., Inc. P. O. Box 3005, Mail Code 60316 Columbus, IN 47202 T: 812-377-5000 F: 812-377-3082 Mark Levett
CYLINK Beijing Office Room 227, Tower Crest Plaza 3 Mai Zi Dian Xi Rd., Beijing 100016 T: 6467-1906 F: 6467-1906 Mr. Li	Communications	Cylink Corp. 910 Hermosa Ct. Sunnyvale, CA 94086 T: 408-735-5800 F: 408-735-6643 Arlene Lightford / C. Petty
D'Arcy Masius Benton & Bowles 601 North Bldg. East Tower 21 Xiaoyun Rd., Beijing 100027 T: 6466-2225 F: 6462-3238 Charlotte Sponholtz	Advertising	D'Arcy Masius Benton & Bowles 1675 Broadway New York, NY 10019 T: 212-468-3622 F: 212-468-4385 Clayton White
Dana China #2625 CWTC Tower 1 Jianguomenwai Dajie, Beijing 100004 T: 6505-5519 F: 6505-5520 Kuang-Ming Lin	Automation Tools	Dana Corp. 4500 Dorr St., P. O. Box 1000 Toledo, OH 43697 T: 419-535-4500 F: 419-535-4544 Gus Franklin / Tom Feely
Deacons/Graham & James CITIC Bldg. #2002 Beijing 100004 T: 6507-8557 F: 6500-2557 Fengming Liu	Law Consulting	Graham & James LLP 801 South Figueroa St., 14/F Los Angeles, CA 90017-5554 T: 213-624-2500 F: 213-623-4582 Hillel Cohn
Deere & Company #C412, Lufthansa Office Center 50 Liangmaqiao Rd., Beijing 100016 T: 6463-7982/83 F: 6463-8078 Ronnie Sonnenburgl	Construction Materials Agricultural Machinery	Deere & Co. John Deere Road Moline, IL 61265 T: 309-765-8000 F: 309-765-5772 Bernard L. Hardiek
Dell Computer Section A, 3/F, Beijing Science Tech Tower 11 Baishiqiao Rd., Beijing 100081 T: 6846-8309 thru 8314 F: 6846-7213 Liu Ling	Computers	Dell Computer Corp. 1 Dell Way Round Rock, TX 78682 T: 512-338-4400 F: 512-338-8700 Mary Jane Lawhorn

China Office	Product/Service	U.S. Head Office
Deloitte Touche Tohmatsu Level 6 Tower A Cofco Plaza 8 Jianguomennei Dajie, Beijing 100005 T: 6526-3899 F: 6526-3898 Clarence Kwan	Accounting Consulting	Deloitte Touche Tohmatsu Int'l Ten Westport Rd. Wilton, CT 06897 T: 203-761-3000 F: 203-834-2200 Dina A. Elliott
Dentsply Room 326 Xinqiao Hotel 2 Dongjiaominxiang, Beijing 100004 T: 6513-3366 x 326 F: 6512-5126 x 326 Charles Estrean	Dental Supply	Dentsply International Inc. 570 W. College Ave. PO Box 872 York, PA 17405 T: 717-845-7511 F: 717-845-2343 Thomas L. Whiting
Dentsu, Young & Rubicam 5/F, Beijing Bond Tak Fiancial Guide Hall 33 Cheng Fang St., Beijing 100032 T: 6607-7558/7560 F: 6607-7559 Mary W. Peng	Advertising	Young & Rubicam 285 Madison Avenue New York, NY 10017 T: 212-210-3000 F: 212-490-9073 James Hood / Mike Samet
DeVLieg-Bullard Inc. Everbright Bldg. #1614 6 Fu Xing Men Wai St., Beijing T: 6856-1418 F: 6856-1419 Max Y. Li	Machines Tools	**DeVLieg-Bullard Inc.** One Gorham Island Westport, CT 06880 T: 203-221-8201 F: 203-221-0780 Richard Lang
DHL-Sinotrans Ltd. 45 Xinyuan St. Chaoyang Dist., Beijing 100027 T: 6466-2211 F: 6467-7826 Michael Goetz	Worldwide Express	DHL Worldwide Express 333 Twin Dolphin Dr. Redwood City, CA 94065 T: 415-593-7474 F: 415-593-1689 Dean Christon / Brian Billings
Digital Equipment China Inc. New Century Office Tower 6/F Beijing 100046 T: 6849-2888 F: 6849-2222 Paul Chan; Thomas Lam	Computer Equipment	Digital Equipment Corp. 111 Powdermill Rd. Maynard, MA 01754 T: 508-493-5111 F: 508-497-7374 Ronald Spinek
DMC China Ltd. Chains City Hotel #2206 4 Gong Ti Dong Rd., Beijing 100027 T: 6501-1227 F: 6501-1227 Andy Pai	Process Control Instruments	Data Measurement Corp. 15810 Gaither Dr. Gaithersburg, MD 20877 T: 301-948-2450 F: 301-670-0506 Leanne Pacheco
Donaldson Far East Ltd. Rm 21 Beijing Goodyear Mansion 9B Xirongxian Hutong, Beijing 100031 T: 6605-8294 F: 6605-5631 H W Ding	Environmental Pollution Sanitation Controls Machining Machinery parts	Donaldson Co., Inc. 1400 W. 94th St., P. O. Box 1299 Minneapolis, MN 55440-1299 T: 612-887-3500 F: 612-887-3377 William Cook
Dorr-Oliver Inc. SCITE Tower #2310 Beijing 100004 T: 6523-2270 F: 6512-3888 Zhiping Wang	Food, Paper, Mineral Chemicals Sugar Industry Pharmaceutical Waste Water Treatment	Dorr-Oliver Inc. 612 Wheeler's Farm Rd. Milford, CT 06460 T: 203-876-5400 F: 203-876-5779 M Smithlin

China Office	**Product/Service**	**U.S. Head Office**
Dow Chemical (China) Ltd. CITIC Bldg. #2303 Beijing 100004 T: 6591-9034 F: 6500-3914 Ringo Leung	Chemical Products Chemicals	Dow Chemical Co. 2030 Willard H Dow Center Midland, MI 48674 T: 517-636-1000 F: 517-636-3518 Dick Sosville
Dow Corning China Ltd. Suite 7-D, CITIC Bldg. 19 Jianguomenwai Dajie, Beijing 100004 T: 6591-9030/31 F: 6591-9032 General Manager	Chemicals`	Dow Corning Corp. 2220 W. Salzburg Rd., PO Box 1767 Midland, MI 48640 T: 517-496-4000 F: 517-496-4586 G. J. Ziarno
Dow Jones & Co., Inc. 1101, 11/F, Tower A, Kelun Bldg. 12 A Guanghua Rd., Beijing 100020 T: 6503-4090 F: 6503-4086 James McGregor	Business Information	Dow Jones & Co., Inc. 200 Liberty St. New York, NY 10281 T: 212-416-2000 F: 212-416-2885 Karen House / James Friedlich
Dresser Industries, Inc. CITIC Bldg. 24/F #3 Beijing 100004 T: 6500-3139 F: 6512-0030 Winnie Ng	Energy Equipment Trading	Dresser Industries, Inc. 2001 Ross Ave. Dallas, TX 75201 T: 214-740-6000 F: 214-740-6584 Albert G. Luke / G. Phillip Tevis
Dresser-Rand China World Tower #3612 Beijing 100004 T: 6505-2511 F: 6505-0936 Wilson Chiu	Compressers Engines & Service	Dresser-Rand Co. 37 Coats Street Wellsville, NY 14895 T: 716-593-1234 F: 716-593-5815 J. A. Gegus
The Drever Group Beijing City Plaza 1-18D Shilipu, Beijing 100025 T: 6556-4856 F: 6556-6378 Weili Chen	Furnaces Industrial Heating Equipment	The Drever Co. P. O. Box 98 Huntington Valley, PA 19006 T: 215-947-3400 F: 215-947-7934 S R Peterson
Du Pont China Limited CITIC Bldg. 6/F, #1 Beijing 100004 T: 6522-7010 F: 6500-3619 Paul Wong	Chemical Products Fibers & Polymers	E I DuPont De Nemours & Co. 1007 Market St. Wilmington, DE 19898 T: 302-774-1000 F: 302-774-7321 Charles O. Holliday, Jr.
Dun & Bradstreet Rm. 318, Dong Yi Commercial Office Bldg. Xibahe Xili, Beisanhuan Donglu, Beijing T: 6420-0661/04 F: 6420-0767 Jane Cheng	Information Service	Dun & Bradstreet Co. One Diamond Hill Rd. Murray Hill, NJ 07974 T: 908-665-5000 F: 908-665-5803 Nick Mancini
E. J. Krause & Associates Inc. 5209 Zi Yu Hotel 55 Zengguang Rd., Beijing 100037 T: 6841-5250 F: 6841-1728 Grace Y. P. Mak	Trade Show Management	E. J. Krause & Associates 6550 Rock Spring Dr., #500 Bethesda, MD 20817 T: 301-493-5500 F: 301-493-5705 Shane Poblete / Sucia Min

China Office	**Product/Service**	**U.S. Head Office**
East Balt Bakery 136 Fahuasi Street Chongwen Dist., Beijing 100061 T: 6713-3761 F: 6712-4349 Jeff J. Brown	Food Products	East Balt Bakery-Florida Inc. 1108 Collins Dr. Kissimmee, FL 34741 T: 407-933-2222 F: 407-933-5367 Jim Pimpinella
Eastern Materials, Inc. (EMI) No. 66 Huayan Beili, Bldg #2, 6/F Chaoyang Dist., Beijing 100029 T: 6235-7112 F: 6235-7115 Paul P. Tung	Industrial Equipment Machinery	Eastern Materials, Inc. 734 Silver Spur Rd., #204 Rolling Hills Estates, CA 90274 T: 310-544-9929 F: 310-541-4304 Paul Tung
Eastman Chemical #704 Lido Commercial Bldg. Jichang Lu, Jiangtai Lu, Beijing 100004 T: 6436-7376 F: 6436-7380 Paul Su	Chemical Products	Eastman Chemical Co. P. O. Box 431 Kingsport, TN 37662 T: 615-229-2000 F: 615-229-1525 A. R. Rothwell
ECOLAB Inc. #4 Lufthansa Office Center 50 Liangmaqiao Rd., Beijing 100016 T: 6465-1254 F: 6465-1240 James K. Smith	Chemicals & Cleaning Eqmt	Ecolab, Inc. Ecolab Center, 370 N. Wabasha St. St. Paul, MN 55102 T: 612-293-2185 F: 612-225-3136 Mike Muenstermann
Edelman Public Relations Worldwide Co. 9/F, Office Tower, Hong Kong Macau Centre Dong Si Shi Tiao Li Jiao Qiao, Beijing 100027 T: 6501-4282/84/86 F: 6501-4271 Serge Dumont; Robert Christensen	Public Relations	Edelman Public Relations Worldwide 200 E. Randolph Dr., #6300 Chicago, IL 60601 T: 312-240-3000 F: 312-240-2900 Diane B. Dalbke
EG&G Fuhua Mansion, 12B, Tower A 8 North Chaoyangmen, Beijing 100027 T: 6502-4525 F: 6506-5692 John Hewis; Jennifer Sullivan	High-Tech Instruments	EG&G, Inc. 45 William St. Wellesley, MA 02181 T: 617-237-5100 F: 617-431-4115 Anthony L. Klemner / Donald M Kerr
Electronic Data Systems (EDS) Ltd. 1205/08 Yanshan Hotel 138A Haidian Rd., Beijing 100086 T: 6256-3388 x 1205 F: 6256-5278 Raymond So	Information Technology	EDS 5400 Legacy Dr. Plano, TX 75024 T: 972-605-6000 F: 972-605-6662 John R. Harris
Elf Atochem 2823 China World Tower 1 Jianguomenwai Dajie, Beijing 100004 T: 6505-3336 F: 6505-2560 Ming Wu	Chemical	Elf Atochem North America, Inc. 2000 Market St. Philadelphia, PA 19103 T: 215-419-7000 Tom Stocker
Eli Lilly Asia Rm. 401, Office Tower B, Ceroil Plaza 8 Jianguomennei Dajie, Beijing 100005 T: 6527-4472/73 F: 6527-4475 James Hsiao	Pharmaceuticals	Eli Lilly & Co. Lilly Corporate Center Indianapolis, IN 46285 T: 317-276-2000 F: 317-276-2095 Gino Santini

China Office	Product/Service	U.S. Head Office
Emerson Electric Holdings Co. 15/F Gateway Bldg. 10 Yabao Rd., Beijing 100020 T: 6592-5321/5325 F: 6592-5320 John Chen	Electric Products Electronic Products	Emerson Electric Co. 8000 Florissant Ave. St. Louis, MO 63136 T: 314-553-2000 F: 314-553-3527 R W Staley
Engelhard Asia Pacific Inc. The Consultation & Info Bldg. of MOFTEC B-12, Guang Hua Rd., Rm. 915, Beijing T: 6505-2255 x 915 F: 6505-1417 x 915 Tim L. Chen	Chemicals	Engelhard Corp. 101 Wood Ave. South Iselin, NJ 08830 T: 732-205-6888 F: 732-205-5915 George C. Hsu
Enron Int'l Inc. Rm. 2512, Silver Tower 2 Dongsanhuanbeilu, Beijing 100027 T: 6410-7455 F: 6410-7458 Lily L. Shui	Oil & Gas	Enron Corp. 333 Clay St. Houston, TX 77002 T: 713-853-6161 F: 713-646-6190 Jack White
Epson Beijing Rep Office 459 Office Bldg., New Century Hotel 6 Capital Gym. Nan Rd., Beijing 100044 T: 6849-2365 F: 6849-2364 General Manager	Computers	Epson America, Inc. 20770 Madrona Ave. Torrance, CA 90503 T: 310-782-0770 F: 310-782-5051 Fredy Seba
Ernst & Young Hua Ming, Beijing 10/F Hong Kong Macau Center Office Bldg. 10/F, Beijing 100027 T: 6501-1520 F: 6501-1519 Peter Chan	Accounting Consulting	Ernst & Young 787 Seventh Ave., 14/F New York, NY 10019 T: 212-773-3000 F: 212-773-6350 Eli Spielman
Esso China Ltd. 8/F China World Tower Beijing 100004 T: 6505-1747 F: 6505-0616 Will Collier; Edward Gallatin	Petroleum Products	Exxon Exploration Co. 233 Benmar Houston, TX 77060 T: 713-423-7765 F:713-423-7799 J. L. Hall, Jr.
Evergreen Int'l Airlines Holiday Inn Lido Office Bldg. #404B, Beijing 100004 T: 6437-6731 F: 6437-6906 Mike Shoaf	Cargo Freight	Evergreen Int'l Airlines 3850 Three Mile Lane McMinnville, OR 97128 T: 503-472-9361F: 503-434-4210 Linda Woodbury
EXIDE Electronics Corp. 205 South Bldg. Hua Peng Mansion Beijing 100020 T: 6592-5140/41 F: 6592-5103 Mei Zhang	Uninterruptable Systems	Exide Electronics Group, Inc. 8609 Six Forks Rd. Raleigh, NC 27615 T: 919-872-3020 F: 919-870-3100 Hermann G. P. Metzler
Exxon Chemical China Inc. China World Tower 7/F Beijing 100004 T: 6505-3880/82 F: 6505-3889 Ernest Chan	Petrochemical	Exxon Corp. 225 E. John W Carpenter Fwry Irving, TX 75062-2298 T: 214-444-1000 F: 214-444-1348 R Dahan

China Office	Product/Service	U.S. Head Office
Far East National Bank Beijing International Hotel #5005 9 Jianguomennei Dajie, Beijing 100005 T: 6512-6688 x 5005 F: 6512-9972 x 5005 Rose Li	Banking	**Far East National Bank** 350 South Grand Ave., #4100 Los Angeles, CA 90071 T: 213-687-1200 F: 213-253-2621 Robert Oehler
Fax Inter. Telecom Software Suite 2D, Guo Men Bldg. No. 1 Zuojiazhuang, Beijing 100028 T: 6460-4491/92/93 F: 6460-4500 Linda Pointer	Software	Unifi Communications 900 Chelmsford St., #312 Lowell, MA 01851 T: 508-551-7500 F: 508-551-7599 Frank Recchia
Federal Express Rm. 401 E.A.S. Tower, 21 Xiaoyun Rd. Dongsanhuanbei Rd., Beijing 100027 T: 6462-3253 F: 6462-3259 Koh Pohyian	Express Mail	Federal Express Corp. 2005 Corporate Ave., 3/F Memphis, TN 38132 T: 901-369-3600 F: 901-395-4858 T Michael Glenn / David Cunningham
Finnigan Mat China Inc. Rm. B-2 Xin Hong Bldg. 8 Chedaogou Dajie, Beijing 100081 T: 6841-8790/92 F: 6841-8793 Xiaobing Yu	Instruments	Finnigan Mat Corp. 355 River Oaks Parkway San Jose, CA 95134 T: 408-433-4800 F: 408-433-4823 T. Z. Chu / Rick Chapman
First National Bank of Chicago CITIC Bldg. #1605 Beijing 100004 T: 6500-3281/3514 F: 6500-3166 Min-Hua Hu	Banking Financial Services	First Chicago NBD Corp. One First National Plaza Chicago, IL 60670 T: 312-732-2755 F: 312-732-5976 Gerald Buldak
Fisher Controls CITIC Bldg., #1103 19 Jianguomenwai Dajie, Beijing 10004 T: 6500-6334 F: 6500-6034 Dale K. Lyle	Machinery Tools Valves	Fisher Controls Int'l Inc. 8000 Maryland Ave. Clayton, MO 63105 T: 314-746-9900 Ron Ward
Fisher-Rosemount, China 318 Duli Dynasty Office Tower 6 Beisanhuan E. Rd., Beijing 100028 T: 6462-3331 F: 6461-9434 Kent Rummelhart	Process Control	Emerson Electric Co. 8000 Florissant Ave. St. Louis, MO 63136 T: 314-553-2000 F: 314-553-3527 R W Staley
Fleishman-Hillard Link, Ltd. A501 Huapeng Mansion 19 Dongsanhuanbeilu, Beijing 100020 T: 6592-5171/72/73/74 F: 6592-5175 Steve Drake	Public Relations	Fleishman-Hillard 200 N. Broadway St. Louis, MO 63102-2796 T: 314-982-1700 F: 314-231-2313 William K. "Bill" Anderson
Fluke Corp. SCITE Tower #2112 Beijing 100004 T: 6512-3435 F: 6512-3437 Chew Siong Teck	Electronic Testing & Measurement Instrument	**Fluke Corp.** 6920 Seaway Blvd. Everett, WA 98203 T: 425-347-6100 F: 425-356-5116 Linda Cheever

China Office	Product/Service	U.S. Head Office

Fluor Daniel China nc.
Landmark Bldg. #2701
Beijing 100004
T: 6506-8015/2033 F: 6506-8024
Jim Rummings

Engineering
Construction
Real Estate

Fluor Corp.
3353 Michelson Dr.
Irvine, CA 92698
T: 714-975-2000 F: 714-975-5976
Jake Easton

FMC Asia-Pacific, Inc.
CITIC Bldg. #604
Beijing 100004
T: 6500-2251 F: 6512-6857
Chi MA

Chemical Products
Food Processing Machinery

FMC Corp.
200 E. Randolph Dr.
Chicago, IL 60601
T: 312-861-6000 F: 312-861-6176
James A MacLung / William Wheeler

Ford Foundation
Rm. 501 International Office Tower
21 Jianguomenwai Dajie, Beijing 100020
T: 6532-6668 F: 6532-5495
Tony Saich

Non-Profit Organization

Ford Foundation
320 E. 43rd St.
New York, NY 10017
T: 212-573-5000 F: 212-599-4584
Susan Berresford

Ford International Business Development Inc.
Unit 1-4, 3/F China World Trade Center
1 Jianguomenwai Dajie, Beijing 100004
T: 6505-2229 F: 6505-0610
Vaughn A Koshkarian

Automobile

Ford Motor Co.
The America Road
Deerborn, MI 48126
T: 313-322-3000
Bob Kramer

Foster Wheeler Energy China
Unit 6 to 26, 4/F, Beijing Ceoil Plaza
8 Jianguomennei Dajie, Beijing 100005
T: 6526-3480/81 F: 6526-3471
David Parham

Power Plant Equipment

Foster Wheeler Energy Corp.
Perryville Corporate Park
Clinton, NJ 08809
T: 908-730-4000 F: 908-236-1274
Gary L. Cable / N William Atwater

Fourth Shift Asia Computer Corp.
F&G, 12/F, Beijing Science Tech & Engr. Twr
75 Baishiqiao Rd., Beijing 100081
T: 6846-3734/35 F: 6846-3736
Mark Grimes

Manufacturing Software

Fourth Shift Corp.
7900 International Dr.
Minneapolis, MN 55425
T: 612-851-1500 F: 612-851-1560
D. J. Bowman

Frank's Place
5 Gong Ti Dong Lu
Beijing 100027
T: 6589-1985 F: 6589-1980
Frank Siegel

Textiles

Frank's Place
Box 307C R D #1
Edinburg, PA 16116
T: 412-654-1008 F: 412-654-1492
Frank Siegel

Gallup China
225 Chaoyang Men Wai Street
China Air SVC, Beijing 100020
T: 6591-4828 F: 6591-4824
Guo Xin

Marketing Research
Management Research

The Gallup Organization
P. O. Box 82513
Lincoln, NE 68501-9645
T: 800-398-8789
H. Gallup, Jr.

General Electric
CITIC Bldg. 3/F
Beijing 100004
T: 6500-6438 F: 6512-7345
Steven Carroll; David Voeller; John Frisbie

Manufacturing
Technology
Service

General Electric Co.
3135 Easton Turnpike
Fairfield, CT 06431
T: 518-869-5555 F: 518-869-2828
Guy Rabbat

China Office	**Product/Service**	**U.S. Head Office**
General Electric Capital Lufthansa Center C714 Chaoyang Dist, Beijing 100016 T: 6465-1068 F: 6465-1070 Betty Deng	Financial Services Leasing	GE Capital P. O. Box 2204 Fort Wayne, IN 46801 T: 219-439-2000 Chuck Devine
General Electric Medical Equipment Co. No. 2 Yong Chang North Road Beijing 100076 T: 6768-1880 F: 6768-1876/77/78 Keith Williams	Medical Equipment	General Electric Co. 3135 Easton Turnpike Fairfield, CT 06431 T: 518-869-5555 F: 518-869-2828 Guy Rabbat
General Motors Overseas Corp. 4/F CVIK Place 22 Jianguomenwi Dajie, Beijing 100004 T: 6522-8002 F: 6515-9799 Rudi Schlais, Jr.; Pat Hawkins	Automotive	**General Motors Corp.** 482-A39-C08, 100 Renaissance Center Detroit, MI 48265-1000 T: 313-556-3527 F: 313-556-5083 Louis Hughes
Gleason Works SCITE Tower #1310 Beijing 100004 T: 6512-3622 F: 6512-3623 Karl Cheung	Gear Machine Tools	Gleason Corp. 1000 University Ave. Rochester, NY 14692 T: 716-473-1000 F: 716-461-4348 J. E. Cronkwright
Glenayre Electronics, Inc. 404/14 Jing Bao Plaza 185 An Wai Dajie, Beijing 100011 T: 6425-6125 F: 6425-6199 Russ Allen	Electronics	Glenayre Technologies Inc. 5935 Carnegie Blvd. Charlotte, NC 28209 T: 704-553-0038 F: 704-553-7878 Lee Ellison
Glocom Inc. 24 Jianguomenwai Dajie, #4-9-2 Beijing 100022 T: 6515-0246/0249 F: 6515-0803 Susan L. Muth; Michael Hou	Trading	Glocom, Inc. 1338 Dogwood Ave. Morgantown, WV 26505 T: 304-599-6888 F: 304-599-9112 Chester Muth
Golden State I/E Enterprise, Inc. Rm. 213, Jing Bao Garden 183 Andingmenwai Dajie, Beijing 100011 T: 6426-2840/41 F: 6426-2821 Peter Jiang	Trading	Golden State Import & Export 2435 Pine Street Pomona, CA 91767 T: 909-392-1078 F: 909-392-1081 Sheni Y. Shieh
Goldman Sachs (China) Landmark Bldg. #1102/04 Beijing 100004 T: 6501-2183/2190 F: 6506-6240 Cherry Li	Investment Banking	Goldman Sachs & Co. 85 Broad St. New York, NY 10004 T: 212-902-1000 F: 212-902-3000 Susan Zuckerman / Mark Evans
Goodyear International Corp. C509 Beijing Lufthansa Center 50 Liangmaqiao Rd., Beijing 100016 T: 6463-7974/75 F: 6463-7976 William B. Ford	Tires	The Goodyear Tire & Rubber Co. 1144 E. Market St. Akron, OH 44316 T: 216-796-2244 F: 216-796-9112 C Perez / William Sharp

China Office	Product/Service	U.S. Head Office
Great Wall Sheraton Hotel Beijing Dong Huan Bei Road Beijing 100026 T: 6500-5566 F: 6508-2580 Leon Larkin	Hotel	ITT Shearton Corp. 60 State St. Boston, MA 02109 T: 617-367-3600 F: 617-367-5543 Dolores Sanchez
Grey-Citic #1801 Capital Mansion 6 Xin Yuan Nan Rd., Beijing 100004 T: 6466-0088 F: 6466-3070 General Manager	Advertising	Grey Advertising 777 Third Ave. New York, NY 10017 T: 212-546-2000 F: 212-546-1495 Barbara Feigin / John D Destler
GT International Inc. Lufthansa Center Office #C553 Beijing 100016 T: 6465-1080/1083 F: 6465-1698 Chuan Ren	Trading	GT International Inc. 1145 Arden Rd. Pasadena, CA 91106 T: 818-583-2000 F: 818-583-2099 Sasong Fu
GTE China Int'l Club, Ritan Road 21 Jianguomenwai Dajie, Beijing 100020 T: 6532-1262 F: 6532-1665 Michael Sacharski	Telecommunications	GTE Corp. One Stamford Forum Stamford, CT 06904 T: 203-965-2000 F: 203-965-2936 Ignacio Santillana
H & A Co. 82 Xin Kai Road Beijing 10005 T: 6524-6466 F: 6522-7470 Angela Lloyd	Aviation & Consulting	H & A Co. 67 Rosewood Dr. Atherton, CA 94027 T: 415-327-8888 F: 415-325-3816 Bob Llyod
Halliburton Int'l Inc. Lido Commercial Bldg. 3/F, Block A2, #303 Beijing 100004 T: 6437-6662 F: 6437-6331 Kai Ping Lo	Oilfield Services Enginnnering Construction	Halliburton Co. 3600 Lincoln Plaza, 500 N. Akard St. Dallas, TX 75201 T: 214-978-2600 F: 214-978-2685 Stephen D. Moore
Hardinge Brothers Inc. Park View Tiantan Hotel #356 Chongwen Dist., Beijing 100061 T: 6711-2277 x 6356 F: 6713-2616 Zhuangkun XU	Precision Machines Machine Tools	Hardinge Brothers Inc. One Hardinge Dr., P. O. Box 1507 Elmira, NY 14902 T: 607-734-2281 F: 607-734-1701 Paula Ameigh
Haythe & Curley Capital Mansion #2303 6 Xinyuan Nanlu, Beijing 100004 T: 6465-4717/18 F: 6465-4728 Jun Wei	Investment Consulting Law	**Haythe & Curley** 237 Park Avenue New York, NY 10017 T: 212-880-6000 Charles E. Dorkey III
Hewlett-Packard Co. World Trade Center West 5/F Beijing 100004 T: 6505-3888 F: 6505-2981 Terry Cheng; Stan Bolle	Computers Electronic Instruments Medical Equipment	Hewlett-Packard Co. 3000 Hanover St. Palo Alto, CA 94304 T: 650-857-1501 F: 650-857-5518 Manuel F. Diaz

China Office	Product/Service	U.S. Head Office
Hill & Knowlton Asia Ltd. 16/F SCITE Tower Beijing 100004 T: 6512-3524/3638 F: 6512-4381 Dian Terry	Public Relations	Hill & Knowlton 420 Lexington Ave. New York, NY 10017 T: 212-885-0300 F: 212-885-0540 Thomas Hoog
HLK Services Ltd. Suite 5, 26/F, CITIC Bldg. 19 Jianguomenwai Dajie, Beijing 100004 T: 6500-2255 x 2650 F: 6500-3896 Zongming Wong	Construction Machinery	HLK Services Ltd. 1111 East Putnam Ave., #301 Riverside, CT 06878 T: 203-698-2888 F: 203-698-2622 Y. T. Li
Hoechst China Ltd. Rm. 15-3 CITIC Bldg. 19 Jianguomenwai Dajie, Beijing 100004 T: 6592-2288 x 554 F: 6500-4456 General Manager	Chemicals & Fibers Plastic Products	Hoechst Celanese Corp. 206 N. Rt. 202 Bridgewater, NJ 08807 T: 908-231-2000 Robert H. Walters
Holiday Inn Crown Plaza 48 Wangfujing Dajie Dongshixikou, Beijing 100006 T: 6513-3388 F: 6513-2513 General Manager	Hotel	Holiday Inns Worldwide 3 Ravina Dr. Atlanta, GA 30346 T: 770-604-2000 Richard L Smith
Honeywell China, Inc. 2/F Zhong Wei Ke Yi Bldg. 34A Donghuanbeilu, Beijing 100020 T: 6595-6898 F: 6591-3001 Ted Gibbon	Process Controls Building Controls	Honeywell, Inc. P. O. Box 524 Minneapolis, MN 55440-0524 T: 612-951-1000 F: 612-951-0075 Larry W. Stranghoener
Hormel Foods Corp. Rm. 1002, 11/F, Guangming Hotel Liangmaqiao Rd., Beijing 100016 T: 6464-2410/13/17 F: 6464-2409 Edward Cheung	Pork Slaughtering Pork Processing	Hormel International Corp. 1 Hormel Place Austin, MN 55912 T: 507-437-5478 F: 507-437-5113 David Dickson / Richard Crane
Hough International, Inc. Lankmark Bldg. #1205 Beijing 100004 T: 6506-4651 F: 6506-4652 Henry You	Feed Mill Machienery Grain Storage Equipment Machinery	Hough International, Inc. 1000 Railroad Ave. Albertville, AL 35950 T: 205-878-8254 F: 205-878-8274 Joseph Woo
Hua Lu (Sino-Lummus) Engineering Co. Ltd. 67A Ande Rd. Xichen Dist., Beijing 100011 T: 6201-4955 F: 6201-4932 General Manager	Engineering Services Construction	ABB Lummus Global Inc. 1515 Broad St. Bloomfield, NJ 07003 T: 201-893-1515 F: 201-893-2000 Y J Chen
Hughes International Corp. Beijing Int'l Club Office #502 21 Jianguomenwai Dajie, Beijing 100020 T: 6532-1631/32/33 F: 6532-1898 K. C. Lang	Aircraft	Hughes Space & Communications Co. P. O. Box 92919 M/S 324 Los Angeles, CA 90009 T: 310-364-6000 Gary Chang / Peter Herron

China Office	Product/Service	U.S. Head Office

Hughes Network Systems Int'l Services Co.
502 SCITE Tower
Jianguomenwai Dajie, Beijing 100004
T: 6512-3592 F: 6512-3593
Zhang Li

Satellite Communications

Hughes Network Systems Inc.
11717 Exploration Lane
Germantown, MD 20876
T: 301-428-7159 F: 301-428-5511
K. C. Kuo

Husi Food Company, Ltd.
4/F Lu Yuan Hotel
101 Weizikeng, Beijing 100025
T: 6578-2473 F: 6500-4491
Michael Boccio

Food Processing
Meat

OSI Industries Inc.
1225 Corporate Blvd.
Aurora, IL 60507
T: 708-851-6600
Gerald Kolschowsky

HYPAC Inc.
Rm. 309, Dongyi Commercial Office
23 Xi Bahe Xili, Beijing 100028
T: 6420-0676 F: 6420-0693
Zia H. Main

Mining Equipment
Construction Equipment

HYPAC Inc.
169 Ballboa St.
San Marcos, CA 92069
T: 619-471-2640 F: 619-471-7638
Carla Sandahl

IBM China Corporation
3/F, Block A2, Lido Commercial Bldg.
Beijing 100004
T: 6437-6677 F: 6437-6439
Robert C. Timpson

Computers (Main Office)

International Business Machines Corp.
Rockwood Dr.
Sleepy Hallow, NY 10591
T: 914-765-1900 F: 914-332-3753
John Dejoy

IBM China/Hongkong Corp.
17/F Everbright Bldg.
6 Fuxingmenwai Dajie, Beijing 100045
T: 6856-1177 F: 6857-1577
John Burgoyne; Wilson Wang

Computers (Exhibition Center)

International Business Machines Corp.
Rockwood Dr.
Sleepy Hallow, NY 10591
T: 914-765-1900 F: 914-332-3753
John Dejoy

ICD Group Inc.
International Club #216
Beijing 100020
T: 6512-9815 F: 6512-9901
Xieping Li

Chemical Products
Dye Products

ICD Group, Inc.
600 Madison Ave.
New York, NY 10022
T: 212-644-1500 F: 212-644-1480
Marty Greenfield

IMAG Industries Inc.
Beijing Hotel #1222
Beijing 100004
T: 6513-7766 x 122 F: 6513-9945
Jiang Wang

Software

IMAG Industries Inc.
3350 Scott Blvd., #54
Santa Clara, CA 95054
T: 408-727-8222 F: 408-727-8438
S Cheung

Infolink International Corp.
Suite F-1 Lufthansa Center Offices
50 Laingmaqiao Rd., Beijing 100016
T: 6465-1312 F: 6465-1240
Lily Lee

Telecommunications

Informix Software (HK) Ltd.
New Century Hotel Office Bldg. #1401
Beijing 100045
T: 6849-2768 F: 6849-2765
Edward Lo

Computer Software
Database Engines
Communication Tools

Informix Software, Inc.
4100 Bohannon Dr.
Menlo Park, CA 94025
T: 650-926-6300 F: 650-926-6593
Kathleen Critchfield

China Office	Product/Service	U.S. Head Office
Ingersoll Milling Machines Rm. 2917 China World Tower Beijing 100004 T: 6505-2190/91 F: 6505-2192 Knox Johnstone	Machine Tools Ball Bearings Compressors	Ingersoll-Rand Co. 200 Chestnut Ridge Rd. Woodcliff Lake, NJ 07675 T: 201-573-0123 F: 201-573-3172 Paul L. Bergen
Ingersoll-Rand 2/F South Wing, Huapeng Mansion 19 Dongsanhuanbeilu, Beijing 100020 T: 6592-5090/91/92 F: 6590-5099 Harris Chan	Construction Machinery Petroleum Machinery Coal Mining Machinery	Ingersoll-Rand Co. 200 Chestnut Ridge Rd. Woodcliff Lake, NJ 07675 T: 201-573-0123 F: 201-573-3172 Paul L. Bergen
Instimpex - Universasl Tech. Support Center 1702/03, CATIC Plaza 18 Beichen E. Rd., Beijing 100101 T: 6494-0566 F: 6494-0569 Jimson Lee	Electronic Assembly Eqmt	Universal Instruments Corp. P. O. Box 825, 90 Bevier Ct. Binghamton, NY 13904 T: 607-779-5184 F: 607-779-7312 Chris Hill
Instron Corp. Beijing Friendship Hotel #60922, Block #9 Suyuan Garden, Beijing 100873 T: 6849-8102 F: 6849-8103 Soloman Shapiro	Instruments	Instron Corp. 100 Royall St. Canton, MA 02021 T: 781-828-2500 F: 781-575-5763 Arthur Hindman
Intel Computer Technology Ltd. Block B, 18/F, Huibin Bldg. 8 Beichen E. Rd., Beijing 100101 T: 6499-4951 F: 6499-3930 General Manager	Computers Semiconductors	Intel Corp. P. O. Box 58119 Santa Clara, CA 95052-8119 T: 408-765-8080 F: 408-765-5590 Leslie Vadasz / William Howe
Intel PRC Corp. Suite 401, Beijing Tong Heng Tower 4 Hua Yuan Rd., Beijing 100088 T: 6238-5130 F: 6238-5110 Joseph Zawadsky; Mike Jun	Computers Semiconductors	Intel Corp. P. O. Box 58119 Santa Clara, CA 95052-8119 T: 408-765-8080 F: 408-765-5590 Leslie Vadasz / William Howe
Interconex International Hotel #4028 9 Jianguomennei Dajie, Beijing 100005 T: 6512-6688 x 4028 F: 6525-4338 Michael Johnsen	Shipping Freight Forwarding	**Interconex Inc.** 55 Hunter Lane Elmsford, NY 10523 T: 914-593-4200 F: 914-347-0131 Phil Hamill
Intergraph China 1201/02 Gateway Bldg. 10 Yabao Rd., Beijing 100020 T: 6592-5270 F: 6592-5268 Stephen Crampton	Computers Interactive Graphic Systems	Intergraph Corp. 1 Madison Industrial Park Huntsville, AL 35894 T: 205-730-2000 F: 205-730-8300 Alan Wilson / Keith Britnell
International Flovors & Fragrances Beijing Hotel #1509 33 Dong Chang St., Beijing 100004 T: 6513-9205 F: 6513-1888 General Manager	Chemicals	International Flavors & Fragrances 521 W. 57th St. New York, NY 10019 T: 212-765-5500 F: 212-708-7132 Frans Nijnens

China Office	Product/Service	U.S. Head Office
International Hua-Mei Glass Engineering Tong Guang Mansion 14/F 12 Nong Zhan Guan Nan Rd., Beijing T: 6500-1168 F: 6500-5467 David Lee	Glass Products	Corning Inc. One Riverfront Plaza Corning, NY 14831 T: 607-974-9000 F: 607-974-8551 Larry Aiello / Ken Kao
International Power Machines (IPM) Lufthansa Center #C414 50 Liangmaqiao Rd., Beijing 100016 T: 6465-1961 F: 6465-1962 Patrick Wong	Electrical Apparatus Uninterruptable Power System	International Power Machines 10451 Brockwood Rd. Dallas, TX 75238 T: 972-272-8000 F: 972-494-2690 Kevin Iao
Itochu Corp. 32/F, China World Trade Center 1 Jianguomenwai Dajie, Beijing 100004 T: 6505-1120/1140 F: 6505-1148/49 Chen Zhong Hui	Equipment & Machinery Aviation, Chemicals & Energy Textile & Garment Metals & Raw Materials Grain & Auto Parts	Itochu International Inc. 335 Madison Ave. New York, NY 10017 T: 212-818-8477 F: 212-818-8420 Albert Ping
ITW Rm. B2008, Vantone New World Plaza No. 2 Fuchengmenwai Dajie, Beijing 100037 T: 6858-8116 F: 6858-8117 Lu Xiaoda	Engineering	ITW Signode 3600 W. Lake Ave. Glenview, IL 60025 T: 847-724-6100 F: 847-724-5910 Frank Ptak
J. P. Morgan CITIC Bldg. #2765 Beijing 100004 T: 6500-8483 F: 6500-8487 Duo Guang	Investment Banking	J. P. Morgan & Co. 60 Wall St. New York, NY 10260 T: 212-648-9528 F: 212-648-5193 Neil Gluckin
J. Walter Thompson China Air Service Bldg. 4/F 225 Chaoyangmenwai Dajie, Beijing 100020 T: 6595-4160/65 F: 6595-4158 Benny Hui	Advertising	J. Walter Thompson Co. 466 Lexington Ave. New York, NY 10017 T: 212-210-7000 F: 212-210-7066 Burt Manning
John Hancock Mutual Life Insurance Co, Landmark Bldg. #1107 8 Dongsanhuanbeilu, Beijing 100004 T: 6506-8040 F: 6506-8041 Peter Yan	Insurance	John Hancock Mutual Life 200 Clarendon St., PO Box 111 Boston, MA 02117 T: 617-572-6000 F: 617-572-6451 Derek Chilvers
Johnson & Higgins #603 Beijing Hilton No. 4 Dongsanhuanbeilu, Beijing 100027 T: 6461-5362 F: 6461-5306 Alice Tak-hing Chen	Insurance Broker	Johnson & Higgins 125 Broad St. New York, NY 10004 T: 212-574-7000 F: 212-574-7676 Norman Barham
Johnson & Johnson China Rep. Office Minzu Cultural Palace #602 Beijing 100046 T: 6605-2940/5618 F: 6602-4776 William Yu	Health Products	Johnson & Johnson One Johnson & Johnson Plaza New Brunswick, NJ 08933 T: 908-524-0400 F: 908-214-0332 Willard D. Nielsen

- - - - - T: Telephone # - - - - - F: Fax # - - - - - Beijing Area Code: (86)10 - - - - -

China Office	**Product/Service**	**U.S. Head Office**
Joy Technologies Inc. Yanshan Hotel #1701/02 Beijing 100086 T: 6256-3388 x 1702 F: 6256-4314 Qin Liu	Coal Mining Equipment Environmental Equipment	Joy Environmental Technologies Inc. 10700 North Freeway Houston, TX 77037 T: 713-878-1000 F: 713-591-2295 William Scott, Sr. / Mark Wray
Jun He Law Office 19/F Peace Hotel, Jin Yu Hutong 3 Wangfujing, Beijing 100004 T: 6512-8833 x 1909 F: 6513-4570 Xiao Wei	Law	Jun He Law Office 1 World Trade Center, #8911 New York, NY 10048 T: 212-775-8610 F: 212-775-8533 Xiao Lin Zhou
Keithley Instruments China 705 Yuan Chen Xin Bldg. 12 Yumin Rd., Beijing 100029 T: 6202-2886 F: 6202-2892 James Zhang	Electronic Instruments Test & Measurement Eqmt	Keithley Instruments Inc. 28775 Aurora Rd. Cleveland, OH 44139 T: 216-248-0400 F: 216-248-6168 Feng Yang
Kellogg China, Inc. CITIC Bldg. #2403 Beijing 100004 T: 6500-3753 F: 6500-4816 Richard Lee; Shidong Lin	Petrochemical Engineering	M W Kellogg Co. 601 Jefferson Ave. Houston, TX 77002 T: 713-753-2000 F: 713-753-5353 Roger N. Aiello / J J Degnan
Kemtech 55 Andingmenwai Dajie, 7/F Beijing 100011 T: 6426-8450/51/52 F: 6426-8455 Alex Kang	Medical Equipment	Kemtech 20488 Chalet Lane Saratoga, CA 95070 T: 408-867-0818 F: 408-867-3693 Shauley Cheng
Kerr-McGee China Petroleum Ltd. 1305/14, Block B, Lucky Tower 3 Dongsanhuanbeilu, Beijing 100027 T: 6461-5789 F: 6461-5715 Colin Murray	Oil & Gas Industrial Chemicals	Kerr-McGee Corp. P. O. Box 25861 Oklahoma City, OK 73125 T: 405-270-1313 F: 405-270-3029 Michael McDonnell
Ketchum Newscan Public Relations Ltd. Rm. 427, 4/F, The Grand Pacific Bldg. 8A Guanghua Rd., Beijing 100026 T: 6506-8222/8333 F: 6608-8288 Kenneth Chu	Public Relations	Ketchum Communications Inc. 292 Madison Ave. New York, NY 10017 T: 212-448-4200 F: 212-448-4499 David R Drobis
Keystone Valve Co., Ltd. 3-7, 10/F, Jing Tai Tower 24 Jianguomenwai Dajie, Beijing 100022 T: 6515-6378 F: 6515-6377 Lee Peng Ann	Valves & Actuators	Keystone International Inc. 9600 W. Gulf Bank Rd., PO Box 40010 Houston, TX 77040 T: 713-937-5355 F: 713-895-4044 Paul Woodward
Kimberly-Clark 8 Hongda Beilu Beijing Eco. Tech Devlp. Zone, Beijing T: 6788-1358 F: 6788-1360 Alan Hagen	Personal Hygienic	Kimberly-Clark Corp. P. O. Box 619100 Dallas, TX 75261 T: 972-281-1200 F: 972-281-1490 Tina S. Barry

- - - - - T: Telephone # - - - - - F: Fax # - - - - - Beijing Area Code: (86)10 - - - - -

China Office	**Product/Service**	**U.S. Head Office**
Kinetics Technology Int'l Rm. 1509 China World Trade center 1 Jianguomenwai Dajie, Beijing 100004 T: 6505-4805 F: 6505-2915 John A Moline	Oil & Gas Chemical Engineering	Kinetics Technology Int'l (KTI) 2300 Clayton Rd., #1490 Concord, CA 94520 T: 510-798-2940 F: 510-798-2944 Tom Gilmore
Kodak (China) Ltd. 4/F Beijing Hau Heng Office Bldg. 31 South Binhe Rd., Beijing 100055 T: 6347-1155 x 8701/02 F: 6347-5639 Victor Chan	Films Imaging Products	Eastman Kodak Co. 343 State St. Rochester, NY 14650 T: 716-724-4000 F: 716-724-0663 Willy Shih / Robert Smith
Korn/Ferry International Rm. 1503 Landmark Office Tower 8 Dongsanhuanbeilu, Beijing 100004 T: 6501-1961 F: 6501-1962 Jean S. Klee	Executive Search	Korn/Ferry International 1800 Century Park East, #900 Los Angeles, CA 90067 T: 310-552-1834 F: 310-553-6452 Kay Kennedy
KPMG Peat Marwick Jing Guang Center #2609 Beijing 100020 T: 6591-3388 F: 6500-4059 Walter Kwauk	Accounting Consulting	KPMG Peat Marwick 530 Chestnut Ridge Rd. Woodcliff, NJ 07675 T: 201-505-3585 F: 201-505-3411 Timothy Pearson

China Office	Product/Service	U.S. Head Office
Kroll Associates Suite 508 Catic Plaza 18 Beichen Road East, Beijing 100101 T: 6494-1370 F: 6494-1270 Albert Louie	Risk Management	Kroll Associates 900 Third Ave. New York, NY 10022 T: 212-593-1000 F: 212-593-2631 Dave Rosenthal
Lehman Brothers Inc. #1203 World Trade center 1 Jianguomenwai Dajie, Beijing 100004 T: 6505-0301/02/03 F: 6505-0304 Jessica Wu	Investment Banking	Lehman Brothers Inc. 3 World Financial Center New York, NY 10285 T: 212-526-7000 F: 212-619-7165 Stephen Roberts
Leo Burnett 12/F, Office Bldg., Hong Kong Macau Ctr Dongsishitiao, Beijing 100027 T: 6501-4212/13 F: 6501-4214 General Manager	Advertising	Leo Burnett Co. 35 W. Wacker Drive Chicago, IL 60601 T: 312-220-5959 F: 312-220-3299 James Oates
Lewis D'Amato, Bisgaard, Buxbaum & Choy #2523 World Trade Center Beijing 100004 T: 6505-2637 F: 6505-2638 David Buxbaum; Lai-Ping NG (Ms.)	Law	Lewis, D'Amato, Brisbois, Buxbaum 221 N. Figueroa St., #1200 Los Angeles, CA 90012 T: 213-250-1800 F: 213-250-7900 David Reynolds
LG China Travel Service Tower 16/F 2 Beisanhuandonglu, Beijing 100028 T: 6461-2645/46/47 F: 6461-2681 Jin Hwan Chun	Chemical Energy Electronics	LG 1000 Sylvan Ave. Englewood Cliffs, NJ 07632-3302 T: 201-816-2011 F: 201-816-0636 Clara Chang
Linc Equipment Services Int'l Ltd. Rm. 413 Lido Holiday Inn Jichang Road, Beijing 100004 T: 6436-3767 F: 6436-2849 Marianne M. Lee	Medical Imaging Equipment	Linc Equipment Services Inc. 303 E. Wacker Dr., #900 Chicago, IL 60601 T: 312-946-7300 F: 312-861-1133 Marketing Manager
Lincoln National (China) Inc. Rm. 511 Bond Tak Financial Bldg. 33 Cheng Fang St., Beijing 100032 T: 6607-7571 F: 6607-7564 Kwan Bok Man	Financial Services Insurance	Lincoln National Corp. 200 E. Berry St. Fort Wayne, IN 46802 T: 219-455-2000 F: 219-455-3514 Barbara Kowalczyk / Stephen Meldrum
Lockheed Martin #2128 China World Tower Beijing 100004 T: 6505-3125 F: 6505-4149 Robert F. Young	Aircraft Electronics Materials	Lockeed Martin Corp. 6801 Rockledge Dr. Bethesda, MD 20817 T: 301-897-6275 F: 301-897-6778 Robert Trice, Jr.
Loctite China Co., Ltd. Rm. 626, Asia Hotel Xingzhongxi Jie, Beijing 100027 T: 6500-7788 x 626 F: 6500-7307 Baosheng Xu	Chemicals Adhesives & Sealants	Loctites Corp. 10 Columbus Blvd. Hartford, CT 06106 T: 860-520-5000 F: 860-520-5073 David Freeman

China Office	Product/Service	U.S. Head Office
Lotus Development Rm. 504, Bond Tak Financial Bldg. 33 Chengfang St., Beijing 100032 T: 6607-7538 F: 6607-7544 Savio Chow	Software	Lotus Development Corp. 55 Cambridge Parkway Cambridge, MA 02142 T: 617-577-8500 F: 617-693-1299 Deborah Besemer
Lovell White Durrant #414 Block B COFCO Plaza 8 Jianguomenwai Dajie, Beeijing 100005 T: 6526-3490/91/93 F: 6526-3492 Virginia Chan	Law	Lovell White & Durrant 527 Madison Ave., 10/F New York, NY 10022-4304 T: 212-758-3773 F: 212-486-0367 P. Gershuny
Lubrizol China Inc. 815 Beijing Tower Crest Plaza 3 Mai Zi Dian W. Rd., Beijing 100016 T: 6467-3326 F: 6467-3321 T. S. Tang	Chemical Additives	Lubrizol Corp. 24900 Lakeland Blvd. Wickliffe, OH 44092 T: 216-943-4200 F: 216-943-5337 Rich Robins
Lucent Technologies 8/F SCITECH Plaza 22 Jianguomenwai Dajie, Beijing 100004 T: 6522-5566 x 2097 F: 6515-7241 General Manager	Computers	Lucent Technologies 600 Mountain Ave. Murray Hill, NJ 07974 T: 908-582-8500 F: 908-508-2576 Tom Uhlman / Carl Hsu
MacNeal-Schwendler Co. Ltd. #5124 Xi Yuan Hotel Erligou, Beijing 100046 T: 6831-3002 F: 6835-4962 Grace Cui	CAD Software	MacNeal-Schwendler Corp. 815 Colorado Blvd. Los Angeles, CA 90041 T: 213-258-9111 F: 213-259-3838 Dennis A Nagy
Makers Int'l Co. A11-H Fuhua Bldg. Dongsishitiao, Beijing T: 6554-1388/89/90 F: 6554-1391 Zhou Bin	Medical	Makers International Inc. 2341 Lincoln Ave. Hayward, CA 94545 T: 510-783-4966 F: 510-783-4965 Hamilton Yong
McCann-Erikson SCITE Tower #706 22 Jianguomenwai Dajie, Beijing 100004 T: 6512-3621 F: 6512-3619 General Manager	Advertising	McCann-Erikson Worldwide 750 Third Avenue New York, NY 10017 T: 212-697-6000 F: 212-867-5177 Marcio Moreira
McDonald's Beijing 31A, Dongchangan St. Beijing 100005 T: 6512-0499/2899 F: 6512-4597 Tim Lai	Fast Food	McDonald's Corp. One McDonald's Plaza Oak Brook, IL 60521 T: 630-623-3000 F: 630-623-8843 James R. Cantalupo
McDonnell Douglas Corp. 402/16 Wangfujing Grand Hotel 57 Wangfujing Dajie, Beijing 100006 T: 6522-3940/42 F: 6522-3943 John W. Burns	Aircraft	McDonnell Douglas Corp. P. O. Box 516 St Louis, MO 63166 T: 314-234-7015 F: 314-234-3826 Rita Luddon

China Office	Product/Service	U.S. Head Office
MCI Global Resources, Inc. Beijing Hotel #1422 Beijing 100004 T: 6513-7766 x 1422 F: 6523-2278 Jun Zhu	Int'l Telecom Service	MCI International 2 International Dr. Rye Brook, NY 10573 T: 914-934-6100 Jane Levene
McKinsey & Co., Inc. 7/F No. 2 CITIC Bldg. 19 Jianguomenwai Dajie, Beijing 100004 T: 6500-5436 F: 6500-5478 Gordon Orr	Management Consultants	McKinsey & Co. Inc. 55 E. 52nd St. New York, NY 10022 T: 212-446-7000 F: 212-446-8575 Stewart Flack
Medtronic China Ltd. 372 Shangri-La Hotel 29 Zizhuyuan Rd., Beijing 100081 T: 6841-2211 x 372 F: 6841-6602 General Manager	Medical Products	Medtronic Inc. 7000 Central Ave. NE Minneapolis, MN 55432 T: 612-514-4000 F: 612-514-4879 Arthur D. Collins, Jr.
Mei United, Inc. Rm. 5208 Exhibition Center Hotel 135 Xizhimenwai Dajie, Beijing 100044 T: 6833-0987 F: 6833-4318 Peter Zanello	Medical Products	Mei United Inc. 1 Court St. Plymouth, MA 02360 T: 508-746-8858 F: 508-746-3335 Peter Zanello
Mentor Graphics anshan Hotel #707/708 Beijing 100086 T: 6256-3638 F: 6256-6339 Felix Wong	CAD/CAM Software	Mentor Graphics Corp. 8005 S. W. Boeckman Rd. Wilsonville, OR 97070 T: 503-685-7000 F: 503-685-1214 Dottie Wanat / P. Hoogerhuis
Merck Sharp & Dohme (China) Ltd. Rm. 1705/06 SCITE Tower 22 Jianguomenwai Dajie, Beijing 100004 T: 6512-7552 F: 6512-7553 Matthew C. K. Chang	Pharmaceutical	Merck & Co. One Merck Dr. Whitehouse Station, NJ 08889 T: 908-423-1000 F: 908-423-1043 Attn: Japan Administration WS-2B-80
Merrill Lynch International #3301 China World Tower 1 Jianguomenwai dajie, Beijing 100004 T: 6505-0290 F: 6505-0278 Dong Ming	Investment Banking	**Merrill Lynch & Co.** World Financial Center North Tower New York, NY 10281 T: 212-449-1000 F: 212-449-7357 Winthrop H. Smith, Jr.
Metal Spray Guang Ming Bldg., #1402 Liangmaqiao Rd., Beijing 100016 T: 6467-8822 x 1402 F: 6466-6790 Heather Lee	Metals Ceramic Powders Thermalspray Equipment Robotics	Metal Spray of Virginia, Inc. 11615 Busy St. Richmond, VA 23236-4059 T: 804-794-1646 F: 804-794-7418 F Easterly
Metropolitan Life Insurance Co. 1006 China World Tower 1 Jianguomenwai Dajie, Beijing 100004 T: 6501-1119 F: 6501-5259 Malone Ma	Insurance	Metropolitan Life Insurance Co. 1 Madison Ave. New York, NY 10010 T: 212-578-7019 F: 212-683-5027 Thomas Laine

China Office	Product/Service	U.S. Head Office
MG International-China, Inc. Zi Yu Hotel #5207 Beijing 100037 T: 6841-5250 F: 6841-1728 Charles Krabek	Computers	E J Krause & Associates 6550 Rock Spring Dr., #500 Bethesda, MD 20817 T: 301-493-5500 F: 301-493-5705 Shane Poblete / Sucia Min
Micrometrics China Xi Yuan Hotel, Bldg. 6, #5609 Beijing 100046 T: 6848-9371 F: 6848-9372 Zhu Hong Zhen	Instruments	Micrometrics Instrument Corp. One Micrometrics Drive Norcross, GA 30093 T: 404-662-3660 F: 404-662-3696 Paul Webb / Andrew Sherwood
Microsoft Corp. F4 Kai Yuan Commercial Bldg. 28 Xhi Chun Li, Beijing 100086 T: 6261-7711 F: 6253-6630 Jia Bin Du	Software	Microsoft Corp. One Microsoft Way Redmond, WA 98052 T: 206-882-8080 F: 206-883-8101 Charles Stevens / Steven A Ballmer
Millipore China Ltd. Rm. 302 Asia Jinjiang Office Bldg. 8 Xizhongxijie, Beijing 100027 T: 6500-8063/8071 F: 6500-7372 Chang Siaoning	Water Purification	Millipore Corp. Ashley Rd. Bedford, MA 01730 T: 781-533-6000 F: 781-533-3110 Thomas Anderson
Mobil Services China Inc. #3701 China World Tower 1 Jianguomenwai Dajie, Beijing 100004 T: 6505-5275/5425 F: 6505-5468 Drew Goodbread	Petrochemical	Mobil Corp. 3225 Gallows Rd. Fairfax, VA 22037-0001 T: 703-846-3000 F: 703-846-4669 Robert Swanson
Monsanto Far East Rm. 1009 Silver Tower 3 Dongsanhuanbeilu, Beijing 100027 T: 6510-6166/71 F: 6410-6161 Charles Martin	Chemicals	Monsanto Co. 800 N. Lindbergh Blvd. St. Louis, MO 63167 T: 314-694-3316 F: 314-694-3635 Nha D. Hoang
Morgan Stanley Asia Ltd. Unit 19-22, Level 37, CWTC 1 Jianguomenwai Dajie, Beijing 100004 T: 6505-4524 F: 6505-3790 C. Y. Wong	Investment Banking	Morgan Stanley & Co. 1585 Broadway New York, NY 10036 T: 212-761-4000 F: 212-762-0094 Jeanmarie McFadden
Motorola (China) Electronics Ltd. 39A Zizhuyuan Lu Haidian Dist., Beijing 100081 T: 6843-7222 F: 6842-0999 P. Y. Lai; Yang Hongqing; Jamie Horsley	Telecommunications	Motorola Inc. 1303 E. Algonquin Rd. Schaumburg, IL 60196 T: 847-576-5000 F: 847-576-4700 Richard W. Younts
MTI Inc. 411 Santra Bldg. 3 Hepingli West St., Beijing 100013 T: 6429-8974 F: 6429-4905 C K Thong	Market Research Management Training Technology Transfer	Management Technologies Int'l (MTI) Dept. 209, 800 Fifth Ave., #101 Seattle, WA 98104 T: 360-779-4430 F: 360-779-4933 Dave Fischer

China Office	Product/Service	U.S. Head Office
MTS System (China) Inc. Xi Yuan Hotel #5674/76 1 San Li He Rd., Beijing 100046 T: 6831-6680 F: 6834-7618 Tommy Lau	Testing Equipment	MTS Systems Corp. 14000 Technology Drive Eden Prairie, MN 55344-2290 T: 612-937-4000 F: 612-937-4515 Karen Odash
Nabisco International #306 Estoril House 2 Jiang Tai Rd., Beijing 100004 T: 6437-9181 F: 6437-9174 Kent Forden	Food Products	RJR Nabisco Holdings 1301 Ave. of the Americas New York, NY 10019 T: 212-258-5600 F: 212-969-9173 Jason H. Wright
National Chemsearch Corp. Rm. 322/24 Olympic Science & Tech Bldg. Beijing 100080 T: 6835-0011 F: 6835-0011 General Manager	Chemical Products	NCH Corp. 2727 Chemsearch Blvd. Irving, TX 75062 T: 972-438-0211 F: 972-438-0802 Irving L Levy
National Power #2302 Capital Mansion 6 Xinyuan Nanlu, Beijing 100004 T: 6466-4139 F: 6466-4149 Andrew R Holt	Power Supplies	American National Power 10000 Memorial Dr., #500 Houston, TX 77024-3411 T: 713-613-4300 F: 713-413-4301 James Moore
National Semiconductor Rm. 614 Sinochem Mansion A2 Fuxingmenwai Dajie, Beijing 100045 T: 6856-8601/02 F: 6856-8606 Xu Jiahui	Computers	National Semiconductor 2900 Semiconductor Drive Santa Clara, CA 95052 T: 408-721-5000 F: 408-733-0293 George Chilton / Keith Kolerus
National Starch & Chemical Ltd. Rm. 511A-B Holiday Inn Lido Jiangtai Rd., Beijing 100004 T: 5436-2862 F: 5436-2861 General Manager	Adhesive & Sealants Resin & Chemicals Food Products Industrial Starch	National Starch & Chemical Co. 10 Finderne Ave. Bridgewater, NJ 08807-3300 T: 908-685-5000 F: 908-685-5005 R. John Forrest
NCR China Ltd. #1808 SCITE Tower Beijing 100004 T: 6512-3609 F: 6512-3544 Johnny Ng	Computers Trading	NCR Corp. 1700 S. Patterson Blvd. Dayton, OH 45479 T: 513-449-2000 F: 513-445-1847 Hideaki Takahashi
NetFrame #418 Kunlun Hotel 2 Xinyuan Nanlu, Beijing 100004 T: 6506-3990 F: 6500-3228 Ray Lei	Computers	NetFrame 1545 Barber Lane Milpitas, CA 95035 T: 408-944-0600 F: 408-474-4190 Steve Huey
Nike 1006 Lucky Tower 3 Dongsanhuanbeilu, Beijing 100027 T: 6461-8495 F: 6461-8494 Nancy Chen	Sportswear Shoes	Nike, Inc. One Bowerman Dr. Beaverton, OR 97005 T: 503-671-6453 F: 503-671-6300 Hilary Smith

China Office	Product/Service	U.S. Head Office
Nordson Corp. Rm 1601 Bei Ren Hotel 48 Dong Shan Hyan Nan Rd, Beijing 100022 T: 6773-0945 F: 6773-0945 General Manager	Industrial Coatings	Nordson Corp. 11475 Lakefield Dr. Duluth, GA 30097 T: 770-497-3400 F: 770-497-3588 Peg Watkins / Daniel Chen
Norman Broadbent Capital Mansion 13/F 6 Xinyuan Nanlu, Beijing 100004 T: 6466-3019 F: 6466-3017 Ivy Chow	Recruitment Consultant	Norman Broadbent Int'l 233 S. Wackler Dr. Chicago, IL 60606 T: 312-876-3300 F: 312-876-3640 R Quick
Northern Telecom Changan Club 3/F 10 Changan Dongjie, Beijing 100006 T: 6523-7788 x 7100 F: 6522-7003 Steven Ting	Telecommunications Eqmt	Northern Telecom P. O. Box 1222 Minneapolis, MN 55440 T: 612-932-8000 F: 612-932-8235 Flo Graham
Northwest Airlines Inc. #L104 China World Trade Center Beijing 100004 T: 6505-3505 F: 6505-1855 Christine Betzler	Airline	Northwest Airlines 2700 Lone Oak Pkwy. Egan, MN 55112 T: 612-726-2111 F: 612-726-0343 Michael E. Levine
Novell, Inc. 6/F, Annex Bldg., Sinochem Mansion A2 Fuxingmenwai Dajie, Beijing 100046 T: 6856-8391/96 F: 6856-8615 Jim King	Networking Software	Novell, Inc. 1555 N. Technology Way Orem, UT 84057 T: 801-222-6000 F: 801-222-7077 Alistair Aitchison
Occidental China, Inc. C407 & C417 Lufthansa Center Office Bldg. Beijing 100016 T: 6465-1614/1624 F: 6465-1634 Zhi-Gang PAN	Petroleum Products Oil & Chemical	Occidental Petroleum Corp. 10889 Wilshire Blvd. Los Angeles, CA 90024 T: 310-208-8800 F: 310-443-6688 John Morgan
Ogilvy & Mather Advertising 4/F, The Everbright Blue Diamond Tower 1 Cheng Gu Zhong Lu, Beijing 100029 T: 6425-6488 F: 6425-6498 Leisa Liang	Advertising	Ogilvy & Mather Worldwide Worldwide Plaza, 309 W. 49th St. New York, NY 10019 T: 212-237-4000 F: 212-237-5515 William Gray
OOCL (China) Ltd. 1608 Capital Mansion 6 Xin Yuan Nan Lu, Beijing 100004 T: 6466-8091/92/93 F: 6466-8097 General Manager	Global Transportation	**OOCL (USA) Inc.** 4141 Hacienda Dr. Pleasanton, CA 94588 T: 510-460-1380 F: 510-460-3109 M. K. Wong / Peter Leng
Oracle System China Ltd. 12 Dahuisi, Haidian Dist. Beijing 100081 T: 62128-1155 x 104 F: 6218-4299 Danny Fung	Software	Oracle Corp. 500 Oracle Parkway Redwood City, CA 94065 T: 415-506-7000 F: 415-506-7200 Raymond Lane / David Roux

China Office	Product/Service	U.S. Head Office
Pacific Solutions Inc. (PSI) Bldg. 12, Chaci Xiao Qu. Dongzhimenwai Dajie, Beijing 100027 T: 6463-7302/07 F: 6463-7308 James H. Spear, Jr.; Laing Tang	Automation	Systems Integrated 2200 North Galffell Orange, CA 92665 T: 714-998-0900 F: 714-998-6059 Susan Corrales-Diaz
Pacific World Trade, Inc. #1213/14 China World Tower Beijing 100004 T: 6505-0658/59 F: 6505-3693 Jean Chu	Diesel Engines & Spare Parts Heavy Duty Trucks Wines & Beers Chemicals	Pacific World Trade 8440 Woodfield Crossing, #370 Indianapolis, IN 46240 T: 317-469-4586 F: 317-469-4588 Shawn Reynolds
Pan-Pacific Enterprises Inc. 2103A Full Link Plaza 18 Chaoyangmenwai dajie, Beijing 100020 T: 6588-2031/34 F: 6588-2038 Hsiao-Li Pan	Medical Equipment Sales Diagnostic Equipment	Pan-Pacific Enterprises Inc. 311 E. 51st St. New York, NY 10022 T: 212-223-3289 F: 212-753-3803 Dru Finley
Paragon Law Offices International Club #116 Beijing 100020 T: 6532-5238 F: 6532-5238 Donald Paragon	Law	Paragon, Donald 2 Mott St., #505 New York, NY 10013 T: 212-964-2032 F: 212-964-4885 Mike Rhee
Parker Hannifin Singapore Pte. Ltd. Suite 1B, 5/F, CITIC Bldg. 19 Jianguomenwai Dajie, Beijing T: 6510-7888 F: 6500-6339 General Manager	Motion Control Products	Parker Hannifin Corp. 17325 Euclid Ave. Cleveland, OH 44112 T: 216-531-3000 F: 216-486-0618 Michael Marrin / Mark Banazak
Paul, Weiss, Rifkind, Wharton & Garrison SCITE Tower #2201 Beijing 100004 T: 6512-3628/30 F: 6512-3631 Yvonne Chan	Law	Paul, Weiss, Rifkind, Wharton & Garri 1285 Avenue of the Americas New York, NY 10019 T: 212-373-3000 F: 212-757-3990 Jerome A Cohen / Jeanette K Chan
Pepper International Associates A8, Gaojing Chaoyangmenwai Dajie, Beijing 100025 T: 6576-5584 F: 6576-5438 Xu Yong Ying	Consulting	Pepper International Associates 2 Logan Square Philadelphia, PA 19103 T: 215-981-4366 J Cahn
Pepsi Cola Int'l 4/F, Jinqiao Bldg. 1A Jianguomenwai Dajie, Beijing 100020 T: 6507-9605/06 F: 6507-9607 Steve Wong	Food & Beverage Catering/Food Provision	PepsiCo International 1 Pepsi Way Somers, NY 10589 T: 914-767-6000 F: 914-767-6553 Keith Hughes
Perkin-Elmer China Inc. 501 Beijing Haowei Bldg. 25 Beitaiping Zhuang Rd., Beijing 100088 T: 6238-1187 F: 6238-1201 Liang Hongsheng	Bio Research Systems	Perkin-Elmer Corp. 761 Main St. Norwalk, CT 06859 T: 203-762-1000 F: 203-762-6000 Leslie O'Carmody

China Office	Product/Service	U.S. Head Office
Philip Morris Asia Inc. Fortune Bldg. #1620 Beijing 100004 T: 6501-7282 F: 6500-3097 Benjamin Shum	Cigarettes	Philip Morris Int'l 800 Westchester Ave. Rye Brook, NY 10573 T: 914-335-1120 F: 914-335-1372 Andreas Gembler
Phillips Petroleum Int'l Co. (Phillips 66) C209 Beijing Lufthansa Center 50 Liangmaqiao Rd., Beijing 100016 T: 6465-1925/1927 F: 6465-1929 W. B. Berry	Petroleum Products Petrochemicals	Phillips Petroleum Co. Plaza Office Bldg. Bartlesville, OK 74004 T: 918-661-6600 F: 918-662-2780 Mike Coffelt
PictureTel Int'l Corp. Suite A1203, Full Link Plaza Chaoyangmenwai Dajie, Beijing 100027 T: 6588-1021 F: 6588-1029 Elisa Tian	Video Conferencing Systems Network Bridging Products	PictureTel Corp. 100 Minuteman Rd. Andover, MA 01810 T: 508-292-5000 F: 508-292-3375 Tom Pesut
Pitney Bowes Golden Bridge Bldg. #405 1A Jianguomenwai Dajie, Beijing 100020 T: 6508-9601/02 F: 6508-9604 Vincente Tang	Postal Equipment Business Supplies	Pitney Bowes Inc. One Elmcroft Rd. Stamford, CT 06926-0700 T: 203-356-5000 F: 203-351-7574 Meredith B. Fischer
Pratt & Whittney Rm. 16-3 CITIC Bldg. 19 Jianguomenwai dajie, Beijing 100004 T: 6500-0403/04 F: 6500-6407 Lyman W. Marshall	Aircraft Engines & Parts	Pratt & Whitney 400 Main St. East Hardford, CT 06108 T: 860-565-4321 James Johnson / A. Anderson
Price Waterhouse 409 East Wing, China World Trade Center 1 Jianguomenwai Dajie, Beijing 100004 T: 6505-1155 F: 6505-5033 Kent Watson	Accounting Consulting	Price Waterhouse LLP 1177 Avenue of the Americas New York, NY 10020 T: 212-596-7000 F: 212-596-8910 James Daley / Robert Gazzi
Principal Mutual Life Insurance Co. Unit B-2003 Vantone New World Plaza 2 Fuchangmenwai Dajie, Beijing 100037 T: 6803-7828 F: 6803-7838 Ruguei Chiang	Insurance	Principal International Inc. 711 High St. Des Moines, IA 50392 T: 515-248-8288 F: 515-248-8049 Steve Hamilton
PRN Grandview Garden Hotel #2204 Beijing 100054 T: 6353-8899 x 2204 F: 6353-9189 x 2204 Margaret Hsu	Consulting	Pro Re Nata, Inc. 26 Murray Place Princeton, NJ 08542 T: 609-683-4337 F: 609-683-4946 M. Hsu
Procter & Gamble Panda Co. #12 Yu Dai He St. Tong County, Beijing 101149 T: 6955-8830 F: 6955-8831 Dirk Beullens	Consumer Goods	Procter & Gamble Co. 1 Procter & Gamble Plaza, PO Box 599 Cincinnati, OH 45201-0599 T: 513-983-1100 F: 513-983-9369 Alan G. Lafley

China Office	Product/Service	U.S. Head Office
Purina Dalian Trade & Consulting Co. 23 Nansanhuandonglu #607 Beijing 100078 T: 6763-2935 F: 6761-1487 Michelle Ye	Food	Ralston Purina International Checkerboard Square St. Louis, MO 63164 T: 314-982-3000 F: 314-982-2752 Jim von der Heydt
Radisson Movenpick Hotel Xiao Tianzhu Village, Shunyi County P. O. Box 6193, Beijing T: 6466-3388 F: 6465-3186 Heinz Schuhmann	Hotel	Radisson Hotel International Carlson Pkwy, P. O. Box 59159 Minneapolis, MN 55459 T: 612-540-5526 F: 612-449-3400 Frank Klare
Ray & Berndtson 929 China Econo. & Trade Consulting Bldg. Jianguomenwai, Beijing T: 6505-1119 F: 6505-1418 Corinne Labonte	Executive Search	Ray & Berndtson 301 Commerce, #2300 Fort Worth, TX 76102 T: 817-334-0500 F: 817-334-0779 D Radden
Raychem Rm. 3, 4/F, Int'l Trading Center 1 Jianguomenwai, Beijing T: 6505-3399 F: 6505-4139 Chao Chang	Material Science	Raychem Corp. 300 Constitution Dr. Menlo Park, CA 94025 T: 650-361-3333 F: 650-361-7377 Scott Wylie
Rayonier China Ltd. SCITE Tower #711 Beijing 100004 T: 6512-3684 F: 6512-4588 Xiancao MA (Ms.)	Forestry Pulp	Rayonier Inc. 1177 Summer St. Stamford, CT 06905 T: 203-348-7000 F: 203-348-0005 Kent B. Smith
Raytek China #221 Zhong Fa Investment Bldg. 12 Jiuxianqiao, Beijing 100016 T: 6437-0264/0284 F: 6437-0285 Cliff Warren	Optical Electronics	Raytek Inc. 1201 Shaffer Rd. Santa Cruz, CA 95060 T: 408-458-1110 F: 408-458-1239 S. Brager
Raytheon Corp. #C808/809 Beijing Lufthansa Center 50 Liangmaqiao d., Beijing 100016 T: 6463-8031/41/42 F: 6463-8043 Jon A. Reynolds	Electronics Air Traffic Control	Raytheon Co. 141 Spring St. Lexington, MA 02173 T: 617-862-6600 F: 617-860-2172 James E. Drumgool
Regus Center Lufthansa Office Center 2/F Beijing 100016 T: 6465-1281/1282 F: 6465-1240 Jenny Quek	Staffed Business Center	OMNI Offices 1117 Perimeter Center W. Atlanta, GA 30338 T: 404-392-3300 F: 404-392-9469 Laurie Wieczyk
Republic National Bank of New York Liang Ma Tower #2201 Chaoyang Dist., Beijing 100004 T: 6506-6549 F: 6506-6943 Chris Lok	Banking	Republic New York Corp. 452 Fifth Avenue New York, NY 10018 T: 212-525-6100 F: 212-525-5678 Joseph DePaolo

China Office	Product/Service	U.S. Head Office
Reynolds Aluminum #2004 Capital Mansion 6 Xinyuan Nanlu, Beijing 100004 T: 6466-2880 F: 6466-2883 Andrew C. Hu	Aluminum Products	Reynolds International Inc. 6601 West Broad St. Richmond, VA 23261 T: 804-281-2265 Gene Voss
Rhone-Poulenc Rorer 11/F Bright China Chang An Bldg. 7 Jianguomenwai Dajie, Beijing 100005 T: 6510-2222 F: 6510-2323 David W. Kuo	Pharmaceutical	Rhone-Poulenc Rorer Inc. 500 Arcola Rd., P. O. Box 1200 Collegeville, PA 19426-0107 T: 215-454-8000 F: 215-454-3812 Alain Audubert
Rice, Fowler, Kingsmill, Flint & Booth #7024 Beijing Int'l Convention Center Beichen Donglu, Beijing 100101 T: 6493-4250 F: 6493-4251 Lixing Zhang	Law Consulting	Rice, Fowler, Kingsmill, Vance, Booth 275 Battery St. San Francisco, CA 94111 T: 415-399-9191 F: 415-399-9192 George Phillips
Rockwell Int'l Overseas Corp. China World Tower #901 1 Jianguomenwai Dajie, Beijing 100004 T: 6505-3334 F: 6505-1676 Philip S. Charmichael	Avionics & Electronics Semiconductor Systems Graphics Communications Industrial Automation	Rockwell International Corp. 600 Anton Blvd., #700 Costa Mesa, CA 92628-5090 T: 714-424-4320 F: 714-424-4360 Derek Wimmer
Rohm & Haas China Inc. C-514 Lufthansa Center Beijing 100016 T: 6461-7006 F: 6465-4001 Thomas Grehl	Chemicals	Rohm & Haas Co. 100 Independence Mall West Philadelphia, PA 19106 T: 215-592-3000 F: 215-592-3377 Rajiv L. Gupta
Rosemount China China World Tower #3301-#3305 1 Jianguomenwai Dajie, Beijing 100004 T: 6505-2218/2230 F: 6505-2328 Warren Young	Industrial Instruments	Rosemount, Inc. 12001 Technology Drive Eden Prairie, MN 55344 T: 612-941-5560 F: 612-828-7795 Ron A. Ward
Royal Crown Int'l Venture Co. (RCI) 3-9-2 Hua Qiao Cun 24 Jian Wai St., Beijing 100022 T: 6515-8921 F: 6515-0110 Larry Tau	Beverages	Triarc Companies, Inc. 280 Park Ave. New York, NY 10017 T: 212-451-3030 F:212-451-3134 Eric Kogan
Salomon Brothers China Ltd. #2109 China World Trade Center 1 Jianguomenwai Dajie, Beijing 100004 T: 6505-5260 F: 6505-5265 Frank Hawke	Invesment Banking	Salomon Brothers Inc. 7 World Trade Center New York, NY 10048 T: 212-783-7000 F: 212-783-2107 Edward White
Santa Cruz Operations, Inc. (SCO) Shangrila Hotel #461 Beijing 100081 T: 6541-2211 x 461 F: 6541-2211 x 461 B. C. Tay; Wang Hui Lin	Open Systems Software	Santa Cruz Operation, Inc. 400 Encinal St. Santa Cruz, CA 95061 T: 408-425-7222 F: 408-458-4227 David McCrabb

China Office	Product/Service	U.S. Head Office
Schenker International Rm. 308, 3/F, Ceroilfood Xingda Bldg. 19B Minwang, Beijing 100013 T: 6429-6520/21/23 F: 6429-6518 Jean-Christopher Brooke	Freight Forwarding	**Schenker International** 150 Albany Ave. Freeport, NY 11520 T: 516-377-3000 F: 516-377-3100 Mike Bujold
Schering-Plough (China) Ltd. #1301 SCITE Tower 22 Jianguomenwai Dajie, Beijing 100004 T: 6512-3652 F: 6512-3568 Stanley Lau	Pharmaceuticals	Schering-Plough Corp. 1 Giralda Farms Madison, NJ 07940 T: 201-822-7000 F: 201-822-7048 Russell Elliott
Schneider Automation Inc. #2502 Landmark Bldg. 8 Dongsanhuanbeilu, Beijing 100004 T: 6592-3331 F: 6506-6541 Zhu Hai	Industrial Automation Programmable Controls	Schneider Automation 1 High St. North Andover, MA 01845 T: 978-794-0800 F: 978-975-9010 Ray Sansouci
Scientific Atlanta Suite 1413/14 Lucky Tower Block B 3 Dongsanhuanbeilu, Beijing 100027 T: 6461-1166 x 5413 F: 6461-5754 C. C. Han	Network System	Scientidic Atlanta Inc. 1 Technology Pkwy. S. Norcross, GA 30092 T: 770-903-5000 F: 770-903-4617 John Buckett / Donald Upton
Sea Land Service (China) Co., Ltd. #2205 Landmark Tower 8 Dongsanhuanbeilu, Beijing 100004 T: 6501-1978 F: 6501-1923 Kevin J. MacDonald	Cargo Transportation	Sea-Land Service Inc. 6000 Carnegie Blvd. Charlotte, NC 28209 T: 704-571-2000 F: 704-571-4613 Clint Eisenhauer
Sensormatic C1406 Huiyuan Int'l Apartments 8 An Li Rd., Beijing 100101 T: 6492-3729 F: 6499-1443 Yeong Wai Hon	Electronic Security	Sensormatic Electronics Corp. 951 Yamato Rd. Boca Raton, FL 33431 T: 954-420-2000 F: 954-420-2017 Terry Price / Ronald Premuroso
SGS-CSTC Standards and Tech Services A-1, Fuxing Road Beijing 100038 T: 6851-7147/52 F: 6852-2311 Tracy Li	Testing & Inspection Certification Services	SGS U.S. Testing Co., Inc. 291 Fairfield Ave. Fairfield, NJ 07004 T: 973-575-5252 F: 973-575-7175 Dave Downic
Shanghai Shen-Mei Beverage & Food Co. #2712 Jing Guang Center Beijing 100020 T: 6501-2890 F: 6501-2809 Andrew Kam	Food & Beverage	Coca-Cola International One Coca-Cola Plaza Atlanta, GA 30313 T: 404-676-2121 F: 404-676-6792 Douglas N. Daft / Sergio Zyman
Shearman & Sterling Capital Mansion #2205 Beijing 100004 T: 6465-4574/75 F: 6465-4578 Mark J. Harty	Law	Shearman & Sterling 599 Lexington Avenue New York, NY 10022 T: 212-848-4000 Mark Kessel

China Office	Product/Service	U.S. Head Office
Silicon Graphics 7/F Sinochem Bldg. #A2, Beijing 100045 T: 6856-8382/87 F: 6856-8299 Kevin Wee	Computers	Silicon Graphics Inc. 2011 N. Shoreline Blvd., PO Box 7311 Mountain View, CA 94039 T: 415-960-1980 F: 415-961-0595 Teruyasu Sekimoto
Sino Fluor Engineering, Inc. Landmark Bldg. #2401 Beijing 100004 T: 6506-8010 F: 6506-8013 Julie Hsu	Engineering	Fluor Corp. 3353 Michelson Drive Irvine, CA 92698 T: 714-975-2000 F: 714-975-5976 Jake Easton
Sinopec Honeywell Ltd. 5th Golden Peacock Arts World Zhuangjiao Bldg., Hepingli, Beijing 100013 T: 6428-9098 F: 6422-7204 B. Schmidt	Building Controls Industrial Controls	Honeywell Inc. P. O. Box 524 Minneapolis, MN 55440 T: 612-951-1000 F: 612-951-0075 Larry W. Stranghoener
Sithe China Holdings Ltd. Suite 308, Asia Hotel Beijing Office Complex 8 Xinzhong Xijie, Beijing 100027 T: 6500-7211 F: 6500-7977 James Spencer	Power Generation	Sithe Energies, Inc. 450 Lexington Ave., #3700 New York, NY 10017 T: 212-450-9000 F: 212-450-9055 James Spencer
Skadden Arps Int'l Consulting Ltd. China World Trade Center 4/F Beijing 100004 T: 6505-5511 F: 6505-5522 Handel Lee	Law	Skadden, Arps, Slate, Meagher & Flom 919 Third Avenue New York, NY 10022 T: 212-735-3000 F: 212-735-2000 William P. Frank
Smith Barney Inc. #1504-1508 China WorldTrade Tower Beijing 100004 T: 6505-5323/24 F: 6505-5319 Catherine Cai	Investment Banking Brokerage	Smith Barney Inc. 388 Greenwich St. New York, NY 10013 T: 212-816-6000 Toni Elliott
Space Systems/Loral Beijing #1728 Han Wei Plaza 7 Guang Hua Lu, Beijing 100020 T: 6561-4083/84/85 F: 6561-4086 Jimmy Kat	Satellite	Loral Space Systems 3825 Fabian Way Palo Alto, CA 94303-4604 T: 650-852-4000 F: 650-852-4788 Peggy Wakeman
Southwestern Bell 6/F Parkview Center 2 Jiang Tai Rd., Beijing 100016 T: 6438-2658 F: 6438-2678 Phillip Essman	Telecommunications	SBC Communications Inc. 175 E. Houston San Antonio, TX 78299 T: 210-821-4105 F: 210-351-2198 Joe W. Walkoviak
Sprint #C-14/F Fu Hua Plaza 8 Chaoyangmenbei Dajie, Beijing 100027 T: 6501-1272 F: 6501-1323 John Savagean	Telecommunications	Sprint International P. O. Box 11315 Kansas City, MO 64112 T: 800-829-0965 Andreas Bande

China Office	**Product/Service**	**U.S. Head Office**
Stanley Works China 1808 CVIK Tower 22 Jianguomenwai Dajie, Beijing 100004 T: 6515-9698 F: 6515-8668 Lian Cheng Ping	Hand Tools & Hardware	The Stanley Works 1000 Stanley Dr., PO Box 7000 New Britain, CT 06050 T: 860-225-5111 F: 860-827-3895 Paul W. Russo
Steelcase Rm. 4H Estoril Court 9 Gongti Beilu, Beijing 100027 T: 6415-5302 F: 6415-5298 Alexis C. T. Chen	Office Furniture	Steelcase Inc. P. O. Box 1967, 901 44th St. SE Grand Rapids, MI 49508 T: 616-247-2710 Mark Greiner / Jerry K Myers
Sterling Enterprises Inc. Rm. 311 Parkview Center, South Side 2 Jiang Tai Rd., Beijing 100016 T: 6438-2680 F: 6438-2710 Paul Cao	Human Resources	Sterling Enterprises 3410 E. University Dr., #300 Phoenix, AZ 85034 T: 602-470-8000 F: 602-470-8008 R. MacDonald
Stratus Computer Inc. 960 New Century Office Tower 6 Shoudu Tiyuguan S. Rd., Beijing 100046 T: 6849-2566 F: 6849-2569 General Manager	Computer Vendor	Stratus Computer 55 Fairbanks Blvd. Marboro, MA 01752-1298 T: 508-460-2000 F: 508-481-8945 Gary Okimoto / Shirley Yee
Strippit, Inc. Rm. 30508, CVIK Palace 22 Jianguomenwai Dajie, Beijing 100004 T:6522-7526 F: 6522-7563 Steven X. Ma	Machinery	Strippit Inc. 12975 Clarence Center Akron, NY 14001-1321 T: 716-542-4511 F: 716-542-5959 Robert Ochs
Subway Rm. 216, No. 11 Jiuxianqiao Jia Chaoyang Dist., Beijing 100016 T: 6435-6670 F: 6435-6674 James L. Bryant	Int'l Restaurant Franchised Business	Subway Franchise 325 Bic Drive Milford, CT 06460 T: 203-877-4281 F: 203-876-6688 Dave Vermilya
Sun Microsystems New Century Hotel 11/F Beijing 100046 T: 6849-2828 F: 6849-2829 Nancy Chao	Computers	Sun Microsystems 2550 Garcia Ave. M/S: UMPK01-16 Mountain View, CA 94043 T: 650-960-1300 F: 650-969-9131 Tim Dwyer / Bob MacRitchie
Sybase China Ltd. New Century Hotel Office Tower #457 Beijing 100046 T: 6849-2216/17/18/19 F: 6849-2606 Xiang Yuan	Software	Sybase, Inc. 6475 Christie Avenue Emeryville, CA 94608 T: 510-596-3500 F: 510-658-9441 Yvonne Van Leeuwen
Tandem PRC, Inc. #1556/58 New Century Hotel Office Tower Beijing 100046 T: 6849-2282 F: 6849-2299 Ashok Raj Pandey	Computers	Tandem Computers Inc. 19333 Valco Pkwy. Cupertino, CA 95014 T: 408-725-6000 F: 408-285-4545 Gerald Peterson / Scott Thompson

China Office	Product/Service	U.S. Head Office
Tektronix China Ltd. Rm. 101, 1/F, Tong Heng Tower 4 Hua Yuan Rd., Beijing 100088 T: 6235-1230 F: 6235-1236 Lingling Zhang	Electronics	Tektronix Inc. 26660 SW Parkway Wilsonville, OR 97070 T: 503-627-7111 F: 503-685-4038 Timothy Thorsteinson
Tellabs, Inc. # 907, Tower 1, Bright China Chang Bldg. 7 Jianguomenwai Dajie, Beijing 100005 T: 6510-1871 F: 6510-1872 General Manager	Voice/Data Accessories	Tellabs Operations Inc. 4951 Indiana Ave. Lisle, IL 60532 T: 630-378-8800 F: 630-852-7346 Peter A Guglielm
Texaco China B. V. #3515 China World Tower Beijing 100004 T: 6505-1875/76 F: 6505-1874 Heidi Wong	Petroleum Products	Texaco Inc. 2000 Westchester Ave. White Plains, NY 10650 T: 914-253-4000 F: 914-253-7839 S. A. Carlson / James W Kinnear
Texas Instruments China, Inc. #705 CITIC Bldg. 19 Jianguomenwai Dajie, Beijing 100004 T: 6500-6427 F: 6500-2705 Luke Chen	Electronics	Texas Instruments Inc. 13500 N Central Expy, PO Box 655474 Dallas, TX 75265 T: 972-995-2011 F: 972-995-4360 Fred Geyer
Textron (Cherry Division) Bldg. 27, San Yuan Li St. P. O. Box 12, Beijing 100027 T: 6467-9066 F: 6467-9066 Xiao-Juan Ren	Aerospace Fastening Systems	Textron Inc. 40 Westminister St. Providence, RI 02903 T: 401-421-2800 F: 401-421-2878 Peter B. S. Ellis / Willard R Gallagher
Textron Lycoming (China) Corp. SCITE Tower #802 Beijing 100004 T: 6512-3432 F: 6512-3433 Michael Cusick, Jr.; Louis Pacini	Gas Turbine Engines	Textron Lycoming 652 Oliver St. Williamsport, PA 17701 T: 717-323-6181 F: 717-327-7101 William McDaniel / Mike Wolf
Time Warner Cable Beijing 74 Xishiku Xicheng Dist., Beijing 100034 T: 6615-6447 F: 6615-6451 Raymond H McCabe	Cable TV Networks Engineering Design Construction	Time Warner Inc. 75 Rockefeller Plaza, 14/F New York, NY 10019 T: 212-484-8000 F: 212-275-3970 Jeanette Lerman / Anne Pappas
TNT Skypak-Sinotrans Ltd. Bldg. 14, Shuguang Xili Chaoyang Dist., Beijing 100028 T: 6465-2227 F: 6467-7894 Wilfred Fong	Courier Service	TNT Skypak Inc. 990 Stewart Ave. Garden City, NY 11530 T: 516-745-9000 Jean-Claude Noel
Trafalgar House Corp. Development Ltd. China World Tower #2616 Beijing 100004 T: 6505-1234/35/36 F: 6505-1237 Cecilia Tse	Engineering Construction	Trafalgar House Holdings Inc. 555 5th Ave. New York, NY 10017 T: 212-880-7516 Charles Buckley

China Office	Product/Service	U.S. Head Office
Transmerica Occidental Life #608 Lufthansa Center 50 Liangqiao Rd., Beijing 100016 T: 6465-1391/92 F: 6465-1390 Peter Kuo	Insurance	Transamerica Occidental Life Co. 1150 S. Olive St. Los Angeles, CA 90015-2211 T: 213-742-3823 F: 213-741-6985 Stephen W. Pinkham
Tritek International 6 Fuguang Lu Xingfu dajie, Beijing 100061 T: 6714-3351 F: 6711-7303 Wang Weimin	Semiconductor Equipment	Tritek International Co. 5000 North Pkwy Calabasas, #304 Calabasas, CA 91302 T: 818-222-9168 F: 818-225-7168 Albert Chiang
Trocha International 717 Jingshan Burlingame Commercial Bldg. 33 Deng Shikou St., Beijing 100006 T: 6522-9679 Ding Wei	Machinery	Trocha International Inc. 17 Meadow Bluss Rd. Parsippany, NJ 07950 T: 973-263-0665 F: 973-984-8141 Calvin Wang
TRW 12B Guang Hua Road Beijing 100020 T: 6505-2797 F: 6505-2814 Da Dong Zhao	Auto Parts Space Systems Communication Systems	TRW Inc. 1900 Richmond Rd. Cleveland, OH 44124 T: 216-291-7000 F: 216-291-7932 Howard Knicely / Richard D McClain
US-China Business Council CITIC Bldg. #2644 Beijing 100004 T: 6592-0727 F: 6512-5854 Piper Lounsbury	Non-Profit Organization	**US-China Business Council** 1818 N St. NW, #200 Washington, DC 20036 T: 202-429-0340 F: 202-775-2476 Robert A Kapp
U.S. Feed Grains Council #1320 China World Tower Beijing 100004 T: 6505-1302/1314 F: 6505-2320 Todd Meyer	Agricultural Products Services	U.S. Feed Grains Council 1400 K St. NW, #1200 Washington, DC 20005 T: 202-789-0789 F: 202-898-0522 Mike Callahan
U.S. Wheat Associates #1318 China World Tower Beijing 100004 T: 6505-1278/3866 F: 6505-2201 Shi Pu Zhao	Wheat Foods Industry Services	U. S. Wheat Associates 1620 I St. NW, #801 Washington, DC 20006 T: 202-463-0999 F: 202-785-1052 Matt Weimar
U.S.-China Environmental Fund #806 Hong De Hang Bldg. 23 Gulouwai St., Beijing 100011 T: 6202-9293 F: 6202-4819 Marc Brody	Environmental	China Environmental Fund 3422 Kelliher Rd. Mt. Horeb, WI 53572-1038 T: 608-767-3888 Marc Brody
U.S.-China Industrial Exchange 7 Xiaopaifang Hutong Beijing 100010 T: 6512-6662 F: 6512-9903 Roberta Lipson; David Hoffman	Marketing Sales Consulting	US-China Industrial Exchange Inc. 7201 Wisconsin Ave., 7/F Bethesda, MD 20814 T: 301-215-7777 F: 301-215-7719 Robert C. Goodwin, Jr.

China Office	Product/Service	U.S. Head Office
Union Carbide Asia Ltd. Rm. 110 Int'l Club Main Bldg. No. 21 Jian wai Ave., Beijing 100020 T: 6532-5841 F: 6532-5940 Oliver X. D. Su	Chemical	Union Carbide Corp. 39 Old Ridgebury Rd. Danbury, CT 06817 T: 203-794-2000 F: 203-794-3170 Lou Agnello
Unison International 1009 Bright Chang An Bldg. 7 Jianguomenwai Dajie, Beijing 100005 T: 6510-1088 F: 6510-1066 Fuming Wang; Richard Young	Consulting	Unison International Corp. 651 Gateway Blvd., #880 South San Francisco, CA 94080 T: 650-877-0846 F: 650-742-0828 Deidra Deamer
Unisys China Services, Ltd. 2/F, Section C 17 Fuchengmenbeijie, Beijing 100037 T: 6836-2233 F: 6836-0430 Kwong Cheung Fu	Computer Sales System Solutions	Unisys Corp. P. O. Box 500 Blue Bell, PA 19424 T: 215-986-6990 F: 215-986-2312 Thomas Yan
United Airlines Lufthansa Center Beijing 100016 T: 6463-1111/8563 F: 6463-8364 Pam Coslett	Airline	United Airlines, Inc. 1200 E. Algonquin Rd. Elk Grove Village, IL 60007 T: 847-952-4000 McDonald Curran
United Parcel Service Unit A, 1/F, Tower B, Kelun Bldg. 12A Guanghua Lu, Beijing 100020 T: 6593-4083 F: 6593-3966 Maggie Zhang	Shipping Service	United Parcel Service of America Inc. 55 Glenlake Pkwy. Atlanta, GA 30328 T: 404-828-6000 F: 404-828-6593 Edward Schroeder
United States Inform. Tech. Office (USITO) C312A, 3/F, Lufthansa Center Offices 50 Liangmaqiao Rd., Beijing 100016 T: 6465-1540/41 F: 6465-1543 Wei-chou Su	Information Technology	USITO 1730 M St. NW, #700 Washington, DC 20036 T: 202-331-1801 F: 202-223-8756 Yusuf A. Khapra
United Technologies Int'l (China) #1603 CITIC Bldg. Beijing 100004 T: 6500-6403/04 F: 6500-4921 Richard Latham	Aero Engines Elevators	United Technologies Corp. United Technologies Bldg. Hartford, CT 06101 T: 860-728-7000 F: 860-728-7901 David C Manke
Universal Leaf Far East Ltd. 1006 Bldg. A, Asia Commercial Mansion Anzhen Xi Li, Chaoyang Dist., Beijing T: 6443-0636 F: 6443-0638 General Manager	Tobacco Products	Universal Corp. P. O. Box 25099 Richmond, VA 23260 T: 804-359-9311 F: 804-254-3582 Jeffrey Leong
Unocal China Ltd. Rm. 6313 Exhibition Center Hotel 135 Xizhimenwai St., Beijing 100044 T: 6834-3133 F: 6835-2469 Allan Armitage	Petroleum	Unocal Corp. 1 Sugar Creek Place, 14141 SW Frwy Sugar Land, TX 77478 T: 281-287-5601 F: 281-287-7345 Glen G. Edwards

China Office	Product/Service	U.S. Head Office
Upjohn Co. Rm. 1014 CATIC Plaza Office Tower 18 Beichendonglu, Beijing 100101 T: 6494-1207/08 F: 6494-1205 Ming Lai	Pharmaceuticals	The Upjohn Company 7000 Portage Road Kalamazoo, MI 49001 T: 616-323-4000 F: 616-323-4077 William N Hubbard
Valley Labs/Pfizer 14/F Swiss Hotel Beijing Hong Kong Macau Center, Beijing 100027 T: 6501-2545/2567 F: 6501-2550 Zhang Hong	Medical Products Pharmaceuticals Animal Health	Pfizer, Inc. 235 E. 42nd St. New York, NY 10017 T: 212-573-2506 F: 212-309-4344 Mohand Sidi Said
Varian China Ltd. Yanshan Hotel #908 138A Haidian Rd., Beijing 100086 T: 6256-5634 F: 6256-5635 Jenson Wu	Medical Semiconductor Instruments Oncology System X-Ray Tube	Varian Associates 3050 Hansen Way Palo Alto, CA 94304 T: 650-493-4000 F: 650-856-4351 Derrel DePasse
Vickers China Services Inc. Rm. 9C, CITIC Bldg. 19 Jianguomenwai Dajie, Beijing 100004 T: 6501-5872 F: 6501-5873 Eddie Cheung	Hydraulic Systems	Vickers, Inc. 3000 Strayer Maumee, OH 43537 T: 419-867-2200 F: 419-867-2650 Michael L. Teadt
VISA International #1601 Landmark Bldg. Beijing 100004 T: 6506-4370/71 F: 6501-1989 Leehun Lee	Financial Service	Visa U.S.A. Inc. 900 Metro Center Blvd. Foster City, CA 94404 T: 650-432-3200 F: 650-432-8100 Michael Beindorff
Voith Hydro, Inc. Rm. 1004 CATIC Bldg. 18 Beichendonglu, Beijing 100101 T: 6494-1468/69 F: 6494-1466 G. E. Pfafflin	Power Generation Equipment	Voith Hydro P. O. Box 712 York, NY 17405 T: 717-792-7000 F: 717-792-7263 Donald A. Bristow / Wolfgang Heine
W R Grace (HK) Ltd. Rm 968 Beijing Towercrest Plaza 3 Mai Zi Dian West Rd., Beijing 100016 T: 6467-4360 F: 6467-4366 General manager	Packaging Materials Chemical Sealant	W R Grace & Co. One Town Center Rd. Boca Raton, FL 33486-1010 T: 407-362-2000 F: 407-362-2193 Bernd A. Schulte
Wang Laboratories Chains City Hotel #1704 4 Gong Ti Dong Rd., Beijing 100027 T: 6500-2517 F: 6500-3549 P. K. Poon	Computers	Wang Laboratories, Inc. 600 Technology Park Dr. Billerica, MA 01821-4149 T: 508-967-5000 F: 508-967-6045 James Hogan
Western Atlas Int'l Inc. Holiday Inn Lido Jichang Rd., Jiang Tai Rd, Beijing 100004 T: 6505-2241/43 F: 6505-2240 Dave Tennant	Oil Well Logging Equipment	Western Atlas Int'l Inc. 360 N. Crescent Dr. Beverly Hills, CA 90210 T: 310-888-2500 F: 310-888-2848 George E. Boullianne

China Office	Product/Service	U.S. Head Office
Western Geophysical Holiday Inn Lido Bldg. Jichang Rd., Jiang Tai Rd, Beijing 100004 T: 6437-9858 F: 6437-9857 Zhao Zhi Yong	Petroleum Exploration	Western Geophysical 10001 Richmond Ave., P. O. Box 2469 Houston, TX 77252 T: 713-789-9600 F: 713-789-0172 Rhonda G. Boone / Chuck Toles
Western Union Rm. 205 Beilou 173 Yong An Lu, Beijing T: 6318-2045 F: 6318-1868 Fun Zhen	Wire Transfer Service	Western Union Financial Services Int'l 1 Mack Center Dr. Paramus, NJ 07652 T: 201-986-5456 F: 201-986-5168 Ray Paske
Westinghouse Electric, China #2001 SCITE Tower Beijing 100004 T: 6512-9997 F: 6512-3540 Fred Sperry	Energy Industrial Technology	Westinghouse Electric Corp. 11 Stanwix St. Pittsburgh, PA 15222 T: 412-642-6000 F: 412-642-3266 Gregory Vereschagin / Gary M Clark
Weyerhaeuser China Ltd. Rm. 414A Commercial Bldg., Lido Center Jichang Rd., Beijing 100004 T: 6436-2865 F: 6436-2867 Kent Wheiler	Forest Timber	Weyerhaeuser Company 33663 Weyerhaeuser Way South Federal Way, WA 98003 T: 206-924-3423 F: 206-924-3332 Montye Male
Wilbur Smith Associates Rm. 403, No. 1 Bldg. Da Bei Office Bldg. Chaoyang Dist., Beijing 100022 T: 6507-1675 F: 6507-1752 Tai Tseng Chang	Engineers Consulting Services Project management	Wilbur Smith Associates 1301 Gervais St., #1600 Columbia, SC 29202 T: 803-758-4500 F: 803-758-4610 John W Bonniville
William Kent Int'l Inc. (WKI China) 1411 SCITECH Tower 22 Jianguomenwai Dajie, Beijing 100004 T: 6512-0843/48 Jim Selman	Consulting	William Kent International (WKI) 2101 Wilson Blvd., #1100 Arlington, VA 22201 T: 703-516-7920 Neal Simon
Xerox Beijing Rep. Office Guomen Bldg. 3/F-A&B No. 1 Zuojiazhuang Rd., Beijing T: 6460-5620 F: 6460-5600 George Carranza	Photocopiers Business Machines Office Automation	**Xerox Corp.** 800 Long Ridge Rd., PO Box 1600 Stamford, CT 06904 T: 203-968-3000 F: 203-968-4458 Allan E. Dugan
Yili-Nabisco Co. 60 Nan Xiange St. Beijing 100053 T: 6326-9133 F: 6326-2688 Chris Wadden	Food Products	RJR Nabisco Holdings Corp. 1301 Ave. of the Americas New York, NY 10019 T: 212-258-5600 F: 201-969-9173 Jason H. Wright
Zen Continental Co., Inc. Rm. 1606, Hui Ya Bldg. 12 N. San Huan Rd., Beijing 100013 T: 6428-9630 F: 6428-9629 Virginia Zhang	Shipping Freight Forwarder	**Zen Continental Co., Inc.** 18111A S. Santa Fe Ave., #168 Rancho Dominquez, CA 90221 T: 310-631-5155 F: 310-631-5222 Rachel Liu

China Office	Product/Service	U.S. Head Office
ABB China Ltd. 2/F, Holiday Inn Chongqing Yangtze Hotel 15 Nanping N. Rd., Chongqing 630060 T: 6280-5679 F: 6280-5369 General Manager	Industrial Automation Power	**ABB** 1515 Broad St. Bloomfield, NJ 07003-3096 T: 201-893-2416 F: 201-893-3150 Y J Chen
Chongqing Cummins Engine Co., Ltd. Lieshimu Chongqing 630031 T: 6531-1941 F: 6531-5379 Hou Gangming	Combustion Engines	Cummins Engine Co., Inc. P. O. Box 3005, Mail Code 60316 Columbus, IN 47202 T: 812-377-5000 F: 812-377-3082 Mark Levett
Chongqing Pepsi-Tianfu Beverage Co. Shipingqiao Jiulongpo Dist., Chongqing 630065 T: 6882-8687/88 F: 6882-1555 General Manager	Soft Drinks	PepsiCo International 1 Pepsi Way Somers, N 10589 T: 914-767-6000 F: 914-767-6553 Keith Hughes
Holiday Inn Yangtze Chongqing 15 Nanping North Rd. Chongqing 630060 T: 6280-3380 F: 6280-0884 General Manager	Hotel	Holiday Inns Worldeide 3 Ravina Dr. Atlanta, GA 30346 T: 770-604-2000 Richard Smith
Merck Sharp & Dohme (China) Ltd. Rm. 1005 Chongqing Mega Hotel 32 Zhongshan Sanlu, Chongqing 630014 T: 6387-3888 x 1005 F: 6387-7512 General Manager	Pharmaceuticals	Merck & Co. One Merck Dr. Whitestone Station, NJ 08889 T: 908-423-1000 F: 908-423-1043 Attn: Japan Administration WS-2B-80
Puyi-Briggs Stratton Engine Co., Ltd. No. 20, Erlang Rd. Shiqiaopu, Chongqing 630039 T: 6860-3494 F: 6861-2508 Li Runnian	Air Cooled Engines	Briggs & Stratton Corp. P. O. Box 702 Milwaukee, WI 53201 T: 414-259-5333 F: 414-259-9594 Mike Schoen
Shanghai Valmont SST Co., Ltd. Rm. 508, No. 88 Wuyi Rd. Chongqing 630010 T: 6384-1559 F: 6383-3063 General Manager	Metal Products	Valmont Industries One Valmont Pkwy., PO Box 358 Valley, NE 68084 T: 402-359-2201 F: 402-359-2848 M. Bay

China Office	Product/Service	U.S. Head Office
3M China Ltd. Block C, 25/F, Fuzhou International Bldg. Fuzhou 350003 T: 782-6142 F: 782-6134 Michelle Yie	Medical Devices Industirial Tapes Commercial Tapes	3M Company 3M Center Bldg., Bldg. 220-14E-02 Saint Paul, MN 55144-1000 T: 612-737-0702 F: 612-733-2095 Tony Gastaldo
Budweiser Wuhan Int'l Brewing Co. Rm. 406, China Tower, Wu Si Rd. Changangdu, Fuzhou 350003 T: 785-1040 F: 785-1040 Tony You	Brewery	Anheuser Busch Co., Inc. 1 Busch Place St. Louis, MO 63118-1852 T: 314-577-2000 F: 314-577-0745 Fred Wolter
Magne Tek Fuzhou 223 Gong Ye Rd. Fuzhou 350004 T: 379-5543 F: 379-4727 Gary Wolfe / Wu Wen Tai	Electric Motors	Magne Tek International 1145 Corporate Lake Dr. St. Louis, MO 63132 T: 314-919-0300 F: 314-692-0282 Staci Rohm
OOCL (China) Ltd. Room A, 30/F, World Trade Plaza No. 71, May 4th St., Fuzhou 350001 T: 754-7190/93 F: 754-7195 General Manager	Global Transportation	**OOCL (USA) Inc.** 4141 Hacienda Dr. Pleasanton, CA 94588 T: 510-460-1380 F: 510-460-3109 M. K. Wong / Peter Leng
Tianjin Smithkline & French Labs, Ltd. 2007/08 Tian Fu Hotel 138 Wu Si Rd., Fuzhou 350003 T: 781-2328 x 2007 F: 781-2308 x 2007 Yin Jiang Hua	Pharmaceuticals	Smithkline Beecham Pharmaceuticals One Franklin Plaza, PO Box 7929 Philadelphia, PA 19101 T: 205-751-4000 F: 215-751-3233 D. Schuma
Allen Bradley Enterprise Xiamen Ltd. 38 Yue Hua Rd. Huli Industrial Dist., Xiamen 361006 T: 602-2084 F: 602-1832 Les Ogden	Industrial Controls	Allen-Bradley Co. 1201 S. Second St., P. O. Box 2086 Milwaukee, WI 53201 T: 414-382-2000 F: 414-382-4444 Richard E. Shelton
Alpha Yunnan Tin Solder Co., Ltd. Room 201, Service Bldg. Torch Hi-Tech Ind. Zone, Xiamen 361006 T: 562-2681 F: 562-2680 J. J. Zhang	Metal Products	Alpha Metals Inc. 600 State Rt. 440 Jersey City, NJ 07304 T: 201-434-6778 F: 201-434-2307 David B. Zerfoss
Arnberger, Kim, Buxbaum & Choy 519 Foreign Trade Center 15 Hu Bin Rd. N., Xiamen 361012 T: 506-3059 F: 511-1044 Zhang Ling	Consulting	Buxaum & Choy 100 Maiden Lane, #1616 New York, NY 10038 T: 212-504-6109 F: 212-412-7016 K. Choy
Boeing Customer Services c/o Xiamen Airlines Gao Qi International Airport, Xiamen 361009 T: 602-8204 F: 602-8205 Paul Liu Yu	Aircraft Servicing	The Boeing Company 7755 E. Marginal Way South Seattle, WA 98108 T: 206-655-2121 F: 206-655-3987 Lawrence W. Clarkson

China Office	**Product/Service**	**U.S. Head Office**
Bourns (Xiamen) Ltd. 4&5/F, Guang Yao Building Torch Hi-Tech Ind. Dev. Zone, Xiamen 361001 T: 603-8194 F: 603-8193 Frank Au	Electronic Components Telecom Equipment	Bourns Inc. 1200 Columbia Ave. Riverside, CA 92507 T: 909-781-5500 F: 909-781-5273 Dennis C Lause
China American Cigarette Co. Ltd. Huli Industrial Zone, S.E.Z. Xiamen 361006 T: 602-3522 F: 602-1462 Zheng Xing Wen	Cigarette Promotion	RJR Nabisco Holdings Corp. 1301 Ave. of the Americas New York, NY 10019 T: 212-258-5600 F: 212-969-9173 Jason H. Wright
Citibank 818 Miramar Hotel, Xing Long Rd. Huli District, Xiamen 361006 T: 603-1666 x 818 F: 602-1615 Timmy Chan	Banking	Citicorp 399 Park Ave. New York, NY 10043 T: 212-559-1000 F: 212-559-5138 Robert Martinsen / Peter Schuring
G. E. International Operations Co. 1901 Hueicheng Business Center Xia He Rd., Xiamen 361003 T: 507-2545 F: 515-0580 Amanda Ke	Electronic Products	General Electric Co. 3135 Easton Turnpike Fairfield, CT 06431 T: 518-869-5555 F: 518-869-2828 Guy Rabbat
Meixia Arts & Handicrafts Co., Ltd. 6/F, CATIC No. 6 Building Hu Li Dist., Xiamen 361006 T: 603-5554 F: 603-5556 Bill Job	Lamps	Forma Vitrum Inc. 20414 N. Main St. Cornelius, NC 28031 T: 704-892-4579 F: 704-892-5438 David MacMahan
OOCL (China) Ltd. 1801 Hui Cheng Commercial Complex 839 Xia He Rd., Xiamen 361004 T: 507-2391/92 F: 507-2474 General Manager	Global Transportation	**OOCL (USA) Inc.** 4141 Hacienda Dr. Pleasanton, CA 94588 T: 510-460-1380 F: 510-460-3109 M. K Wong / Peter Leng
Philip Morris Asia Corp. 1128 Hot Spring Hotel 218 Wu Si Rd., Xiamen 360003 T: 785-1818 x 1128 F: 783-5108 Jade Wang	Cigarette Promotion	Philip Morris Int'l 800 Westchester Ave. Rye Brook, NY 10573 T: 914-335-1120 F: 914-335-1372 Andreas Gembler
Xiamen World Gear Sports Goods Co. Eqmt No. 12 Hou Pu Enterprise Dist. 2 He Shan, Xiamen 361009 T: 523-1121/22 F: 523-1120 Michael Carmen Bruno	Exercise & Gymnasium	**1998 Fairs & Exhibitions China** Details on 260+ fairs & exhibitions in 19 cities of China. Bilingual. Tel: 310-325-0100 Fax: 310-325-2583
Zen Continental Co. Inc. 9F-B Temao Bldg. Hu Bin N. Rd., Xiamen 361012 T: 505-5986 F: 505-5990 Kevin Li	Shipping	**Zen Continental Co., Inc.** 18111A S. Santa Fe Ave., #168 Rancho Dominguez, CA 90221 T: 310-631-5155 F: 310-631-5222 Rachel Liu

China Office	Product/Service	U.S. Head Office
DonGeneral Managerei Food Co., Ltd. 38 Zhou Mian Fang Dongguan 511700 T: 222-2660 F: 222-1007 Guo Qun Hong	Foodstuff	Kraft Foods Int'l Inc. 800 Westchester Ave. Rye Brook, NY 10573 T: 914-335-2500 F: 914-335-1522 James King / James Ko
Dongguan Mei Dong Mirror, Ltd. Industrial Road Shi Long Town, Dongguan 511721 T: 661-4597 F: 661-4597 Yu Ming Xiong	Glass Products	

China Office	Product/Service	U.S. Head Office
Dongguan Molex South China Connector Co. #1 Xin Wei Cun, Wei Xin Lu Hung Mien 2nd Rd., Dongguan 511721 T: 661-1376 F: 661-2716 Wu Guo Sheng	Connectors	Molex, Inc. 2222 Wellington Ct. Lisle, IL 60532 T: 630-969-4550 F: 630-969-1352 John Krehbiel, Jr.
Foshan Crown Can Co., Ltd. 20 Qinggong San Lu Foshan 528000 T: 221-9400 F: 221-3295 Louis K. M. Chui	Aluminum Can Mfg.	Crown Cork & Seal Co., Inc. 9300 Ashton Rd., PO Box 63290 Philadelphia, PA 19114 T: 215-698-5100 F: 215-676-7245 William Voss / Nigel Gilson
Foshan Kohler Limited Shan Shui Le Ping Town 2nd Industrial Area, Foshan 528137 T: 738-8238 F: 738-8128 Edward Clark	Ceramic Sanitary Ware	**Kohler Co.** 444 Highland Dr. Kohler, WI 53044-1500 T: 920-457-1271 F: 920-457-1595 Bernhard H. Langel

China Office	Product/Service	U.S. Head Office

3M China Ltd.
Rm. 601 T. P. Plaza
109-9 Liuhua Rd., Guangzhou 510010
T: 8381-4662 F: 8381-8815
Simon C. Lee

Office Supplies
Office Equipment
Safety Equipment

3M Company
3M Center Bldg. Bldg. 220-14E-02
Saint Paul, MN 55144-1000
T: 612-737-0702 F: 612-733-2095
Tony Gastaldo

A C Nielsen SRG
3-4/F Yin Nong Bldg.
174 Dong Feng W. Rd., Guangzhou 510180
T: 8318-2792 F: 8318-2987
General Manager

Market Research

A C Nielsen
177 Broad St.
Stamford, CT 06901
T: 203-961-3300 F: 203-961-3170
Nicholas Trivisonno

AEM Inc.
Rm. 1515 Dong Fang Hotel
120 Liu Hua Rd., Guangzhou 510016
T: 8667-3804 F: 8667-3814
Wei Chiu Sou

Electronics Components

AEM, Inc.
6827 Nancy Ridge Dr.
San Diego, CA 92121
T: 619-587-8285 F: 619-455-5528
Daniel H. Chang

AIA Information Technology Co. Ltd.
Rm. 919-920 South Twr, GZ World Trade Ctr.
371-375 Huan Shi Rd E., Guangzhou 510095
T: 8778-4398 F: 8778-5768
Xie Yong Yao

Information Technology

American International Group
70 Pine St.
New York, NY 10270
T: 212-770-7000 F: 212-770-7821
Evan Greenberg / Martin J. Sullivan

Air Products Corporation
GETDD
Huangpu Dist., Guangzhou
T: 8223-5877
General Manager

Chemicals

Air Products & Chemicals Inc.
7201 Hamilton Blvd.
Allentown, PA 18195
T: 610-481-4911 F: 610-481-5900
Joseph J Kaminiski

AIU Insurance Company
13/F, Guang Fa Center
No. 83 Nong Lin Xia Rd., Guangzhou 510080
T: 8731-1888 F: 8731-0166
David Peng

Insurance

American International Group
70 Pine St.
New York, NY 10270
T: 212-770-7000 F: 212-770-7821
Evan Greenberg / Martin J. Sullivan

Allen Filters Inc.
Rm. 1105 New Century Plaza
2-6 Hongde Rd., Guangzhou 510235
T: 8432-8571/73 F: 8432-8576
Rick Carter

Oil Purification
Oil Recycling

Allen Filters Inc.
522 N. Fremont Ave., PO Box 747
Springfield, MO 65802
T: 417-865-2844 F: 417-865-2469
K. A. Allen

Allergan Asia Ltd.
Rm. 2307 South Twr, GZ World rade Ctr.
371-375 Huan Shi Rd. E., Guangzhou 510095
T: 8775-5280 F: 8778-9078
Hu Zhi Hong

Eye & Skin Care Products

Allergan Inc.
2525 DuPont Dr., P O Box 19534
Irvine, CA 92612
T: 714-246-4500 F: 714-246-4359
Jacqueline J. Schiavo

Alliance Refrigeration Supply Inc. USA
Rm. 1741 Airport Hotel
Bai Yun Int'l Airport, Guangzhou 510406
T: 8665-9017 x 1741 F: 8665-9007
Chen Shui Xi

Refrigeration

China Office	Product/Service	U.S. Head Office
Allied Signal Friction Materials Co., Ltd. GETDD Guangzhou 510730 T: 8222-0466 F: 8222-0248 Joseph Yu	Automotive	Allied Signal International Inc. 101 Columbia Road, P O Box 2245 Morristown, NJ 07962 T: 201-455-2000 F: 201-455-4807 Paul R. Schindler
American Chamber of Commerce Unit M-2E10, Guangdong Int'l Hotel 339 Huan Shi Rd. E., Guangzhou 510098 T: 8331-1888 x 70205 F: 8332-1642 Catherine Lee	Business Facilitation	**S.E.S. International Express, Inc.** 神龍國際運通有限公司 International Freight Forwarder Tel: 310-673-9937 Fax: 310-673-9935
American Express International Inc. C1, G/F, Guangdong Int'l Hotel 339 Huan Shi Rd. E., Guangzhou 510095 T: 8331-1771 F: 8331-3535 Liu Xian Sheng	Travel Related Service	American Express Travel Related Co. 200 Vessey St. New York, NY 10285 T: 212-640-2000 F: 212-619-8802 Stephen Friedman / John Sutphen
American International Assurance Co., Ltd. 18/F Guangda Finance Center 83 Nonglinxia Rd., Guangzhou 510080 T: 8731-1888 F: 8731-0675 Ooi Kim Chai	Insurance	American International Group Inc. 70 Pine St. New York, NY 10270 T: 212-770-7000 F: 212-770-7821 Evan Greenberg / Martin J. Sullivan
American President Lines Rm. 1307/08 South Twr, GZ World Trade Ctr. 371-375 Huan Shi Rd. E., Guangzhou 510095 T: 8766-4629 F: 8778-3228 Catherine Ng	Shipping Freight Forwarding	APL Limited 1111 Broadway Oakland, CA 94607 T: 510-272-8000 F: 510-272-7941 Keith Mackie
AMF Bowling Inc. 2/F Pacific Ocean Bldg. 97 Si You Rd. S., Guangzhou 510600 T: 8737-0009 F: 8737-0106 Rover Wang	Bowing Products	AMF Bowling Inc. 8100 AMF Dr. Mechanicsville, VA 23111 T: 804-730-4325 F: 804-730-0923 B Morin
AMP Products Pacific Ltd. Rm. 713 China Hotel Office Tower Liu Hua Rd., Guangzhou 510015 T: 8666-3388 x 2713 F: 8667-9840 Patrick Pedron	Connectors	AMP Inc. 470 Friendship Rd., P O Box 3608 Harrisburg, PA 17105-3608 T: 717-564-0100 F: 717-780-6130 Hebert M. Cole / Ted L. Dalymple
Amway (China) Co., Ltd. 8 Guangzhou Book Shopping Center 123 Tianhe Rd., Guangzhou 510620 T: 8759-6868 F: 8753-1006 Gan Chee Eng	Personal Care Products	Amway Corp. 7575 E Fulton Rd. Ada, MI 49355 T: 616-787-4193 F: 616-787-4770 David Brenner / Dan DeVos
Amway (China) Co., Ltd. 8/F, Guangzhou Book Centre No. 123 Tain He Rd., Guangzhou 510620 T: 8759-6868 F: 8753-6589 Audie Wong	Personal Care Products	Amway Corp. 7575 E Fulton Rd. Ada, MI 49355 T: 616-787-4193 F: 616-787-4770 David Brenner / Dan DeVos

China Office	**Product/Service**	**U.S. Head Office**
Apple Computer Int'l Ltd. Rm. 1009 Main Tower, GITIC Hitel 339 Huan Shi Rd. E., Guangzhou 510098 T: 8331-3228 F: 8331-1337 Freddie Lam	Computers	Apple Computer Inc. One Infinite Loop Cupertino, CA 95014 T: 408-996-1010 F: 408-974-2113 Dave Manovich
Armstrong Insulation Panyu Ltd. Quan Qiao Cun, Sjilou Town Panyu City, Guangzhou 511447 T: 8486-5693 F: 8486-5692 Timothy Pierce	Insulation Products	Armstrong World Industries Inc. 313 W. Liberty St. Lancaster, PA 17603 T: 717-397-0611 F: 717-396-4477 Alan L. Burnaford
AST Research Inc. 1705 North Tower, GZ World Trade Center 371-375 Huanshi E. Rd., Guangzhou 510095 T: 8778-6186 F: 8761-9053 General Manager	Computers	AST Research Inc. 16215 Alton Parkway Irvine, CA 92619 T: 714-727-4141 F: 714-727-8584 Hoon Choo / Scott Bower
AT&T China Co., Ltd. Suite 706, GITIC Plaza 339 Huan Shi Rd. E., Guangzhou 510098 T: 8335-0208 F: 8335-0108 Julius Low	Telecommunication Service	AT&T International 295 N. Maple Ave., Rm. I-14 Basking Ridge, NJ 07920 T: 248-262-6646 F: 248-952-5095 Elizabeth Mallek
ATC International Inc. Rm. 605 GITIC Commercial Center 1 Huang Tian Zhi Jie, Guangzhou 510050 T: 8350-1150 F: 8350-1156 Don Bai	Aviation Petrochemicals	ATC International Inc. 1776 Yorktown, #340 Houston, TX 77056 T: 713-622-3047 F: 713-622-1864 Bruce Bentley
Aura Systems Inc. Rm. 2002, Tao Jin Commercial Centre 98 Heng Fu Rd., Guangzhou 510095 T: 8332-2965 F: 8358-2863 Allen Chan	Audio Equipment	Aura Systems Inc. 2335 Alaska Ave. El Segundo, CA 90245 T: 310-643-5300 F: 310-643-8719 Mark Drake
Avon Products Inc. 2/F, Lian Wei Building 420-1 Huan Shi Rd. E., Guangzhou 510075 T: 8761-0088 F: 8760-6239 Barry Wong	Personal Care Products	Avon Products Inc. 1345 Ave. of the Americas New York, NY 10105-1096 T: 212-282-5000 F: 212-282-6149 Marcia L. Worthing
Bank of America Rm. 1325/33 Dong Fang Hotel 120 Liu Hua Rd., Guangzhou 510015 T: 8668-5864 F: 8667-8063 Alfred Lam	Banking	BankAmerica Corp. 315 Montgomery St., M/S-10540 San Francisco, CA 94104 T: 415-622-2507 F: 415-622-5719 John Mauney
Baxter Healthcare (GZ) Co., Ltd. Rm. 906 T. P. Plaza 109-9 Liuhua Rd., Guangzhou 510010 T: 8666-8334/35 Michael Cheah	Medical Products CAPD Dialysis Solution	Baxter International Inc. One Baxter Parkway Deerfield, IL 60015 T: 847-948-2000 F: 847-948-2887 John F. Gaither, Jr.

China Office	Product/Service	U.S. Head Office
Becker ^ Poliakoff, P. A. 1506 Guangzhou World Trade Center 371-375 Huanshi E. Rd., Guangzhou 510065 T: 8775-7808 F: 8777-9738 Michael Zhang	Law	Becker ^ Poliakoff & Streitfeld 33 N. Garden Ave., #960 Clearwater, FL 34615 T: 813-443-3781 F: 813-443-4079 Robert Tankel
Black Clawson Company Rm. 1503 North Twr, GZ World Trade Center 371-375 Huan Shi Rd. E., Guangzhou 510095 T: 8778-1783 F: 8776-6588 Andrew Gan	Polution Control Pulp, Paper & Plastics Converting Industries	Black Clawson Co. 405 Lexington Ave., 61/F New York, NY 10174 T: 212-916-8000 F: 212-916-8057 Carl C. Landegger
Block Drug Company, Inc. Rm. 1808 GITIC Hotel 339 Huan Shi Rd. E., Guangzhou 510060 T: 8331-2228 F: 8331-2468 Frank F. Yan	Toothpaste Denture Cleanser Denture Adhesives	Block Drug Co. 257 Cornelison Ave. Jersey City, NJ 07302 T: 201-434-3000 F: 201-332-7899 Anthony Englese
Boeing Customer Support Office Rm. 303 China Southern Airline Engr. Bldg. Bai Yun Airport, Guangzhou 510405 T: 8659-7994 F: 8657-0719 Robert Anderson	Aircraft Servicing	**The Boeing Company** 7755 E. Marginal Way South Seattle, WA 98108 T: 206-655-7300 F: 206-544-2791 Raymond J. Waldmann
Budweiser Wuhan Int'l Brewing Co., Ltd. Rm. 2002, South Twr, GZ World Trade Ctr. 371-375 Huan Shi Rd. E., Guangzhou 510065 T: 8775-0630 F: 8776-4148 Rico Ho	Brewery	Anheuser Busch Co., Inc. 1 Busch Place St. Louis, MO 63118-1852 T: 314-577-2000 F: 314-577-0745 Fred Wolter
Burson-Marsteller Rm. 1201 Parkview Square 960 Jie Fang Rd., Guangzhou T: 8666-5666 x 1201 F: 8666-9101 Peter Lam	Public Relations	Burson-Marsteller 230 Park Ave. New York, NY 10003-1566 T: 212-614-4000 F: 212-614-4262 Thomas D. Bell, Jr.
Butler Manufacturing Co. Rm. 1304 North Twr, GZ World Trade Ctr. 371-375 Huan Shi Rd. E., Guangzhou 510095 T: 8778-8823 F: 8778-2681 Shaker (Chuck) A. Hijazi	Building Systems	Butler Manufacturing Co. BMA Tower, 310 S. W. Traffic Way Kansas City, MO 64141 T: 816-968-3293 Pauline Jung
C. Melchers GmBH & Co. Rm. 1108, T. P. Plaza 9/109 Liu Hua Rd., Guangzhou 510010 T: 8666-8700 F: 8667-7845 Nancy Chow	General Trading	C. Melchers America 55 New ontgomery St. #888 San Francisco, CA 94105 T: 415-974-6210 F: 415-974-1640 Hellmuth Starnitzky
Caltex China Ltd./ Caltex Langton Investment Rm. 1106 North Twr, GZ World Trade Ctr. 371-375 Huan Shi Rd. E., Guangzhou 510095 T: 8775-7549 F: 8778-0448 Gary Yang	Petroleum Products Business Management	Caltex Petroleum Corp. 125 E. John Carpenter Freeway Irving, TX 92675 T: 972-830-1000 F: 972-830-3034 H. S. Nichols

China Office	Product/Service	U.S. Head Office
Carrier China Ltd. Rm. 544 Garden Hotel Office Tower 368 Huna Shi Rd. E., Guangzhou 510064 T: 8333-8999 x 544 F: 8332-5414 Peter Chiu	Air Conditioner Service & Parts	Carrier International Carrier Pkwy., P. O. Box 4808 Syracuse, NY 13221 T: 315-432-3352 F: 315-432-7216 Robert Fiesinger
Chemtex International Inc. Jiao Yuan Rd., Dongji Section GETDZ, Guangzhou 510730 T: 8221-5863 x 230 F: 8221-9121 Zhang Zhan Bin	Polyester Products	Chemtex International Inc. 560 Lexington Avenue New York, NY 10022 T: 212-752-5220 F: 212-752-0872 Nitoshi Kono
China Hewlett-Packard Co., Ltd. 7/F, T. P. Plaza 9/109 Liu Hua Rd., Guangzhou 510010 T: 8331-1888 x 71202 F: 8331-1413 He Xiao Qiang	Computer Products Medical Equipment Analytical Equipment	Hewlett-Packard Co. 3000 Hanover St. Palo Alto, CA 94304 T: 650-857-1501 F: 650-857-5518 Manuel F. Diaz
CIGNA Corp. Rm. 2810 Peace World Plaza 362-366 Huan Shia Rd. E., Guangzhou 510060 T: 8387-2309 F: 8387-2706 Amy Lan	Insurance	CIGNA Corp. One Liberty Place, 1650 Market St. Philadelphia, PA 19192 T: 215-761-1000 F: 215-761-5505 B. Kingsley Schubert / Ed Loughman
Citibank N.A. 1703 Main Bldg., GITIC Hotel 339 Huan Shi Rd. E., Guangzhou 510098 T: 8332-1711 F: 8331-1323 Andrew Tung	Banking	Citicorp. 399 Park Ave. New York, NY 10043 T: 212-559-1000 F: 212-559-5138 Robert Martinsen / Peter Schuring
Clorox (Guangzhou) Co., Ltd. 3001A, 3/F, 158 Dong Feng Rd. E. Guangzhou 510170 T: 8188-2248 F: 8188-3418 Raymond Lee	Insecticide Products	The Clorox Co. 1221 Broadway, PO Box 24305 Oakland, CA 94612 T: 510-271-7327 F: 510-208-1501 Mark Chichak
Coca-Cola China Ltd. Rm. 1114 GITIC Plaza Main Bldg. 339 Huanshi E. Rd., Guangzhou 510060 T: 8279-8228 F: 8279-8707 Franky Sze	Soft Drinks Bottler	Coca-Cola Co. One Coca-Cola Plaza Atlanta, GA 30313 T: 404-676-2121 F: 404-676-6792 Douglas N. Daft / Sergio Zyman
Coherent 1006 South Tower, GZ World Trade Center Huan Shi Rd. E., Guangzhou 510095 T: 8778-5888 General Manager	Medical Products Laser Products Optical Systems	Coherent Inc. 5100 Patrick Henry Dr. Santa Clara, CA 95054 T: 408-764-4129 F: 408-970-9998 Edwina DeRousse
Colgate (Guangzhou) Co., Ltd. 16-17F, Metro Plaza 183 Tian He Bei Rd., Guangzhou 510620 T: 8755-1991 x 383 F: 8755-2511 Lim Kim Seng	Personal Care Products	Colgate-Palmolive Co. 300 Park Ave. New York, NY 10022 T: 212-310-2000 F: 212-310-3301 Stephen A Lister / Carlos Velasquez

China Office	Product/Service	U.S. Head Office
Colgate-Palmotive Company 16-17F, Metro Plaza 183 Tian He Rd., Guangzhou 510620 T: 8758-8112 F: 8758-8248 Chester Fong	Personal Care Products	Colgate-Palmolive Co. 300 Park Ave. New York, NY 10022 T: 212-310-2000 F: 212-310-3301 Stephen A Lister / Carlos Velasquez
Compaq Computer HK Ltd. Rm. 8078 T. P. Plaza 9-109 Liuhua Rd., Guangzhou 510010 T: 8669-5829 F: 8669-5061 General Manager	Computers	Compaq Computer Corp. 20555 State Highway 249 Houston, TX 77070 T: 281-370-0670 F: 281-514-1740 Machael Heil
Coopers & Lybrand Unit B, 10/F, Tower A, GITIC Hotel 339 Huan Shi Rd. E., Guangzhou 510060 T: 8331-1529 F: 8332-4717 Sonny Doo	Accounting Taxation Consulting	Coopers & Lybrand 1530 Wilson Blvd. Arlington, VA 22209-2447 T: 703-908-1500 F: 703-908-1695 Bob Rourke
Cosa Crown Worldwide Ltd. 18 Hua Le Lu Guangzhou 510060 T: 8382-2308 F: 8382-3365 Lai Chung Hang	Shipping Freight Forwarding	Crown Pacific 5252 Argosy Dr. Huntington Beach, CA 92649 T: 714-898-0955 F: 714-898-5640 James Thompson
Coulter Electronics Guangzhou Office Rm. A303 Shui Feng Bldg. Xian Lie Zhong Lu, Guangzhou 510095 T: 8730-4484 F: 8760-9697 Yu Yong Jin	Electronic Products Medical Equipment	Coulter Corp. 11800 S. W. 147th St., PO Box 169015 Miami, FL 33116-9015 T: 305-380-3800 F: 305-380-8312 Mike Crochu / James Schepp
CPC (Guangzhou) Foods Ltd. 2/F, 170-174 Zhan Yi Street Lin He Rd. E., Guangzhou 510610 T: 8757-3413 F: 8757-3422 Chow Thin Wai	Food Products	CPC International inc. P. O. Box 8000, Int'l Plaza Englewood Cliffs, NJ 07632 T: 201-894-4000 F: 201-541-5304 Robert J. Gillespie
Cultor (Guangzhou) Co., Ltd. 2/F Yong Star Bldg. 1&3 Jin Xiu Rd., GETDD, Guangzhou 510730 T: 8221-9531 F: 8221-9532 Lawrence A. Burkholder	Food Ingredients	Cultor Food Science 430 Saw Mill River Rd. Ardsley, NY 10502 T: 914-674-6300 F: 914-674-6898 Ariella Gastel
Deacons Guangzhou Office Rm. 2108 South Twr, GZ World Trade Ctr. 371-375 Huan Shi Rd. E., Guangzhou 510095 T: 8778-5678 F: 8777-0488 Rose Baochun Zeng	Law	Graham & James 801 South Figueroa St., 14/F Los Angeles, CA 90017 T: 213-624-2500 F: 213-623-4581 Hillel Cohn
Dehaan Corporation 2821 Dong Shan Plaza 69 Xian Lie Zhong Rd., Guangzhou 510095 T: 8732-1706 F: 8732-1070 Cary Au	Industrial Eqmt Sales Installation & Repair	Dehaan Corp. P. O. Box 3105 Carlsbad, CA 92009 T: 760-930-8066 F: 760-930-8046 Kurt Dehaan

China Office	Product/Service	U.S. Head Office
Deloitte Touche Tohmatsu Rm. 2002 Peace World Plaza 362-366 Huanshi E. Rd., Guangzhou 510060 T: 8387-8555 F: 8387-0199 General Manager	Accounting	Deloitte Touche Tohmatsu Int'l Ten Westport Rd. Wilton, CT 06897 T: 203-761-3000 F: 203-834-2200 Dina A. Elliott
Dentsu, Young & Rubicam Rm. 506/07, 5/F, Parkview Square 960 Jie Fang d., Guangzhou 510030 T: 8666-7733 F: 8666-7723 Manny Tonogbanua	Advertising	Young & Rubicam Inc. 285 Madison Ave. New York, NY 10017 T: 212-210-3000 F: 212-490-9073 James Hood / Mike Samet
DHL Sino-Trans Ltd. Express Bldg., Jichang North Rd. Guangzhou 510410 T: 8664-4668 F: 8654-3293 Bob Vickers	Express Mail Service	DHL Worldwide Express 333 Twin Dolphin Dr. Redwood City, CA 94065 T: 650-593-7474 F: 650-593-1689 Dean Christon / Brian Billings
Digital Equipment China Inc. Rm. 908 South Twr, GZ World Trade Ctr 371-375 Huan Shi Rd. E., Guangzhou 510095 T: 8778-4228 x 2828 F: 8760-9065 Paul Chiu	Computer Equipment	Digtal Equipment Corp. 111 Powermill Rd. Maynard, MA 01754 T: 508-493-5111 F: 508-497-7374 Ronald Spinek
Dongguan Molex South China Connector Rm. 1344/45 Garden Tower Hotel 368 Huanshi E. Rd., Guangzhou 510064 T: 8333-8999 x 1345 F: 8335-5779 Mendy Lee	Connectors	Molex Inc. 2222 Wellington Ave. Lisle, IL 60532 T: 708-969-4550 F: 708-969-1352 J. Krehbiel
Dow Chemical (China) Ltd. Rm. 1352/53 China Hotel Office Tower Liu Hua Rd., Guangzhou 510015 T: 8611-1222 F: 8666-6407 Michael Chow	Chemical Products	Dow Chemical Co. 2030 Dow Center Midland, MI 48674 T: 517-636-1000 F: 517-636-3518 Dick Sosville
Dow Jones Markets (HK) Ltd. 1108 GITIC Plaza 339 Huanshi E. Rd., Guangzhou 510060 T: 8331-1357 F: 8331-2748 General Manager	Business Information	Dow Jones & Co., Inc. 200 Liberty St. New York, Ny 10281 T: 212-416-2000 F: 212-416-2885 Karen House / James Friedlich
Dupont Agricultural Chemicals Ltd. Rm. 801 Garden Tower East 368 Huan Shi Rd. E., Guangzhou 510064 T: 8386-5356 F: 8386-6022 Chen Feng	Agricultural Chemicals	E I Dupont De Nemours & Co. 1007 Market St. Wilmington, DE 19898 T: 302-774-1000 F: 302-774-7321 Charles O. Holliday, Jr.
Duracell Asia Ltd. Rm. 1009 T. P. Plaza 9/109 Liu Hua Rd., Guangzhou 510010 T: 8669-5205 F: 8669-5202 Robert C. K. Choi	Batteries	Duracell Int'l Inc. Berkshire Corporate Park Bethel, CT 06801 T: 203-796-4000 F: 203-796-4516 Bob Giacolone

China Office	Product/Service	U.S. Head Office
Eagle International Investment Group Ming Zhu Rd., GETDD Guangzhou 510730 T: 8221-1549 F: 8221-5593 Xiao Ren Mian	Electric Generation	Eagle Int'l Investment 821 S. Garfield Ave. Alhambra, CA 91801 T: 626-300-0648 F: 626-300-8876 K. Au
Eastern American Ind.Developemnt Co. Guangzhou Guangdong T: 8750-7101 Clark Friedman	Metal Buildings	**Eastern American** 77 Oak St. Newton, MA 02164 T: 617-926-4025 Clark Friedman
Edelman Public Relations Suite 706 Garden Tower, Garden Hotel 368 Huan Shi Rd. E., Guangzhou 510064 T: 8385-0212 F: 8381-5315 Ruby Ong	Public Relations	Edelman Public Relations Worldwide 200 E. Randolph Dr., #6300 Chicago, IL 60601 T: 312-240-3000 F: 312-240-2900 Diane B. Dalbke
EDS Manufacturer Systems Rm. 611-613 Holiday Inn City Centre 28 Huan Shi Rd. E., Guangzhou 510060 T: 8776-6999 x 611/13 F: 8775-3126 x 612 Yang Xi Xie	Computer Software	EDS 5400 Legacy Dr. Plano, TX 75024 T: 972-605-6000 F: 972-605-6662 John R. Harris
Eli Lilly Asia Inc. Rm. 2703 Yi An Plaza Jian She 6 Rd., Guangzhou 510060 T: 8383-7402 F: 8387-1613 Hank Yuan	Pharmaceutical Products	Eli Lilly & Co. Lilly Corporate Center Indianapolis, IN 46285 T: 317-276-2000 F: 317-276-2095 Gino Santini
Ernst & Young Rm. 1110/11 Main Office Tower, GITIC 339 Huan Shi Rd. E., Guangzhou 510060 T: 8331-2788 F: 8331-2868 Albert Cheung	Accounting Consulting	Ernst & Young 787 Seventh Ave., 14/F New York, NY 10019 T: 212-773-3000 F: 212-773-6350 Eli Spielman
Esso Hong Kong Ltd.. Rm. 29E Annex A, Guangdong Int'l Hotel 339 Huanshi E. Rd., Guangzhou 510615 T: 8331-3666 F: 8331-2818 Raymond Ma	Petrochemical Products	Exxon Corp. 225 E. John W Carpenter Freeway Irving, TX 75062 T: 214-444-1000 F: 214-444-1348 R Dahan
Eternit Guangzhou Co., Ltd. 203-1 Fang Cun Da Dao, PO Box 1051 Guangzhou 510360 T: 8189-2299 F: 8180-3536 R-Xavier Thiebaud	Building Materials Fiber Cement Panels Fire Protection Boards Roofing Slates	Eternit Corp. Berks Corp. Center, 210 Corporate Dr. Reding, PA 19605 T: 610-926-0100 F: 610-926-9232 Ron Hruz
FedEx Guangzhou Rep. Office Rm. 1004A, T. P. Plaza 9/109 Liu Huan Rd., Guangzhou 510010 T: 8667-5719 F: 8667-5991 Florence Liang	Express Mail Service	Federal Express Corp. 2005 Corporate Ave., 3/F Memphis, TN 38132 T: 901-369-3600 F: 901-395-4858 T Michael Glenn / David Cunningham

China Office	Product/Service	U.S. Head Office

China Office

Product/Service

U.S. Head Office

Fourth Shift Asia Computer Corp.
Rm. 1801 GITIC Hotel
339 Huan Shi Rd. E., Guangzhou 510098
T: 8331-1500 F: 8331-1247
Tim Fare

Computer Software

Fourth Shift Corp.
7900 International Dr.
Minneapolis, MN 55425
T: 612-851-1500 F: 612-851-1560
D. J. Bowman

Frederick Hong Law Office
1503, North Tower, GZ World Trade Center
371-375 Huanshi E. Rd., Guangzhou 510095
T: 8760-9933 F: 8760-9896
Frederick Hong

Law

> **The next edition of
> "American Business in China"
> will be published
> in January, 2000.**

Frito-Lay Co., Ltd.
57 Dun He Rd., Haizhu Dist.
Guangzhou 510300
T: 8445-9553 F: 8445-1685
Jeffrey A Goh

Food Products

Frito-Lay Inc.
P. O. Box 660634
Dallas, TX 75266
T: 214-334-5500 F: 214-334-5611
M. E. Howell

G.E. (China) Co. Ltd.
Rm. 1212 Yi An Plaza
38 Jian She 6 Rd., Guangzhou 510060
T: 8387-2818 F: 8387-3128
General Manager

Industrial Products

General Electric Co.
3135 Easton Turnpike
Fairfield, CT 06431
T: 518-869-5555 F: 518-869-2828
Guy Rabbat

G.E. Aircraft Engines China
4/F, Maintenance Engineering Bldg.
Bai Yun Airport, Guangzhou 510405
T: 8612-2145 F: 8663-4079
David Settergren

Aircraft Engine Servicing

General Electric Co.
3135 Easton Turnpike
Fairfield, CT 06431
T: 518-869-5555 F: 518-869-2828
Guy Rabbat

G.E. Capital Corp.
Rm. 1512 Yi An Plaza
38 Jian She 6 Rd., Guangzhou 510060
T: 8380-4995 F: 8380-3076
Sue Li

Financial Services

GE Capital
P. O. Box 2204
Fort Wayne, IN 46801
T: 219-439-2000
Chuck Devine

Gameco (Lockeed Aircraft Service Int'l)
Bai Yun International Airport
Guangzhou 510405
T: 8657-9761 F: 8657-9757
Dan Lange

Aircraft Servicing

Lockeed Martin Corp.
6801 Rockledge Dr.
Bethesda, MD 20817
T: 301-897-6275 F: 301-897-6778
Robert Trice, Jr.

Gar-Sun Co. / General United Co.
Flat F, 10/F, No. 18 Si You Er Ma Rd.
Guangzhou 510600
T: 8739-6304 F: 8739-0288
Alexander Peng

Flour Additives
Electronic Products

Gar-Sun Company
309 Klamath St.
Brisbane, CA 94005
T: 415-587-0118 F: 415-587-1911
Gary Mui

Gillette Guangzhou Office
Rm. 2706 Yi An Mansion
Jian She 6 Rd., Guangzhou 510064
T: 8381-2606 F: 8381-3350
Deng Ying

Blades & Razors
Cosmetics & Toiletries

The Gillette Co.
Prudential Tower Bldg.
Boston, MA 02199
T: 617-421-7000 F: 617-421-7123
Peter Kent

China Office	Product/Service	U.S. Head Office
Glenayre Electronics Inc. Rm. 515/16 Parkview Square 960 Jiefang North rd., Guangzhou 510030 T: 8666-9148 F: 8666-8861 General Manager	Electronics	Glenayre Technologies Inc. 5935 Carnegie Blvd. Charlotte, NC 28209 T: 704-553-0038 F: 704-553-9338 Lee Ellison
Global One GZ Office Unit 1312/13 Main Tower, GITIC 339 Huan Shi Rd. E., Guangzhou 510098 T: 8331-2822 F: 8333-6606 Tina Fan	Telecommunications	Global One 12490 Sunrise Valley Dr. Reston, VA 20196 T: 703-689-6000 F: 703-689-6458 Sybil Mewman
Grey Advertising Co., Ltd. Rm. 3101 North Twr, GZ World Trade Ctr. 371-375 Huan Shi Rd. E., Guangzhou 510095 T: 8778-4286 F: 8775-2412 Sandy T. C. Ng	Advertising	Grey Advertising Inc. 777 Third Ave. New York, NY 10017 T: 212-546-2000 F: 212-546-1495 Barbara Feigin / John D Destler
GTE China 12/F, Tower 3, Dong Jun Plaza 836 Dong Feng Rd. E., Guangzhou 510080 T: 8760-5512 F: 8760-5582 Arnold E. Marks	Telecommunications Services	GTE Corp. One Stamford Forum Stamford, CT 06904 T: 203-965-2000 F: 203-965-2936 Ignacio Santillana
Guangdong Guangxin McDonald's Food Co. Rm. 813-820, 8/F, Sapphire Bldg. 668 Ren Min Rd. North, Guangzhou 510180 T: 8136-1356 F: 8136-2987 Joe Lau/Paul Yee	Fast Food Real Estate	McDonald's Corp. One McDonald's Plaza Oak Brook, IL 60521 T: 630-623-3000 F: 630-623-8843 James R. Cantalupo
Guangmei Foods Co. Ltd. Yuancun Fourth Sideroad, Tianhe Dist. East Suburb of Guangzhou T: 8552-5117 F: 8552-5846 K. C. Ng	Food Products Beverage	Coca-Cola International One Coca-Cola Plaza NW Atlanta, GA 30313 T: 404-676-2121 F: 404-676-6792 Douglas N. Daft / Sergio Zyman
Guangtong Food Co. Ltd. 2 Tian He Rd. Tian He Dist. Guangzhou T: 8776-5693 F: 8776-5418 Edward Yeung	Food Maxwell House Coffee	Kraft General Foods Int'l Inc. 800 Westchester Ave. Rye Brook, NY 10573 T: 914-335-2500 F: 914-335-1522 James King / James Ko
Guangzhou Asian-American Polyester Co. Jiao Yuan Rd., Dongji Section GETDZ, Guangzhou 510730 T: 8221-5863 x 230 F: 8221-9121 Zhang Zhan Bin	Polyester Products	Chemtex International Inc. 560 Lexington Ave. New York, NY 10022 T: 212-752-5220 F: 212-752-0872 Nitoshi Kono
Guangzhou Coca-Cola Company 2 Gang Qian Rd. Huangpu, Guangzhou T: 8227-5984 F: 8227-9562 Xie Yan'er	Soft Drinks Bottler	Coca-Cola International One Coca-Cola Plaza, NW Atlanta, GA 30313 T: 404-676-2121 F: 404-676-6792 Douglas N. Daft / Sergio Zyman

China Office	Product/Service	U.S. Head Office
Guangzhou Harris Telecommunications Co. 181 Xin Gang Rd. West Guangzhou 510300 T: 8445-1701 x 3316 F: 8445-1781 Franky Cheung	Telecommunications Services	Harris Corp. 1025 W. NASA Blvd. Melbourne, FL 32919 T: 407-727-9260 F: 407-727-9644 Larry Smith
Guangzhou M.C. Pakaging Ltd. GETDD, Huanpu Guangzhou 510730 T: 8221-2998 F: 8221-2458 Jiang Wei Shi	Packaging Materials	Ball Corp. 345 S. High St. Munice, IN 47305 T: 317-747-6100 F: 317-747-6808 G. Sissel / W. L. Peterson
Guangzhou Otis Elevator Co., Ltd. Xia Mao Guang Hua Road Guangzhou 510425 T: 8662-0060 F: 8662-0061 Vir Santos	Elevators Escalators Moving Wallways	Otis Elevators Co. 10 Farm Springs Farmington, CT 06032 T: 860-676-6000 F: 860-676-6970 Steve Page
Guangzhou Pepsi-Cola Beverage Co. 57 Dun He Road, Henan Guangzhou 510300 T: 8429-3622 F: 8422-8316 Richard Amrozowicz	Beverages	PepsiCo International 1 Pepsi Way Somers, NY 10589 T: 914-767-6000 F: 914-767-6553 Keith Hughes
Guangzhou Pepsico Food International 57 Dun He Lu Guangzhou 510300 T: 8445-9553 F: 8445-1685 Jeffrey Goh	Food - Snack	PepsiCo International 1 Pepsi Way Somers, NY 10589 T: 914-767-6000 F: 914-767-6553 Keith Hughes
Guangzhou Quaker Oats Beverage & Food Co. 5/F, Golden Lake Bldg. 2 Dong Hu Rd. West, Guangzhou 510100 T: 8384-2198 F: 8385-6253 Zhang Yong Jian	Food & Beverages	Quaker Oats Co. 321 N. Clark St. Chicago, IL 60610 T: 312-222-7267 F: 312-222-8304 Barb Allen
Guangzhou Reltec Communication Technology Science & Tehnology Bldg. 1, 4/F, GETDZ Chuang Ye Road, Guangzhou 510730 T: 8222-0413/0423 F: 8222-1092 Felix Yao	Telecommunications Equipment Installation	Reltec 2100 Reliance Pkwy. Bedford, TX 76021 T: 817-267-3141 F: 817-540-8240 Teryl Jones
Guangzhou SuiJia Petroleum Products Co. Rm. 708 Di Zhi Bldg. 739 Dong Feng Rd. E., Guangzhou 510080 T: 8766-4845 F: 8766-3324 Ringo Kwan	Petroleum	Caltex Petroleum Corp. 125 E. John Carpenter Frwy. Irving, TX 92675 T: 972-830-1000 F: 972-830-3034 H. S. Nichols
H. B. Fuller (China) Adehesives Co. Ltd. 10 Bihua St., GETDZ, Huangpu Guangzhou 510730 T: 8221-4333 F: 8221-4818 S. W. Chiu	Adhesive Products Sealants & Coatings	H B Fuller Co. 3724 Lexington Ave. N. St. Paul, MN 55126 T: 612-645-3401 F: 612-236-3163 Al Longstreet

China Office	**Product/Service**	**U.S. Head Office**
HAVI Group (Far East) L. P. Rm. 1308 GITIC Plaza 339 Huanshi E. Rd., Guangzhou 510060 T: 8331-2948 F: 8331-2986 Richard Ho	Trading	HAVI Group 1010 Executive Dr., #100 Westmont, IL 60559 T: 630-986-5880 F: 630-986-9734 Alicia Lutz
Heinz-UFE Ltd. Yan Tang, Sha He, Guangzhou 510507 T: 8770-6218 F: 8770-5808 Shirley Cheung	Baby & Snack Food	H J Heinz Co. 600 Grant St. Pittsburgh, PA 15219 T: 412-456-5700 F: 412-456-6128 Anthony O'Reilly
Holiday Inn City Centre 28 Guang Ming Lu, Hua Qiao Xin Cun Huan Shi Rd. E., Guangzhou 510095 T: 8776-6999 F: 8776-3126 Michael Wu	Hotel	Holiday Inns Worldwide 3 Ravina Dr. Atlanta, GA 30346 T: 770-604-2000 Richard L Smith
Hua Mei Sanitary Ware Co. Ltd. Rm. 1512/13 GITIC Hotel 339 Huan Shi Rd. E., Guangzhou 510060 T: 8332-1573 F: 8332-1634 Yang Jian Hong	Sanitary Ware	American Standard, Inc. 1 Centennial Plaza Piscataway, NJ 08855 T: 908-980-3000 F: 908-980-3219 Alan Silver
I. T. W. (China) Rm. 557 Garden Tower, Garden Hotel 368 Huan Shi Rd. E., Guangzhou 510064 T: 8384-0122 F: 8384-0123 Carey Allen	Tire Testing Machinery	ITW Signode 3600 W. Lake Ave. Glenview, IL 60025 T: 847-724-6100 F: 847-724-5910 Frank Ptak
IBM China Co. 20/F, Metro Plaza 183 Tian He Bei Rd., Guangzhou 510620 T: 8778-7268 F: 8778-7238 Patrick Leung	Computers	International Business Machines Corp. Rockwood Dr. Sleepy Hallow, NY 10591 T: 914-765-1900 F: 914-332-3753 John Dejoy
Informix Software (China) Co. Ltd. 16/F, Unit B, Office Tower, GITIC Hotel 339 Huan Shi Rd. E., Guangzhou 510098 T: 8335-0638 F: 8335-0932 Lawrence Huang	Computer Software	Informix Software, Inc. 4100 Bohannaon Dr. Menlo Park, CA 94025 T: 650-926-6300 F: 650-926-6593 Kathleen Critchfield
Ingersoll-Rand Far East Co. Rm. 2005 North Twr, GZ World Trade Ctr. 371-375 Huanshi E. Rd., Guangzhou 510060 T: 8775-7757 F: 8775-7727 General Manager	Bearings & Compressors	Ingersoll-Rand Co. 200 Chestnut Ridge Rd. Woodcliff Lake, NJ 07675 T: 201-573-0123 F: 201-573-3172 Paul L. Bergen
Intel Architectural Developemnt Co. Rm. 1410 GITIC Hotel 339 Huan Shi Rd. E., Guangzhou 510098 T: 8332-3333 F: 8331-1888 x 1410 Jim Jarrett	Computers & Software	Intel Corp. P. O. Box 58119 Santa Clara, CA 95052-8119 T: 408-765-8080 F: 408-765-5590 Leslie Vadasz / William Howe

China Office	Product/Service	U.S. Head Office
International Flavors & Fragrances Ltd. Rm. 1960 Dongfang Hotel 120 Liuhua Rd., Guangzhou 510016 T: 8666-1298 F: 8666-7888 Peter Smith	Chemicals - Aroma	International Flavors & Fragrances 521 W. 57th St. New York, NY 10019 T: 212-765-5500 F: 212-708-7132 Frans Nijnens
J Walter Thompson Rm. 606, 6/F, T. P. Plaza 9-109 Liuhua Rd., Guangzhou 510095 T: 8666-8790/93 F: 8666-8897 Helen Tao	Advertising	J. Walter Thompson Co. 466 Lexington Ave. New York, NY 10017 T: 212-210-7000 F: 212-210-7066 Burt Manning
Johnson Controls International Inc. Rm. 3102, Tower 2, Dong Jun Plaza 836 Dong Feng Rd. E., Guangzhou 510060 T: 8760-5881 F: 8760-5735 S. H. Ling	Control Systems Batteries & Plastics	Johnson Controls Inc. 5757 N. Green Bay Ave. Milwaukee, WI 53209 T: 414-228-1200 F: 414-228-2077 William P. Killan
Kellogg's (China) Ltd. Bei Wei Industrial Dist., GETDD Hangpu, Guangzhou 510730 T: 8221-1151 F: 8221-7269 Eduardo T. Cadiz, Jr. (Dodie)	Food Products	Kellogg Co. One Kellogg Square Battle Creek, MI 49016 T: 616-961-2000 F: 616-961-2871 Arnold G. Langbo
Ketchum-Newscan Public Relations Rm. 724 Garden Tower Hotel 368 Huanshi E. Rd., Guangzhou 510064 T: 8385-2532 F: 8385-2476 General Manager	Public Relations	Ketchum Communications Inc. 6 PPG Place Pittsburgh, PA 15222 T: 412-456-3500 Daniel Madia / David Drobis
Keystone Guangzhou Office Rm. 1602 North Twr, GZ World Trade Center 371-375 Huan Shi Rd. E., Guangzhou 510095 T: 8778-2018 F: 8765-9959 Victor Wan	Valve and Actuator	Keystone International Inc. 9600 W. Gulf Bank Rd., PO Box 40010 Houston, TX 77040 T: 713-937-5355 F: 713-895-4044 Paul Woodward
Kimberly-Clark Paper (GZ) Co., Ltd. Rm. 2901/02 Peace World Plaza 362-366 Huan Shi Rd. E., Guangzhou 510095 T: 8387-2183 F: 8387-0355 Jeff Chang	Paper Products	Kimberly-Clark Corp. P. O. Box 619100 Dallas, TX 75261 T: 972-281-1200 F: 972-281-1490 Tina S. Barry
Kimberly-Clark Paper (GZ) Co., Ltd. 1/F, Tong Xing Industrial Bldg. Chuang Ye Rd., GETDZ, Guangzhou 510730 T: 8221-7820 F: 8221-7827 James Deng	Paper Products	Kimberly-Clark Corp. P. O. Box 619100 Dallas, TX 75261 T: 972-281-1200 F: 972-281-1490 Tina S. Barry
Kodak China Ltd. 6/F, East Tower, GZ Int'l Financial Bldg. 197-199 Dong Feng Rd. E., Guangzhou 510180 T: 8319-8888 x 6101 F: 8333-1810 Jonna Li	Film Products	Eastman Kodak Co. 343 State St. Rochester, NY 14650 T: 716-724-4000 F: 716-724-0663 Willy Shih / Robert Smith

China Office	Product/Service	U.S. Head Office
KPMG Peat Marwick Rm. 712 South Tower, GZ World Trade Center 371-375 Huanshi E. Rd., Guangzhou 510095 T: 8765-9966 F: 8765-9955 General Manager	Accounting	KPMG Peat Marwick 530 Chestnut Ridge Rd. Woodcliff, NJ 07675 T: 201-505-3585 F: 201-505-3411 Timothy Pearson
Leo Burnett China Ltd. Rm. 1003/04 GITIC Hotel 339 Huan Shi Rd. E., Guangzhou 510060 T: 8331-1183 F: 8331-1123 Jeff Bradley	Advertising	Leo Burnett Co. 35 W. Wacker Drive Chicago, IL 60601 T: 312-220-5959 F: 312-220-3299 James Oates
Liebert Rm. 1101 Da ad Square 111 Liu Hua Rd., Guangzhou 510015 T: 8669-5386 F: 8666-8814 Timothy Chung	Computer Support Systems	Liebert Corp. 1050 Dearborn Dr. Columbus, OH 43229 T: 614-888-0246 F: 614-841-6022 Dennis Webb / Joe Filippi
Lincoln National (China) Inc. Rm. 629 Garden Tower, Garden Hotel 368 Huan Shi Rd. E., Guangzhou 510064 T: 8333-8999 x 629 F: 8381-8809 Phoebe Yeung	Insurance	Lincoln National Corp. 200 E. Berry St. Fort Wayne, IN 46802 T: 219-455-2000 F: 219-455-3514 Barbara Kowalczyk / Stephen Meldrum
Lotus Development Asia Pacific Ltd. Rm. 2215 South Twr, GZ World Trade Ctr. 371-375 Huan Shi Rd. E., Guangzhou 510095 T: 8777-1088 F: 8776-9868 Kent Choi	Computer Software	Lotus Corp. 55 Cambridge Parkway Cambridge, MA 02142 T: 617-577-8500 F: 617-693-1299 Deborah Besemer
Louis Berger International Inc. Zhongcun, Shabei, West Dist. Guangzhou 510610 T: 8199-9911 x 2654 F: 8199-9911 x 2336 John McMonagle	Construction - Highway Engineering Consultancy	Louis Berger International, Inc. 100 Halsted St. East Orange, NJ 07019 T: 201-678-1960 F: 201-672-4284 Lee Ahlstrom
Lucent Technology (China) Co., Ltd. Suite 710, GITIC Plaza 339 Huan Shi Rd. E., Guangzhou 510098 T: 8331-1600 F: 8331-2218 Louis Tong	Telecommunications	Lucent Technologies 600 Mountain Ave. Murray Hill, NJ 07974 T: 908-582-8500 F: 908-508-2576 Tom Uhlman / Carl Hsu
Map Info China Suite 1506 North Twr, GZ World Trade Ctr. 371-375 Huan Shi Rd. E., Guangzhou 510095 T: 8778-1663 F: 8777-9738 Holly He	Computer Software	Map Info Corp. 1 Global View Troy, NY 12180 T: 518-285-6000 F: 518-285-6060 Tom Muro
Massachusetts Port Authority Office Rm. 1207 Friendship Commercial Bldg. 369 Huan Shi Rd. E., Guangzhou 510095 T: 8357-5761 F: 8357-1070 Dinah Wu	Trade Promotion	Massachusetts Port Authority 1 Harborside Dr., #200S East Boston, MA 02128-2909 T: 617-568-1000 F: 617-478-411 Charlie Yelen

China Office	Product/Service	U.S. Head Office

May Lee International Inc.
Rm. 512 China Hotel Office Tower
Liuhua Rd., Guangzhou
T: 8666-3388 x 2512 F: 8667-7024
David Buxbaum

Trading
Consulting
Law

Buxaum & Choy
100 Maiden Lane, #1616
New York, NY 10038
T: 212-504-6109 F: 212-412-7016
K. Choy

McCall's Center (U.S.C.I.)
P. O. Box 544
Guangzhou 510010
T: 8663-3338 F: 8664-6545
Paul Condrell

Direct Mail Marketing

McCann-Erickson Ltd.
11/F, Guang Hai Hotel
932 Jie Fang Rd. N., Guangzhou 510030
T: 8339-5461 F: 8336-4668
Simon Liang

Advertising

McCann-Erickson Worldwide
750 Third Ave.
New York, NY 10017
T: 212-697-6000 F: 212-867-5177
Marcio Moreira

McCormick (Guangzhou) Food Co., Ltd.
Dong Ji Industry Dist., GETDZ
Guangzhou 510730
T: 8222-0832 F: 8221-3530
Victor Sy

Food
Condiments & Seasonings

McCormick & Co., Inc.
18 Loventon Circle
Sparks, MD 21152
T: 410-771-7830 F: 410-527-8195
Gary Zimmerman

Mead Johnson (Guangzhou) Ltd.
Xia Yuan Rd., Dong Ji Industry Dist.
GETDZ, Guangzhou 510730
T: 8221-4741 F: 8221-1277
James Mullen

Food - Milk Powder

Mead Johnson Nutritional Group
2400 W. Lloyd Expwy.
Evansville, IN 47721
T: 812-429-5000 F: 812-429-8994
Leroy G. McBrien

Merck Sharp & Dolune China
Rm. 605 Municipal Bldg.
348 Huan Shi Rd. E., Guangzhou 510060
T: 8384-3396 F: 8384-3405
Eva Law

Pharmaceutical Products

Merck & Co.
One Merck Dr.
Whitestone Station, NJ 08889
T: 908-423-1000 F: 908-423-1043
Attn: Japan Administration WS-2B-80

Mezzullo & McCandlish
Suite 1411 Guangdong International Hotel
339 Huan Shi Rd. E., Guangzhou 510098
T: 8331-3676 F: 8331-3675
Shao Long Zhu

Law
Consulting

Mezzullo & McCandlish
1111 E. Main St., #1500
Richmond, VA 23219-3500
T: 804-775-3884 F: 804-775-3800
R. Harmon

Microsoft (China) Co., Ltd.
Unit 1, 9/F, Broadway Plaza
233 Dong Feng Rd. W., Guangzhou 510180
T: 8318-0779 F: 8318-0575
Anny Wong

Computer Software

Microsoft Corp.
One Microsoft Way
Redmond, WA 98052
T: 206-882-8080 F: 206-883-8101
Charles Stevens / Steven A Ballmer

Mobil Asia Pacific Pte. Ltd.
Rm. 1101/04 GITIC Plaza
339 Huan Shi Rd. E., Guangzhou 510098
T: 8331-1443 F: 8331-1445
Geoffrey Cheng

Petroleum

Mobil Corp.
3225 Gallows Rd.
Fairfax, VA 22037-0001
T: 703-846-3000 F: 703-846-4669
Robert Swanson

- - - - - T: Telephone # - - - - - F: Fax # - - - - - Guangzhou Area Code: (86)20 - - - - -

China Office	**Product/Service**	**U.S. Head Office**
Moen Guangzhou Faucet Co., Ltd. Dhang Yuan Gang, Sha He Tian He Dist., Guangzhou 510655 T: 8773-4317 F: 8773-4484 Peter P. Wang	Faucets	Moen Inc. 377 Woodland Ave. Elyria, OH 44035 T: 2126-962-2000 F: 216-329-2743 H. Griffin / N. North
Motorola (China) Electronics Ltd. 271 Huangpu Da Dao West Tian He Dist., Guangzhou 510620 T: 8753-7798 F: 8753-8008 Helen Du	Telecommunications Products	Motorola Inc. 1303 E. Algonquin Rd. Schaumburg, IL 60196 T: 847-576-5000 F: 847-576-4700 Richard W. Younts
National Starch & Chemical Ltd. Rm. 1006 Huagong Bldg. 808 Dongfeng E. Rd., Guangzhou 510080 T: 8776-3888 x 1006 F: 8765-6483 General Manager	Adhesive & Sealants Resin & Chemicals Food Products Industrial Starch	National Starch & Chemical Co. 10 Finderne Ave. Bridgewater, NJ 08807-3300 T: 908-685-5000 F: 908-685-5005 R. John Forrest
NCR Corp. 6/F, Main Tower GITIC Plaza 339 Huan Shi Rd. E., Guangzhou 510098 T: 8335-1511 F: 8335-0788 Ken Chu	Computers & Software	NCR Corp. 1700 S. Patterson Blvd. Dayton, OH 45479 T: 513-449-2000 F: 513-445-1847 Hideaki Takahashi
Nike, Inc. 25/F North Twr, GZ World Trade Ctr. 371-375 Huan Shi Rd. E., Guangzhou 510095 T: 8778-2893 F: 8778-2348 Ron Hartfield	Athletic Footwear	Nike, Inc. One Bowerman Dr. Beaverton, OR 97005 T: 503-671-6453 F: 503-671-6300 Hilary Smith
Northern Telecom Global Corp. Unit E, 2/F, GITIC Plaza 339 Huanshi E. Rd., Guangzhou 510098 T: 8331-1639 F: 8331-1637 General Manager	Telecommunications Eqmt	Northern Telecom P. O. Box 1222 Minneapolis, MN 55440 T: 612-932-8000 F: 612-932-8235 Flo Graham
Occidental Chemical China Ltd. Rm. 735 Garden Tower Hotel 368 Huanshi E. Rd., Guangzhou 510064 T: 8333-8999 x 735 F: 8335-8979 Charles Choi	Chemical Products	Occidental Petroleum Corp. 10889 Wilshire Blvd. Los Angeles, CA 90024 T: 310-208-8800 F: 310-443-6688 John Morgan
Ogilvy & Mather Advertising Area B, 8/F, Sui Feng Bldg. Yong Tai Cun Kou, Guangzhou 510095 T: 8730-4687 F: 8730-4622 Ramsey Leung	Advertising	Ogilvy & Mather Worldwide Worldwide Plaza, 309 W. 49th St. New York, N 10019 T: 212-237-4000 F: 212-237-5515 William Gray
OOCL (China) Ltd. Rm. 932 Guangzhou Int'l Financial Bldg. 197Dong Feng Rd. E., Guangzhou 510180 T: 8337-8996 F: 8337-8995 General Manager	Global Transportation	**OOCL (USA) Inc.** 4141 Hacienda Dr. Pleasanton, CA 94588 T: 510-460-1380 F: 510-460-3109 M. K. Wong / Peter Leng

China Office	Product/Service	U.S. Head Office
Opel China GmbH, GZ Rep. Office Suite 1501, GITIC Bldg. 339 Huan Shi Dong Rd., Guangzhou 510098 T: 8333-6256 F: 8333-6382 Frank Chou	Business Development	General Motors Corp. 482-A39-C08, 100 Renaissance Center Detroit, MI 48265-1000 T: 313-556-3527 F: 313-556-5083 Louis Hughes
Oracle Systems China Ltd. 1108 North Tower, GZ World Trade Center 371-375 Huanshi E. Rd., Guangzhou 510060 T: 8778-0378 F: 8775-4786 General Manager	Software	Oracle Corp. 500 Oracle Parkway Redwood City, CA 94065 T: 415-506-7000 F: 415-506-7200 Raymond Lane / David Roux
Owens Corning Rm. 1306 GITIC Hotel 339 Huan Shi Rd. E., Guangzhou 510098 T: 8331-3558 F: 8331-3566 Hu Hong Shan	Insulation Products - Fiberglass	Owens-Corning Fiberglass Corp. Fiberglass Tower Toledo, OH 43659 T: 419-248-8000 F: 419-248-8445 Michael Wachtell
Owens Corning Fiberglass Co., Ltd. Xia Yuan Rd., Dong Ji Industry Dist. GETDZ, Guangzhou 510730 T: 8221-9821 F: 8222-0239 Gary Wan	Insulation Products - Fiberglass	Owens-Corning Fiberglass Corp. Fiberglass Tower Toledo, OH 43659 T: 419-248-8000 F: 419-248-8445 Michael wachtell
PairGain, the Copperoptics Co. Suite 719 Garden Tower, Garden Hotel 368 Huan Shi Rd. E., Guangzhou 510064 T: 8333-8999 x 719 F: 8387-3011 Steven Z. Li	Copperoptics Telecom Equipment	PairGain Technologies 2701 Dow Ave. Tustin, CA 92780 T: 714-832-9922 F: 714-832-9908 Lucia Ratinoff
Panduit (GZ Office) Rm. 1712 Ho King Hotel 313 Huan Shi Rd. E., Guangzhou 510095 T: 8359-2738 F: 8359-2728 Fu Xiao Bin	Communication Products Wiring Products	**Panduit Corp.** 17301 S. Ridgeland Ave. Tinley Park, IL 60477 T: 708-532-1800 F: 708-614-0254 John Kwong / William Wholley
Pepsi-Cola Int'l (Asia Division) GETDD Guangzhou 510730 T: 8221-5014 F: 8221-5013 Huang Dong Wei	Food Beverage Concentrate	PepsiCo International 1 Pepsi Way Somers, NY 10589 T: 914-767-6000 F: 914-767-6553 Keith Hughes
Pepsico (China) Ltd. Jin Bi Road GETDD, Guangzhou 510730 T: 8221-4888 F: 8221-1351 Frederick Yiu	Food - Cola	PepsiCo International 1 Pepsi Way Somers, NY 10589 T: 914-767-6000 F: 914-767-6553 Keith Hughes
Perkin-Elmer China Inc. Rm. 1203/05 South Twr, GZ World Trade Ctr. 371-375 Huan Shi Rd. E., Guangzhou 510095 T: 8778-5868 F: 8778-5368 George G. J. Gao	Medical Instruments Analytical Instruments	Perkin-Elmer Corp. 761 Main St. Norwalk, CT 06859 T: 203-762-1000 F: 203-762-6000 Leslie O'Carmody

China Office	Product/Service	U.S. Head Office
Petrocorp Exploration China Ltd. Rm. 955/58 China Hotel Office Tower Liuhua Rd., Guangzhou T: 8666-3388 x 2955 F: 8611-1225 John Frisbie	Petroleum Exploration	Santa Fe Energy Resources 1616 S. Voss Rd., #1000 Houston, TX 77057-2694 T: 713-507-5000 F: 713-507-5341 Bill Schaefer / Larry Leavell
Philip Morris Asia Inc. Rm. 2743 Dong Fang Hotel 120 Liu Hua Rd., Guangzhou 510016 T: 8667-7328 F: 8667-7218 Michael Wong	Cigarette Promotion	Philip Morris Int'l 800 Westchester Ave. Rye Brook, NY 10573 T: 914-335-1120 F: 914-335-1372 Andreas Gembler
Pioneer Motors Ltd. Rm. 903 Dong Jun Plaza 838 Dong Feng Rd. E., Guangzhou 510080 T: 8760-5426 F: 8760-5402 Lin Gao Hui	Automotive	Chryster Motors Corp. 1000 Chrysler Drive Auburn Hill, MI 48326 T: 810-576-5741 Joseph E. Cappy / P. J. Trimmer
Pizza Hut (Guangzhou Pizza Co. Ltd.) A 3/F, Fu Hai Commercial Center 82 Da Nan Rd., Guangzhou 510115 T: 8319-2235 F: 8318-2531 Henry Yip	Fast Food Franchised Business	Pizza Hut 9111 East Douglas Wichita, KS 67207 T: 316-681-9000 F: 316-687-8218 Allan Huston
Price Waterhouse Rm. 1808 Yi An Plaza 38 Jianshe Liumalu, Guangzhou 510060 T: 8380-0922 F: 8380-0941 Jim Warren/Charles Fung	Accounting Consulting	Price Waterhouse 1177 Ave. of the Americas New York, Ny 10020 T: 212-596-7000 F: 212-596-8910 James Daley / Robert Gazzi
Procter & Gamble (China) Ltd. 2-4F, Aether Square 986 Jie Fang Rd. N., Guangzhou 510030 T: 8669-8828 x 2060 F: 8669-3569 Michael Qiu	Personal Care Products Detergents Paper	Procter & Gamble Co. 1 Procter & Gamble Plaza, PO Box 599 Cincinnati, OH 45201-0599 T: 513-983-1100 F: 513-983-9369 Alan G. Lafley
Procter & Gamble (Guangzhou) Ltd. 1 Pin He Rd. Huangpu, Guangzhou T: 8221-8828 x 2100 F: 8221-5501 Bonnie Curtis (Ms.)	Personal Care Products Detergents Paper	Procter & Gamble Co. 1 Procter & Gamble Plaza, PO Box 599 Cincinnati, OH 45201-0599 T: 513-983-1100 F: 513-983-9369 Alan G. Lafley
Rhone-Poulenc Guangzhou Rm. 1154 China Hotel Office Tower Liuhua Rd., Guangzhou 510015 T: 8666-3388 x 1154 F: 8667-1682 General Manager	Pharmaceuticals	Rhone-Poulenc Rorer Inc. 500 Arcola Rd., P. O. Box 1200 Collegeville, PA 19426-0107 T: 215-454-8000 F: 215-454-3812 Alain Audubert
Schenker (HK) Ltd. Rm. 713 International Golf Plaza 486 Huanshi E. Rd., Guangzhou 510075 T: 8767-6175 F: 8767-6301 General Manager	Freight Forwarding	**Schenker International** 150 Albany Ave. Freeport, NY 11520 T: 516-377-3000 F: 516-377-3100 Mike Bujold

China Office	**Product/Service**	**U.S. Head Office**
Sealand China Co., Ltd. Rm. 1905/06 South Twr, GZ World Trade Ctr. 371-375 Huan Shi Rd. E., Guangzhou 510095 T: 8766-0001/03 F: 8776-4298 Jon Whalen	Shipping Cargo Transportation	Sea-Land Service Inc. 6000 Carnegie Blvd. Charlotte, NC 28209 T: 704-571-2000 F: 704-571-4613 Clint Eisenhauer
Shanghai Shen-Mei Beverage & Food Corp. Rm. 1114, Main Bldg., GITIC Plaza 339 Huan Shi Rd. E., Guangzhou 510098 T: 8331-1546/47 F: 8331-1569 Matt Kittredge	Food - Concentrate	Coca-Cola Co. One Coca-Cola Plaza Atlanta, GA 30313 T: 404-676-2121 F: 404-676-6792 Douglas N. Daft / Sergio Zyman
Silicon Graphics Computer Systems Rm. 1804 North Twr, GZ World Trade Ctr. 371-375 Huan Shi RD. E., Guangzhou 510095 T: 8778-5148 F: 8777-0108 Stephen Kwok	Computer Equipment	Silicon Graphics Inc. 2011 N. Shoreline Blvd., PO Box 7311 Mountain View, CA 94039 T: 415-960-1980 F: 415-961-0595 Teruyasu Sekimoto
Singer-Hunan Sewing Machine Co. No. 2 Cao Fang Wei Nan Hua E. Rd., Guangzhou T: 8441-7806/07 F: 8441-7805 Jeremy Watson	Sewing Machines	Singer Co. 6245 State Rd. Philadelphia, PA 19135 T: 215-624-4800 Robert Cantor
SK&F (Tianjin Smith Kline & French Labs.) Rm. 1201/11 South Twr, GZ World Tarde Ctr. 371-375 Huan Shi Rd. E., Guangzhou 510095 T: 8778-7688 F: 8778-7698 He Yun Xian	Pharmaceutical Products	Smith Kline & French P. O. Box 80809 Lincoln, NE 68501 T: 402-475-4541 Harold Byram
Stratus Computer Inc. Rm. 1803 North Twr, GZ World Trade Ctr. 371-375 Huan Shi Rd. E., Guangzhou 510095 T: 8778-6448 F: 8778-5178 Bosco Lau	Computer Equipment Fault Tolerance Computers	Stratus Computer 55 Fairbanks Blvd. Marboro, MA 01752-1298 T: 508-460-2000 F: 508-481-8945 Gary Okimoto / Shirley Yee
Sun Microsystems China Ltd. Rm. 2908/13 South Twr, GZ World Trade Ctr. 371-375 Huan Shi RD. E., Guangzhou 510095 T: 8777-9913 F: 8775-6189 Charles Tien	Network Computing System	Sun Microsystems 2550 Garcia Ave. M/S: UMPK01-16 Mountain View, CA 94043 T: 415-960-1300 F: 415-969-9131 Tim Dwyer / Bob MacRitchie
Sunrider (Guangzhou) Co., Ltd. 269 Huang Pu Da Dao West Tian He Dist., Guangzhou 510620 T: 8756-7888 F: 8754-2731 Peter Ng	Health Food Products Personal Care Products	Sunrider International 1625 Abalone Ave. Torrance, CA 90501 T: 310-781-3808 F: 310-222-9273 Tei Fu Chen
Sybase Software Rm. 1112/13 Office Tower Int'l Hotel 339 Huanshi E. Rd., Guangzhou 510098 T: 8331-3501/02 F: 8331-2083 General Manager	Software	Sybase Inc. 6475 Christie Avenue Emeryville, CA 94608 T: 510-596-3500 F: 510-658-9441 Yvonne Van Leeuwen

China Office	Product/Service	U.S. Head Office
Tai Wing Hong USA Group Rm. 908 North Twr, GZ World Trade Ctr. 371-375 Huan Shi Rd. E., Guangzhou 510095 T: 8777-9878 F: 8777-1348 Michael Ng	Trading	Tai Wing Hong 1300 Metropolitan Ave. Brooklyn, NY 11237 T: 718-381-3388 F: 718-381-0678 Linda Ta
Tandem PRC Ltd. Rm. 3303 North Twr, GZ World Trade Ctr. 371-375 Huan Shi Rd. E., Guangzhou 510095 T: 8777-0848 F: 8775-0778 Joseph Wu	Computer Software Network Promotion	Tandem Computers Inc. 19333 Valco Pkwy. Cupertino, CA 95014 T: 408-725-6000 F: 408-285-4545 Gerald Peterson / Scott Thompson
Tektronix China Ltd. 845 Garden Hotel Office Tower 368 Huanshi E. Rd., Guangzhou 510064 T: 8333-8999 x 845 F: 8384-2952 General Manager	Electronics	Tektronix Inc. 26660 SW Parkway Wilsonville, OR 97070 T: 503-627-7111 F: 503-685-4038 Timothy Thorsteinson
Tupperware (China) Co., Ltd. 1/F, No. 26-28 Huifu West Road Guangzhou 510120 T: 8188-8966 F: 8188-9033 Greg Voyik	Direct Sales of Household Products	**Tupperware Corp.** P. O. Box 2353 Orlando, FL 32802 T: 407-826-5050 F: 407-826-8849 Gaylin Olson
U.S.-China Industrial Exchange Inc. Rm. 636/637 Garden Tower, Garden Hotel 368 Huan Shi Rd. E., Guangzhou 510064 T: 8333-8999 x 636 F: 8331-7757 Roberta Lipson	Hi-Tech & Analytical Instrum. Constructtion & Mining Eqmt.	US-China Industrial Exchange Inc. 7201 Wisconsin Ave., 7/F Bethesda, MD 20814 T: 301-215-7777 F: 301-215-7719 Robert C. Goodwin, Jr.
U.S. Kraft General Food Guangzhou Rm. 743 Garden Tower Hotel 368 Huanshi E. Rd., Guangzhou 510064 T: 8776-5633 F: 8335-0467 x 743 Phillip Shen / Eric Hsia	Food Products	Kraft Foods Int'l Inc. 800 Westchester Ave. Rye Brook, NY 10573 T: 914-335-2500 F: 914-335-1522 James King / James Ko
Underwriters Laboratories Inc. Rm. 665 Garden Tower, Garden Hotel 368 Huan Shi Rd. E., Guangzhou 510064 T: 8387-7427 F: 8384-7745 Dorothy K. Yuan	Product Certification	Underwriters Laboratories 333 Pfingsten Rd. Northbrook, IL 60062 T: 847-272-8800 F: 847-272-8129 Steve Wasserman
Union Carbide Asia Ltd. Rm. 1207A, T. P. Plaza 9/109 Liu Hua Rd., Guangzhou 510010 T: 8669-5599 F: 8668-2555 Vincent Zeng	Chemical Products	Union Carbide Corp. 39 Old Ridgebury Rd. Danbury, CT 06817 T: 203-794-2000 F: 203-794-3170 Lou Agnello
Unisys China Service Inc. Rm. 607/08 T. P. Plaza 9-109 Liuhua Rd., Guangzhou 510010 T: 8669-5825 F: 8669-5835 General Manager	Computer Sales System Promotion	Unisys Corp. P. O. Box 500 Blue Bell, PA 19424 T: 215-986-6990 F: 215-986-2312 Thomas Yan

China Office	Product/Service	U.S. Head Office
UPS Parcel Delivery Service Ltd. Rm. 2103 South Twr, GZ World Trade Ctr. 371-375 Huna Shi RD. E., Guangzhou 510095 T: 8775-5778 F: 8775-6178 T. H. Lim	Delivery Service	United Parcel Service of America Inc. 55 Glenlake Pkwy. Atlanta, GA 30328 T: 404-828-6000 F: 404-828-6593 Edward Schroeder
Valleylab China 127 Guang Ta Lu Guangzhou 510180 T: 8186-2482 F: 8186-2482 Fang Ming Jie	Hospital Products Pharmaceuticals	Pfizer, Inc. 235 E. 42nd St. New York, NY 10017 T: 212-573-2506 F: 212-309-4344 Mohand Sidi Said
W. R. Grace (Hong Kong) Ltd. Rm. 3104 North Twr, GZ World Trade Ctr. 371-375 Huan Shi Rd. E., Guangzhou 510095 T: 8777-9208 F: 8778-9278 Morgan Cen	Waterproofing Systems Adhesive Membrane Liquid Membrane	W R Grace & Co. One Town Center Rd. Boca Raton, FL 33486-1010 T: 561-362-2000 F: 561-362-2193 Bernd A. Schulte
Warner-Lambert (Guangzhou) Ltd. Jiao Yuan Road, Dong Ji Industrial Dist. GETDZ, Guangzhou 510630 T: 8222-0771 F: 8221-4000 Santiago Echeverry	Health Care Products Pharmaceuticals	Warner-Lambert Co. 201 Tabor Road Morris Plains, NJ 07950 T: 201-540-2000 F: 201-540-3761 Philip Gross / Frank Ritt
Westinghouse Electric Co., Ltd. Rm. 652/653 Garden Tower, Garden Hotel 368 Huan Shi Rd. E., Guangzhou 510064 T: 8387-8752 F: 8387-8777 Fred Sperry	Power Generation Process Control Transportation Refrigeration Air Traffic Control	Westinghouse Electric Corp. 11 Stanwix St. Pittsburgh, PA 15222 T: 412-642-6000 F: 412-642-3266 Gregory Vereschagin / Gary M Clark
Wrigley Chewing Gum Co. Ltd. Friendship Road East GETDZ, Guangzhou 510730 T: 8221-8816 F: 8221-5107 Du Wen Jim	Chewing Gum	WM Wrigley Jr. Co. 410 N. Michigan Ave. Chicago, IL 60611 T: 312-644-2121 F: 312-644-0015 Douglas S. Barrie / Stefan Pfander
Xerox of Shanghai Ltd. Rm. 10501 Jincheng Hotel 168 Donghua North Rd., Guangzhou 510080 T: 8775-4888 x 10501 F: 8775-4888 x 10528 Jiang Chang Qin	Maintenance Service Center Copy Machines	Xerox Corp. 800 Long Ridge Rd., PO Box 1600 Stamford, CT 06904 T: 203-968-3000 F: 203-968-4458 Allan E. Dugan
York Guangzhou Office Rm. 3402 North Twr, GZ World Trade Ctr. 371-375 Huan Shi Rd. E., Guangzhou 510095 T: 8761-0818 F: 8761-9476 Liu Zhen Chang	Refrigerating Equipment	York International Corp. 631 S. Richland Ave., P. O. Box 1592 York, PA 17405 T: 717-771-7890 F: 717-771-6819 Jeff Cook

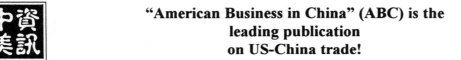

- - - - - T: Telephone # - - - - - F: Fax # - - - - - Guangzhou Area Code: (86)20 - - - - -

China Office	Product/Service	U.S. Head Office
Agip (Overseas) Ltd. 410 Shekou Industrial Zone Bldg. 4 Gang Wang Rd. 1, Shenzhen 518067 T: 668-4915 F: 668-5034 Giovanni Ferraro	Petroleum	Agip Petroleum Co. 2950 North Loop West, #300 Houston, TX 77092 T: 713-688-6281 F: 713-688-6091 S. Fantini
Amoco Orient Petroleum Co. 15/F, Chiwan Petroleum Bldg. Chiwan, Shekou, Shenzhen T: 685-2672 F: 685-1110 Joern Boe-Hansen	Petroleum	AMOCO Chemical Corp. 200 E. Randolph Dr. Chicago, IL 60601 T: 312-856-2777 F: 312-856-3800 Enrique J. Sosa
ARCO China Ltd. 17/F, Finance Center, Tai Zi Rd. Shekou Ind. Zone, Shenzhen 518067 T: 667-1212 F: 667-1211 James D. Weeks	Petroleum	**Atlantic Richfield Co.** 515 S. Flower St. Los Angeles, CA 90071 T: 213-486-3511 F: 213-486-1544 Walter A. Coyne
Arnberger, Kim, Buxbaum & Choy 2103A, Shenzhen Development Center Ren Min Nan Lu, Shenzhen 518001 T: 229-8009 F: 229-8011 Li Yan	Law Consulting	Buxum & Choy 100 Maiden Lane, #1616 New York,N 10038 T: 212-504-6109 F: 212-412-7016 K. Choy
Arthur Andesen Business Consulting Co. 28/F, International Financial Bldg. 23 Jian She Rd., Shenzhen 518001 T: 229-8288 F: 228-0044 Peter Mak	Accounting Consulting	Arthur Andersen & Co. 69 W. Washington St. Chicago, IL 60602 T: 312-580-0069 F: 312-507-6748 Richard Measelle
Caltex China Ltd. Unit B, 17/F, Real Estate Bldg. Ren Min Nan Lu, Shenzhen 518002 T: 232-1550 F: 232-4107 Patrick Ho	Petroleum Products	Caltex Petroleum Corp. 125 E. John Carpenter Freeway Irving, TX 75602 T: 972-830-1000 F: 972-830-3034 H. S. Nichols
Chia Tai Conti (Shenzhen) Ltd. Nan Tau Shanzhen 518062 T: 663-0422 F: 663-0528 Too Shu Wing	Livestock	Continental Grain Co. 277 Park Avenue, 50/F New York, NY 10172 T: 212-207-5100 F: 212-207-5181 Thomas Coyle / Peter Schroeder
China American Int'l Engineering Inc. 14/F, Liancheng Lianhe Bldg. Wen Jin Du, Chun Feng Rd., Shenzhen T: 232-6540 F: 232-7421 Wang Jin	Engineering	Bechtel Group Inc. 50 Beale St. San Francisco, CA 94105 T: 415-768-1234 F: 415-768-2154 Riley P Bechtel
China Bicycle Co. Holdings Ltd. 1 Buxin, Shuibei Industrial Zone Shenzhen 518019 T: 551-6998 F: 551-6620 Jerome Sze	Bicycles	Schwinn Bicycle Co. 217 N. Jefferson St. Chicago, IL 60606 T: 312-454-7400 F: 312-454-7525 M. Martinsen

China Office	**Product/Service**	**U.S. Head Office**
China Corelab Ltd. 2/F, Bldg. 6, Nanshui Industrial Block 5 Industrial Rd., Shenzhen 518066 T: 669-1696 F: 669-6214 Satish Kumar	Inspection Oil Services	Core Laboratories 5295 Hollister Rd. Houston, TX 77040 T: 713-460-9600 F: 713-690-3947 Satish Kumar
China Hewlett-Packard Co., Ltd. 4/F, Hua Dian Tong Xun Bldg. Shang Bu Dist., Shenzhen 518031 T: 336-8608 F: 336-3154 General Manager	Computers Medical Equipment	Hewlett-Packard Co. 3000 Hanover St. Palo Alto, CA 94304 T: 650-857-1501 F: 650-857-5518 Manuel F. Diaz
China Nanhai Magcobar Mud Corp. 519/26, China Merchants Shekou Ind. Zone Bldg., Shenzhen 518067 T: 669-1870 F: 669-2643 Robert R. Harvey	Petroleum	M-I Drilling Fluids Co. Three Greenway Plaza, #2008 Houston, TX 77242 T: 713-308-9402 F: 713-297-2181 Eveleana Chang
China Sun Oil Company Hai Wan Road Shekou, Shenzhen T: 669-1499 F: 669-5009 Mr. Huang	Petroleum	
Chun Wang Industrial Gases Ltd. Song Hu Rd., China Merchants Shekou Ind. Zone, Shenzhen 518067 T: 669-1208 F: 669-2845 Peter Ren	Industrial Gases	
Citibank N.A. 37/f, Shenzhen Int'l Financial Bldg. 23 Jinn She Rd., Shenzhen 518001 T: 223-2338 F: 223-1238 Thomas Tsang	Banking	Citicorp 399 Park Ave. New York, Ny 10043 T: 212-559-1000 F: 212-559-5138 Robert Martinsen / Peter Schuring
Compaq Computer Technologies (China) Co. Overseas Chinese Town, Easter Ind. Dist. D Block 1, Shenzhen 518053 T: 660-9090 F: 660-9226 Yip Keng Xhin	Computers	Compaq Computer Corp. 20555 State Highway 249 Houston, TX 77070 T: 281-370-0670 F: 281-514-1740 Michael Heil
Crown Worldwide (China) Ltd. 426 SKIZ Bldg., Shekou Ind. Zone Shekou, Shenzhen 518067 T: 668-4809 F: 668-4807 Robert Fisch	Freight Forwarding	Crown Pacific 5252 Argosy Dr. Huntington Beach, CA 92649 T: 714-898-0955 F: 714-898-5640 James Thompson
CWI International China, Inc. 210 Kwei Lan Hsing Village Guan Lan Town, Bao An Dist, Shenzhen T: 802-0387 F: 802-0304 General Manager	Plumbing Supplies	Waxman Industries, Inc. 24460 Aurora Rd. Bedford Heights, OH 44146 T: 440-439-1830 F: 440-439-0227 Jimmy Xu

China Office	**Product/Service**	**U.S. Head Office**
Deloitte Touch Tohmatsu 806 Shenzhen Development Centre Bldg. Ren Min Nan Lu, Shenzhen 518001 T: 228-0161 F: 228-0163 Ted Lee	Accounting	Deloitte Touche Tohmatsu Int'l Ten Westport Rd. Wilton, CT 06897 T: 203-761-3000 F: 203-834-2200 Dina A. Elliott
Delta Magnetic Technology Ltd. 3/F, SEG Industrial Bldg. Huang Qiang Rd. N., Shenzhen 518031 T: 324-1604 F: 336-0902 Guan Gui Xian	Computer Hard Disk Parts	*DART EXPRESS GROUP* Worldwide Air/Ocean Freight Services Tel: 310-649-3641 Fax: 213-776-6132 www.dartexpress.com
Dow Jones Economic Research 1705, 17/F, SITIC Building 7 Hong Ling Zhong Rd., Shenzhen 518001 T: 557-4701 F: 557-4275 Peter C. Wonacott	Consultant	Dow Jones & Co., Inc. 200 Liberty St. New York, NY 10281 T: 212-416-2000 F: 212-416-2885 Karen House / James Friedlich
DuPont China Holding Co., Ltd. District No. 5, Che Gong Miao Ind. Area Shenzhen 518040 T: 330-7848 F: 330-7047 Li Shang Sin	Engineering Polymer Non-woven Fabrics Photoresist Dry Film	E I DuPont De Nemours & Co. 1007 Market St. Wilmington, DE 19898 T: 302-774-1000 F: 302-774-7321 Charles O. Holliday, Jr.
Ernst & Young 2B, 8/F, Shenzhen Development Center Bldg. Ren Min Nan Lu, Shenzhen 518001 T: 228-0788 F: 228-0077 T. T. Chan	Accounting	Ernst & Young 787 Seventh Ave., 14/F New York, NY 10019 T: 212-773-3000 F: 212-773-6350 Eli Spielman
Flextronics Industry Shenzhen Co., Ltd. Block 9, Second Industrial Zone Xi Xiang, Shenzhen 518126 T: 749-7333 F: 749-7222 Ash Bhardwaj	Electronic Products	Flextronics Int'l Inc. 2090 Fortune Dr. San Jose, CA 95131 T: 408-428-1300 F: 408-576-7454 David Garcia
GKI 3/F, Great Wall Bldg. Science & Industry Park, Shenzhen 518057 T: 663-0785 F: 663-0362 Arthur J. Yarzumbeck	Computers & Software	International Business Machines Corp. Rockwood Dr. Sleepy Hallow, NY 10591 T: 914-765-1900 F: 914-332-3753 John Dejoy
Guangdong Float Glass Co., Ltd. 8 Hai Wan Rd. Shekou Industrial Zone, Shenzhen 518067 T: 669-2135 F: 669-6593 Y. Z. Yang	Float Glass Products	PPG Industries, Inc. 1 PPG Place Pittsburgh, PA 15272 T: 412-434-2049 F: 412-434-2125 Valentino Buttignol
Halliburton International Inc. 401 Seaview Commercial Bldg. East Block, Xin Hua Rd., Dhenzhen 518067 T: 669-2470 F: 668-3061 Brian Huculak	Oil & Gas	Halliburton Co. 3600 Lincoln Plaza, 500 N. Akard St. Dallas, TX 75201 T: 214-978-2600 F: 214-978-2685 Stephen D. Moore

China Office	Product/Service	U.S. Head Office
Hirson, Wexler, Perl & Stark Suite F, 19/F, 2nd Bldg., Nanguo Dasha Hong Ling Zhong Rd., Shenzhen T: 558-1687 F: 321-8719 Liping Epps	Law	Hirson, Wexler, Perl & Stark One Park Plaza, #950 Irvine, CA 92714 T: 714-251-8844 F: 714-251-1545 Liping Epps
Int'l Software Development Co., Ltd. Block B, Teaching Bldg. Shenzhen University, Shenzhen 518060 T: 666-1406 F: 666-1414 Charles Chow	Software	International Business Machines Corp. Rockwood Dr. Sleepy Hallow, NY 10591 T: 914-765-1900 F: 914-332-3753 John Dejoy
Interquip Electronics (Shekou) Ltd. 3/F, Hua Fa Building Industrial Rd., Shenzhen 518067 T: 669-3119 F: 669-5033 Vivian Leung	Electronic Products Crystal Resonator Oscillator	Interquip 2935 Byberry Rd. Hatboro, PA 19040 T: 215-957-9107 K Sobon
Johnson Controls International Inc. 1602 Tian An International Bldg., Complex C Ren Min Nan Lu, Shenzhen 518005 T: 229-5066 F: 218-0864 General Manager	Controls	Johnson Controls Inc. 5757 N. Green Bay Ave. Milwaukee, WI 53209 T: 414-228-1200 F: 414-228-2077 William P. Killan
KPMG Peat Marwick 3/F, 207 Shen Man Rd. East Shenzhen 518001 T: 556-6184 F: 556-6184 General Manager	Accounting	KPMG Peat Marwick 530 Chestnut Ridge Rd. Woodcliff, NJ 07675 T: 201-505-3585 F: 201-505-3411 Timothy Pearson
Phillips China Inc. 9/F, Finance Centre Tai Zi Rd., Shenzhen 518066 T: 669-1786 x 1786 F: 669-1162 Tom Schreoder	Petroleum Products Oi & gas Exploration	Phillips Petroleum Co. Plaza Office Bldg. Bartlesville, OK 74004 T: 918-661-6600 F: 918-662-2780 Mike Coffelt
Price Waterhouse 1802/04, Block A, Tian An Int'l Bldg. Ren Min Nan Lu, Shenzhen 518001 T: 217-7333 F: 217-7666 W. K. Tsang	AccountingPrice	Price Waterhouse LLP 1177 Ave. of the Americas New York, N 10020 T: 212-596-7000 F: 212-596-8910 James Daley / Robert Gazzi
Seagate Technology 3/F, Kia Fa Complex, Cai Tian Rd. Fu Tian Ind. Dist., Shenzhen 518026 T: 323-3168 F: 323-8819 Eddie Lui	Computer Disc Drives	Seagate Technology 920 Disc Drive Scotts Valley, CA 95066 T: 408-438-6550 F: 408-438-4127 Woody Monroy
Sealand China Division 1902 Hai Yang Ge, Hai Bin Garden Shekou, Shenzhen T: 668-1268 F: 668-1068 William Liu	Shipping Freight Forwarding	Sea-Land Service Inc. 6000 Carnegie Blvd. Charlotte, NC 28209 T: 704-571-2000 F: 704-571-4613 Clint Eisenhauer

China Office	**Product/Service**	**U.S. Head Office**
Segky Electronic Co., Ltd. 8/F, Kangle Electronic Bldg. Huaqiang Bei Road, Shenzhen T: 335-4442 F: 336-0801 Xiao Jiehui	Floppy Disk	Media Factory 1930 Junction Ave. San Jose, CA 95121 T: 408-456-9189 F: 408-456-9337 Willie Chow
Shenzhen Pspsi-Cola Beverage Co., Ltd. 10 Thien Pui Dong North Wen Jin Rd., Shenzhen 518020 T: 553-4418 F: 553-4679 Kelly Chan	Soft Drinks	PepsiCo International 1 Pspsi Way Somers, NY 10589 T: 914-767-6000 F: 914-767-6553 Keith Hughes
Tong Guang-Nortel Ltd. 186 Chi Wan Rd. Shekou, Shenzhen 518068 T: 669-3039 F: 669-3742 Jackson Wu	Telecommunications	Northern Telecom P. O. Box 1222 Minneapolis, MN 55440 T: 612-932-8000 F: 612-932-8235 Flo Graham
Trammell Crow International 6/F, Shekou Ind. Zone Bldg. Shekou, Shenzhen 518067 T: 689-1900 F: 689-1901 Andrea K. Richey	Real Estate	Trammell Crow 2000 Ross Ave., #3400 Dallas, TX 75201 T: 214-863-3000 F: 214-978-4479 Bill Starnes
U.S-China Business Center of Shenzhen The Statistics & Information Bureau Bldg. No. 1 Tong Xin Rd., Shenzhen 518027 T: 224-3034 F: 224-1559 John Li	Business Facilitation	**China Business Register 1997/1998** Contains information on 23,000 Chinese enterprises, including annual sales and fax number. Bilingual. Search by SIC. Tel: 310-325-0100 Fax: 310-325-2583
Universal Instruments (Shenzhen) Co., Ltd. 2/F, Block 541, Baqua San Rd. Bagualing Industrial Area, Shenzhen 518029 T: 240-1233 F: 226-4735 Jimson Lee	Electronic Assembly Eqmt	Universal Instruments Corp. P. O. Box 825, 90 Bevier St. Binghamton, NY13901 T: 607-779-5184 F: 607-779-7312 Chris Hill
Wal*Mart China Co., Ltd. 4/F, HuQing Block, Lake View Garden Hong Hu Rd., Shenzhen 518020 T: 560-7063 F: 560-5749 Joe Hatfield	Retailing	Wal-Mart Stores, Inc. 702 S. W. Eighth St. Bentonville, AR 72716-8611 T: 501-273-4000 F: 501-273-4329 Millard Baron
Wal*Mart China Co. - Sam's Club Xiang Mei Rd., Honey Lake Futian Dist., Shenzhen 518034 T: 370-0923 F: 370-0793 John Reaves	Warehouse Club	Wal-Mart Stores, Inc. 702 S. W. Eighth St. Bentonville, AR 72716-8611 T: 501-273-4000 F: 501-273-4329 Millard Baron
Weatherford Oil Field Services & Rentals No. 1 Warehouse, Shekou Ind. Zone Shekou, Shenzhen T: 669-7407 F: 669-7407 Tom Norrdell	Petroleum - Oil & Gas	Weatherford International Inc. 515 Post Oak Blvd., #600 Houston, TX 77027 T: 713-693-4000 F: 713-693-4245 John Hincir

China Office	Product/Service	U.S. Head Office
A. O. Smith Fiberglass Products Co.,Ltd. 32 Gong Bing Rd. Xing Xiangfang Dist., Harbin 150038 T: 532-3761 F: 532-3759 Jerry Kennedy	Fiberglass Products	A. O. Smith Corp. 11270 W. Park Pl., #1200 Milwaukke, WI 53224 T: 414-359-4000 F: 414-359-4180 R. O'Toole
Coca-Cola Beverage Co., Ltd. 16/F Tobacco Bldg. 127 Gexin Ave. Nangang Dist., Harbi T: 260-5450 F: 260-5452 Huang Zhengyi	Soft Drinks	Coca-Cola Co. One Coca-Cola Plaza Atlanta, GA 30313 T: 404-676-2121 F: 404-676-6792 Douglas N. Daft / Sergio Zyman
Harbin Hotel Inter Continental Corp. No. 47 Xia Man St. Dao Li Dist., Harbin 150010 T: 469-6496 F: 469-6466 Tou Junji	Hotel	Inter-Continental Hotel 111 E. 48th St. New York, NY 10017 T: 212-755-5900 F: 212-906-3133 F. De Roode
Warner Candy Co., Ltd. 66 Shangjiang St. Daoli Dist., Harbin T: 460-6074/75 F: 460-6073 Christen Chardlard / Guo Fengyun	Confectionery Products	Warner-Lambert Co. 201 Tabor Road Morris Plains, NJ 07950 T: 201-540-2000 F: 201-540-3761 Philip Gross / Frank Ritt

China Office	Product/Service	U.S. Head Office
3Com Asia Ltd. 24/F Lipochun Chambers 189 Des Voeux Rd., Central, Hong Kong T: 2501-1111 F: 2537-1149 Matthew Kapp	Computer Systems Networking Products	3Com Corp. 5400 Bayfront Plaza Santa Clara, CA 95052 T: 408-764-5000 F: 408-764-5001 Matthew Kapp
3M Hong Kong Ltd. 5/F Victoria Center, 15 Watson Road Causeway Bay, Hong Kong T: 2806-6111 F: 2807-1308 Joann Fernandez	Chemical Products Medical Equipments Automotive Products Office & Telecom Products Consumer & Safety Products	**3M Company** 3M Center Bldg. Bldg. 220-14E-02 Saint Paul, MN 55144-1000 T: 612-737-0702 F: 612-733-2095 Tony Gastaldo
A & A International 1406/1411 World Commerce Centre Harbour City, Tsim Sha Tsui, Hong Kong T: 2730-0226 F: 2730-8430 Andrew W T Chan	Consumer Electronics	Tandy Corp. 1800 One Tandy Center Fort Worth, TX 76102 T: 817-390-3700 F: 817-390-2647 Al Esquival / Lou Ann Balylock
A C Nielsen SRG 2/F Warwick House East Wing 979 King's Rd., Hong Kong T: 2563-9688 F: 2564-2097 Juling Ngai	Market Research	A C Nielsen 177 Broad St. Stamford, CT 06901 T: 203-961-3300 F: 203-961-3170 Nicholas Trivisonno
A T Kearney Inc. Level 31, One Pacific Place 88 Queensway, Hong Kong T: 2530-2688 F: 2530-1545 William J Best	Management Consultants Executive Search	A T Kearney Inc. 222 West Adams St. Chicago, IL 60606 T: 312-648-0111 F: 312-223-6200 William J Best
AA Cargo Express Co., Ltd. G/F 29 Sheung Heung Rd. Kowloon, Hong Kong T: 2363-4302 F: 2764-2731 C Y Lau	Freight Forwarder	AA Cargo Express Co., Ltd. 175/01 Rockaway Blvd. Jamaica, NY 11434-5502 T: 718-244-6606 F: 718-244-0865 Ronnie Sum
Abbott Laboratories Ltd. B605, 6/F, SeaView Estate 2-8 Watson Rd., North Point, Hong Kong T: 2566-8711 F: 2807-2917 Paul Kuen Chung	Pharmaceuticals Medical Equipment Nutritional Products/services	Abbott Laboratories 100 Abbott Park Rd. Abbott Park, IL 60064 T: 847-937-6100 F: 847-937-1511 Robert Parkinson
Ademco Asia Pacific Ltd. Flat A&B, 7/F, China Dyeing Workds Bldg. 388 Castle Peak Rd., Tsuen Wan, Hong Kong T: 2405-2323 F: 2415-3112 N H Lam	Security Systems Fire/Burglary Systems	Ademco International 180 Michael Dr. Syosset, NY 11791 T: 516-921-6704 F: 516-496-7454 Alan Wachtel
Advance Watch Co. Ltd. 12/F Phase 1, Kingford Industrial Bldg. 26-32 Kwai Hei St., Kwai Chung, Hong Kong T: 2614-5873 F: 2614-1878 Chun Hung Chu	Watches & Clocks	Advance Watch Co. 26400 W. 8 Mile Rd. Southfield, MI 48034-3689 T: 810-353-5130 F: 810-353-3637 M Schechter

China Office	**Product/Service**	**U.S. Head Office**
Advanced Controls (HK) Ltd. Flat A, 7/F, Loyang Court 212-220 Lockhart Rd., Wanchai, Hong Kong T: 2893-3885 F: 2838-2003 Tong Joe Fang	PCB Drilling Equipment Printed & Etched Circuits	Advanced Controls Inc. 16901 Jamboree Rd. Irvine, CA 92606-5188 T: 714-863-9300 F: 714-863-3049 Robert Quest
Advanced Micro Devices Far East Ltd. Suite 2007-2011 Tower 2 The Gateway 25 Canton Rd., Tsim Sha Tsui, Hong Kong T: 2956-0388 F: 2956-0599 Philip Chu	Electronic Components	Advanced Micro Devices Inc. (AMD) One AMD Place, P. O. Box 3453 Sunnyvale, CA 94088-3453 T: 408-732-2400 F: 408-749-3127 Giuliano Meroni / Gerald A. Lynch
AETNA International Inc. 2818 Two Pacific Place 88 Queensway, Hong Kong T: 2829-0088 F: 2829-0011 Patrick Poon	Insurance	AETNA International Ltd. 151 Farmington Ave. Hartford, CT 06156 T: 860-273-0123 F: 860-275-2677 Frederick C Copeland, Jr.
AFS Intercultural Exchanges Ltd. 8/F Shun Feng Int'l Centre 182 Queens Rd. E., Wanchai, Hong Kong T: 2802-0383 F: 2802-4181 Audrey Schroeder	Education & Training	AFS Intercultural Programs, Inc. 71 West 23rd St., 17/F New York, NY 10010 T: 212-807-8686 F: 212-807-1001 Tara Boyce
Air Express International (HK) Ltd. Rm. 28, 1/F, Pacific Trade Center 2 Kai Hing Rd., Kowloon Bay, Hong Kong T: 2796-3668 F: 2750-7323 Bobby Chao	Freight Forwarder	Air Express Int'l Corp. (AEI) 120 Tokeneke Rd., P O Box 1231 Darien, CT 06820 T: 203-655-5809 F: 203-655-5840 Ken Nieze
Air Products Asia Inc. 5507-10 Hopewell Center 183 Queen's Rd. East, Wanchai, Hong Kong T: 2527-1922 F: 2527-1827 Mike McNallen	Chemicals	Air Products & Chemicals Inc. 7201 Hamilton Blvd. Allentown, PA 18195 T: 610-481-4911 F: 610-481-5900 Joseph J Kaminski
Airborne Freight Corp. 7E Sunshine Kowloon Bay Cargo Centre 59 Tai Yip St., Kowloon Bay, Hong Kong T: 2796-3223 F: 2796-3881 Francis Lo	Freight Forwarder Int'l Courier Service Custom Brokerage Logistics Services	Airborne Freight Corp. 3101 Western Ave., P O Box 662 Seattle, WA 98121 T: 206-285-4600 F: 206-281-3890 John J Cella / Bruce E. Grout
Alberto Culver (HK) Ltd. Rm. 1110/11 Stanhope House 738 King's Rd., Quarry Bay, Hong Kong T: 2516-7318 F: 2563-8946 Paul Garf	Consumer Goods	Alberto Culver Co. 2525 Armitage Ave. Melrose Park, IL 60160 T: 708-450-3000 F: 708-450-3435 John Ibeling / Kristin B Muntean
Alcoa International (Asia) Ltd. 1301 Admiralty Centre 18 Harcourt Rd., Hong Kong T: 2529-2333 F: 2529-2322 Celia Chan	Metal Products	Aluminum Co of America (Alcoa) Alcoa Bldg., 425 Sixth Ave. Pittsburgh, PA 15219-1850 T: 412-553-4545 F: 412-553-4585 Robert F. Slagle

China Office	Product/Service	U.S. Head Office
Allen-Bradley Co. 27/F Citicorp Centre 18 Whitfield Rd., Causeway Bay, Hong Kong T: 2887-4788 F: 2510-9436 Bing-Hian Co	Industrial Automation Process Controls	Allen-Bradley Co. 1201 S. Second St., P. O. Box 2086 Milwaukee, WI 53201 T: 414-382-2000 F: 414-382-4444 Richard E. Shelton
Allergan Asia Ltd. Unit 3001 New Metroplaza Tower 1 223 Hing Fong Rd., Kwai Fong, Hong Kong T: 2480-3330 F: 2424-0213 Anthony Mak	Eye & Skin Care Products	Allergan Inc. 2525 DuPont Dr., P O Box 19534 Irvine, CA 92612 T: 714-246-4500 F: 714-246-4359 Jacqueline J. Schiavo
Allied Pickfords Ltd. 17/F Hong Kong Computer Centre 54 Lockhart Rd., Wanchai, Hong Kong T: 2736-6032 F: 2375-1065 Nicki Bradley	Moving Service Storage & Trucking	Allied International 215 W. Diehl Rd. Naperville, IL 60563 T: 630-717-3500 F: 630-717-3496 Mike Cosnett / Dave Buth
Allison and Asociates 2/F Shui On Centre Hong Kong T: 2824-8229 F: 2824-8001 Richard Allison / George Liu	Marketing & Finance	**Allison and Associates** Two Midamerica Plaza, Suite 800 Oakbrook, IL 60181 T: 630-575-2938 F: 630-368-9091 Richard Allison
Alltel Information Services HK Ltd. 2403 Admiralty Centre 18 Harcourt Rd., Hong Kong T: 2866-9178 F: 2866-8737 John Millea	Data Processing Services	Alltel Information Services Inc. 4001 Rodney Parham Rd. Little Rock, AK 72212 T: 800-874-7359 F: 501-220-5100 Dodd Miles
Aloha Airlines 15/F United Overseas Bank Bldg. 54-58 Des Voeux Rd., Central, Hong Kong T: 2826-9111 F: 2845-9560 Connie Lio	Airline Services	Aloha Air Group 371 Aokea Place Honolulu, HI 96819 T: 808-836-4101 F: 808-836-4193 Glenn R. Zander
Alpha Metals Ltd. 1/F, Block A, 21 Tung Yuen St. Yau Tong Bay, Kowloon, Hong Kong T: 2347-7112 F: 2347-5301 Richard Ertmann	Metal Products Chemicals	Alpha Metals Inc. 600 State Rt. 440 Jersey City, NJ 07304-1059 T: 201-434-6778 F: 201-434-2307 David B. Zerfoss
Amdahl International Corp. 701B, 7/F, Caroline Centre 28 Yun Ping Rd., Causeway Bay, Hong Kong T: 2882-7938 F: 2808-0380 John Wholley	Computers & Software Data Storage Products Info-technology Solutions	Amdahl Corp. 1250 E Arques Ave., P O Box 3470 Sunnyvale, CA 94088-3470 T: 408-746-6000 F: 408-773-0833 Orval J. Nutt / Linda T. Alepin
Amerasia International Ltd. 1915Asian House 26 Des Voeux Rd., Central, Hong Kong T: 2866-9088 F: 2866-3818 Alice Ho	Raw Cotton Products	Plains Cotton Cooperative Associates 3301 E. 50th St. Lubbock, TX 79408 T: 806-763-8011 F: 806-762-7400 David Stanford

China Office	**Product/Service**	**U.S. Head Office**
Amerex Int'l (HK) Ltd. 2/F, Block B, Eldex Industrial Bldg. 21 Ma Tau Wei Rd., Kowloon, Hong Kong T: 2356-6600 F: 2764-1733 C R Lawson	Apparel & Accessories	Amerex Inc. 512 7th Ave. New York, NY 10018 T: 212-719-2444 F: 212-391-8702 Lenny Blumenthal
American & Efird (HK) Ltd. 1501/08, 15/F, Tsuen Wan Industrial Centre 220-248 Texaco Rd., Tsuen Wan, Hong Kong T: 2407-6595 F: 2407-5433 Ching Cheong Lam	Industrial Thread & Yarns Consumer Sewing Products	American & Efird Inc. 22 American St., P. O. Box 507 Mt. Holly, NC 28120 T: 704-827-4311 F: 704-822-6054 John Hoyle
American Airlines 2904 Central Plaza 18 Harbour Rd., Wanchai, Hong Kong T: 2826-9269 F: 2845-9560 Bruce Frederick Jarman	Airlines	American Airlines Inc. 4333 Amon Carter Blvd. Ft. Worth, TX 76155 T: 817-963-1234 F: 817-967-3816 Hans Mirka
American Appraisal Hong Kong Ltd. Suite 2901, Central Plaza 18 Harbour Rd., Hong Kong T: 2511-5200 F: 2511-9626 K K Ip/Keith Yan	Asset Valuation Real Estate Developer	American Appraisal Associates 411 East Wisconsin Avenue Milwaukee, WI 53202 T: 414-225-2005 F: 414-271-1041 George H. Liu
American Brands Int'l Corp. 4003, 40/F, Lee Gardens 33 Hysan Rd, Causeway Bay, Hong Kong T: 2506-0660 F: 2506-0671 Dennis Liang Gin-Hung	Household Products	American Brands Inc. 1700 E Putnam Ave. Old Greenwich, CT 06870 T: 203-698-5000 F: 203-637-2580 Charles McGill / Salvatore Costantino
American Bureau of Shipping 15/F Queen's Centre 58-64 Queen's Rd. E., Wanchai, Hong Kong T: 2527-8478 F: 2861-3403 Peter Schmitz	Marine Products Marine Services	American Bureau of Shipping 2 World Trade Center, 106/F New York, NY 10048 T: 212-839-5000 F: 212-839-5130 Robert D Somerville
American Express Bank Ltd. 35/F One Pacific Place 88 Queensway, Hong Kong T: 2844-0688 F: 2845-3637 J Dennis Dunn	Banking Financial Services	American Express Company 200 Vessy St. New York, NY 10285 T: 212-640-2000 F: 212-619-8802 David Beeman
American Express Int'l Ltd. 18/F Somerset House, Taikoo Place 979 King's Rd., Quarry Bay, Hong Kong T: 2811-6888 F: 2811-2445 Li Jun Jia	Travel-Related Services	American Express Travel Related Co. 200 Vesey St. New York, NY 10285 T: 212-640-2000 F: 212-619-8802 Stephen Friedman / John Sutphen
American Int'l Assurance Co., Ltd. 14/F New World Centre West Wing 20 Salisbury Rd., Hong Kong T: 2731-0333 F: 2311-5266 Piu Fat Pete Chan	Insurance	American Int'l Group (AIG) Inc. 70 Pine St. New York, NY 10270 T: 212-770-7000 F: 212-770-7821 Evan Greenberg / Martin J. Sullivan

- - - - - T: Telephone # - - - - - F: Fax # - - - - - Hong Kong Area Code: (852) - - - - -

China Office	Product/Service	U.S. Head Office
American National Can Asia Pacific Ltd. Rm. 2504/06 Windsor House 311 Gloucester Rd, Causeway bay, Hong Kong T: 2837-9808 F: 2837-9888 Stephen D Franklin	Catering Food Provision	American National Can Co. 8770 W Bryn Mawr Ave. Chicago, IL 60631 T: 773-399-3000 F: 773-399-3330 Gerard Hauser
American President Lines Ltd. 16/F, New T & T Centre 7 Canton Rd., Hong Kong T: 2738-7333 F: 2730-5870 Torey Presti	Shipping	APL Limited 1111 Broadway Oakland, CA 94607 T: 510-272-8000 F: 510-272-7941 Keith Mackie
AMF Bowling Centers (HK) Int'l Inc. 9/F, Chung Nam Bldg. 1 Lockhart Rd., Wanchai, Hong Kong T: 2866-6466 F: 2866-6299 Vincent Au Kwok-Chuen	Sporting Goods Recreation Services	AMF Bowling Inc. 8100 AMF Dr. Mechanicsville, VA 23111 T: 804-730-4325 F: 804-730-0923 B Morin
Ammirati Puris Lintas 23/F Chinachem Exchange Square 1 Hoi Wan St., Quarry Bay, Hong Kong T: 2960-8688 F: 2960-1606 Sandy Kornberg	Advertising	Ammirati Puris Lintas 1 Dag Hammerskjold Plaza New York, NY 10017 T: 212-605-8000 F: 212-605-4708 Kenneth L Robbins / Terry Rosenquist

China Office	**Product/Service**	**U.S. Head Office**
AMOCO Chemical Asia Pacific Ltd. 16/F Great Eagle Centre 23 Harbour Rd., Wanchai, Hong Kong T: 2586-8899 F: 2827-6810 Arthur R McCaughan	Chemicals	Amoco Chemical Co. 200 E Randolph Dr. Chicago, IL 60601 T: 312-856-2777 F: 312-856-3800 Enrique J. Sosa
AMP Products Pacific Ltd. Rm. 1301 Ocean Centre 5 Canton Rd., Tsim Sha Tsui, Hong Kong T: 2735-1628 F: 2735-0243 Joseph Tang	Electrical Connectors	AMP Inc. 470 Friendship Rd., P. O. Box 3608 Harrisburg, PA 17105-3608 T: 717-564-0100 F: 717-780-6130 Herbert M. Cole / Ted L. Dalrymple
Amphenol East Asia Ltd. Unit 3-12, 10/F, Wah Luen Indus. Centre 15-21 Wong Chuk Yeung St., Hong Kong T: 2699-2663 F: 2691-1774 T K Yeung	Electronic Components Interconnect Systems	Amphenol/Time Fibers Commun. Inc. 358 Hall Ave. Wallingford, CT 06492 T: 203-265-8500 F: 203-265-8628 Gary Williams
Amway Asia Pacific Ltd. 38/F Lee Gardens 33 Hysan Rd., Causeway Bay, Hong Kong T: 2969-6333 F: 2503-3903 Eva Cheng	Personal Care Products Houseware Products Cosmetics & Toiletries	Amway Corp. 7575 E Fulton Rd. Ada, MI 49355 T: 616-787-4193 F: 616-787-4770 David Brenner / Dan DeVos
Andersen Consulting Ltd. 23-25/F Wing On Centre 111 Connaught Rd., Central, Hong Kong T: 2852-0388 F: 2850-8956 Alex W Lau	Consultants Business Management	Arthur Andersen & Co. 69 W. Washington St. Chicago, IL 60602 T: 312-580-0069 F: 312-507-2548 George T. Shaheen
Anju Jewelry Ltd. Blk A, 4/F Kaiser Estate Phase 1 51 Man Yue St., Kowloon, Hong Kong T: 2365-9081 F: 2764-0514 Siri Subphon	Jewelry	Town & Country Corp. 25 Union St. Chelsea, MA 02150 T: 617-884-8500 F: 617-889-6707 Irene Shea
ANSAC 2401A Great Eagle Centre 23 Harbour Rd., Wanchai, Hong Kong T: 2827-5511 F: 2827-5199 Robert Choy	Chemicals	ANSAC 15 Riverside Ave. Westport, CT 06880 T: 203-226-9056 F: 203-227-1484 J Skelly
Anthony Au & Associates Ltd. 2016 Two Pacific Place 88 Queensway, Hong Kong T: 2526-1133 F: 2868-4596 Anthony Au	Executive Search	Ward Howell International Inc. 99 Park Ave. New York, NY 10016 T: 212-697-3730 F: 212-697-1398 George J Donnelley / Judy Seto
Aon Risk Services Hong Kong 9/F Asian House 1 Hennessy Rd., Hong Kong T: 2862-4288 F: 2865-0623 Helen Tang	Insurance	Aon Corp. 123 N. Wacker Dr. Chicago, IL 60606 T: 312-701-4592 F: 312-701-4359 Philip Gawthorpe

China Office	Product/Service	U.S. Head Office
Apple Computer Int'l Ltd. 2401 NatWest Tower, Times Square 1 Matheson St., Causeway Bay, Hong Kong T: 2506-8888 F: 2506-2833 Pauline Ho	Computers & Software Information Technology	Apple Computer Inc. One Infinite Loop Cupertino, CA 95014 T: 408-996-1010 F: 408-974-2113 Dave Manovich
ARCO Chemical Asia Pacific Ltd. 41/F, The Lee Gardens 33 Hysan Rd., Causeway Bay, Hong Kong T: 2882-2668 F: 2840-1690 Edward V. Zenzola	Chemicals	ARCO Chemical Co. 3801 W. Chester Pike Newton Square, PA 19073 T: 610-359-2000 F: 610-359-2722 Edward V. Zenzola
ARCO China Ltd. J W Marriott Business Center 88 Queensway, Hong Kong T: 2841-3759 F: 2845-7921 Jerry Owens	Chemicals	Atlantic Richfield Co. 515 S. Flower St. Los Angeles, CA 90071 T: 213-486-3511 F: 213-486-1544 Walter A. Coyne
ARCO Toys Ltd. 13/F South Tower, World Financial Centre 17-18 Canton Rd., Tsim Sha Tsui, Hong Jong T: 2738-8000 F: 2730-4088 Jone Nichelson	Toys	Mattel Inc. 333 Continental Blvd. El Segundo, CA 90245 T: 310-252-2000 F: 310-252-2179 Alexander Welch / Larry Morgan
Armstrong World Industries (HK) Ltd. 19/F Cindic Tower 128 Gloucester Rd., Wanchai, Hong Kong T: 2585-7800 F: 2598-7113 Tom McEvoy	Building Materials Construction Equipment	Armstrong World Industries Inc. 313 W. Liberty St. Lancaster, PA 17603 T: 717-397-0611 F: 717-396-4477 Alan L. Burnaford
Arthur Andersen & Co. 25/F Wing On Centre 111 Connaught Rd., Central, Hong Kong T: 2852-0222 F: 2815-0548 Allan Aw	Accounting	Arthur Andersen & Co. 69 W. Washington St. Chicago, IL 60602 T: 312-580-0069 F: 312-507-6748 Richard L Measelle
Arthur D Little 7/F Bank of America Tower 12 Harbour Rd., Wanchai, Hong Kong T: 2845-6221 F: 2845-5271 Shum Foong Leng	Management Consultants	Arthur D Little Int'l Inc. 25 Acorn Park Cambridge, MA 02140 T: 617-498-5000 F: 617-498-7200 Alfred E Wechsler
Asiachem (Hong Kong) Ltd. 26/F CMA Bldg. 64-66 Connaught Rd., Central, Hong Kong T: 2541-0434 F: 2541-3103 Alan Fishman	Chemicals Agricultural Products	Plexchem Int'l Inc. 1121 Old Walt Whitman Rd. Melville, NY 11747 T: 516-271-0670 F: 516-271-0034 Edward Nassberg
The Asian Wall Street Journal 2/F AIA Bldg. 1 Stubbs Rd., Wanchai, Hong Kong T: 2573-7121 F: 2834-5291 William Peter Adamopoulos	Publishing	Dow Jones & Co. Inc. 200 Liberty St., World Financial Center New York, NY 10281 T: 212-416-2000 F: 212-416-2885 Karen House / James Friedlich

China Office	Product/Service	U.S. Head Office
Associated Merchandising Corp. 5/F West Wing, Tsim Sha Tsui Centre 66 Mody Rd., Lowloon, Hong Kong T: 2733-7333 F: 2721-7193 Bob Chang	Global Sourcing Product Development	Associated Merchandising Corp. 1440 Broadway New York, NY 10018 T: 212-596-4000 F: 212-575-2993 Richard Kuzmich / Douglas Bertsch
AST Asia Pacific 29/F Citicorp Centre 18 Whitefield Rd., Hong Kong T: 2806-4333 F: 2807-0599 Robert McFarland	Computers	AST Research Inc. 16215 Alton Parkway Irvine, CA 92619 T: 714-727-4141 F: 714-727-8584 Hoon Choo / Scott Bower
AT&T Asia Pacific Inc. 30/F Shell Tower, Times Square 1 Matheson St., Causeway Bay, Hong Kong T: 2506-5111 F: 2506-2100 JoAnn Patrick-Ezzell	Telecommunications	AT&T International 295 N. Maple Ave., Rm. I-14 Basking Ridge, NJ 07920 T: 248-262-6646 F: 248-952-5095 Elizabeth Mallek
AT&T Global Information Solutions Ltd. 34-35/F Shun Tak Centre 200 Connaught Rd., Central, Hong Kong T: 2859-6888 F: 2858-2478 Mike Darch	Computers Information Technology	AT&T Corp. 32 Ave. of the Americas New York, NY 10013 T: 212-387-5400 F: 212-841-4715 Victor A Pelson / Gail J McGovern
Autodesk Far East Ltd. 2803A Central Plaza 18 Harbour Rd., Wanchai, Hong Kong T: 2824-2338 F: 2824-3228 Stephaine J Mitchell	CAD/CAM Software	Autodesk Inc. 111 McInnis Parkway San Rafael, CA 94903 T: 415-507-5000 F: 415-507-5100 Tom Norring
AVCO Financial Services (Asia) Ltd. 8/F Sunning Plaza 10 Hysan Ave., Causeway Bay, Hong Kong T:2894-5555 F: 2504-1332 Gilbert A Tony Travers	Financial Services	AVCO Financial Services Inc. 600 Anto Blvd., P O Box 5011 Costa Mesa, CA 92628-5011 T: 714-435-1200 F: 714-445-7052 Eugene R Schutt
Avery Dennison Asia Pacific Group Rm. 2705/08 Shui On Centre 6-8 Harbour Rd., Wanchai, Hong Kong T: 2802-9618 F: 2588-1344 Christian Simcic	Office Products Labels & Tags	Avery Dennison Corp. 150 N. Orange Grove Blvd. Pasadena, CA 91103 T: 818-304-2000 F: 818-792-7312 Kim A. Caldwell / Robert Fletcher
Avery Dennison (HK) Ltd. G/F Tseung Kwan O Ind. Estates 7 Chun Wing St.,NT, Hong Kong T: 2555-9441 F: 2518-4164 Eddy Cheung	Office Products Labels & Tags	Avery Dennison Corp. 150 N. Orange Grove Blvd. Pasadena, CA 91103 T: 818-304-2000 F: 818-792-7312 Kim A Caldwell / Robert Fletcher
Aviall Airstocks Ltd. 604 New Bright Bldg. 11 Sheung Yuet Rd., Hong Kong T: 2318-0233 F: 2331-9222 Yenho Tree	Aircraft Parts	Aviall Inc. 2075 Diplomat Dr. Dallas, TX 75234 T: 972-406-6515 F: 972-406-6502 Pat Manning

- - - - - T: Telephone # - - - - - F: Fax # - - - - - Hong Kong Area Code: (852) - - - - -

China Office	Product/Service	U.S. Head Office
AVIS Hong Kong Bonaventure House 85-91 Leighton Rd., Hong Kong T: 2890-6988 F: 2895-3686 General Manager	Car Rental Services	AVIS Inc. 900 Old Country Rd. Garden City, NY 11530 T: 516-222-3000 F: 516-222-6633 Michael Collins
Avnet WKK Components Ltd. WKK Bldg. 10/F 418A Kwun Tong Rd., Hong Kong T: 2357-8888 F: 2790-2182 Nicholas Leung	Computers & Peripherals Electronic Components	Avnet Inc. 80 Cutter Mill Rd. Great Neck, NY 11027 T: 516-466-7000 F: 516-466-1203 Keith Williams / Mark Woods
AVON Cosmetics Hong Kong Ltd. 16/F, Tower II, Enterprise Square 9 Sheung Yuet Rd., Hong Kong T: 2751-5000 F: 2751-5941 Carrie Miller	Cosmetics & Toiletries Fashion Jewelry Gifts & Collectibles	Avon Products Inc. 1345 Ave. of the Americas New York, NY 10105-1096 T: 212-282-5000 F: 212-282-6149 Marcia L. Worthing
AVX/Kyocera Asia Ltd. 3/F Hilder Centre 2 Sung Ping St., Hung Hom, Hong Kong T: 2363-3303 F: 2765-8185 Charles Lau	Multilayer Ceramic Capacitors	Avx Corp. 750 Lexington Ave. New York, NY 10019 T: 212-935-6363 Benedict Rosen
B F Goodrich Chemical (Far East) Ltd. 2208 Fortress Tower 250 King's Rd., Quarry Bay, Hong Kong T: 2508-1021 F: 2512-2241 S L Wong	Chemicals	B F Goodrich Co. 9911 Brecksville Rd. Cleveland, OH 44141 T: 216-447-5000 F: 216-447-5740 Abbas N. Sitabkhan
Bain & Co. (Hong Kong) 10/F One Pacific Place 88 Queensway, Hong Kong T: 2978-8800 F: 2978-8801 Rick Yan	Market Survey & Research	Bain & Co., Inc. 2 Copley Piace Boston, MA 02116 T: 617-572-2000 F: 617-572-2427 Sue Blake
Baker & McKenzie 14/F Hutchison House 10 Harcourt Rd., Central, Hong Kong T: 2846-1888 F: 2845-0476 Lawrence Lee	Law	Baker & McKenzie 1 Prudential Plaza 130 E. Randolph Dr. Chicago, IL 60601 T: 312-861-8000 F: 312-861-8823 Teresa A. Townsend / Jennifer Flynn
Baldwin Printing Controls Ltd. Unit A, 26/F, Sea View Plaza 283 Shau Kei Wan Rd., Hong Kong T: 2811-2987 F: 2811-0641 Simon Li	Prepress Equipment Printing Equipment	Baldwin Technology Co., Inc. 65 Rowayton Ave. Rowayton, CT 06853 T: 203-838-7470 F: 203-852-7040 Akira Hara
Bank of America (Asia) Ltd. 11/F Devon House, Taikoo Plaza 979 King's Rd., Quarry Bay, Hong Kong T: 2597-2805 F: 2597-2799 Samuel N Tsien	Banking	BankAmerica Corp. 315 Montgomery St., M/S-10540 San Francisco, CA 94104 T: 415-622-2507 F: 415-622-5719 John Mauney

- - - - - T: Telephone # - - - - - F: Fax # - - - - - Hong Kong Area Code: (852) - - - - -

China Office	Product/Service	U.S. Head Office
Bank of America NT & SA 2/F Bank of America Tower 12 Harcourt Rd., Central, Hong Kong T: 2847-6088 F: 2847-6080 Robert Morrow	Banking	BankAmerica Corp. 231 S. LaSalle St., #927 Chicago, IL 60604 T: 312-828-5116 F: 312-974-6518 Harry W Garschagen
Bank of California NA 1006/08, 10/F, Asia Pacific Finance Tower Citibank Plaza, 3 Garden Rd., Hong Kong T: 2826-0600 F: 2877-2666 Terry Flanagan	Banking	Union Bank of California 400 California St. San Francisco, CA 94104 T: 415-765-0400 F: 415-765-2979 Roger Min / Tony Rivano
Bank of Hawaii 2203 Vicwood Plaza 199 Des Voeux Rd.,Central, Hong Kong T: 2805-2960 F: 2805-2933 Kenneth Lam	Banking	Bank of Hawaii 130 Merchant St. Honululu, HI 96813 T: 808-847-8888 F: 808-521-7602 Kenneth M K Wong
Bank of New York 7/F New Henry House 10 Ice House St., Central, Hong Kong T: 2840-9888 F: 2810-5279 Michael J Ranieri	Banking	Bank of New York 48 Wall St. New York, NY 10286 T: 212-495-3007 F: 212-495-2413 Thomas A. Renyi

China Office	**Product/Service**	**U.S. Head Office**
Bankers Trust Co. 36/F Two Pacific Place 88 Queensway, Hong Kong T: 2533-8000 F: 2845-1868 Edward B Lo	Banking	Bankers Trust Co. 280 Park Ave. New York, NY 10017 T: 212-454-3047 F: 212-454-3110 Karen Horn
Bard International 1629 Star House 3 Salisbury Rd., Hong Kong T: 2317-7232 F: 2375-2382 Bosco Chan	Health Care Products	C R Bard Inc. 730 Central Ave. Murray Hill, NJ 07974 T: 908-277-8000 F: 908-277-8240 Louis G. Salgueiro
Batts Far East Ltd. Flat B, 1/F, The Grande Bldg. 398-400 Kwun Tong Rd., Hong Kong T: 2341-6373 F: 2343-4835 Thomas Chung / Danny Yeung	Plastics Products	Batts Inc. 200 N Franklin St. Zeeland, MI 49464 T: 616-772-4635 F: 616-772-1668 Jim Batts
Bausch & Lomb (HK) Ltd. 412 Mount Parker House 1111 King's Rd., Taikoo Shing, Hong Kong T: 2579-5488 F: 2590-6422 Steeve Chow	Vision Care Products	Bausch & Lomb Inc. One Bausch & Lomb Place Rochester, NY 14604 T: 716-338-6000 F: 716-338-6007 Alexander E. Izzard
Baxter Healthcare Ltd. 2003 Evergo House 38 Gloucester Rd., Hong Kong T: 2802-4535 F: 2802-0096 Andrew D S Lau	Disposable Medical Products	Baxter International Inc. One Baxter Parkway Deerfield, IL 60015 T: 847-948-2000 F: 847-948-2887 John F. Gaither, Jr.
BBDO Asia Pacific Ltd. 35/F Doroset House 979 King's Rd., Quarry Bay, Hong Kong T: 2820-1888 F: 2877-2167 Wick Smith	Advertising	BBDO Worldwide 1285 Ave. of the Americas New York, NY 10019 T: 212-459-5000 Philippe Krakowsky
Bear Stearns Asia/Far East Ltd. 26/F, Citibank Tower, Citibank Plaza 3 Garden Rd., Hong Kong T: 2593-2700 F: 2593-2871 Pascal J. Lambert	Investment Banking	Bear Stearns Co., Inc. 245 Park Ave. New York, NY 10167 T: 212-272-2000 F: 212-272-5143 Michael Conway
Beckman Instruments Inc. 15/F Gee Chang Hong Centre 65 Wong Chuk Hang Rd., Hong Kong T: 2814-7431 F: 2873-0652 Mike Belen	Medical Equipment Diagnostic Systems	Beckman Instruments Inc. 2500 Harbor Blvd. Fullerton, CA 92634 T: 714-871-4848 F: 714-773-8898 Barbara Keeler
Bel Components / Bel Fuse Ltd. 8/F Luk Hop Industrial Bldg. 8 Luk Hop St., Kowloon, Hong Kong T: 2325-5244 F: 2352-3706 Joseph Meccariello	Hybrids & Magnetic Products Fuses & Delay Lines Electronic Components	**Bel Fuse Inc.** 198 Van Vorst St. Jersey City, NJ 07302 T: 201-432-0463 F: 201-432-9542 Donald Morehouse / Dennis Akerman

China Office	**Product/Service**	**U.S. Head Office**
Bernard Chaus Int'l Inc. Block G, 9/F, Kaiser Estate Phase II 51 Man Yue St., Hungham, Hong Kong T: 2764-3732 F: 2764-3530 Donna Poach	Apparel & Accessories	Bernard Chaus Inc. 1410 Broadway New York, NY 10018 T: 212-354-1280 F: 212-302-8713 Joseph Janicki
BGF Industries Inc. 22/F Mirage Tower 13-15 Thompson Rd., Hong Kong T: 2527-7733 F: 2865-2885 Philippe Peters	Textiles	BGF Industries Inc. 401 Amherst Ave. Altavista, VA 24517 T: 804-369-4751 F: 804-369-7032 Ken Lowry
Bidermann Co. Ltd. 930 Ocean Centre Harbour City, Hong Kong T: 2795-2655 F: 2754-8275 Bility Yin	Apparel & Accessories	Bidermann Industries Corp. 575 5th Ave. New York, NY 10017 T: 212-984-8900 F: 212-984-8925 B Marsal
Binnie Consultants Ltd. 11/F New Town Tower Pak Hok Ting St., Shatin, Hong Kong T: 2601-1000 F: 2601-3331 Arnold Derrek	Engineering Services Architectural Services	Black & Veatch International 8400 Ward Pkwy., P O Box 8405 Kansas City, MO 64114 T: 913-458-2000 F: 913-458-7677 Ronald E. Zitterkopf
Bio-Rad Pacific (HK) Ltd. Unit 1111, New Kowloon Plaza 38 Tai Kok Tsui Rd., Kowloon, Hong Kong T: 2789-3300 F: 2789-1257 Y L. Lo	Analytical Instruments Clinical Diagnostics Life Science Resrch Products	Bio-Rad Laboratories Inc. 1000 Alfred Nobel Dr. Hercules, CA 94547 T: 510-724-7000 F: 510-724-3167 Warren R. Howell
Black & Veatch Power Asia Ltd. #5102 Central Plaza 18 Harbour Rd., Wanchai, Hong Kong T: 2802-3112 F: 2519-3589 Tom Kalin	Engineering Architectural Services	Black & Veatch International 8400 Ward Pkwy., P O Box 8405 Kansas City, MO 64114 T:913-458-2000 F: 913-458-7677 Ronald E. Zitterkopf
Bloomberg Co. 16/F Standard Chartered Bank Bldg. 4 Des Voeux Rd., Central, Hong Kong T: 2521-4500 F: 2521-4900 David Gillen	Financial Services	Bloomerg Financial Markets 499 Park Ave. New York, NY 10022 T: 212-318-2000 F: 212-893-5999 Ted Merz
Bonded Services International #7&8, 11/F, Block B, Tung Chun Ind. Bldg. 11-13 Tai Yuen St., Kwai Chung, Hong Kong T: 2425-6036 F: 2480-5935 Phillip Chu	Film/Tape Libraries Storage & Service	Bonded Services 520 Main St. Fort Lee, NJ 07024 T: 201-592-9044 F: 201-592-5946 Christopher W Preuster
Bonnie International Ltd. 907, Tower II, China Hong Kong City 33 Canton Rd., Kowloon, Hong Kong T: 2730-4886 F: 2730-9730 A Charish	Handbags	Bonnie International 5801 Jefferson St. West New York, NJ 07093 T: 201-868-9400 Allan Ginsburg

China Office	Product/Service	U.S. Head Office
Boston Consulting Group 34/F Shell Tower, Times Square 1 Matheson St., Causeway Bay, Hong Kong T: 2506-2111 F: 2506-9084 Richard Foyston	Management Consultants	Boston Consulting Group 53 State St., Exchange Place Boston, MA 02109 T: 617-973-1200 Phillip Catchings
Bourns Asia Pacific Inc. Unit 2, 2/F, Fook Hong Ind. Bldg. 19 Sheung Yuet Rd., Hong Kong T: 2736-0308 F: 2317-0836 C H Fan	Panel Controls & Switches PTC Resettable Fuses Precision Potentiometers Resistive Components Inductive Components	Bourns Inc. 1200 Columbia Ave. Riverside, CA 92507 T: 909-781-5500 F: 909-781-5273 Dennis C Lause
Bowne of Hong Kong 3402 Citibank Tower 3 Garden Rd., Central, Hong Kong T: 2526-0688 F: 2526-1200 Paul Dalton	Language Translation Book Printing	Bowne International Inc. 345 Hudson St. New York, NY 10014 T: 212-924-5500 F: 212-229-3410 Thomas J. Vos
Boyden International Ltd. 10/F, 1 On Hing Terrace Wyndham St., Central, Hong Kong T: 2868-3882 F: 2810-6198 Amy Lau	Executive Search	Boyden Consulting Corp. 55 Madison Ave. Morristown, NJ 07960 T: 973-267-0980 F: 973-267-6172 Joseph F. DiPiazza
Bozell Ltd. 6/F Sino Plaza 256 Gloucester Rd., Hong Kong T: 2892-8678 F: 2892-8797 Howard Wang	Advertising	Bozell, Jacobs, Kenyon & Eckhardt Inc. 40 W. 23rd St. New York, NY 10010 T: 212-727-5000 F: 212-727-5041 David Bell
Branson Ultrasonics (Asia Pacific) Co. Unit 5A, Pioneer Ind. Bldg. 213 Wai Yip St., Hong Kong T: 2790-3393 F: 2341-2716 Wing Eng	Ultrasonic Cleaning Eqmt	Branson Ultrasonics Corp. 41 Eagle Rd. Dansbury, CT 06813 T: 203-796-0400 F: 203-796-9813 Sylvio Mainolfi
Brennan Beer Gorman/Architechs Ltd. 13/F Lyndhurst Tower 1 Lyndhurst Terrace, Central, Hong Kong T: 2525-9766 F: 2525-9850 Jeffrey Williams	Architects Interior Designers Space Planners	Brennan Beer Gorman 515 Madison Ave., #4 New York, N 10022 T: 212-888-7663 F: 212-935-3868 Peter Gorman
Brighton Information Technology Corp. Unit B, 14/F, Aik San Factory Bldg. 14 Westlands Rd., Hong Kong T: 2571-7231 F: 2807-2919 Kit Kung	Computer Products Software	Brighton Industries Corp. 6 Pearl Court Allendale, NJ 07401 T: 201-818-2889 F: 201-818-0983 K. Kung
Brink's Hong Kong Ltd. #1022W, Asia Terminals Centre A, Berth 3 Kwai Chung Container Termical, Hong Kong T: 2612-2988 F: 2612-2993 Gilbert K H Chan	Security Transportation	Brink's Inc. One Thorndale Circle Darien, CT 06820 T: 203-662-7800 F: 203-662-7929 J. T. Walsh

China Office	**Product/Service**	**U.S. Head Office**
Bristol-Myers Squibb (HK) Ltd. 17/F Manulife Tower 169 Electric Rd., North Point, Hong Kong T: 2510-6000 F: 2510-6000 Anthony Cheng	Pharmaceuticals Health/Hygiene Products Medical Equipment	Bristol-Myer Squibb Co. 345 Park Ave. New York, NY 10154 T: 212-546-4000 F: 212-546-9585 Donald J. Hayden, Jr.
Brown & Wood 49/F Bank of China Tower 1 Garden Rd., Hong Kong T:2509-7888 F: 2509-3110 Mark Wiltshire	Law	Brown & Wood One World Trade Center New York, NY 10048 T: 212-839-5300 F: 212-839-5599 Thomas Amico
Brunswick International Ltd. Rm. 801 Energy Plaza 92 Granville Rd., Kowloon, Hong Kong T: 2367-8080 F: 2367-6112 Steve Jones	Sporting Goods Recreation Products Marine Engines	Brunswick Corp. One N. Fileld Ct. Lake Forest, IL 60045 T: 847-735-4700 F: 847-735-4765 Jerry Perkins
Buck Consultants Suite 608/09 Tower 1, Admiralty Centre 18 Harcourt Rd., Hong Kong T: 2802-1846 F: 2802-1828 Robert Kilvert	Employee Benifit Consulting Service	Buck Consultants Inc. 500 Plaza Dr. Secaucus, NJ 07096 T: 201-902-2300 F: 201-902-2450 Wil Gaitan
Bull HN Information Systems Ltd. #1081/04, 18/F, Chinachem Exchange Square 1 Hoi Wan St., Quarry Bay, Hong Kong T: 2960-5111 F: 2811-5862 Albert Tang	Computers & Software	Bull HN Information Systems Inc. 300 Concord Rd. Billerica, MA 01821 T: 508-294-6000 D Zereski
Bulova Watch Int'l Ltd. Unit 2-3, 3/F, Siu Wai Industrial Centre 29-33 Wing Hong St., Kowloon, Hong Kong T: 2310-8871 F: 2370-1800 John Mak	Watchs & Clocks Timepieces	Bulova Corp. One Bulova Ave. Woodside, NY 11377 T: 718-204-3300 F: 718-204-3546 Frances Abraham
Burlington Air Express Ltd. 2/F Sunhing Chekiang Godown 8 Sze Shan St., Yau Tong, Hong Kong T: 2379-9280 F: 2379-9700 Andrew Jillings	Freight Forwarder	**Burlington Air Express** 2005 W. 14th St., Suite 130 Tempe, AZ 85281 T: 602-966-5094 F: 602-921-8111 Larry Manrose
Burlton Int'l Ltd. 1307 New Treasure Centre 10 Ng Fong St., Hong Kong T: 2721-2213 F: 2723-1117 Benjamin K T Cheung	Fibers & Textiles	Cone Mills Corp. 3101 N. Elm St. Greensboro, NC 27408 T: 910-379-6165 F: 910-379-6187 John Bayersdorfer
Burson-Marsteller 14/F Stanhope House 738 King's Rd, North Point, Hong Kong T: 2880-0229 F: 2856-1101 Shirley Dirkin	Public Relations	Burson-Marsteller 230 Park Ave. New York, NY 10003-1566 T: 212-614-4000 F: 212-614-4262 Thomas D. Bell, Jr.

- - - - - T: Telephone # - - - - - F: Fax # - - - - - Hong Kong Area Code: (852) - - - - -

China Office	Product/Service	U.S. Head Office
Bush Boake Allen Ltd. 11/F Fortei Bldg. 98 Texaco Rd., Tsuen Wan, Hong Kong T: 2408-7170 F: 2407-6067 Steven John Howland	Paper Products Chemicals Wood Products Packaging Products	Union Camp Corp. 1600 Valley Rd. Wayne, NJ 07470 T: 201-628-2000 F: 201-628-2722 C. S. Howell
Business Week International 27/F Alexandra House 16-20 Chater Rd., Central, Hong Kong T: 2912-3000 F: 2912-3028 Mary F Bellman	Magazine Publishing	McGraw-Hill Inc. 1221 Avenue of the Americas New York, NY 10020 T: 212-512-2000 F: 212-512-2186 James Glionna
C & K Systems (HK) Ltd. 12/F, Tower II, Grant Central Plaza 138 Shatin Rural Committee Rd., Hong Kong T: 2391-5311 F: 2789-2062 Albert Lam	Secutiry Services Electronic Products	C & K Systems, Inc. 625 Coolidge Dr. Folsom, CA 95630 T: 916-353-5300 F: 916-985-0352 Marilyn Tenney
Cabot Plastics HK Ltd. Tai Po Industrial Estate 18 Dai Kwai St., Tai Po, Hong Kong T: 2666-2666 F: 2666-0807 Alfred Li	Plastics Products	Cabot Corp. 75 State St. Boston, MA 02109 T: 617-345-0100 F: 617-342-6103 Ken Burnes
Calcomp Asia Pacific Ltd. 701/04 Chinachem Exchange Square 1 Hoi Wan St., Quarry Bay, Hong Kong T: 2963-9600 F: 2960-1842 Don Lightfoot	Computer Graphics Products	Calcomp Inc. 2411 W La Palma Ave. Anaheim, CA 92801 T: 714-821-2000 F: 714-821-2832 Winfried Rohloff / Donald Lightfoot
Caltex China Ltd. / Caltex Oil HK Ltd. 42/F Central Plaza 18 Harbour Rd., Wanchai, Hong Kong T: 2802-8338 F: 2802-8966 P Y Chen	Petroleum Products	Caltex Petroleum Corp. 125 E John Carpenter Freewy Irving, TX 75602 T: 972-830-1000 F: 972-830-3034 H. S. Nichols
Camp Dresser & McKee Int'l Inc. 5-10, 43/F, Metroplaza Tower 1 223 Hing Fong Rd., Kwai Fong, Hong Kong T: 2428-2332 F: 2424-9114 P. Y. Chung	Consulting Engineers	Camp Dresser & McKee Int'l Ten Bridge Center Cambridge, MA 02142 T: 617-252-8000 F: 617-621-2565 B Callahan
Campbell Soup Asia Ltd. 19/F Cornwall House 28 Tong Chong St., Hong Kong T: 2811-3806 F: 2564-3249 David Wells	Food Products	Campbell Soup Co. Campbell Place Camden, NJ 08103 T: 609-342-4800 F: 609-342-3965 Robert Subin / Francis DuVernois
Cargill Hong Kong Ltd. 37/F Dorset House, Taikoo Place 979 King's Rd., Quarry Bay, Hong Kong T: 2968-9888 F: 2968-1681 James Bassett	Food Ingredients Meats Animal Nutrition Food Products	Cargill, Inc. 15407 McGinty Rd. Minnetonka, MN 55391 T: 612-742-6000 F: 612-742-2185 Dan Huber

China Office	**Product/Service**	**U.S. Head Office**
Carley of California (HK) Ltd. 8/F Man Hing Industrial Centre 4 Yip Fat St., Wong Chuk Hang, Hong Kong T: 2554-1113 F: 2873-4003 J A Carley	Interior Designers Space Planners	Carley Lamps, Inc. 1502 W. 228th St. Torrance, CA 90501 T: 310-534-3860 F: 310-534-2912 J A Carley
Carrier Hong Kong Ltd. 2/F Sun King Factory Bldg. 1-7 Shing Chuen Rd., Shatin, Hong Kong T: 2694-5333 F: 2691-2642 Allan Richard Jones	Air Conditioning Refrigeration	Carrier Corp. 7310 W. Morris Indianapolis, IN 46231 T: 317-240-5328 F: 317-240-5182 Roger Lawandowski
Carrier Transicold (HK) Ltd. 1702 Vicwood Plaza 199 Des Voeux Rd., Hong Kong T: 2880-0389 F: 2880-0314 Peter Shank	Air Conditioning	Carrier International Carrier Pkwy., P. O. Box 4808 Syracuse, NY 13221 T: 315-432-3352 F: 315-433-4744 Robert Fiesinger
Caterpillar China Ltd. 37/F The Lee Gardens 33 Hysan Ave., Causeway Bay, Hong Kong T: 2848-0333 F: 2848-0440 Dick Kahler	Contruction Equipment Earth Handling Machinery Mining Machinery Engines	Caterpillar Inc. 100 N E Adams St. Peoria, IL 61629 T: 309-675-1000 F: 309-675-1717 Siegfried R. Ramseyer
Cathay Bank 103 Takshing House 20 Des Voeux, Central, Hong Kong T: 2522-0071 F: 2810-1652 Paul Li	Banking	**Cathay Bank** 777 N. Broadway Los Angeles, CA 90012 T: 213-625-4700 F: 213-625-1368 Dunson Cheng
Central National Hong Kong Ltd. 1504 New Trend Centre 704 Prince Edward Rd. E., Hong Kong T: 2398-7666 F: 2398-7570 Ian King Yuen Fung	Pulp & Paper Products	Central National-Gotlesman Inc. 3 Manhattanville Rd. Purchase, NY 10577 T: 914-696-9000 F: 914-696-1066 Kenneth L. Wallach
Centralab Hong Kong Ltd. 3/F Block B, Hoplite Industrial Centre 3-5 Wang Tai Rd., Kowloon, Hong Kong T: 2757-8911 F: 2799-0525 William Paul Winther	Electronic Products	Philips Electronics 100 E 42nd St., #4 New York, NY 10017 T: 212-850-5000 F: 212-850-5362 S Tumminello
Chase Manhattan Asia Ltd. Chase manhattan Tower, Grand Central Plaza 138 Shatin Rural Committee Rd., Hong Kong T: 2685-5111 F: 2685-5099 Anthony Leung	Banking Financial Services	Chase Manhattan Corp. 270 Park Ave., #220 New York, NY 10017 T: 212-270-6000 F: 212-270-2613 Donald H. Layton
Cherasia Ltd. 14/F Block B, North Point Industrial Bldg. 499 King's Rd., North Point, Hong Kong T: 2565-6678 F: 2565-6827 Howard Chan	Electrical Switches Electronic Keyboards Controls & Displays Semiconductors	The Cherry Corp. 3600 Sunset Ave., PO Box 718 Waukegan, IL 60087 T: 708-662-9200 F: 708-662-2990 Peter B Cherry

- - - - - T: Telephone # - - - - - F: Fax # - - - - - Hong Kong Area Code: (852) - - - - -

China Office	**Product/Service**	**U.S. Head Office**
Chesterton Petty Ltd. 28/F Jardine House 1 Connaught Place, Central, Hong Kong T: 2840-1177 F: 2840-0600 Peter John Feely	Real Estate	Chesterton Binswanger Int'l Two Logan Square, 4/F Philadelphia, PA 19103 T: 215-448-6000 F: 215-448-6238 Ellen R. Weiss
China Phone Book Co. Ltd. 24/F Citicorp Centre 18 Whitfield Rd., Causeway Bay, Hong Kong T: 2508-4448 F: 2503-1526 Kang Sun Tsang	Directory Publishing	Dow Jones & Co., Inc. 200 Liberty St. New York, NY 10281 T: 212-416-2000 F: 212-416-2885 Karen House / James Friedlich
Ciba Corning Diagnostics (HK) Ltd. 20/F Gee Chang Hong Centre 65 Wong Chuk Hang Rd., Hong Kong T: 2814-7337 F: 2873-4245 Daniel J Sullivan	Therapeutics & Vaccines Diagnostics & Ophthalmics	Chiron Corp. 4560 Horton St. Emeryville, CA 94608 T: 510-601-2412 F: 510-655-9910 Rajen K. Dalal
CIGNA (Insurance Co of North America) 9/F Cityplaza 3 14 Taikoo Wan Rd., Taikoo Shing, Hong Kong T: 2539-9222 F: 2886-3722 Chor Chin Mak	Insurance	CIGNA Corp. One Liberty Place, 1650 Market St. Philadelphia, PA 19192 T: 215-761-1000 F: 215-761-5505 B. Kingsley Schubert / Ed Loughman
Cincom Systems Inc. 2106 Harcourt House 39 Gloucester Rd., Wanchai, Hong Kong T: 2866-2060 F: 2527-9332 Paul Greening	Computer Software	Cincom Systems Inc. 55 Merchant St. Cincinnati, OH 45246 T: 513-612-2300 F: 513-612-2000 Barry Sargeant
Circle International Ltd. Unit 1, Basement, Kai Fuk Ind. Centre 1 Wang Tung St., Hong Kong T: 2796-6340 F: 2796-3352 Sam Chung	Freight Forwarder	Circle International 260 Townsend St., P O Box 77933 San Francisco, CA 94107-1719 T: 415-978-0600 F: 415-978-0699 John Himoff
The CIT Group Commercial Services Ltd. 42/F Gloucester Tower 11 Pedder St, Central, Hong Kong T: 2913-5300 F: 2810-5539 Kenneth Choi	Factoring Financial Services	CIT Financial Corp. 135 W. 50th St. New York, NY 10020 T: 212-408-6000 F: 212-408-6068 S Nectow
Citicorp International 40-50/F Citibank Tower, Citibank Plaza 3 Garden Rd., Central, Hong Kong T: 2868-6666 F: 2868-8111 Stephen Long	Banking Financial Services	Citicorp 399 Park Ave. New York, NY 10043 T: 212-559-1000 F: 212-559-5138 Robert Martinsen / Peter Schuring
Clarcor Inc. Flat 1, 10/F, Block U, Alberdeen Centre 1 Nam Ming St., Hong Kong T: 2552-1481 F: 2555-6167 David Lee	Filtration Products Consumer Packaging Products	Clarcor Inc. 2323 Sixth St., P O Box 7007 Rockford, IL 61125 T: 815-962-8867 F: 815-962-0417 David Anderson

China Office	Product/Service	U.S. Head Office
Clarly Ltd. Suite 3802, 38/F, Shell Tower, Times Square 1 Matheson St., Causeway Bay, Hong Kong T: 2506-3399 F: 2506-3177 Kelvin K W Yao	Market & Trade Research Shipping Services Financial Services	Rototech Electrical Components Inc. 120 S. Wood Ave., #618 Iselin, NJ 08830 T: 908-494-5411 F: 908-494-6542 Kevin Yao
Cleary Gottlieb Steen & Hamilton 56/F Bank of China Tower 1 Garden Rd., Hong Kong T: 2521-4122 F: 2845-9026 Christopher Austin	Law	Cleary, Gottlieb, Steen & Hamilton 1 Liberty Plaza New York, NY 10006 T: 212-225-2000 F: 212-225-3999 S Alpert
Clorox International 19/F Centre Pointe 183-185 Gloucester Rd., Hong Kong T: 2891-4894 F: 2572-7187 Thomas Yang	Household Products Insecticides	Clorox Co. 1221 Broadway Oakland, CA 94612 T: 510-271-7327 F: 510-208-1501 Mark Chichak
CMC Far East Ltd. Unit C, 12/F, Cindic Tower 128 Gloucester Rd., Hong Kong T: 2511-0218 F: 2507-2617 Jimmy Dee	Metal Products Steel Mills	Commercial Metals Co. 7800 Stemmons Freeway Dallas, TX 75247 T: 214-689-4300 F: 214-689-4320 Murray McClear / Walter Kammann
COBA Technomic 19/F, 80 Gloucester Rd. Wanchai, Hong Kong T: 2511-2831 F: 2519-9503 Tan Wai Kee	Market Analysis Strategic Planning	COBA Technomic 500 Skokie Blvd., #575 Northbrook, IL 60062-2830 T: 847-291-1212 F: 847-291-1277 Steve H. Ganster
Coca-Cola Far East Ltd. 39/F Shell Tower, Times Square 1 Matheson St., Causeway Bay, Hong Kong T: 2599-1333 F: 2506-1425 John Farrell	Soft Drinks Catering/Food Provision Syrups & Concentrates	Coca-Cola Co. One Coca-Cola Plaza Atlanta, GA 30313 T: 404-676-2121 F: 404-676-6792 Douglas N. Daft / Sergio Zyman
Coherent Pacific 1515/18, Tower II, Grand Century Plaza 193 Prince Edward Rd. W., Hong Kong T: 2174-2800 Simon Chu	Laser Products Optical Systems	Coherent Inc. 5100 Patrick Henry Dr., PO Box 54980 Santa Clara, CA 95056 T: 408-764-4129 F: 408-970-9998 Edwina DeRousse
Colgate-Palmolive (HK) Ltd. 11/F Caroline Centre 28 Yun Ping Rd., Causeway Bay, Hong Kong T: 2830-1833 F: 2882-8031 Daniel Li / Patrick Fung	Pharmaceuticals Cosmetics & Toiletries Detergents Household Products	Colgate-Palmolive Co. 300 Park Ave. New York, NY 10022 T: 212-310-2000 F: 212-310-3301 Stephen A Lister / Carlos Velasquez
Compaq Computer HK Ltd. 27/F, Windsor House 311 Gloucester Rd., Hong Kong T: 2867-1600 F: 2524-9533 Philip Leung	Computers	Compaq Computer Corp. 20555 State Highway 249 Houston, TX 77070 T: 281-370-0670 F: 281-514-1740 Michael Heil

- - - - - T: Telephone # - - - - - F: Fax # - - - - - Hong Kong Area Code: (852) - - - - -

China Office	**Product/Service**	**U.S. Head Office**
Computer Associates Int'l Ltd. 3008 Convention Centre Office Tower 1 Harbour Rd., Wanchai, Hong Kong T: 2587-1388 F: 2587-1018 Linda Chan	Business Application Software Information Management	Computer Associates Int'l Inc. One Computer Associates Plaza Islandia, NY 11788 T: 516-342-2811 F: 516-342-4864 Kurt Seibert
Computer Products Asia-Pacific Ltd. 13-15 Shing Wan Rd. Tai Wai, Shatin, Hong Kong T: 2699-2868 F: 2699-1770 Wai-Kwok Lo	Electronic Components Computers	Computer Products Inc. 7900 Glades Rd., #500 Boca Raton, FL 33434 T: 561-451-1000 F: 561-451-1050 Joe O'Donnell
Computerland 5/F Zung Fu Bldg. 1067 King's Rd., Quarry Bay, Hong Kong T: 2811-9800 F: 2811-3631 Kenny Kwong	Computers	Synnex Corp. 3797 Spinnaker Ct. Fremont, CA 94538 T: 510-668-8200 F: 510-440-3763 C K Cheng
Computervision Asia Ltd. 2506 Vicwood Plaza 199 Des Voeux Rd., Hong Kong T: 2831-4600 F: 2891-9235 David Ko	Computers Data Management Software	Computervision Corp. 100 Crosby Dr., MS 21-17 Bedford, MA 01730 T: 617-275-1800 F: 617-275-2670 Richard Moore
Concurrent Computer HK Ltd. 1701 Stanhope House 738 King's Rd., Quarry Bay, Hong Kong T: 2880-0802 F: 2880-0664 K K Tay	Computers	Concurrent Computer Corp. 2101 W. Cypress Creek Rd. Ft. Lauderdale, FL 33309 T: 954-974-1700 F: 954-977-5580 George Chapman
Connell Bros Co (HK) Ltd. 601 Stanhope House 738 King's Rd., North Point, Hong Kong T: 2565-5123 F: 2564-7634 Rob Harringtpn Johnson	Consumer Electronics Foods; Fibers & Textiles Construction Materials Chemicals	Wilbur-Ellis Co. Ltd. 320 California St., #200 San Francisco, CA 94104 T: 415-772-4000 F: 415-772-4011 Frank Brown
Consumer Testing Laboratories Ltd. 703/04, 7/F, Riley House 88 Lei Muk Rd., Hong Kong T: 2423-7161 F: 2480-4758 Willy Leung	Quality Control Product Standards/Testing	Consumer Testing Labs Inc. 480 Neponset St. Canton, MA 02021 T: 617-828-8060 F: 617-828-8518 Stewart A Satter
Continental Conair Ltd. 15/F Tower II, World Trade Square 123 Hoi Bun Rd., Hong Kong T: 2751-4688 F: 2751-8920 Ying Hung Tam	Household Appliances Personal Care Products	Conair Corp. One Cummings Rd. Stamford, CT 06904 T: 203-351-9000 F: 203-351-9180 Ralph Coccaro / Jaime Morozowski
Continental Enterprises Ltd. 35/F United Centre 95 Queensway, Hong Kong T: 2823-6111 F: 2861-1826 Christian Topuz	Feed Additives	Continental Grain Co. 277 Park Ave., 50/F New York, NY 10172 T: 212-207-5100 F: 212-207-5181 Thomas Coyle / Paul Schroeder

China Office	Product/Service	U.S. Head Office
Continental Insurance Asia Pacific 19/F Asia Orient Tower, Town Place 33 Lockhart Rd., Wanchai, Hong Kong T: 2576-4705 F: 2529-9499 Oliver Wayne Shilling	Insurance	Continental Insurance (CNA) 180 Maiden Lane New York, NY 10038 T: 212-440-3000 F: 212-440-7130 John H Bretherick, Jr.
Coopers & Lybrand 23/F Sunning Plaza 10 Hysan Ave., Causeway Bay, Hong Kong T: 2839-4321 F: 2576-5356 Roderick E D Chalmers	Accounting Consulting	Coopers & Lybrand 1530 Wilson Blvd. Arlington, VA 22209-2447 T: 703-908-1500 F: 703-908-1695 Bob Rourke
Corstates Bank NA 17/F Asia Pacific Finance Tower 3 Garden Rd., Central, Hong Kong T: 2509-0888 F: 2845-2073 Stevens S Nicholas	Banking	Corstates Financial Corp. 1500 Market St. Philadelphia, PA 19101 T: 215-973-3100 F: 215-973-1761 Michael Heavener
Corning (Hong Kong) Ltd. Chinachem Exchange Square 1 Hoi Wan St., Quarry Bay, Hong Kong T: 2807-2723 F: 2807-2152 William Sha Fu	Construction Materials Optical Products	Corning Inc. One Riverfront Plaza Corning, NY 14831 T: 607-974-9000 F: 607-974-8551 Larry Aiello /Ken Kao
Coudert Brothers 25/F Nine Queen's Rd Central, Hong Kong T: 2810-4111 F: 2845-9021 Owen D Nee Jr.	Law	Coudert Brothers 1114 Avenue of the Americas New York, NY 10036-7794 T: 212-626-4400 F: 212-626-4120 Robert Hornick
Coulter Electronics (HK) Ltd. Unit B, 13/F, Gee Chang Hong Centre 85 Wong Chuk ang Rd., Hong Kong T: 2814-0481 F: 2873-4511 Jackey Ho	Blood Analysis System Flow Cytometers Medical Equipment	Coulter Corp. 11800 S. W. 147th St., PO Box 169015 Miami, FL 33116-9015 T: 305-380-3800 F: 305-380-8312 Mike Crochu / James Schepp
CPC-AJI Ltd. / CPC Asia Ltd. 1408 Cityplaza 4 Taikoo Wan Rd., Taikoo Shing, Hong Kong T: 2523-0061 F: 2845-2914 Heribert H Gruenert	Food Products	CPC International Inc. P. O. Box 8000, Int'l Plaza Englewood Cliffs, NJ 07632 T: 201-894-4000 F: 201-541-5304 Robert J. Gillespie
CPC/AJI (Hong Kong) Ltd. Tai Po Industrial Estate 6 Dai Fu St., Tai Po, Hong Kong T: 2664-2011 F: 2664-2845 C E Lloyd	Food Products	CPC International Inc. P. O. Box 8000, Int'l Plaza Englewood Cliffs, NJ 07632 T: 201-894-4000 F: 201-541-5304 Robert J. Gillespie
Credit Suisse First Boston (HK) Ltd. 16/F One Exchange Square 8 Connaught Place, Central, Hong Kong T: 2101-6091 F: 2101-7781 Bonnie Wu	Investment Banking	Credit Suisse First Boston Inc. 11 Madison Ave. New York, NY 10010 T: 212-325-2000 F: 212-325-6665 Stephen E. Stonefield

China Office	Product/Service	U.S. Head Office
Crown Can Hong Kong Ltd. Tai Po Industrail Estate 8-10 Dai Kwai St., Tai Po, Hong Kong T: 2665-6312 F: 2664-3837 Terry Cartwright	Metal Products Packaging Products	Crown Cork & Seal Co. Inc. 9300 Ashton Rd., PO Box 63290 Philadelphia, PA 19114 T: 215-698-5100 F: 215-676-7245 William Voss / Nigel Gilson
Cummins Engine Hong Kong Ltd. 2/F, Unison Industrial Centre 27-31 Au Pui Wan St., Fo Tan, Hong Kong T: 2606-5678 F: 2687-3552 Saw Guan	Power Generation Petroleum Products Mining Equipment Marine Products	Cummins Engine Co. Inc. P. O. Box 3005, Mail Code 60316 Columbus, IN 47202 T: 812-377-5000 F: 812-377-3082 Mark Levett
Cuno Filtration Asia Pte Ltd. 2510 Technology Park 18 On Lai St., Hong Kong T: 2388-4988 F: 2388-5322 Paul Chung	Hydraulic Components Fluid Purification Systems Preengineered Buildings Stamped Metal Products	Commercial Intertech Corp. 1775 Logan Ave. P O Box 239 Youngstown, OH 44501 T: 216-746-8011 F: 216-746-1148 Paul J Powers
D'Arcy Masius Benton & Bowles Unit 606/11 Devon House, Taikoo Place 979 King's Rd., Quarry Bay, Hong Kong T: 2590-5888 F: 2856-9905 Alan Thompson	Advertising	D'Arcy Masius Benton & Bowles 1675 Broadway New York, NY 10019 T: 212-468-3622 F: 212-468-4385 Clayton White
Dana Asia Pacific 1602 Fairmont House 8 Cotton Tree Dr., Central, Hong Kong T: 2521-0226 F: 2521-8542 Charles F Heine	Automotive Products	Dana Corp. 4500 Dorr St., P. O. Box 1000 Toledo, OH 43697 T: 419-535-4500 F: 419-535-4544 Gus Franklin / Tom Feely
Dart Express (Hong Kong) Ltd. 1/F Wan Tung Bldg. 115 Tam Kung Rd., Kowloon, Hong Kong T: 2715-7613 F: 2760-0850 Joseph Pang	Freight Forwarder	**Dart Express** 821 W. Arbor Vitae St. Inglewood, CA 90301 T: 310-649-3641 F: 213-776-6132 Vincent Lai
Data General HK Sales & Service Ltd. 11/F Warwick House West Wing 979 King's Rd., Hong Kong T: 2599-6688 F: 2506-0221 Leonard Lee	Computer Products	Data General Corp. 4400 Computer Dr. Westboro, MA 01580 T: 508-898-5000 F: 508-898-4003 Joel Schwartz / Angelo Guadagno
Dataquest Asia Pacific Ltd. 5904 Central Plaza 18 Harbour Rd., Hong Kong T: 2824-6168 F: 2824-6139 Bruce Witney	Market & Trade Research	Dataquest Inc. 251 Rivers Oak Pkwy. San Jose, CA 95134 T: 408-468-8000 F: 408-954-1780 Tom McCall
DDB Needham Worldwide DIK Ltd. 33/F Sun Hung Kai Centre 30 Harbour Rd., Hong Kong T: 2828-0328 F: 2827-2700 Twiggy Lam	Advertising	DDB Needham Worldwide Inc. 437 Madison Ave. New York, NY 10022 T: 212-415-2000 F: 212-415-3562 Bernard Brochard

Dart Express is committed to the effective service and efficient transportation of goods worldwide. Our staff has the knowledge and ability to facilitate and promote international trade. With stations and agents in most major gateway cities of the world, we are able to meet the increasing demands and needs of importers and exporters worldwide. Dart Express Group offers the following services:

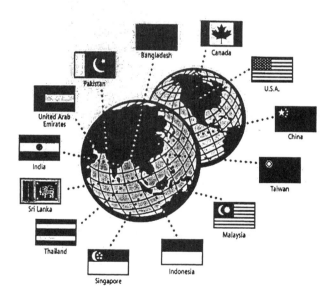

Worldwide Air/Ocean Freight Services
Ground Transportation
International Documentation
Crating and Handling
Export Declaration
Banking/Letter of Credit/Bank Presentation
Certificate of Origin
Warehousing/Distribution
Import Transaction
US Customs Clearance (Advanced ABI Systems
Cargoes Consolidation

Dart Express (LAX) Inc.
821 W. Arbor Vitae Street
Inglewood, Ca. 90301

Tel: 310-649-3641 Fax: 213-776-6132
www.dartexpress.com

China Office	Product/Service	U.S. Head Office
DDI Asia/Pacific Int'l Ltd. 2102 Chinachem Hollywood Centre 1 Hollywood Rd., Central, Hong Kong T: 2526-1188 F: 2537-9575 Alice Law	Education & Training	Development Dimensions Int'l Inc. 1225 Washington Pike Bridgeville, PA 15017 T: 412-257-0600 F: 412-257-0614 Ron Dalesio
Deacoms/Graham & James 3-6/F Alexandra House Chater Rd., Central, Hong Kong T: 2825-9211 F: 2810-0431 Sally Harpole	Law	Graham & James 801 South Figueroa St., 14/F Los Angeles, CA 90017 T: 213-624-2500 F: 213-623-4581 Hillel Cohn
Dean Witter Reynolds (HK) Ltd. Rm. 3408 Edinburgh Tower 15 Queen's Rd., Central, Hong Kong T: 2521-3322 F: 2845-2028 Tony K C Lee	Securities & Commodities Investment Banking Money Management	Dean Witter Reynolds Inc. 2 World Trade Center, 66/F New York, NY 10048 T: 212-392-2222 Richard Powers / Philip J Purcell
Del Monte Fresh Produce Int'l Inc. 936/37 New World Office Bldg. 24 Salisbury Rd., Kowloon, Hong Kong T: 2723-7011 F: 2311-3187 Francis Cheung	Agricultural Products	Del Monte Fresh Produce Int'l Inc. 800 Douglas Entrance North Tower Coral Gables, FL 33134 T: 305-520-8400 F: 305-520-8495 Bryce Edmonson
Deloitte Touche Tohmatsu 26/F Wing On Centre 111 Connaught Rd., Central, Hong Kong T: 2545-0303 F: 2541-1911 Patrick Cheng	Accounting Consulting	Deloitte Touche Tohmatsu Int'l Ten Westport Rd. Wilton, CT 06897 T: 203-761-3000 F: 203-834-2200 Dina A. Elliott
Delta International (HK) Ltd. Suite 2915/21Two Pacific Place 88 Queensway, Hong Kong T: 2926-6280 F: 2537-1900 Kwok Kun Wai	Airlines	Delta Air Lines Inc. Hartsfield Atlanta Int'l Airport Atlanta, GA 30320 T: 404-715-2600 F: 404-715-2731 Robert Coggin / Michael Medlicott
Dentsply International Inc. 23/F Gee Chang Hong Centre 65 Wong Chuk Rd., Aberdeen, Hong Kong T: 2870-0336 F: 2870-0620 Charles T Kean	Dental Equipment Dental Supplies	Dentsply Int'l Inc. 570 W. College Ave., P. O. Box 872 York, PA 17405 T: 717-845-7511 F: 717-854-2343 Thomas L. Whiting
Dentsu Young & Rubicam Ltd. 418 Mount Parker House 1111 King's Rd., Quarry Bay, Hong Kong T: 2884-6668 F: 2886-0989 Eddie Gonzalez	Advertising	Young & Rubicam Inc. 285 Madison Ave. New York, NY 10017 T: 212-210-3000 F: 212-490-9073 James Hood / Mike Samet
Development Consultants Int'l Ltd. 1205 Hong Kong Arts Centre 2 harbour Rd., Hong Kong T: 2893-3649 F: 2802-2100 J. Sandhu	Engineering Services Construction Management	The Kuljian Co. 3624 Science Center Philadelphia, PA 19104 T: 215-243-1900 John A Burckhardt

China Office	Product/Service	U.S. Head Office
Dexter Asia Pacific Ltd. Suite 1201, Tower 6, Ching Hong Kong City 33 Canton Rd., Tsim Sha Tsui, Hong Kong T: 2730-1101 F: 2730-1119 Alice Lam	Polymer Products Magnetic Materials Biotechnology	Dexter Corp. 1 Elm St. Windsor Locks, CT 06096 T: 860-292-7675 F: 860-292-7673 Horst Geldmacher
DHL International (HK) Ltd. DHL House 13 Mok Cheong St. Tokwawan, Kowloon, Hong Kong T: 2764-4888 F: 2764-0641 Po Chung	Courier Service	DHL Worldwide Express 333 Twin Dolphin Dr. Redwood City, CA 94065 T: 650-593-7474 F: 650-593-1689 Dean Christon / Brian Billings
Dietz Trading Co., Ltd. 3/F United Ind. Bldg. 50 Heung Yip Rd., Hong Kong T: 2553-9261 F: 2873-0301 Jackson Mak	Kitchen Utensils Trading	R E Dietz Co. 639 N Salina St. Syracuse, NY 13208 T: 315-478-4723 T Gschwender
Digital Equipment HK/PRC Ltd. 16-22/F Cityplaza 4 12 Taikoo Wan Rd., Hong Kong T: 2805-3111 F: 2805-4200 Frank Fortunato	Computers	Digital Equipment Corp. 111 Powermill Rd. Maynard, MA 01754 T: 508-493-5111 F: 508-497-7374 Ronald Spinek
Dillingham Construction (HK) Ltd. 29-37/F Sing Mei Ind. Bldg. Hong Kong T: 2401-0897 F: 2401-0476 Jennis Fer	General Contrcting	Dillingham Construction Corp. 5960 Inglewood Dr. Pleasanton, CA 94588 T: 510-463-3300 F: 510-847-7800 Lenore J. Thielen
Direct Container Line Inc. Suite 4904 Central Plaza 18 Harbour Rd., Wanchai, Hong Kong T: 2507-3026 F: 2802-1806 Michael C Tsui	Shipping Freight Consolidating	Direct Container Line Inc. 857 E. 230th St. Carson, CA 90745 T: 310-518-1773 F: 310-830-5316 Owen G Glenn
Dole China Ltd. 803 Wing On Centre 111 Connaught Rd., Central, Hong Kong T: 2854-6302 F: 2854-6391 John Casazza	Agricultural Products Food Crops	Dole Packaged Food Inc. 5795 Lindero Canyon Rd. Westlake Village, CA 91362 T: 818-874-4687 F: 818-874-4966 Philip M. FitzPatrick
Donaldson Far East Ltd. Unit A, 21/F, CDW Bldg. 388 Castle Peak Rd, Tsuen Wan, Hong Kong T: 2402-2830 F: 2493-2928 Rolfe E Sobolik	Filtration Products	Donaldson Co Inc. 1400 W. 94th St., PO Box 1299 Minneapolis, MN 55440 T: 612-887-3500 F: 612-887-3377 William Cook / Steve Mulder
Donaldson, Lufkin & Jenrette 29/F One Exchange Square 8 Connaught Palce, Hong Kong T: 2501-3800 F: 2501-3833 Alfred Pang	Investment Management	Donaldson Lufkin & Jenrette Inc. 277 Park Ave., 11/F New York, NY 10172 T: 212-892-3000 Charles Hale

China Office	Product/Service	U.S. Head Office
Dow Chemical Pacific Ltd. 47/F Sun Hung Kai Centre 30 Harbour Rd., Wanchai, Hong Kong T: 2879-7333 F: 2827-6019 Andrew Liveris	Chemicals Agricultural Products	Dow Chemical Co. 2030 Dow Center Midland, MI 48674 T: 517-636-1000 F: 517-636-3518 Dick Sosville
Dow Corning Asia 19/F East Point Centre 533 Hennessy Rd., Causeway bay, Hong Kong T: 2835-0350 F: 2836-6650 Scott Barber	Chemicals	Dow Corning Corp. 2220 W Salzburg Rd., P O Box 1767 Midland, MI 48640 T: 517-496-4000 F: 517-496-4586 G. J. Ziarno
Draco International Ltd. 16/F First Pacific Bank Centre 51-57 Gloucester Rd., Wanchai, Hong Kong T: 2866-9913 F: 2861-3588 Tick Pang Leung	Flame Retardant Concentrates	Hanna Engrd Matrs/Monmouth Inc. 4955 Avalon Ridge Pkwy., #300 Norcross, GA 30071 T: 770-243-7000 F: 770-243-7024 Tom Moccia
Drake Beam Morin (Hong Kong) 16/F Printing House 6 Duddell St., Central, Hong Kong T: 2840-0838 F: 2877-3721 John R Newnam	Business Mgmt Consultants	Drake Beam Morin Inc. 100 Park Ave. New York, NY 10017 T: 212-692-7700 F: 212-953-0194 Donald E Stevens
Dresser-Rand Co. Suite 1408 Prince's Bldg. Chater Rd., Hong Kong T: 2526-1859 F: 2537-1629 Alf Cheung	Energy Industry Equipment Technical Service	Dresser-Rand Co.. 37 Coats St. Wellsville, NY 14895 T: 716-593-1234 F: 716-593-5815 J. A. Gegus
Drew Ameroid International Corp. Fook Lee Commercial Centre Town Place, Hong Kong T: 2520-2010 F: 2865-6472 Mr. Lee	Chemicals	Ashland Chemical Inc. 5200 Paul G. Memorial Pkwy. Dublin, OH 43017 T: 614-889-3333 F: 614-790-3823 G. A. Cappeline
Du Pont China Ltd. 1122 New World Office Bldg. East Wing 24 Salisbury Rd., Kowloon, Hong Kong T: 2734-5345 F: 2724-4458 David Pang	Chemicals	E I Du Pont de Nemours & Co. 1007 Market St. Wilmington, DE 19898 T: 302-774-1000 F: 302-774-7321 Charles O. Holliday, Jr.
Dun & Bradstreet (HK) Ltd. 12/F, K Wah Centre 191 Java Rd., North Point, Hong Kong T: 2516-1350 F: 2562-6147 James B Barnett	Business Information Business Mgmt Concultants Marketing Services	Dun & Bradstreet Co. One Diamond Hill Rd. Murray Hill, NJ 07974 T: 908-665-5000 F: 908-665-5803 Nick Mancini
Dunavant Asia Ltd. 2020A Jardine House 1 Connaught Place, Central, Hong Kong T: 2522-5076 F: 2810-4879 David G Hardoon, Jr.	Cotton Products	Dunavant Enterprises Inc. 3797 New Getwell Rd. Memphis, TN 38118-6065 T: 901-369-1500 F: 901-369-1608 H. J. Weathersby

China Office	Product/Service	U.S. Head Office
Duracell Asia Ltd. 16/F Island Place 510 King's Rd., North Point, Hong Kong T: 2506-2121 F: 2506-2185 Edwin Ko	Batteries	Duracell Int'l Inc. Berkshire Corporate Park Bethel, CT 06801 T: 203-796-4000 F: 203-796-4516 Bob Giacolone
E I Freight (HK) Ltd. 201 South Seas Centre, Tower 2 75 Mody Rd., Lowloon, Hong Kong T: 2739-2399 F: 2721-9734 Thomas Moopenn	Freight Forwarder	Expeditors International P. O. Box 69620 Seattle, WA 98168-9620 T: 206-246-3711 F: 206-674-3459 James L. K. Wang
E J Krause & Associates (HK) Ltd. Rm. 2013 Hang Lung Centre 2-20 Paterson St., Causeway Bay, Hong Kong T: 2577-3343 F: 2577-6426 Emily Tung	Exhibition Organizer Trade Show Management	E J Krause & Associates 6550 Rock Spring Dr., #500 Bethesda, MD 20817 T: 301-493-5500 F: 301-493-5705 Shane Poblete / Sucia Min
East Asia Aetna Insurance Group 28/F East Asia Aetna Tower 308 Des Voeux Rd., Central, Hong Kong T: 2850-2333 F: 2850-3838 Patrick Poon	Insurance	AETNA International 151 Farmington Ave. Hartford, CT 06156 T: 860-273-0123 F: 860-275-2677 Frederick C Copeland, Jr.
Eastman Chemical Ltd. Yuen Long Ind. Est. 1-3 Wang Lok St., Hong Kong T: 2473-7188 F: 2474-0913 James Ron Hilderbrand	Chemicals Fibers & Plastics Photo & Plastic Products	Eastman Chemical Co. P. O. Box 431 Kingsport, TN 37662 T: 615-229-2000 F: 615-229-1525 A. R. Rothwell
Eaton Technologies Ltd. 10/F, 100 Canton Rd. Tsim Sha Tsui, Hong Kong T: 2736-3811 F: 2736-3781 Lincoln Lee	Vehicle Components	Eaton Corp. Eaton Center, 1111 Superior Ave. Cleveland, OH 44114-2584 T: 216-523-5000 F: 216-479-7014 Laurence M. Ivan
Ecolab Ltd. 50/F Lu Plaza 2 Wing Yip St., Hong Kong T: 2341-4202 F: 2797-9030 Johnny C C Choy	Chemicals Cleaning Equipment Sanitation Controls	Ecolab Inc. Ecolab Center, 370 N. Wabasha St. St. Paul, MN 55102 T: 612-293-2185 F: 612-225-3136 Mike Muenstermann
Economist Group Asia Pacific Ltd. 25/F Dah Sing Financial Centre 108 Gloucester Rd., Hong Kong T: 2585-3888 F: 2802-7638 Monica Chan	Publishing Information Management	**Economist Intelligent Unit (E.I.U.)** 111 W. 57th St. New York, NY 10019 T: 212-554-0600 F: 212-586-1181 Nigel Ludlow
Edelman Public Relations Worldwide 3701/02, 37/F, Windsor House 311 Gloucester Rd., Hong Kong T: 2804-1338 F: 2804-1303 Clara Shek	Public Relations	Edelman Public Relations Worldwide 200 E. Randolph Dr., #6300 Chicago, IL 60601 T: 312-240-3000 F: 312-240-2900 Diane B. Dalbke

China Office	Product/Service	U.S. Head Office
Electroflow Hong Kong Ltd. 8/F Block B, Veristrong Ind. Centre 34 Au Pui Wan St., Shatin, Hong Kong T: 2695-8318 F: 2695-3944 Vivien Chan	Electronic Components	Electenergy Technologies Inc. 1816 Grindstone Ave. Columbia, MO 65201 T: 573-442-2520 J A Fraser
Electronic Data Systems (HK) Ltd. 1302 Stanhope House 738 King's Rd., Quarry Bay, Hong Kong T: 2811-3130 F: 2811-4447 Susan Young	Software	EDS 5400 Legacy Dr. Plano, TX 75024 T: 972-605-6000 F: 972-605-6662 John R. Harris
Eli Lilly (Asia) Inc. 3/F Hua Fu Commercial Bldg. 111 Queen's Rd. W., Hong Kong T: 2572-0160 F: 2572-7893 Michael Kong	Pharmaceuticals	Eli Lilly & Co. Lilly Corporate Center Indianapolis, IN 46285 T: 317-276-2000 F: 317-276-2095 Gino Santini
EMC Computer Systems Ltd. Rm. 1101/03 CityPlaza 4 Taikoo Shing, Hong Kong T: 2839-9600 F: 2576-1362 Freeman Nung	Computers	EMC Corp. 35 Parkwood St. Hopkinton, MA 01748 T: 508-435-1000 F: 508-435-5222 Colin Patterson
Emerson Electric (Asia) Ltd. Rm. 3904 Central Plaza 18 Harbour Rd., Wanchai, Hong Kong T: 2802-9223 F: 2827-8665 Danny Lay	Automotive Products Aerspace/Aviation Air Conditioning Consumer Products	Emerson Electric Co. 8000 Florissant Ave. St. Louis, MO 63136 T: 314-553-2000 F: 314-553-3527 R W Staley
Emerson Radio Hong Kong Ltd. 705/11, Gateway Bldg., Tower II 25 Canton Rd., Hong Kong T: 2956-7900 F: 2956-1333 Ron Gulett	Consumer Electronics	Emerson Radio Corp. PO Box 430, 9 Entin Rd. Parsippany, NJ 07054 T: 201-884-5800 F: 201-428-2033 John Raab
Engelhard Hong Kong Ltd. 6/F Block B2 Eldex Industrial Bldg. 21 Ma Tau Wei Rd., Kowloon, Hong Kong T: 2365-0301 F: 2765-6406 Roger Wong	Precious Metals	Engelhard Corp. 101 Wood Ave. S. Iselin, NJ 08830 T: 732-205-6888 F: 732-205-5915 George C. Hsu
Enthon-Omi (HK) Co Ltd. 8/F Hale Weal Industrial Bldg. 22-28 Tai Chung Rd., Hong Kong T: 2499-7299 F: 2415-2225 Thomas Lam / Ben Leung	Chemicals & Minerals Nonferrous Metals	Asarco Inc. 180 Maiden Lane New York, NY 10038 T: 212-510-2000 F: 212-510-1835 Jerry W. Cooper
Erie-Watala Glass Co. Ltd. Unit 401/05 Worldwide Industrial Centre 43-47 Shan Mei St., Shatin, Hong kong T: 2694-1838 F: 2691-9150 Derek Ngai	Dental Products Orthodontic Products	Sybron Int'l Corp. 411 E. Wisconsin Ave., 24/F Milwaukee, WI 53202 T: 414-274-6600 F: 414-274-6561 Eileen Short

China Office	Product/Service	U.S. Head Office
Ernst & Young Indochina Ltd. 15/F Hutchison House 10 Harcourt Rd., Central, Hong Kong T: 2846-9888 F: 2868-4432 Brian Stevenson	Accounting Consulting	Ernst & Young 787 Seventh Ave., 14/F New York, NY 10019 T: 212-773-3000 F: 212-773-6350 Eli Spielman
ERTL (Hong Kong) Ltd. 7/F Prosperous Centre 1 Knutsford Terrace, Kowloon, Hong Kong T: 2366-1778 F: 2366-1492 Frederick Liu	Die Casting Toys	The ERTL Co. PO Box 500, Highway 136 & 20 Dyersville, IA 52040 T: 319-875-2000 F: 319-875-8263 Jim Cavanaugh
ESSO Petroleum China Ltd. 19/F Central Plaza 18 Harbour Rd., Wanchai, Hong Kong T: 2829-6868 F: 2802-7117 Kim Teck Neo	Petroleum Products	Exxon Corp. 225 E. John W Carpenter Freeway Irving, TX 75062 T: 214-444-1000 F: 214-444-1348 R Dahan
Estee Lauder (HK) Ltd. 1107 New T & T Centre 7 Canton Rd., Hong Kong T: 2378-0600 F: 2317-6169 Hermia Pavanetto	Cosmetic Products	Estee Lauder Int'l Inc. 767 Fifth Ave. New York, NY 10153 T: 212-572-4200 F: 212-572-4655 Muriel Gonzalez
Eveready Battery Co Asia Pacific Inc. 1601 New World Office Bldg. East Wing 24 Salisbury Rd., Kowloon, Hong Kong T: 2731-3300 F: 2739-7258 T J Moran	Battery Products Lighting Equipment	Eveready Battery Co. 801 Chouteau Ave. St. Louis, MO 63102 T: 314-982-2000 F: 314-982-2320 D. P. Hatfield / W. M. Klein
Eveready HK Co. / Eveready Batteries HK Co. Rm. 1109/12 Tower 1, Gateway, Harbour City 25 Canton Rd., Tsim Sha Tsui, Hong Kong T: 2956-2333 F: 2956-1221 Wai Man Shum	Battery Products Lighting Equipment	Eveready Battery Co. 801 Chouteau Ave. St. Louis, MO 63102 T: 314-982-2000 F: 314-982-2320 D. P. Hatfield / W. M. Klein
Everex Systems Inc. Unit 3C, Sime Darby Ind. Centre 420 Kwun Tong Rd., Kowloon, Hong Kong T: 2354-3599 F: 2341-4040 Chung Kwok Kwong	Computers	Everex Systems Inc. 5020 Brandin Ct. Fremont, CA 94538 T: 510-498-1111 F: 510-683-2025 Dolly Wu
Evergreen International Airlines Inc. 111 Air Cargo Terminal Bldg. HK Int'l Airport, Hong Kong T: 2382-7373 F: 2382-5804 Catherine Cole	Cargo Freight	Evergreen Int'l Airlines 3850 Three Mile Lane McMinnville, OR 97128 T: 503-472-9361 F: 503-434-4210 Linda Woodbury
Exxon Chemical International Ltd. 22/F Central Plaza 18 Harbour Rd., Wanchai, Hong Kong T: 2582-0888 F: 2802-0279 Tan Jin Cher	Chemicals	Exxon Corp. 225 E. John W Carpenter Freeway Irving, TX 75062-2298 T: 214-444-1000 F: 214-444-1348 R Dahan

- - - - - T: Telephone # - - - - - F: Fax # - - - - - Hong Kong Area Code: (852) - - - - -

China Office	**Product/Service**	**U.S. Head Office**
Exxon Energy Ltd. 10/F St. George Bldg. 2 Ice House St., Central, Hong Kong T: 2826-3000 F: 2845-9068 G L Graves	Petroleum Products Power Generation	Exxon Corp. 225 E. John W Carpenter Freeway Irving, TX 75062-2298 T: 214-444-1000 F: 214-444-1348 R Dahan
Fabricators International Ltd. 11/F Safety Godown Industrial Bldg. 56 Ka Yip St., Hong Kong T: 2896-4451 F: 2897-0294 Ching Chung Chui	Portable DC Battery Chargers Electronic Components	International Components Corp. 107 Maxess Rd. Melville, NY 11747 T: 516-293-1500 F: 516-293-4983 Irwin Friedman
Federal Express (HK) Ltd. 606, 6/F, Ocean Centre 5 Canton Rd., Hong Kong T: 2193-1111 F: 2375-1511 Grace Lo / Raymond Wong	Express Mail Courier Service	Federal Express Corp. 2005 Corporate Ave., 3/F Memphis, TN 38132 T: 901-369-3600 F: 901-395-4858 T Michael Glenn / David Cunningham
Federal Insurance Co. 1801 Harcourt House 39 Gloucester Rd., Wanchai, Hong Kong T: 2861-3668 F: 2861-2681 Mike Howey	Insurance	**The Chubb Corp.** 15 Mountain View Rd. Warren, NJ 07059 T: 908-903-2000 F: 908-903-2003 Robert M Lynyak
Federal-Mogul World Trade Hong Kong Ltd. 305 Join In Hang Sing Centre 71-75 Container Port Rd., Hong Kong T: 2612-2807 F: 2419-8549 Paul Wan	Vehicle Components	Federal-Mogul Corp. P. O. Box 1966 Detroit, MI 48235 T: 313-354-7700 F: 313-354-8950 James J Zamoyski
Feeco Ltd. 9C Fortune Bldg. 150 Lockhart Rd., Wanchai, Hong Kong T: 2507-4802 F: 2598-0661 Kim Shepard	Consumer Electronics	Fleishman-Hillard Inc. 200 N. Broadway St. Louis, MO 63102 T: 314-982-1700 F: 314-231-2313 Alan W. Akerson
Felton Int'l Ltd. 711 Nan Fung Commercial Centre 19 Lam Lok St., Hong Kong T: 2750-2380 F: 2318-1962 Mike Wong	Essential Oils & Extracts Perfumes & Flavor Material Aromatic Chemicals	Felton International Inc. 599 Johnson Ave. Brooklyn, NY 11237 T: 212-497-4664 Philip Rosner
Ferro Far East Ltd. Rm. 1014 Penninsula Centre 67 Mody Rd., Kowloon, Hong Kong T: 2724-6193 F: 2724-6837 R L Klassen	Chemicals & Coatings Plastics & Refractories	Ferro Corp. 1000 Lakeside Ave. Cleveland, OH 44114 T: 216-641-8580 F: 216-566-1464 Charles M. Less
Fidelity Investments Management (HK) Ltd. 16/F Citibank Tower 3 Garden Rd., Central, Hong Kong T: 2848-1700 F: 2845-9051 Robert Auld	Fund Management Investment	Fidelity Investment (FMR Corp.) 82 Devonshire St. Boston, MA 02019 T: 617-563-7000 F: 617-476-5979 Roger T. Serrison

China Office	Product/Service	U.S. Head Office
Fiduciary Trust Int'l Asia Ltd. 1903/04 Two Pacific Place 88 Queensway, Hong Kong T: 2877-1931 F: 2877-0206 Tom Duffy	Investment Management	Fiduciary Trust Co. Int'l 2 World Trade Center, #9400 New York, NY 10048 T: 212-466-4100 F: 212-313-2677 Henry C. Barkhorn, III
First Brands Asia Ltd. Rm. 2803 Central Plaza 18 Harbour Rd., Wanchai, Hong Kong T: 2802-9100 F: 2802-4090 Robert Kam	Automotive Products Plastic Wraps & Bags Pet Products	First Brands Corp. 83 Wooster Hights Rd. Danbury, CT 06813 T: 203-731-2300 F: 203-731-2518 J. S. Gracie
First National Bank of Boston Suite 801/09 Jardine House 1 Connaught Place, Central, Hong Kong T: 2526-4361 F: 2845-9222 Russ Magarity	Banking Financial Services	BankBoston Corp. 100 Federal St. Boston, MA 02110 T: 617-434-2200 Clark W Miller
First National Bank of Chicago 13/F Jardine House 1 Connaught Place, Central, Hong Kong T: 2844-9222 F: 2844-9318 Richard Kolehmainen	Banking Financial Services	First Chicago NBD Corp. One First National Plaza Chicago, IL 60670-0758 T: 312-732-2755 F: 312-732-5976 Gerald Buldak
Fischer Imaging (China) Ltd. 714 Concordia Plaza Science Museum Rd., Kowloon, Hong Kong T: 2723-3132 F: 2723-3711 Simon Tam	Medical Equipment	Fischer Imaging Corporation 12300 N. Grant St. Denver, CO 80241 T: 303-452-6800 F: 303-450-4335 Simon Tam
Fleishman-Hillard Hong Kong 12B Shun Ho Tower 24-30 Ice House St., Central, Hong Kong T: 2530-0228 F: 2845-0363 Anthony Phillips	Public Relations	Fleishman-Hillard, Inc. 200 North Broadway St. Louis, MO 63102-2796 T: 314-982-1700 F: 314-231-2313 William K. "Bill" Anderson
Flextronics Purchasing (HK) Ltd. Unit A, Block A, 11/F, Wo Kee Hong Bldg. 585-609 Castle Peak Rd., Hong Kong T: 2489-9813 F: 2480-4490 S L Tsui	Board Assembly	Flextronics Int'l Inc. 2241 Lundy Ave. San Jose, CA 95131 T: 408-428-1300 Dennis Straford
FMC Asia-Pacific Inc. 12/F Caroline Centre 28 Yun Ping Rd., Causeway Bay, Hong Kong T: 2839-6600 F: 2576-2918 Milton Steele	Chemicals & Machinery Food Ingredients	FMC Corp. 200 E. Randolph Dr. Chicago, IL 60601 T: 312-861-6000 F: 312-861-6176 James A MacLung / William Wheeler
Foote, Cone & Belding Ltd. 2/F Harbour Centre 25 Harbour Rd., Wanchai, Hong Kong T: 2886-0933 F: 2568-5080 Ben Barnes	Advertising	Foote, Cone & Belding Communictns 101 E. Erie St. Chicago, IL 60611 T: 312-751-7000 F: 312-751-3501 Mark Modesto

China Office	**Product/Service**	**U.S. Head Office**
Four Winds Removals Ltd. 5/F Len Shing Industrial Bldg. 4A Kung Ngam Village Rd., Hong Kong T: 2885-9666 F: 2567-7954 Chris Wilkinson	Removal & Storage Third Party Logistics	Four Winds Int'l Group 1500 SW Forst Ave., #850 Portland, OR 97201 T: 503-241-2732 F: 503-241-1829 Stephen C Standring
Franklin Mint Far East Ltd. Unit 5-7, 19/F, Tower III, Enterprise Square 19 Sheung Yuet Rd., Kowloon, Hong Kong T: 2707-7988 F: 2798-1215 Howard P Lucker	Collectibles/Luxury Items	The Franklin Mint US Rte. 1 Franklin Center, PA 19091 T: 610-459-6000 F: 610-459-6880 Don Fisher
Fred Kort Int'l Ltd. 501/02 Peninsula Centre 67 Mody Rd., Kowloon, Hong Kong T: 2369-9545 F: 2724-2651 Fred Kort	Toys	Imperial Toy Corp. 2060 E. 7th St. Los Angeles, CA 90021-1399 T: 213-489-2100 F: 213-489-4467 Fred Kort
Fritz Transportation Int'l Ltd. Unit 1-7, 20/F, Kowloon Plaza 485 Castle Peak Rd., Kowloon, Hong Kong T: 2371-6888 F: 2370-2922 Billy Tse	Freight Forwarder	Fritz Companies Inc. 706 Mission St., #900 San Francisco, CA 94103 T: 415-904-8360 F: 415-904-8661 John H. Johung
Fulbright & Jaworski LLP 19/F Hong Kong Club Bldg. 3A Chater Rd., Hong Kong T: 2523-3200 F: 2523-3255 Jeffrey A Blount	Law	Fulbright & Jaworski 1301 McKinney St., #5100 Houston, TX 77010 T: 713-651-5151 F: 713-651-5246 George H Liu
G L Transearch China Ltd. 17C On Hing Bldg. 1 On Hing Terrace, Central, Hong Kong T: 2868-1008 F: 2810-6420 George U Lim	Executive Search	Johnson Smith Knisely 100 Park Ave. New York, NY 10017 T: 212-661-0339 G Knisely
Galco Int'l Toys Ltd. Rm. 1205, 12/F, Wang Chin St. Kowloon, Hong Kong T: 2378-1111 F: 2730-8230 Ronnie Soong	Toys	Galoob Toys Inc. 500 Forbes Blvd. S. San Francisco, CA 94080 T: 650-952-1678 F: 650-875-1668 Ron Hirchfeld
GAP Int'l Sourcing Ltd. 21-22/F Tower 3 China Hong Kong City 33 Canton Rd., Kowloon, Hong Kong T: 2377-0060 F: 2730-5466 James Cunningham	Apparel	The GAP Co. 1 Harrison St. San Francisco, CA 94105 T: 415-427-5219 F: 415-427-5297 Edward Dunlop
Gates Rubber Co. 7/F Duke Wellington House 14-24 Wellington St., Central, Hong Kong T: 2525-1306 F: 2810-4289 A Van Es	Rubber Products Automotive Products	Gates Rubber Co. P. O. Box 5887 Denver, CO 80217-5887 T: 303-744-1911 F: 303-744-4000 John M. Riess

China Office	Product/Service	U.S. Head Office
Gavin Anderson & Co. Ltd. 2704 Universal Trade Centre 3 Arbuthnot Rd., Central, Hong Kong T: 2523-7189 F: 2810-1239 Walter Jennings	Public Relations Corp Financial Consultants	Gavin Anderson & Co Worldwide 1633 Broadway, 26/F New York, NY 10019 T: 212-373-0200 F: 212-307-9278 Gavin Anderson
GE Appliance - Asia 10/F The Lee Gardens 33 Hysan Ave., Causeway Bay, , Hong Kong T: 2100-6800 F: 2526-9842 Bill Abdallah	Household Products	GE Appliance Appliance Park Louisville, KY 50211 T: 502-452-4311 F: 502-452-0644 Steven C Reidel
GE Capital Asia Pacific Ltd. 16/F, Three Exchange Square 8 Connaught Place, Central, Hong Kong T: 2100-6700 F: 2810-5025 Steve Bertamini	Financial Services Leasing	GE Capital P. O. Box 2204 Fort Wayne, IN 46801 T: 219-439-2000 Chuck Devine
GE Plastics HK Ltd. Rm. 1008, 10/F, The Gateway Tower I 25 Canton Rd., Kowloon, Hong Kong T: 2629-0888 F: 2629-0800 Art Harper	Plastic Products	GE Plastics One Plastics Ave. Pittsfield, MA 01201 T: 413-448-7110 Jean M. Heuschen
GE Power System Asia-Pacific 15/F The Lee Gardens 33 Hysan Ave., Causeway Bay, Hong Kong T: 2100-6600 F: 2530-2598 Debert L Williamson	Power Generation	GE Power Systems One River Rd. Schenectady, NY 12345 T: 518-869-5555 F: 518-869-2828 Ronald R. Pressman
General Datacomm Int'l Corp. 11/F Kailey Tower 14-16 Stanley St., Central, Hong Kong T: 2526-5511 F: 2525-9944 Art Landro	Computers	General Datacomm Int'l Inc. 1579 Straits Turnpike, P O Box 1299 Middlebury, CT 06762-1299 T: 203-574-1118 F: 203-758-8507 Robert Francis
General Motors Overseas Corp. 1101, 11/F, Sino Plaza 256 Gloucester Rd., Hong Kong T: 2846-4500 F: 2840-1192 Ian Stones	Automotive Products	General Motors Corp. 482-A39-C08, 100 Renaissance Center Detroit, MI 48265-1000 T: 313-556-3527 F: 313-556-5083 Louis Hughes
Gerber Far East Ltd. Unit D, Block 5, HK Spinners Ind. Bldg. 760 Cheung Sha Wan RD., Hong Kong T: 2785-8881 F: 2786-4960 Becky Fu	Trading Sundries	J. Gerber & Co. 11 Penn Plaza, #1020 New York, NY 10041 T: 212-631-1200 F: 212-631-1316 C. Tan
Getz Bros & Co (HK) Ltd. 8/F Wyler Centre I 200 Tai Lin Pai Rd., Hong Kong T: 2429-1292 F: 2480-4691 Steven Lee	Trading Travel Services	Getz Bros & Co Inc. 150 Post St., #500 San Francisco, CA 94108 T: 415-772-5500 F: 415-772-5659 James J Beeman

China Office	Product/Service	U.S. Head Office
Gibson Dunn & Crutcher 1602 Double Bldg. 22 Stanley St., Central, Hong Kong T: 2526-6816 F: 2845-9144 Hsiao Chiung Li	Law	Gibson, Dunn & Crutcher 333 S. Grand Ave. Los Angeles, CA 90071 T: 213-229-7000 Ronald Beard
Gillette Far East Trading Ltd. 16/F Island Place 510 King's Rd., Hong Kong T: 2539-9800 F: 2513-7391 Anita To	Blades & Razors Cosmetics & Toiletries	The Gillette Co. Prudential Tower Bldg. Boston, MA 02199 T: 617-421-7000 F: 617-421-7123 Peter Kent
Glenayre Electronics (Hong Kong) Ltd. 304, 3/F, Sino Plaza 255-257 Gloucester Rd., Hong Kong T: 2838-3236 F: 2838-3231 Henry Tsang	Electronics	Glenayre Technologies Inc. 5935 Carnegie Blvd. Charlotte, NC 28209 T: 704-553-0038 F: 704-553-7878 Lee Ellison
Goldman Sachs (Asia) LLC 37/F Asia Pacific Finance Tower 3 Garden Rd., Central, Hong Kong T: 2978-1000 F: 2978-0396 Philip Murray	Investment Banking Fund Management	Goldman, Sachs & Co. 85 Broad St. New York, NY 10004 T: 212-902-1000 F: 212-902-3000 Susan Zuckerman / Mark Evans
Goodyear International Corp. 15/F Radio City 505 Hennessy Rd., Hong Kong T: 2543-3320 F: 2541-5119 Andrew Woo	Rubber Products	Goodyear Tire & Rubber Co. 1144 E. Market St. Akron, OH 44316 T: 216-796-2244 F: 216-796-9112 C Perez / William Sharp
Goulds Pumps (Asia) Ltd. 1501, 15/F, Argyle Centre, Phase I 688 Nathan Rd., Kowloon, Hong Kong T: 2396-0536 F: 2544-0052 Chris Choi	Pumps Sanitation Controls	Gould Pumps Inc. 240 Fall St. Seneca Falls, NY 13148 T: 315-568-7214 F: 315-568-5737 Frank Zonarich
Graco Hong Kong Ltd. 1203 The Goldmark Bldg. 502 Hennessy Rd., Causeway Bay, Hong Kong T: 2576-5411 F: 2576-8609 Agnes Lam	Fluid Handling Equipment	Graco Inc. 4050 Olson Memorial Hy, PO Box 1441 Minneapolis, MN 55440-1441 T: 612-623-6000 F: 612-623-6942 Pam Dovenmuehler
Grandprix Electronics 4/F, Unit A, Big Star Centre 8 Wang Kwong Rd., Kowloon, Hong Kong T: 2795-5838 F: 2795-3588 Randy Chang	Electronic Products	GPX Electronics 108 Madison St. St. Louis, MO 63102 T: 314-621-1555 F: 314-621-0869 Tony Jenkins
Grant Thornton International 37/F Wu Chung House 213 Queen's Rd E., Wanchai, Hong Kong T: 2838-0099 F: 2840-0789 Gabriel Azedo	Accounting	Grant Thorton International 800 Prudential Plaza, 130 E. Randolph Chicago, IL 60601 T: 312-856-0001 F: 312-861-1340 Robert A Kleckner

- - - - - T: Telephone # - - - - - F: Fax # - - - - - Hong Kong Area Code: (852) - - - - -

China Office	Product/Service	U.S. Head Office
Graphics International (HK) Ltd. 901 Stanhope House 734-738 King's Rd, Quarry Bay, Hong Kong T: 2563-1222 F: 2561-8101 Daniel S Krouse	Trading	Hallmark Cards Inc. 2501 McGee St. Kansas City, MO 64108 T: 816-274-5111 F: 816-274-7276 Jim Toohey / Mark Schwab
Great Lakes Chemical Far East Ltd. Printing House Hong Kong T: 2537-4238 F: 2973-0029 Rita Lew	Bromine & Derivatives Furfural & Derivatives	Great Lakes Chemical Corp. One Great Lakes Blvd. W. Lafayette, IN 47906 T: 317-497-6100 F: 317-497-6234 David Hall / Greg Griffith
Grey Advertising Asia/Pacific 34/F Manulife Tower 169 Electric Rd., North Point, Hong Kong T: 2586-1048 F: 2510-7541 Benjamin Samuel Barnes	Advertising	Grey Advertising Inc. 777 Third Ave. New York, NY 10017 T: 212-546-2000 F: 212-546-1495 Barbara Feigin / D. Destler
Griffith Laboratories Inc. 8/F Supreme Industrial Bldg. 15 Shan Mei St., Shatin, Hong Kong T: 2604-5008 F: 2694-9149 Alex Lei	Food Ingredients	Griffith Laboratories Worldwide Inc. 1 Griffith Center Alsip, IL 60658 T: 708-371-0900 F: 708-597-3294 Thomas Burrows
Guy Carpenters & Co (Asia) Ltd. 2118, 21/F, Miramar Tower 1-23 Kimberley Rd., Hong Kong T: 2582-3500 F: 2827-5551 Chon K Chen	Insurance	Guy Carpenter & Co. 2 World Trade Center New York, NY 10048-0086 T: 212-323-1000 F: 212-313-4970 Brandon Sweitzer
H B Fuller International Inc. Suite 2605, 26/F, Sino Plaza 255-257 Gloucester Rd., Hong Kong T: 2832-9622 F: 2892-1680 Alan Longstreet	Adhesive Products	H B Fuller Co. 1200 Willow Lake Blvd. St. Paul, MN 55164 T: 612-415-5900 F: 612-481-1828 Al Longstreet
Hamlin Electronics Laws Commercial Plaza 788 Cheung Sha Wan Rd., Hong Kong T: 2559-2041 F: 2858-2555 Bill Au	Electronic Products	Hamlin Inc. 612 E. Lake St. Lake Mills, WI 53551 T: 920-648-3000 F: 920-648-3001 Sue Robbins
Handy & Harman (HK) Ltd. 11/F King Fook Bldg. 30-32 Des Voeux Rd., Central, Hong Kong T: 2523-7061 F: 2810-6704 Thomas A Longo	Precious Metals	Handy & Harman 250 Park Ave. New York, NY 10177 T: 212-661-2400 Robert M. Thompson
Harris Semiconductor HK Ltd. 83 Austin Rd. Hong Kong T: 2723-6339 F: 2724-4369 Frank Chao / Kascien Chan	Communications Equipment	Harris Corp. 1025 W. NASA Blvd. Melbourne, FL 32919 T: 407-727-9260 F: 407-727-9644 Larry Smith

China Office	**Product/Service**	**U.S. Head Office**
The Hartford Steam Boiler Inspection Co. 2705 Universal Trade Centre 3 Arbuthnot Rd., Central, Hong Kong T: 2523-1016 F: 2868-1686 C J Steggles	Inspection & Insurance Quality Assurance	Hartford Steam Boiler Inspection Co. PO Box 5024, 1 State St. Hartford, CT 06102 T: 860-722-1866 F: 860-722-5106 R Bjork
Hartmarx Far East Ltd. 714B, Tower I, Chung Sha Wan Plaza Cheung Sha Wan Rd., Kowloon, Hong Kong T: 2310-8128 F: 2310-8096 Dick Pang	Apparel	Hartmarx Corp. 101 N Wacker Dr. Chicago, IL 60606 T: 312-372-6300 F: 312-444-2710 Gilbert L. Bachman
Hasbro Far East Ltd. 1308 World Commercial Centre 11 Canton Rd., Kowloon, Hong Kong T: 2736-8373 F: 2736-5705 Jack Harris	Toys	Hasbro Inc. 1027 Newport Ave. Pawtuket, RI 02862 T: 401-431-8467 F: 401-727-5779 Norman C. Walker
Heller Ehrman White & McAuliffe 1902/08, Peregrine Tower, Lippo Centre 89 Queensway, Hong Kong T: 2526-6381 F: 2810-6242 Simon Luk	Law	Heller Ehrman White & McAulife 333 Bush St., #3100 San Francisco, CA 94104-2878 T: 415-772-6488 F: 415-772-6268 Christopher Armstrong
Hercules China Ltd. Rm. 1907/08 Harcourt House 39 Gloucester Rd., Wanchai, Hong Kong T: 2527-2638 F: 2528-1598 Gerard W Cross	Chemicals	Hercules Inc. 1313 North Market St. Wilmington, DE 19894 T: 302-594-6600 F: 302-594-5400 Harry Tucci / Frazer Reid
Hewlett-Packard Asia Pacific Ltd. 17-21/F Shell Tower, Times Square 1 Matheson St., Causeway Bay, Hong Kong T: 2599-7777 F: 2506-9261 Dick Warmington	Computers Electronic Products	Hewlett-Packard Co. 3000 Hanover St. Palo Alto, CA 94304 T: 650-857-1501 F: 650-857-5518 Manuel F. Diaz
Hill & Knowlton Asia Ltd. 35/F Windsor House 311 Gloucester Rd., Hong Kong T: 2577-9025 F: 2576-3551 Vivian Lines	Public Relations	Hill & Knowlton 466 Lexington Ave. New York, NY 10017 T: 212-885-0300 F: 212-885-0540 Thomas Hoog
Hitachi Data Systems 3909 Lippo Tower, Lippo Centre 89 Queensway, Hong Kong T: 2525-2385 F: 2868-4023 S K Cheung	Computers	Hitachi Data Systems 750 Central Parkway Santa Clara, CA 95050 T: 408-970-1000 F: 408-982-0108 W David Turner / James Balassone
Hoechst Celanese Far East Ltd. 2205 Shell Tower, Times Square 1 Matheson St., Causeway Bay, Hong Kong T: 2506-3133 F: 2506-4010 Thomas Franklin Surrency	Chemicals & Fibers Plastic Products	Hoechst Celanese Corp. 206 N. Rt. 202 Bridgewater, NJ 08807 T: 908-231-2000 Robert H. Walters

- - - - - T: Telephone # - - - - - F: Fax # - - - - - Hong Kong Area Code: (852) - - - - -

China Office	Product/Service	U.S. Head Office
HOK Int'l (Asia/Pacific) Ltd. 33/F The Lee Gardens 33 Hysan Ave., Causeway Bay, Hong Kong T: 2824-1903 F: 2824-1874 Ernest Cirangle	Architectural Services	Hellmuth, Obata & Kassabaum 71 Stevenson St., #2200 San Francisco, CA 94105 T: 415-243-0555 F: 415-882-7763 Patrick MacLeamy
Holiday Inn Worldwide 20/F, Tower III, China Hong Kong City 33 Canton Rd., Kowloon, Hong Kong T: 2736-6955 F: 2735-2005 Bob Poole	Hotel	Holiday Inns Worldwide 3 Ravina Dr. Atlanta, GA 30346 T: 770-604-2000 Richard L Smith
Honeywell Asia Pacific Inc. 3213/25 Sun Hung Kai Centre 30 Harbour Rd., Wanchai, Hong Kong T: 2829-8298 F: 2824-1226 Samuel Hawkins	Industrial Automation Process Controls	Honeywell Inc. 2701 4th Ave. S. Minneapolis, MN 55440-0524 T: 612-951-1000 F: 612-951-0075 Larry W. Stranghoener
Horwath Management Service Ltd. 2001, 20/F, Central Plaza 18 Harbour Rd., Wanchai, Hong Kong T: 2526-2191 F: 2810-0502 Alan Johnson	Accounting Travel & Tourism Executive Search	Horwath International 415 Madison Ave. New York, NY 10017 T: 212-838-5566 F: 212-838-3636 Werner E Rotach
Houghton Oils & Chemicals Co. Ltd. Unit B Full Win Commercail Centre 573 Nathan Rd., Hong Kong T: 2770-8211 F: 2385-3623 Kelvin Chow	Chemicals & Lubricants Hydraulic Fluids	Houghton Int'l Inc. Madison & Van Buren, P. O. Box 930 Valley Forge, PA 19482 T: 610-666-4000 F: 610-666-1376 W. J. Pearcy
HPC Ltd. Unit A, 2/F, Kowloon Teck Ind. Bldg. 26 Wong Chuk Hang Rd., Hong Kong T: 2580-1878 F: 2870-2663 T. W. Lui	Electronic Equipment	PCA Electronics Inc. 16799 Schoenborn St. Sepulveda, CA 91343 T: 818-892-0761 F: 818-894-5791 Morris Weinberg
Hunton & Williams 23/F CITIC Tower 1 Tim Mei Avenue, Central, Hong Kong T: 2841-9100 F: 2841-9191 Edward B. Koehler	Law	Hunton & Williams 951 E Byrd St. East Tower Richmond, VA 23219 T: 804-788-8200 F: 804-788-8218 Thurston R Moore
Hyatt Regency Hong Kong 67 Nathan Rd. Tsim Sha Tsui, Kowloon, Hong Kong T: 2311-1234 F: 2739-8701 Larry Tchou	Hotel	Hyatt Int'l Corp. 200 West Madison St., 39/F Chicago, IL 60606 T: 312-750-1234 F: 312-750-8570 John Wallis
I J K Ltd. 929/33 Star House 3 Salisbury Rd., Kowloon, Hong Kong T: 2735-9165 F: 2735-7493 Yuen Pui Poon	Floral Products	Reliance Trading Corp of America 4949 W. 65th St. Chicago, IL 60638 T: 708-563-2515 F: 708-563-2931 Ira Kleinberg

China Office	Product/Service	U.S. Head Office
IBM China/Hong Kong Corp. 10/F Hong Kong Telecom Tower 979 King's Rd., Quarry Bay, Hong Kong T: 2825-6222 F: 2810-0210 Samuelson Young	Computers	Int'l Business Machines Corp. Rockwood Rd. Sleepy Hallow, NY 10591 T: 914-765-1900 F: 914-332-3753 John Dejoy
ICC (Hong Kong) Ltd. Rm. 1110 New World Office Bldg. West Wing 20 Salisbury rd., Kowloon, Hong Kong T: 2366-1678 F: 2367-1609 Helen Ho	Chemicals	International Chemical Corp. 1887 E. 71st St. Tulsa, OK 74136 T: 918-496-7711 F: 918-492-1719 Brad Thomas
Idab Wamac Pacific Ltd. 1703/04 Trinity House 165-171 Wanchai Rd., Hong Kong T: 2893-9255 F: 2893-0715 Henry Barman	Material Handling Equipment	Ryson International Inc. 161 Enterprise Dr. Newport News, VA 23603 T: 757-888-1010 F: 888-2766 Ole B. Rygh
Industrial Acoustics Co. 2501 Hopewell Centre 183 Queen's Rd., Wanchai, Hong Kong T: 2866-7188 F: 2866-7132 Alvin Leung	Acoustic Products	Industrial Acoustics Co. 1160 Commerce Ave. Bronx, NY 10462 T: 718-931-8000 F: 718-863-1138 John M. Handley
Informix Software (HK) Ltd. 2801 Central Plaza 18 Harbour Rd., Wanchai, Hong Kong T: 2824-0981 F: 2824-1863 Denny Lo Yiu-Chung	Software	Informix Software Inc. 4100 Bohannon Dr. Menlo Park, CA 94025 T: 650-926-6300 F: 650-926-6593 Ken Coulter
Ingersoll-Rand Far East Suite 1201/03 Central Plaza 18 Harbour Rd., Wanchai, Hong Kong T: 2527-0183 F: 2529-5976 Richard Johannessen	Costruction Equipment Ball Bearings Compressers Pumps & Rock Drills	Ingersoll-Rand Co. 200 Chestnut Ridge Rd. Woodcliff Lake, NJ 07675 T: 201-573-0123 F: 201-573-3172 Paul L Bergren
Innovative Time Corp (HK) Ltd. 4/F, 15 Cameron Rd. Tsim Sha Tsui, Kowloon, Hong Kong T:2721-1661 F: 2721-3130 Nicholas Gikas	Watches & Clocks	Innovative Time Corp. 5858 Edison Place Carlsbad, CA 92008 T: 760-438-0595 F: 760-438-4588 Mickey Novak
Institute for Int'l Research (IIR) 20 Siu On Centre 188 Lockhart Rd., Wanchai, Hong Kong T: 2531-6100 F: 2586-1999 Laurence McCormick	Conference Organizer	Institute for Int'l Research (IIR) 708 Third Ave., #4 New York, NY 10017-4201 T: 212-661-3500 F: 212-599-2192 A Oakes
Intel Semiconductor Ltd. 32/F Two Pacific Place 88 Queensway, Hong Kong T: 2844-4555 F: 2868-1989 David A Shrigley	Semiconductor Products Microprocessors	Intel Corp. 2200 Mission College Blvd. Santa Clara, CA 95052 T: 408-765-8080 F: 408-765-5590 David House / Leslie Vadasz

- - - - - T: Telephone # - - - - - F: Fax # - - - - - Hong Kong Area Code: (852) - - - - -

China Office	**Product/Service**	**U.S. Head Office**
Interbold Paciifc Ltd. 192, A-1 Business Centre Kowloon, Hong Kong T: 2595-1126 General Manager	Automated Banking Systems	Diebold Inc. 5995 Mayfair Rd., P. O. Box 8320 Canton, OH 44711 T: 330-489-4000 F: 330-490-4549 Edgar Petersen
Interconex Far East Ltd. 2612/24, Level 26, Metro Plaza, Tower I 223 Hing Fong Rd., Kwai Chong, Hong Kong T: 2480-3122 F: 2428-2881 Phil Hamill	Freight Forwarder	**Interconex, Inc.** 55 Hunter Lane Elmsford, NY 10523 T: 914-593-4200 F: 914-347-0130 Phil Hamill
Intermec East Asia 1603/04 Causeway Bay Plaza I 489 Hennessy Rd., Hong Kong T: 2574-9777 F: 2574-9725 John Roberts	Data Collection Systems	Intermec Technologies Corporation 6001 36th Ave. W., P O Box 4280 Everett, WA 98203 T: 206-348-2600 F: 206-355-9551 Michael Ohanian
International Data Corp Asia Ltd. 2901/02, 29/F, Universal Trade Centre 3 Arbuthnot Rd., Central, Hong Kong T: 2530-3831 F: 2537-7347 Dennis Philbin	Market & Trade Research	International Data Group (IDG) One Exter Plaza Boston, MA 02116 T: 617-534-1200 F: 617-859-8642 Chris McAndrews
International Flavors & Fragrances FE Ltd. 11/F Watson Centre 16 Kung Yip St., Kwai Chung, Hong Kong T: 2427-7021 F: 2480-5391 Todd Rossuck	Cosmetics & Toiletries	International Flavors & Fragrances Inc. 521 W. 57th St. New York, NY 10019 T: 212-765-5500 F: 212-708-7132 Frans Nijnens
International Paper (Far East) Ltd. 2607/18 Shui On Centre 6-8 Harbour Rd., Wanchai, Hong Kong T: 2824-3000 F: 2824-3035 Albert Lau	Paper Products Wood Products	International Paper 2 Manhattanville Rd. Purchase, NY 10577 T: 914-397-1500 F: 914-397-1650 Gerald C. Marterer
Intertek Testing Services (Formerly ETL) 2/F Garment Centre 576 Castle Peak Rd., Kowloon, Hong Kong T: 2746-8600 F: 2785-5487 Raymond Wong	Testing & Inspection Certification Services	Intertek Testing Services (ETL Lab) 3933 US Route 11 Cortland, NY 13045 T: 607-753-6711 F: 607-756-9891 Sheryl Shaffer
Intertrans Cargo Services (HK) Ltd. G/F, 2 Hang Fung Ind. Bldg. 2G Hok Yuen St., Hong Kong T: 2334-7664 F: 2365-7589 Wai Chung Lam	Freight Forwarder	Intertrans Corp. 125 E. John Carpenter Frwy. Irving, TX 75062 T: 214-830-8888 F: 214-830-7488 Carsten S Anderson
ITT Defense & Electronics Int'l 8/F Bank of America Tower 12 Harbour Rd., Central, Hong Kong T: 2584-6120 F: 2537-5655 Thomas C Roberts	Defense Equipment	ITT Defense & Electronics 1650 Tysons Blvd., #1700 McLean, VA 22102-3915 T: 703-790-6300 F: 703-790-6360 Frank Parker

China Office	**Product/Service**	**U.S. Head Office**
J C Penney Purchasing Corp. 1301/09 New T & T Centre 7 Canton Rd., Hong Kong T: 2317-3800 F: 2317-0732 Hal Snell / Philip See	Buying Services Retail Servicing	J C Penney Purchasing Corp. P. O. Box 10001 Dallas, TX 75301-2318 T: 214-431-1000 F: 214-431-9466 Kenneth T. Russo
J P Morgan Securites Asia Ltd. 24/F Edinburgh Tower 15 Queen's Rd., Central, Hong Kong T: 2841-1311 F: 2868-5070 K H Kwok	Investment Banking	J P Morgan & Co. Inc. 60 Wall St. New York, NY 10260 T: 212-648-9528 F: 212-648-5193 Neil Gluckin
J Walter Thompson Co Ltd. 3/F Shui On Centre 6-8 Harbour Rd., Wanchai, Hong Kong T: 2584-4668 F: 2802-4383 Alan Fairnington	Advertising	J Walter Thompson Co. 466 Lexington Ave. New York, NY 10017 T: 212-210-7000 F: 212-210-7066 Burt Manning
Jockey Far East Ltd. 6/F Easey Commercial Bldg. 253-261 Hennessy Rd., Wanchai, Hong Kong T: 2511-1167 F: 2507-3637 Hanson Fung	Apparel & Accessories	Jockey International Inc. 2300 60th St. Kenosha, WI 53140 T: 414-658-8111 F: 414-658-0036 Steven Tolensky / Ed Emma
Johnson & Higgins HK/Far East Ltd. 2118, 21/F, Miramar Tower 1-23 Kimberley Rd., Hong ong T: 2301-7700 F: 2576-6419 Grace Lai	Insurance Brokerage	Johnson & Higgins Inc. 125 Broad St. New York, NY 10004 T: 212-574-7000 F: 212-574-7676 Norman Barham
Johnson & Johnson (HK) Ltd. 13/F, Tower I, Grand Century Place 193 King Edward Rd. W., Hong Kong T: 2738-2888 F: 2738-0572 Tristan de la Rosa	Health Care Products	Johnson & Johnson One Johnson & Johnson Plaza New Brunswick, NJ 08933 T: 908-524-0400 F: 908-214-0332 Willard D. Nielsen
Johnson Controls HK/Int'l Ltd. 1501, 15/F, Devon House, Taikoo Place 979 King's Rd., North Point, Hong Kong T: 2590-0033 F: 2516-5648 Wing-On Yau	Batteries & Plastics Auto Seating Control Systems	Johnson Controls Inc. 5757 N. Green Bay Ave. Milwaukee, WI 53209 T: 414-228-1200 F: 414-228-2077 William P. Killan
Jones Day Reavis & Pogue 29/F Entertainment Bldg. 30 Queen's Rd., Central, Hong Kong T: 2526-6895 F: 2868-5871 William Anthony Stewart	Law	Jones, Day, Reavis & Pouge North Point, 901 Lakeside Cleveland, OH 44114 T: 216-586-3939 F: 216-579-0212 David F. Clossey
Jones International Ltd. 804/06 Tower 1 Cheung Sha Wan Plaza 833 Cheung Sha Wan, Hong Kong T: 2745-8998 F: 2744-0100 Sidney Kimmel	Apparel	Jones Apparel Group Inc. 250 Rittenhouse Circle Bristol, PA 19007 T: 215-785-4000 F: 215-785-1795 Jackwyn Nemerov

China Office	Product/Service	U.S. Head Office
Jordache International (HK) Ltd. 15/F Highgrade Bldg. 117 Chatham Rd., Hong Kong T: 2721-7798 F: 2721-7761 Anissa Ng	Apparel	Jordache Enterprises 1411 Broadway New York, NY 10018-3501 T: 212-643-8400 F: 212-643-8508 Kaaryn Denig
K Mart Far East Ltd. 18/F United Centre 95 Queensway, Hong Kong T: 2823-3111 F: 2527-0109 Tony Vaal	Buying Services	KMART Corp. 3100 W. Big Beaver Rd. Troy, MI 48084 T: 313-643-1000 F: 313-643-5249 Thomas Watkins
Kaye Scholer Fierman Hays & Handler 18/F, 9 Queen's Rd. Central, Hong Kong T: 2845-8989 F: 2845-2389 Franklin D Chu	Law	Kaye Scholer Fierman Hays 425 Park Ave., #8 New York, NY 10022 T: 212-836-8000 F: 212-836-8689 F Freundlich
Keesal, Young & Logan 1603 The Central Mark 287 Queen's Rd., Central, Hong Kong T: 2854-1718 F: 2541-6189 Jon W Zinke	Law	Keesal, Young & Logan 400 Oceangate Ave. Long Beach, CA 90802 T: 562-436-2000 F: 562-436-7416 Michelle Conn
Kepner-Tregoe SEA Ltd. 4/F, Dina House, Ruttonjee Centre 11 Duddell St., Central, Hong Kong T: 2532-8348 David Choo	Management Consulting	Kepner-Tregoe Inc. 17 Research Rd. Skillman, NJ 08558 T: 609-921-2806 F: 609-497-0130 Bill Fellows
Keystone Valves Hong Kong Ltd. 1704 Shanghai Ind. Investment Bldg. 48-62 Hennessy Rd., Hong Kong T: 2861-3078 F: 2527-4607 Jonathan Tan	Valves & Actuators	Keystone Int'l Inc. 9600 W. Gulf Bank Rd., PO Box 40010 Houston, TX 77040 T: 713-937-5355 F: 713-895-4044 Paul Woodward
Kimberly-Clark (Hong Kong) Ltd. 34/F, 311 Gloucester Rd. Hong Kong T: 2334-3361 F: 2362-6309 B Y Lau	Lumber/Paper Products Personal Care Products	Kimberly-Clark Corp. P. O. Box 619100 Dallas, TX 75261 T: 972-281-1200 F: 972-281-1490 Tina S. Barry
Knight-Ridder Financial Asia 708/12 One Pacific Place 88 Queensway, Hong Kong T: 2820-2500 F: 2810-0260 Peter Coker	Newspaper Publishing Information Services	Knight-Ridder Inc. One Herald Plaza Miami, FL 33132 T: 305-376-3800 F: 305-376-3865 Jerome S. Tilis
Knoll Inc. c/o Comer Co Ltd. 801 Eton Tower Hysan Avenue, Hong Kong T: 2881-8734 F: 2895-6385 Valerie Blaisdell	Office Furnishing	The Knoll Group 105 Wooster St. New York, NY 10021 T: 212-343-4000 F: 212-343-4170 Andrew Cogan

China Office	Product/Service	U.S. Head Office
Kodak Export Sales Ltd /Kodak Far East Ltd. Kodak House 1 321 Java Rd., North Point, Hong Kong T: 2564-9333 F: 2565-7474 Janice Koo	Photographic Products	Eastman Kodak Co. 343 State St. Rochester, NY 14650 T: 716-724-4000 F: 716-724-0663 Willy Shih / Robert Smith
Korn/Ferry International (HK) Ltd. 2104 Gloucester Tower, The Landmark Bldg. 15 Queen's Rd., Central, Hong Kong T: 2521-5457 F: 2810-1632 Alan Choi	Executive Search	Korn/Ferry International 1800 Century Park E., #900 Los Angeles, CA 90067 T: 310-552-1834 F: 310-553-6452 Kay Kennedy
KPMG Peat Marwick 8/F Prince's Bldg. 10 Chater Rd., Central, Hong ong T: 2522-6022 F: 2845-2588 Sandor J Weiss	Accounting Consulting	KPMG Peat Marwick 530 Chestnut Ridge Rd. Woodcliff Lake, NJ 07675 T: 201-505-3585 F: 201-505-3411 Timothy Pearson
Kraft General Foods (Asia/Pacific) Ltd. 15/F One Pacific Place 88 Queensway, Hong Kong T: 2848-0800 F: 2525-4930 Victor Chua	Food Products	Kraft Foods Int'l Inc. 800 Westchester Ave. Rye Brook, NY 10573 T: 914-335-2500 F: 914-335-1522 James King / James Ko
Kras Asia Ltd. 1-4/F Kras Asia Industrial Bldg. 79 Hung To Rd., Kwun Tong, Hong Kong T: 2344-4141 F: 2343-4819 Mark W M Parker	Precision Tools Machinery Electronic Components	Kras Corp. 99 Newbold Rd. Fairless Hills, PA 19030 T: 215-736-0981 F: 215-736-8953 Anita Tracey
Kroll Associates (Asia) Ltd. 906/11 Mount Parker House 1111 King's Rd., Taikoo Shing, Hong Kong T: 2884-7788 F: 2568-8505 Stephen G Vickers	Consulting	Kroll Associates 900 Third Ave. New York, NY 10022 T: 212-593-1000 F: 212-593-2631 Dave Rosenthal
Kulicke & Soffa (Asia) Ltd. 21/F Yan Sheng Centre 64 Hoi Yuen Rd., Kwun Tong, Hong Kong T: 2955-3668 F: 2955-3666 Raymond Chan	Semiconductor Products	Kulicke & Soffa Industries Inc. 2101 Blair Mill Rd. Willow Grove, PA 19090 T: 215-784-6000 F: 215-659-7588 Asuri Raghavan / James Chiafery
Kurt Salmon Associates Inc. 1114/15 Ocean Centre 5 Canton Rd., Hong Kong T: 2723-4212 F: 2721-5156 Guido Schild	Management Consultants	Kurt Salmon Associates Inc. 1355 Peachtree St. NE Atlanta, GA 30309 T: 404-892-0321 F: 404-898-9590 John Beddows
Lafitte Garner Ltd. World Finance Centre Hong Kong T: 2375-4880 F: 2375-5300 Stephen H Croll	Toys	Landor Associates 1001 Front St. San Francisco, CA 94111 T: 415-955-1400 F: 415-986-1857 Clay Timon

China Office	Product/Service	U.S. Head Office
Landor Associates 17/F Kin Wick Centre 32 Hollywood Rd., Central, Hong Kong T: 2851-8173 F: 2544-9199 Steve Pask	Corporate Designers	Landor Associates 1001 Front St. San Francisco, CA 94111 T: 415-955-1400 F: 415-986-1857 Clay Timon
Larami Co. Ltd. 910/11 New World Office Bldg. East Wing 24 Salisbury Rd., Kowloon, Hong Kong T: 2367-0161 F: 2722-7050 Peter To	Toys	Larami Ltd. 303 Fellowship Rd. Mt. Laurel, NJ 08054 T: 609-439-1717 F: 609-439-9732 Myung Song
Leach & Garner (HK) Ltd. 2105 Chung Kiu Commercial Bldg. 47-51 Shan Tung St., Kowloon, Hong Kong T: 2770-0323 F: 2780-5231 Dragon Young	Jewelry Products	Leach & Garner Co. 57 John L Dietsch Square N. Attleboro, MA 02761 T: 508-695-7800 F: 508-695-4031 Edwin F Leach II
Learning International (HK) Ltd. 1201/02 Harcourt House 39 Gloucester Rd., Wanchai, Hong Kong T: 2864-6880 F: 2865-1004 Craig Topp	Education	Learning International 680 Wahsington Blvd. Stamford, CT 06094 T: 203-965-8400 F: 203-965-8602 Debra Dinnocenzo
LeaRonal SE Asia Ltd. 207, 2/F, Kafat Bldg. 70-80 Sung Wong Toi Rd., Hong Kong T: 2365-9071 F: 2765-7139 Friedric Hunkizer	Chemicals	LeaRonal Inc. 272 Buffalo Ave. Freeport, NY 11520 T: 516-868-8800 F: 516-868-4781 David Schram
Leo A Daly Pacific Ltd. 10/F, CNAC Group Bldg. 10 Queen's Rd., Hong Kong T: 2567-4321 F: 2885-3507 Richard Woodling	Engineering Services Architectural Services	Leo A Daly 8600 Indian Hills Dr. Omaha, NE 68114 T: 402-391-8111 F: 402-391-7209 John L. Whisler
Leo Burnett Ltd. 6/F Citiplaza 3 14 Taikoo Wan Rd., Quarry Bay, Hong Kong T: 2567-4333 F: 2885-3209 Dennis Wong	Advertising	Leo Burnett Co., Inc. 35 West Wacker Dr. Chicago, IL 60601 T: 312-220-5959 F: 312-220-3299 James G. Oates
Levi Strauss (Far East) Ltd. Units A&B, 10/F, CDW Bldg. 388 Castle Peak Rd., Hong Kong T: 2412-8088 F: 2402-3067 Wan Kong Ting	Apparel	Levi Strauss & Co. 1155 Battery St. San Francisco, CA 94111 T: 415-544-6000 F: 415-501-3939 Joyce Fung
Levi Strauss Eximco Ltd. Units A, B &C, 23/F, CDW Bldg. 388 Castle Peak Rd., Hong Kong T: 2411-9900 F: 2411-5668 Y S Chan	Apparel	Levi Strauss & Co. 1155 Battery St. San Francisco, CA 94111 T: 415-544-6000 F: 415-501-3939 Joyce Fung

China Office	Product/Service	U.S. Head Office
Liebert Asia Ltd. 19/F Causeway Bay Plaza I 489 Hennessy Rd., Hong Kong T: 2572-2201 F: 2831-0114 Victor Ma	Air Conditioning Refrigeration	Liebert Corp. 1050 Dearborn Dr. Columbus, OH 43229 T: 614-888-0246 F: 614-841-6022 Dennis Webb / Joe Filippi
Line Analysis Ltd. 1407B Sea View Estate 2-8 Watson Rd., North Point, Hong Kong T: 2678-5839 Neil G. Sutherland	Instruments	Micrometrics Instrument Corp. One Micrometrics Dr. Norcross, GA 30093 T: 770-662-3660 F: 770-662-3696 Paul Webb / Andrew Sherwood
Linear HK Manufacturing Ltd. 19/F Honour Industrial Centre 6 Sun Yip St., Chaiwan, Hong Kong T: 2557-1133 F: 2897-8584 Nicholas Hung	Security Systems RF Transmitters & Receivers	Linear Corp. 2055 Corte Del Nogal Carlbad, CA 92009 T: 619-438-7000 F: 619-438-7043 Ted Odolecki
Liz Claiborne International Ltd. 8/F Trade Square 681 Cheng Sha Wan Rd., Hong Kong T: 2304-2100 F: 2725-3491 Rick Tsui	Apparel	Liz Claiborne 1441 Broadway New York,NY 10018 T: 212-354-4900 F: 212-626-1594 Robin Scheer-Ettinger
LoBue Associates Inc. 1133 Central Bldg. 1 Pedder St., Central, Hong Kong T: 2841-7758 F: 2810-1868 Chris Zaske	Financial Services	LoBue Associates Inc. 2342 Dolphin Ct. Green Valley, NV 89014 T: 702-898-6940 F: 702-433-4021 Janet Buckstein / Robert Andrzejewski
Lockheed Martin Ltd. / Martin Marietta Inc. Suite 1907 Two Pacific Place 88 Queensway Hong Kong T: 2810-0773 F: 2810-1280 Bernard P Miller	Aerospace/Aviation	Lockeed Martin Corp. 6801 Rockledge Dr. Bethesda, MD 20817 T: 301-897-6275 F: 301-897-6778 Robert Trice, Jr.
Loctite (Asia) Ltd. 2014 Sung Hung Kai Centre 30 Harbour Rd., Wanchai, Hong Kong T: 2827-1223 F: 2827-0525 G Martin Wiley	Industrial Adhesives Sealants Automotive Products	Loctite Corp. 10 Columbus Blvd. Hartford, CT 06106 T: 860-520-5000 F: 860-520-5073 David Freeman
MacDermid Hong Kong Ltd. 9/F Tai Ping Ind. Park 51 Ting Kok Rd., Hong Kong T: 2667-8283 F: 2667-1000 General Manager	Chemicals	MacDermid Inc. 245 Freight St. Waterbury, CT 06702 T: 203-575-5700 F: 203-575-7900 Terrence Copeland / Anita Miller
Maitland-Smith Fine Furnishing Ltd. 2818 Ocean Terminal Tsim Sha Tsui, Hong Kong T: 2317-6610 F: 2317-1000 Emily Chan	Home Furnishing Products	Masco Corp. 21001 Van Born Rd. Taylor, MI 48180 T: 313-274-7400 F: 313-374-6135 George Herrera

China Office	Product/Service	U.S. Head Office
Manhattan Industries (Far East) Ltd. 930 Ocean Centre Harbor City, Kowloon, Hong Kong T: 2337-4111 F: 2352-2427 Nicholas Paolo	Apparel	Salant Corp. 1114 Avenue of the Americas New York, NY 10036 T: 212-221-7500 F: 212-354-3471 Elliott M. Lavigne
Manpower Inc. 1216 Prince's Bldg. Chater Rd., Central, Hong Kong T: 2868-2328 F: 2868-5803 Deborah Morgan	Temporary Help Service	Manpower International Inc. 5301 N. Ironwood Rd., P O Box 2053 Milwaukee, WI 53201-2053 T: 414-961-1000 F: 414-961-3255 Jeffrey Joerres / Joel W Biller
Marriott International Inc. 1603 East Wing, New World Office Bldg. 24 Salisbury Rd., Kowloon, Hong Kong T: 2724-4622 F: 2311-9731 Geoff Garsid	Hotel	Marriott International Inc. 10400 Fernwood Rd. Bethesda, MD 20817 T: 301-380-8990 F: 301-380-8997 Edwin D. Fuller
Mast Industries (Far East) Ltd. 14/F New World Office Bldg. East Wing 24 Salisbury Rd., Kowloon, Hong Kong T: 2734-4213 F: 2724-4736 John R Welch	Apparel	Mast Industries Inc. 100 Old River Rd. Andover, MA 01810 T: 508-794-0660 F: 508-975-6700 Judy Lam
Mastercard Int'l Ltd. 1401/04 Dah Shing Financial Centre 108 Gloucester Rd., Wanchai, Hong Kong T: 2598-0548 F: 2598-4015 Rosaling Tam	Financial Services	Mastercard International 2000 Purchase St. Purchase, NY 10577 T: 914-249-4600 F: 914-249-4151 James A. Cassin
Mattel Toys (HK) Ltd. 11/F South Tower, World Finance Centre Harbour City, Canton Rd., Hong Kong T: 2737-4500 F: 2737-4489 Ron W Drwinga	Toys	Mattel Inc. 333 Continental Blvd. El Segundo, CA 90245 T: 310-252-2000 F: 310-252-2179 Alexander Welch / Larry Morgan
Maxtor Hong Kong Ltd. Rm. 3818 Sun Hung Kai Centre 30 Harbour Rd., Wanchai, Hong Kong T: 2727-5461 F: 2585-4577 Francis K Yu	Magnetic Storage Products	Maxtor Corp. 510 Cottonwood Dr. Milpitas, CA 95035 T: 408-432-1700 F: 408-432-4510 William Roach
May Department Stores Int'l Inc. 15/F South Tower, World Finance Centre Harbour City, Kowloon, Hong Kong T: 2738-5388 F: 2736-2479 Lawrence Chan	Retailing	May Department Stores Co. 611 Olive St. St. Louis, MO 63101 Tel: 314-342-6300 F: 314-342-4461 William D. Edkins
McCann-Erickson (HK) Ltd. 1/F Sunning Plaza 10 Hysan Ave., Causeway Bay, Hong Kong T: 2808-7888 F: 2576-9136 Joop Broeren	Advertising	McCann-Erickson Worldwide 750 Third Ave. New York, NY 10017 T: 212-697-6000 F: 212-867-5177 Marcio Moreira

China Office	**Product/Service**	**U.S. Head Office**
McGraw-Hill Int'l Enterprises Inc. Suite 2309/11, 1 Hung To Rd. Kwun Tong, Kowloon, Hong Kong T: 2730-6640 F: 2730-2085 Jason Ho	Book Publishing	McGraw-Hill Inc. 1221 Avenue of the Americas New York, NY 10020 T: 212-512-2000 F: 212-512-2186 James Glionna
MCI International 3507 Edinburgh Tower, The Landmark Bldg. 15 Queen's Rd., Central, Hong Kong T: 2526-4403 F: 2537-1603 Yen Pao	Telecommunications	MCI International 2 International Dr. Rye Brook, NY 10573 T: 914-934-6100 Jane Levene
McKinsey & Co Inc. 31/F Asia Pacific Finance Tower Citibank Plaza, 3 Garden Rd., Hong Kong T: 2868-1188 F: 2845-9985 Dominic Casserley	Management Consultants	McKinsey & Co. 55 E. 52nd St. New York, NY 10022 T: 212-446-7000 F: 212-446-8575 Stewart Flack
Mearl Corp HK Ltd. Rm. 1001/02 Yuen Foong Centre 150-160 Castle Rd., Yuen Long, Hong Kong T: 2479-5700 F: 2479-0018 Joseph Cheung	Pearlescent Luster Pigments Decorative Iridescent Film Mica & Kaolin Catalyst	Engelhard Corp. 101 Wood Ave. Iselin, NJ 08830 T: 732-205-7125 F: 732-494-9009 Charles Eggert
Medtronic International Ltd. 2002 CC Wu Bldg. 308 Hennessy Rd., Wanchai, Hong Kong T: 2891-4068 F: 2891-6830 Michael J Costello	Medical Products	Medtronic Inc. 7000 Central Ave. NE. Minneapolis, MN 55432 T: 612-514-4000 F: 612-514-4879 Arthur D. Collins, Jr.
Mellon Asia Ltd. 29 Queen's Rd. Hong Kong T: 2878-1030 F: 2810-4594 Ye T. Ho	Trade & Commercial Banking	Mellon Bank NA One Mellon Bank Center Pittsburgh, PA 15258 T: 412-234-5000 F: 412-234-6265 Stewart E. Sutin
Merck Sharp & Dohme (Asia) Ltd. 15/F Caroline Centre 28 Yun Ping Rd., Causeway Bay, Hong Kong T: 2574-4241 F: 2834-5386 Marc Cugnon	Pharmaceuticals	Merck & Co., Inc. One Merck Dr. Whitehouse Station, NJ 08889 T: 908-423-1000 F: 908-423-1043 Attn: Japan Administration WS-2B-80
Merrill Lynch Asia Pacific Ltd. 18/F Asia Pacific Finance Tower 3 Garden Rd., Central, Hong Kong T: 2536-3888 F: 2536-3789 Bob Grievs	Investment Banking Financial Services	Merrill Lynch & Co. World Financial Center North Tower New York, NY 10281 T: 212-449-1000 F: 212-449-7357 Winthrop H. Smith, Jr.
Metron Semiconductor HK Ltd. Unit 5, 5/F, China Overseas Bldg. 139 Hennessy Rd., Wanchai, Hong Kong T: 2891-7128 F: 2574-5800 John Peter Thompson	Semiconductor Products	Fluoroware Inc. 3500 Lyman Blvd. Chaska, MN 55318 T: 612-448-3131 F: 612-448-2950 Stan Geyer

China Office	Product/Service	U.S. Head Office
Metropolitan Life Insurance HK Ltd. 11/F Bank of East Asia Bldg. 10 Des Voeux Rd., Central, Hong Kong T: 2973-4000 F: 2826-9189 Joseph Yau	Insurance	Metropolitan Life Insurance Co. 1 Madison Ave. New York, NY 10010 T: 212-578-2211 F: 212-578-7385 Richard F. Wiseman
Microsemi (Hong Kong) Ltd. 5-7/F Meeco Industrial Bldg. 53-55 Au Pui Wan St., Fo Tan, Hong Kong T: 2692-1202 F: 2691-0544 Felix Lai	Semiconductor Products	Microsemi Corp. 2830 S. Fairview St. Santa Ana, CA 92704 T: 714-979-8220 F: 714-557-5989 T S Andy Yuen / Robert Vecck
Microsoft Hong Kong 11/F City Plaza 4 12 Taikoo Wan Rd., Quarry Bay, Hong Kong T: 2804-4200 F: 2560-6247 Laurie Kan	Software	Microsoft Corp. One Microsoft Way Redmond, WA 98052 T: 206-882-8080 F: 206-883-8101 Charles Stevens / Steven Ballmer
Milbank Tweed Hadley & McCloy 3007 Alexandra House 16-20 Chater Rd., Central, Hong Kong T: 2971-4888 F: 2840-0792 Douglas Tanner	Law	Milbank Tweed Hadley & McCloy 1 Chase Manhattan Plaza New York, NY 10005 T: 212-530-5000 F: 212-530-5219 F Logan
Millipore Asia Ltd. 1401 Cityplaza 4 12 Taikoo Wan Rd., Hong Kong T: 2803-9111 F: 2513-0313 Jean-Paul Mangeolle	Precision Filters Liguid Chromatography Instr.	Millipore Corp. Ashby Rd. Bedford, MA 01730 T: 781-533-6000 F: 781-533-3110 Thomas Anderson
Mobil Oil Hong Kong Ltd. 12/F Ocean Centre, Harbour City Tsim Sha Tsui, Kowloon, Hong Kong T: 2738-4222 F: 2736-8763 George Good	Petroleum Products Petrochemiclas & Chemicals Petroleum Exploration	Mobil Corp. 3225 Gallows Rd. Fairfax, VA 22037-0001 T: 703-846-3000 F: 703-846-4669 Robert Swanson
Molex HK/China Ltd. Block A, 2/F, Shatin Industrial Centre 5-7 Yuen Shun Circuit, Shatin, Hong Kong T: 2637-3111 F: 2637-5990 Sandy Tang	Connectors Electronic Components	Molex Inc. 2222 Wellington Ave. Lisle, IL 60532 T: 630-969-4550 F: 630-969-1352 J Joseph King
Monroe Systems for Business Inc. Rm. 505 Wang Yip Industrial Bldg. 1 Elm St., Kowloon, Hong Kong T: 2390-5351 F: 2789-8733 Phaeson Chung	Office Equipment Business Machines	Monroe Systems for Business Inc. 1000 American Rd. Morris Plains, NJ 07950 T: 201-993-2000 F: 201-993-2643 Robert Lakeland
Monsanto Far East Ltd. 2/F Cityplaza V, Tower III 14 Tai Koo Wan Rd.., Hong Kong T: 2832-8800 F: 2831-9193 Anthony Tan	Chemicals Pharmaceuticals	Monsanto Co. 800 N. Linbergh Blvd. St. Louis, MO 63167 T: 314-694-3316 F: 314-694-3635 Nha D. Hoang

- - - - - T: Telephone # - - - - - F: Fax # - - - - - Hong Kong Area Code: (852) - - - - -

China Office	Product/Service	U.S. Head Office
Montgomery Ward (HK) Ltd. Rm. 901/06 World Commercial Centre Harbour City, 11 Canton Rd., Hong Kong T: 2377-6666 F: 2376-3580 Terry Leung	Retailing	Montgomery Ward & Co Inc. Montgomery Ward Plaza Chicago, IL 60671 T: 312-467-2000 F: 312-467-3975 Al Digangi / John Istwan
Moog Controls Hong Kong Ltd Unit 5, 11/F, Citimark 28 Yuen Shun Circuit, Shatin, Hong Kong T: 2635-3200 F: 2635-4505 General Manager	Precision Controls	Moog Inc. Seneca St. at Jamison Rd. East Aurara, NY 14052 T: 716-652-2000 F: 716-687-4406 Stephen Huckvale
Morgan Guaranty Trust Co of New York 23/F Edinburgh Tower, The Landmark Bldg. 15 Queen's Rd., Central, Hong Kong T: 2841-1311 F: 2868-1473 Martyn Goosen	Banking Financial Services	Morgan Guaranty Trust Co. 60 Wall St. New York, NY 10260 T: 212-483-2323 F: 212-648-5193 Neil Gluckin
Morgan Stanley Asia Ltd. 31/F Three Exchange Square 8 Connaught Place, Central, Hong Kong T: 2848-5200 F: 2845-1012 John Spencer Wadsworth	Investment Banking	Morgan Stanley & Co. 1585 Broadway New York, NY 10036 T: 212-761-4000 F: 212-762-0094 Jeanmarie McFadden
Morrison & Foester 23/F Entertainment Bldg. 30 Queen's Rd., Central, Hong Kong T: 2585-0888 F: 2585-0800 Jonathan Lemberg	Law	Morrison & Foester 345 California St. San Francisco, CA 94104-2675 T: 415-677-7000 F: 415-677-7522 Carl E. Anduri, Jr.
Morton International Inc. Rm. 438, 4/F, Tung Ying Bldg. 100 Nathan Rd., Kowloon, Hong Kong T: 2722-1111 F: 2366-0388 General Manager	Adhesives & Coatings Special Chemicals	Morton International Inc. 100 N. Riverside Plaza Chicago, IL 60606 T: 312-807-2000 F: 312-807-3150 Alan Goldberg
Motorola Asia Pacific Ltd. 34/F NatWest Tower, Times Square 1 Matheson St., Causeway Bay, Hong Kong T: 2966-3000 F: 2506-2454 Richard A Rigsbee	Telecommunications	Motorola Inc. 1303 E. Algonquin Rd. Schaumburg, IL 60196 T: 847-576-5000 F: 847-576-4700 Richard W. Younts
Motorola Semiconductors HK Ltd. Silicon Harbour Centre, 2 Dai King St. Taipo Industrial Estate, Tai Po, Hong Kong T: 2666-8333 F: 2666-6123 Joseph Yiu	Electronic Products	Motorola Inc. 1303 E. Algonquin Rd. Schaumburg, IL 60196 T: 847-576-5000 F: 847-576-4700 Richard W. Younts
MTS Systems (HK) Inc. Rm. 601/02 Golden Gate Commercial Bldg. 136-138 Austin Rd., Kowloon, Hong Kong T: 2301-2200 F: 2722-7240 Vincent P Lei	Testing & Simulation	MTS Systems Corp. 14000 Technology Dr. Eden Prairie, MN 55344-2290 T: 612-937-4000 F: 612-937-4515 Karen Odash

- - - - - T: Telephone # - - - - - F: Fax # - - - - - Hong Kong Area Code: (852) - - - - -

China Office	Product/Service	U.S. Head Office
Nalco Chemical (HK) Ltd. 1806 Tower 6, China Hong Kong City 33 Canton Rd., Kowloon, Hong Kong T: 2736-3033 F: 2736-1317 Peter T Leung	Water Treatment Chemicals Oil Products & Refining	Nalco Chemical Co. One Nalco Center Naperville, IL 60563 T: 630-305-1000 F: 630-305-2900 Stephen D. Newlin
National Semiconductor (HK) Ltd. 13-15/F, Straight Block, Ocean Centre 5 Canton Rd., Kowloon, Hong Kong T: 2737-1800 F: 2736-9931 Michael Burger	Semiconductor Products	National Semiconductor Corp. 2900 Semiconductor Dr. Santa Clara, CA 95052 T: 408-721-5000 F: 408-733-0293 George Chilton / Keith Kolerus
National Starch & Chemical Co. 513/14 Cheung Sha Wan Plaza, Tower II 833 Cheung Sha Wan Rd., Hong Kong T: 2745-7799 F: 2745-7063 Eddie Ng	Adhesives & Sealants Resins & Chemicals Food Products Industrial Starch	National Starch & Chemical Co. 10 Finderne Ave. Bridgewater, NJ 08807-3300 T: 908-685-5000 F: 908-685-5005 R. John Forrest
NCR (Hong Kong) Ltd. 24-25/F Office Tower,Convention Plaza 1 Harbour Rd., Wanchai, Hong Kong T: 2859-6888 F: 2858-2478 Mike Darch	Computers	NCR Corp. 1700 S. Patterson Blvd. Dayton, OH 45479 T: 937-445-2000 F: 937-445-1847 Hideaki Takahashi
Nellcor Ltd. 1602 Evergo House 38 Gloucester Rd., Hong Kong T: 2529-0363 F: 2528-3599 Stanley Carl Lipin	Medical Equipment Safety Instrument	Nellcor Puritan Bennett Inc. 4280 Hacienda Dr. Pleasanton, CA 94588-2719 T: 510-463-4000 F: 510-463-4420 Boudewijn Bollen
New York Life Insurance Worldwide Ltd. 8/F, Ming An Plaza, Phase I 8 Sunning Rd., Causeway Bay, Hong Kong T: 2881-5988 F: 2881-0043 Stan Silberstein	Insurance	New York Life Insurance Co. 51 Madison Ave. New York, NY 10010 T: 212-576-7000 F: 212-576-8145 Richard Wecker / William F Yelverton
Newsweek Inc. 47/F Bank of China Tower 1 Garden Rd., Central, Hong Kong T: 2921-2928 F: 2921-2953 Lam Tang	Publishing	Newsweek Inc. 251 W. 57th St. New York, NY 10019 T: 212-445-4000 F: 212-445-4757 Peter J. Luffman
Nike Hong Kong Ltd. 801/06 Tower II, Enterprise Square 9 Sheung Yuet Rd., Hong Kong T: 2751-4988 F: 2755-4978 Adam T C Koo	Footwear	Nike Inc. 1 Bowerman Dr. Beaverton, OR 97005 T: 503-671-6453 F: 503-671-6300 Hilary Smith
Nordson Application Equipment Inc. Rm. 718 Shatin Galleria 18-24 Shan Mei St., Shatin, Hong Kong T: 2693-0345 F: 2602-0663 Bradley C Davis	Machinery & Parts	Nordson Corp. 11475 Lakefield Dr. Duluth, GA 30097 T: 770-497-3400 F: 770-497-3588 Peg Watkins / Daniel Chen

China Office	Product/Service	U.S. Head Office
Northwest Airlines Inc. 2908 Alexandra House 16-20 Chater Rd., Central, Hong Kong T: 2810-4288 F: 2868-4148 James Webster O'Brien	Airlines	Northwest Airlines 2700 Lone Oak Pkwy. Egan, MN 55112 T: 612-726-2111 F: 612-726-0343 Michael E. Levine
Norwest Bank Minnesota, NA 9/F The Peninsula Office Tower 18 Middle Rd., Kowloon, Hong Kong T: 2315-9500 F: 2721-0044 Kenny Wong	Banking Financial Services	Norwest Corp. Norwest Center, 6th & Marquette Minneapolis, MN 55479 T: 612-667-1234 F: 612-667-4947 Darin P Narayana
Novell Hong Kong Ltd. 4601/05 China Resources Bldg. 26 Harbour Rd., Wanchai, Hong Kong T: 2588-5288 F: 2588-5188 Agnes Ao	Software	Novell Inc. 1555 N. Technology Way Orem, UT 84057 T: 801-222-6000 F: 801-222-7077 Alistair Aitchison
Nynex Network Systems Co. 1306 Two Exchange Square 8 Connaught Place, Central, Hong Kong T: 2844-2688 F: 2810-1422 John DeShaw	Telecommunications	NYNEX Corp. 1095 Avenue of the Americas New York, NY 10036 T: 212-395-2121 F: 212-921-2917 Donald Reed / Patricia Hennebry
Nypro Hong Kong Ltd. Unit B, 8/F, Sun Ping Industrial Bldg. 916-922 Cheung Sha Wan Rd., Hong Kong T: 2745-9723 F: 2745-9707 Nelson Ngai	Plastic Products	NYPRO Inc. 101 Union St. Clinton, MA 01510 T: 508-365-9721 F: 508-365-4352 G Lankton
O'Melveny & Myers 1905 Peregrine Tower, Lippo Center 89 Queensway, Central, Hong Hong T: 2523-8266 F: 2522-1760 Larry Tu	Law	O'Melveny & Myers 54/F, Citicorp Center, 153 E. 53rd St. New York, NY 10022-4611 T: 212-326-2000 F: 212-326-2061 Ko-Yung Tung
Occidental Chemical China/Far East Ltd. Rm. 4106, 41/F, Central Plaza 18 Harbour Rd., Wanchai, Hong Kong T: 2507-2033 F: 2827-9905 Richard John Glover	Chemicals	Occidental Petroleum Corp. 10889 Wilshire Blvd. Los Angeles, CA 90024 T: 310-208-8800 F: 310-443-6688 John Morgan
Ogilvy & Mather (HK) Pte Ltd. 8/F Mount Parker House, Taikoo Shing, 1111 King's Rd., Quarry Bay, Hong Kong T: 2568-0161 F: 2885-3215 Mike Murphy	Advertising Public Relations	Ogilvy & Mather Worldwide Worldwide Plaza, 309 W. 49th St. New York, NY 10019 T: 212-237-4000 F: 212-237-5515 William Gray
Olin Industrial (HK) Ltd. 1111 Peninsula Centre 67 Mody Rd., Kowloon, Hong Kong T: 2366-8303 F: 2367-1309 Peter C C Lo	Chemicals Metals Applied Physics	Olin Corp. 501 Merritt 7 Norwalk, CT 06856 T: 203-750-3000 F: 203-356-3595 Patricia McClean / William M Smith

China Office	Product/Service	U.S. Head Office

China Office

OMC Asia Ltd.
35-47 Tsing Yi Rd.
Tsing Yi Island, Hong Kong
T: 2431-2200 F: 2433-0185
Grainger McFarland

Oracle Systems HK Ltd.
39/F The Lee Gardens
33 Hysan Ave., Causeway Bay, Hong Kong
T: 2865-2626 F: 2865-5206
Pak Wah Pong

Orient Overseas Container Line Ltd.
31/F Harbour Centre
25 Harbour Rd., Wanchai, Hong Kong
T: 2833-3888 F: 2531-8234
Ted Wang

Orion Research Far East Inc.
904 Federal Bldg.
369 Lockhart Rd., Wanchai, Hong Kong
T: 2836-0933 F: 2834-5160
General Manager

Osmonics Asia Pacific Ltd.
201, 2/F, Enterprise Centre
4 Hart Ave., Kowloon, Hong Kong
T: 2311-1829 F: 2721-1466
Claude P Reynaud

Otis Far East Holdings Ltd.
12/F Mount Parker House
111 King's Rd., Quarry Bay, Hong Kong
T: 2567-4411 F: 2885-0054
Vern K Stait

Oxford Products Int'l Ltd.
19/F, Tower 1, Metroplaza
223 Hing Fong Rd., Kwai Chung, Hong Kong
T: 2481-2000 F: 2422-1104
Michael Cheng

Pacific Waste Management Ltd.
917 Sun Hung Kai Centre
30 Harbour Rd., Wanchai, Hong Kong
T: 2827-1383 F: 2827-1541
Thomas G Smith

Pagoda Asia Pacific Ltd.
3/F Two Harbour Front
22 Tak Fung St., Hung Hom, Hong Kong
T: 2621-5151 F: 2621-0888
Howard Herman

Product/Service

Marine Engines
Boats & Accessories

Software

Global Transportation

Industrial Products
Laboratory Products

Fluid Filtration Equipment
Sanitation Controls

Elevators & Escalators

Apparel

Environmental Services

Footwear

U.S. Head Office

Outboard Marine Corp.
100 Sea Horse Dr.
Waukegan, IL 60085
T: 847-689-6200 F: 847-689-7292
Paul Rabe

Oracle Corp.
500 Oracle Parkway
Redwood Shores, CA 94065
T: 650-506-7000 F: 650-506-7200
Raymond Lane / David Roux

OOCL (USA) Inc.
4141 Hacienda Dr.
Pleasanton, CA 94588
T: 510-460-3180 F: 510-460-3109
M. K. Wong / Peter Leng

> **The next edition of
> "American Business in China"
> will be published
> in January, 2000.**

Osmonics Inc.
5951 Clearwater Dr.
Minnetonka, MN 55343
T: 612-933-2277 F: 612-933-0141
Ken E Jondahl

Otis Elevators Co.
10 Farm Springs
Farmington, CT 06032
T: 860-676-6000 F: 860-676-6970
Steve Page

Oxford Industries Inc..
222 Piedmont Ave. NE.
Atlanta, GA 30308
T: 404-659-2424 F: 404-653-1545
Ben B. Blount, Jr.

WMX Technologies Inc.
3003 Butterfield Rd.
Oak Brook, IL 60521
T: 630-572-8800 F: 630-572-0355
Ed Falkman / Patrick Yip

Brown Group Inc.
8300 Maryland Ave.
St. Louis, MO 63105
T: 314-854-4000 F: 314-854-4274
Ronald Durchfort / Donald Damask

China Office	**Product/Service**	**U.S. Head Office**
Paine Webber Int'l Ltd. 32/F Citibank Tower Citibank Plaza, 3 Garden Rd., Hong Kong T: 2842-0600 F: 2509-3939 David King	Stock Brokerage	Paine Webber Group Inc. 1285 Avenue of the Americas New York, NY 10019 T: 212-713-2000 F: 212-713-1054 Joseph Grano / Lynn Waldvogel
Pan Pacific Services Ltd. 2612/24, 26/F, Tower 1, Metroplaza 223 Hing Fong Rd., Kwai Chung, Hong Kong T: 2418-4488 F: 2494-9129 Warren Lam	Removals & Storage Freight Forwarder	**Interconex Inc.** 50 Main St. White Plains, NY 10606 T: 914-328-7600 F: 914-328-7644 Monika Adee
Panduit Hong Kong 3310, 33/F, Tower I, The Gateway 25 Canton Rd., Kowloon, Hong Kong T: 2956-0380 F: 2956-1802 William Yip	Electricical Wiring Products Communication Products	**Panduit Corp.** 17301 Ridgeland Ave. Tinley Park, IL 60477 T: 708-532-1800 F: 708-614-0254 John Kwong / William Wholley
Paradyne Far East Corp. Rm. 901 Wing On Centre 111 Connaught Rd., Central, Hong Kong T: 2543-0083 F: 2541-3767 Cherry Kwan	Telecommunications	Paradyne Corp. 8545 126th Ave. N. Largo, FL 33773 T: 813-530-2000 F: 813-530-2575 Dennis Krutzler
Paramount Cards Asia Ltd. 12A Tsuen Wan Int'l Centre Wang Lung St., Tsuen Wan, Hong Kong T: 2555-1333 F: 2870-0378 Joseph Chai	Greeting Cards	Paramount Cards Inc. 400 Pine St. Pawtucket, RI 02860 T: 401-726-0800 F: 401-723-0920 Linda Flamand
Parker Hannifin Hong Kong Ltd. Unit A, 10/F, Chung Shum Knitting Centre 1-3 Wing Yip St., Hong Kong T: 2428-8008 Joseph Whiteman	Motion Control Products	Parker Hannifin Corp. 17325 Euclid Ave. Cleveland, OH 44112 T: 216-531-3000 F: 216-486-0618 Michael Marrin / Mark Banazak
Parsons Brinckerhoff (Asia) Ltd. 7/F Devon House, Taikoo Place 979 King's Rd., Quarry Bay, Hong Kong T: 2579-8899 F: 2856-9902 Keith Hawksworth	Construction Management Engineering Consultants	Parsons Brinckerhoff Int'l Inc. One Penn Plaza, 2/F New York, NY 10119 T: 212-465-5000 F: 212-465-5096 Robert Prieto
Paul, Weiss, Rifkind, Wharton & Garrison 13/F Hong Kong Club Bldg. 3A Chater Rd., Central, Hong Kong T: 2536-9933 F: 2536-9622 Jerome A Cohen	Law	Paul, Weiss, Rifkind, Wharton 1285 Ave. of the Americas New York, NY 10019 T: 212-373-3000 F: 212-757-3990 Jerome A. Cohen / Jeanette K Chan
Pavilion Investment Ltd. 608 Harbour Centre 1 Hoi Tin St., Kowloon, Hong Kong T: 2334-9488 F: 2764-8711 Andre Rofe	Handbags	Holiday Fair Inc. 1 E. 33rd St. New York, NY 10016 T: 212-725-8227 F: 212-725-0499 S Hedaya

- - - - - T: Telephone # - - - - - F: Fax # - - - - - Hong Kong Area Code: (852) - - - - -

China Office	**Product/Service**	**U.S. Head Office**
Perkin Elmer Hong Kong Ltd. Rm. 1409 Kodak House, Phase II 39 Healthy St. East, North Point, Hong Kong T: 2590-0238 F: 2590-0513 Otto Shek	Scientific Instruments Thermal Spray Coatings	Perkin-Elmer Corp. 761 Main Ave. Norwalk, CT 06859 T: 203-762-1000 F: 203-762-6000 Leslie O'Carmody
Philip Morris Asia Inc. 23/F Two Pacific Place 88 Queensway, Hong Kong T: 2825-1600 F: 2524-6394 Peter L Barnes	Cigaretts	Philip Morris Int'l 800 Westchester Ave. Rye Brook, NY 10573 T: 914-335-1120 F: 914-335-1372 Andreas Gembler
Phillips Petroleum Int'l Inc. 8/F Dina House 11 Duddell St., Central, ong Kong T: 2526-5591 F: 2810-0125 Monizer Fok / Adrian Lee	Oil/Gas Exploration	Phillips Petroleum Co. Plaza Office Bldg. Bartlesville, OK 74004 T: 918-661-6600 F: 918-662-2780 Mike Coffelt
Phillips-Van Heusen Co. 14/F TAL Bldg. 49 Austin Rd., Kowloon, Hong Kong T: 2738-6500 F: 2730-2398 Tony Wong C K	Garment	Phillips-Van Heusen Corp. 1290 Ave. of the Americas New York, NY 10104-0307 T: 212-468-7095 F: 212-468-7184 Ken Wyse
Picker International Inc. Rm. 1303 CC Wu Bldg. 302/08 Hennessy Rd., Wanchai, Hong Kong T: 2892-1238 F: 2838-4302 Stephen Choi	Diagnostic Imaging Eqmt	GE Medical Systems P. O. Box 414 Milwaukee, WI 53201 T: 414-544-3011 Surge Huot / Peter Holman
PictureTel Int'l Corp. Citibank Tower 3 Garden Rd., Hong Kong T: 2821-4700 F: 2821-4800 Peter Woo Kam Lun	Video Conferencing Systems Network Bridging Products	PictureTel Corp. 100 Minuteman Rd. Andover, MA 01810 T: 508-292-5000 F: 508-292-3375 Tom Pesut
Pillsbury Madison & Sutro LLP 603/04, 6/F, Asia Pacific Finance Tower Citibank Plaza, 3 Garden Rd., Hong Kong T: 2509-7100 F: 2509-7188 Timothy Jacobs	Law	Pillsbury Madison & Sutro 235 Montgomery St., #1668 San Francisco, CA 94104 T: 415-983-1000 F: 415-983-1200 D Stanley Rowland
Pinkerton Consulting & Investigation Services 1808 Tower II, The Gateway Bldg. 25 Canton Rd., Kowloon, Hong Kong T: 2956-1888 F: 2956-1111 Stephen J S Payne	Investigative Services Security Services	Pinkerton's Inc. 15910 Ventura Blvd., #900 Encino, CA 91436 T: 818-380-8800 F: 818-380-8997 Mike Stugrin
Pitney Bowes Inc. 1001/02, 10/F, Asia Orient Tower 33 Lockhart Rd., Wanchai, Hong Kong T: 2528-9011 F: 2527-4077 Robert Y Laban	Business Equipment Business Supplies	Pitney Bowes Inc. One Elmcroft Rd. Stamford, CT 06926-0700 T: 203-356-5000 F: 203-351-7574 Meredith B. Fischer

China Office	**Product/Service**	**U.S. Head Office**
Plough Co. Ltd. 23/F Tung Hip Commercial Bldg. 244 Des Voeux Rd., Central, Hong Kong T: 2545-3113 F: 2543-8072 Hui King Yuen	Drug & Cosmetic Products	Plough Inc. 3030 Jackson St., P. O. Box 377 Memphis, TN 38151 T: 901-320-2011 R. Modjeski / R R Mohling
Polaroid Far East Ltd. 32/F Windsor House 311 Gloucester Rd., Hong Kong T: 2894-0333 F: 2895-1382 Joseph O'Leary	Photographic Products	Polaroid Corp. 549 Technology Square Cambridge, MA 02139 T: 781-386-3284 F: 781-386-9333 Carole Uhrich
Polo Ralph Lauren Sourcing Co. 10/F, Unit C, CDW Bldg. 388 Castle Peak Rd., Tsuen Wan, Honng Kong T: 2611-4333 F: 2414-1188 John W Cox	Apparel	Polo Ralph Lauren Corp. 650 Madison Ave. New York, NY 10022 T: 212-318-7000 F: 212-888-5780 Tracy Nelson / Dolores Barrett
PPC Industries 1980 Ltd. 1/F Efficiency House 35 Tai Yau St., Hong Kong T: 2320-8280 F: 2320-3586 General Manager	Fans Electronic Housewares	Windmere Durable Corp. 5980 Miami Lakes Dr. Hialeah, FL 33014 T: 305-362-2611 F: 305-364-0635 Barbara Friedson Garrett
PPG Industries Int'l Inc. Units A2-A3, 13/F, United Centre 95 Queensway, Central, Hong Kong T: 2861-0918 F: 2804-2859 Joe Pinto	Glass Products Automotive Paints Industrial Chemicals Industrial Paints	PPG Industries, Inc. 1 PPG Place Pittsburgh, PA 15272 T: 412-434-3131 F: 412-434-2125 Valentino Buttignol
Praxair Asia Inc. 508/11 Tower II, The Gateway Bldg. 25 Canton Rd., Kowloon, Hong Kong T: 2956-1138 F: 2956-2267 Jose L Travassos	Chemicals	Praxair Inc. 39 Old Ridgebury Rd. Danbury, CT 06810 T: 203-837-2000 F: 203-837-2505 Jose L. Travassos
Precision Fabrics Group Inc. 1307, 13/F, New Treasure Centre 10 Ng Fong St., San Po Kong, Hong Kong T: 2721-2213 F: 2723-1117 Benjamin K T Cheung	Impression Fabric	Precision Fabrics Group Inc. 6012 High Point Rd. Greensboro, NC 27407 T: 910-888-2544 F: 910-888-2524 Dick Reed
Price Waterhouse 22/F Prince's Bldg. Central, Hong Kong T: 2826-2111 F: 2810-9888 Patrick B Paul	Accounting	Price Waterhouse LLP 1177 Ave. of the Americas New York, NY 10020 T: 212-596-7000 F: 212-596-8910 James Daley / Robert Gazzi
Prime Source Holdings Ltd. Yeung Yiu Chung No. 8 Bldg. 20 Wang Hoi Rd., Kowloon, Hong Kong F: 2795-2088 David To	Electronic Products	C & K Components Inc. 57 Stanley Ave. Watertown, MA 02172 T: 617-926-6400 F: 617-926-6846 J Walsh

China Office	**Product/Service**	**U.S. Head Office**
Priority Management (HK) Ltd. One Exchange Square Hong Kong T: 2858-0285 F: 2858-0299 Richard Pearson	Management Consultant	Priority Management Systems Inc. 2035 120th Ave. N.E. Bellevue, WA 98004 T: 206-454-7686 F: 206-454-5506 Erika Herrmann
Procter & Gamble Hong Kong Ltd. 6/F Shui On Centre 6-8 Harboutr Rd., Wanchai, Hong Kong T: 2582-9333 F: 2802-4267 Brad Casper	Consumer Products	Procter & Gamble Co. 1 Procter & Gamble Plaza, PO Box 599 Cincinnati, OH 45201-0599 T: 513-983-1100 F: 513-983-9369 Alan G. Lafley
Prudential Asia Investments Ltd. 32/F Alexandra House 18 Chater Rd., Central, Hong Kong T: 2844-1000 F: 2868-0195 Victor K Fung	Insurnace	Prudential Insurance Co of America 751 Broad St., 16/F Newark, NJ 07102 T: 201-802-6000 F: 201-802-7486 Roger Lawson
Prudential-Bache Securities (HK) Ltd. 40/F Asia Pacific Finance Tower 3 Garden Rd., Central, Hong Kong T: 2841-2800 F: 2841-2881 Desmond Liu	Fund Management	Prudential Securities Inc. 199 Water St. New York, NY 10292 T: 212-214-1000 Michael Madigan
Pulse Components Ltd. 19/F China United Plaza 1008 Tai Nan W. St., Hong Kong T: 2788-6588 F: 2776-1055 Maria Fung	LAN Products	Pulse Engineering Inc. 12220 World Trade Dr., P O Box 12235 San Diego, CA 92112 T: 619-674-8100 F: 619-674-8334 Bill Fister
Pypun Group Consultants Ltd. 301 Asian House 1 Hennessy Rd., Wanchai, Hong Kong T: 2866-3688 F: 2529-5056 Hugh D McBride	Engineering Services	Brown & Root Inc. 4100 Clinton Dr. Houston, TX 77020 T: 713-676-3011 F: 713-676-4109 Susan Moore
Quaker Chemical Ltd. 2603, 26/F East Asia Aetna Tower 308 Des Voeux Rd., Central, Hong Kong T: 2854-3311 F: 2854-2320 Daniel S. Ma	Chemicals	Quaker Chemicals Corp. Elm & Lee Streets Conshohocken, PA 19428-0809 T: 610-832-4000 F: 610-832-8682 Daniel S. Ma
Quill Co (Far East) Ltd. 20/F Tung Ning Bldg. 2 Hiller St., Central, Hong Kong T: 2545-4423 F: 2854-0456 Michael Woody	Trading	Quill Co. Inc. 2080 Plainfield Pike Cranston, RI 02921 T: 401-946-0030 F: 401-946-0358 Edward Wong
R J Reynolds Int'l Ltd. / RJR Nabisco Ltd. 7/F Sung Hung Kai Centre 30 Harbour Rd., Wanchai, Hong Kong T: 2585-9211 F: 2827-5807 T A McCoy	Agricultural Products	RJR Nabisco Holdings Corp.. 1301 Ave. of the Americas New York, NY 10019 T: 212-258-5600 F: 212-969-9173 Jason H. Wright

China Office	Product/Service	U.S. Head Office
R R Donnelley / Leefung-Asco (HK) Ltd. 10/F Wing On House 71 Des Voeux Rd., Central, Hong Kong T: 2522-7746 F: 2524-2977 John G Gottman	Printing & Publishing	R R Donnelley & Sons Co. 77 W. Wacker Dr. Chicago, IL 60601 T: 312-326-8000 F: 312-326-8543 Steven J. Baumgartner
Ralston Purina International 21/F Devon House, Taikoo Place 979 King's Rd., Quarry Bay, Hong Kong T: 2922-2489 F: 2563-7954 J Stephen Crotty	Consumer Products	Ralston Purina International Checkboard Square St. Louis, MO 63164 T: 314-982-3000 F: 314-982-2752 Jim von der Heydt
Rank Xerox (Hong Kong) Ltd. 8/F Cityplaza 3 14 Taikoo Wan Rd., Hong Kong T: 2513-2888 F: 2560-6433 Allan Lin	Business Machines	Xerox Corp. 800 Long Ridge Rd., P O Box 1600 Stamford, CT 06904 T: 203-968-3000 F: 203-968-4458 Allan E. Dugan
Raychem (Hong Kong) Ltd. 601 South Tower, World Finance Tower Harbour City, Kowloon, Hong Kong T: 2738-3388 F: 2735-1185 Wendy Lee	Telecommunications	Raychem Corp. 300 Constitution Dr. Menlo Park, CA 94025 T: 650-361-3333 F: 650-361-7377 Scott Wylie
Rayovac Far East Ltd. Rm. 720/23 Hollywood Plaza 610 Nathan Rd., Mongkok, Hong Kong T: 2782-2343 F: 2782-4091 Stephen So	Watches & Clocks Trading	Rayovac Corp. 601 Rayovac Dr. Madison, WI 53711 T: 608-275-3340 F: 608-275-4577 Roger Warren
Reader's Digest Association Far East Ltd. 3 Ah Kung Ngam Village Rd. Shaukiwan, Hong Kong T: 2884-5678 F: 2885-2805 Steve Wiles	Publishing	Reader's Digest Associations Inc. P. O. Box 235 Pleasantville, NY 10570 T: 914-238-1000 F: 914-238-5324 Peter Davenport
Reebok Trading (Far East) Ltd. 1303/12 Tower II The Gateway Bldg. 25-27 Canton Rd., Hong Kong T: 2956-3883 F: 2521-1111 Polly Chan	Footwear	Reebok International Ltd. 100 Technology Center Dr. Stoughton, MA 02072 T: 617-341-5000 F: 617-341-7402 Bruce Nevins
Republic National Bank of New York 6/F Jardine House 1 Connaught Place, Central, Hong Kong T: 2526-6941 F: 2845-9095 Ian Pollock	Banking	Republic New York Corp. 452 Fifth Ave. New York, NY 10018 T: 212-525-6100 F: 212-525-5678 Joseph DePaolo
Respironics Hong Kong Ltd. 3/FMicrontron Bldg. 38 Hung To Rd., Hong Kong T: 2343-4218 F: 2343-2680 David Groll	Medical Products	Respironics Inc. 1001 Murry Ridge Dr. Murrysville, PA 15668-8550 T: 412-733-0200 F: 412-733-0299 Robert Crouch / Kam-Kwen Ng

China Office	Product/Service	U.S. Head Office
Review Publishing Co Ltd. 25/F Citicorp Centre 18 Whitfield Rd., Causeway Bay, Hong Kong T: 2508-4300 F: 2503-1530 Karen Mullis	Publishing	Dow Jones & Co. Inc. 200 Liberty St. New York, NY 10281 T: 212-461-2000 F: 212-416-2885 Karen House / James Friedlich
Revlon (Hong Kong) Ltd. 3/F Etaon Tower 8 Hysan Ave., Causeway Bay, Hong Kong T: 2576-4042 F: 2576-2617 Meyer Hoffman	Cosmetic Products	Revlon Inc. 625 Madison Ave. New York, NY 10022 T: 212-572-5000 Annette M. McEvey
Reynolds Aluminum Asia Pacific 2416 Sun Hung Kai Centre 30 Harbour Rd., Wanchai, Hong Kong T: 2827-4369 F: 2827-5207 Gresham P Sackett	Metal Products	**Reynolds Int'l Inc.** 6601 West Broad St. Richmond, VA 23261 T: 804-281-2000 F: 804-281-3695 Gene Voss
Rhone-Poulenc Asia Ltd. 18/F Manulife Tower 169 Electric Rd., North Point, Hong Kong T: 2570-0221 F: 2887-1874 Daniel Grout	Pharmaceuticals	Rhone-Poulenc Rorer Inc. 500 Arcola Rd., P. O. Box 1200 Collegeville, PA 19426-0107 T: 215-454-8000 F: 215-454-3812 Alain Audubert
Rich Products Corp. 1102 CRE Bldg. 303 Hennessy Rd., Hong Kong T: 2529-3880 F: 2520-0710 Jay Gmerek	Non-Dairy Products	Rich Products Corp. 1150 Niagara St. Buffalo, NY 14213 T: 716-878-8000 F: 716-878-8765 Richard Ferranti
Ritz-Carlton Hong Kong 3 Connaught Rd. Central, Hong Kong T: 2877-6666 F: 2877-6778 Des Pugson	Hotel	Ritz-Carlton Hotels 3414 Peachtree Rd. NE, #300 Atlanta, GA 30326 T: 404-237-5500 F: 404-365-9643 Dan Collins
Rockwell Int'l Ltd. / Rockwell Overseas Corp. Rm. 1308/10 Harbour Centre 25 Harbour Rd., Wanchai, Hong Kong T: 2827-0181 F: 2827-6488 Jonathan Lam	Automotive Products Aerospace/Aviaition	Rockwell Int'l Corp. 600 Anton Blvd., #700 Costa Mesa, CA 92628-5090 T: 714-424-4320 F: 714-424-4360 Derek Wimmer
Rogers Tool Works Inc. 1903 Shiu Lam Bldg. 23 Luard Rd., Wanchai, Hong Kong T: 2520-6978 F: 2529-9972 Martyn Russell	Rotary Cutting Tools	Greenfield Industries Inc. 470 Old Evans Rd. Evans, GA 30809 T: 706-863-7708 F: 706-860-8559 Mark Richards / John Woodridge
Rohm & Haas (Far East) Ltd. 17A On Hing Bldg. 1 On Hing Terrace, Central, Hong Kong T: 2868-1383 F: 2845-2555 Albert Pow	Chemicals	Rohm & Haas Co. 100 Independence Mall West Philadelphia, PA 19106 T: 215-592-3000 F: 215-592-3377 Rajiv L. Gupta

China Office	Product/Service	U.S. Head Office
Rubbermaid Int'l Sales Corp. 4404/05 Hopewell Centre 183 Queen's Rd. E., Hong Kong T: 2865-1102 F: 2865-0389 Alex Lou Kwok-Yau	Plastic Products	Rubbermaid Inc. 1147 Akron Rd. Wooster, OH 44691 T: 330-264-6464 F: 330-287-2864 L. B. Ahrens, Jr.
Russell Reynolds Associates Inc. 3801/04 Edinburgh Tower 15 Queen's Rd., Central, Hong Kong T: 2523-9123 F: 2845-9044 Raymond C P Tang	Executive Search	Russell Reynolds Associates Inc. 200 Park Avenue, #2300 New York, NY 10166 T: 212-351-2000 F: 212-370-0896 Raymond C. P. Tang
Rust Asia Pacific Ltd. 3/F Devon House, Taikoo Place 979 King's Rd., Quarry Bay, Hong Kong T: 2590-9333 F: 2590-9897 Patrick Yip	Environmental Pollution Engineering Service	WMX Technologies Inc. 3003 Butterfield Rd. Oak Brook, IL 60561 T: 630-572-8800 F: 630-572-0355 Ed Falkman / Patrick Yip
S C Johnson Ltd. 20/F OTB Bldg. 160 Gloucester Rd., Wanchai, Hong Kong T: 2575-5655 F: 2838-1807 Teddy Hui	Consumer Products Specialty Chemicals	S C Johnson & Son Inc. 1525 Howe St. Racina, WI 53403 T: 414-631-2000 F: 414-260-2632 John R. Buerkle
Saatchi & Saatchi 51/F Sung Hung Kai Centre 30 Harbour Rd., Wanchai, Hong Kong T: 2582-3333 F: 2802-0213 Michael John Cooper	Advertsing	Saatchi & Saatchi Worldwide 375 Hudson St. New York, NY 10014 T: 212-463-2000 F: 212-463-9855 Joe Cronin / Dick O'Brien
Salomon Brothers Hong Kong Ltd. 20/F Three Exchange Square Central, Hong Kong T: 2501-2000 F: 2501-8146 Robert Morse	Investment Banking Fund Management	Salomon Brothers Inc. 7 World Trade Center, 40/F New York, NY 10048 T: 212-783-7000 F: 212-783-2107 Edward White
Sandra Kan Industrial (1981) Ltd. 1/F Ching Cheong Industrial Bldg. 1-7 Kwai Cheong Rd., Hong Kong T: 2429-7631 F: 2480-2702 Jay Kramer	Toys	Life Like Products Inc. 1600 Union Ave. Baltimore, MD 21211 T: 410-889-1023 F: 410-889-0503 Jay Kramer / Ting Wai Shing
Sara Lee Corp. 17/F Allied Kajima Bldg. 138 Gloucester Rd., Wanchai, Hong Kong T: 2820-8600 F: 2827-2360 John Hannsz	Apparel	Sara Lee Corp. 3 First National Plaza, 70 W Madison Chicago, IL 60602 T: 312-726-2600 F: 312-726-3712 Jeffrey Smith
Schenker (Hong Kong) Ltd. 3801/05 China Resources Bldg. 26 Harbour Rd., Wanchai, Hong Kong T: 2585-9688 F: 2827-5363 Dieter Borkert	Freight Forwarder	**Schenker Int'l Inc.** 150 Albany Ave. Freeport, NY 11520 T: 516-377-3000 F: 516-377-3100 Mike Bujold

China Office	**Product/Service**	**U.S. Head Office**
Schering-Plough / SOL Ltd. 19/F Citicorp Centre 18 Whitfield Rd., Causeway Bay, Hong Kong T: 2578-9811 F: 2807-2423 Susan Oh Young-Mee	Pharmaceuticals	Schering-Plough Corp. USA 1 Giralda Farms Madison, NJ 07940-1000 T: 201-822-7000 F: 201-822-7048 Russell Elliott
Schlumberger Industries Int'l 3204/05, Tower 2, The Gateway Bldg. 25-27 Canton Rd., Kowloon, Hong Kong T: 2956-3331 F: 2956-1055 Jack Lui	Quality Control Oilfield Services	Schlumberger Ltd. 277 Park Ave., 44/F New York, NY 10172 T: 212-350-9400 F: 212-350-8129 Victor E. Grijalva
Scientific Atlanta Suite 56/57, 51/F, New Henry House 10 Ice House St., Central, Hong Kong T: 2522-5059 F: 2522-5624 Bob Burkholder	Telecommunications Test & Measurement Device	Scientific Atlanta Inc. 1 Technology Pkwy. S. Norcross, GA 30092 T: 770-903-5000 F: 770-903-4617 John Buckett / Donald Upton
Sea-Land Service Inc. 13/F Asia Terminal Centre B, Berth 3 Kwai Chung Container Terminal, Hong Kong T: 2489-4888 F: 2489-8100 William F. Flynn	Shipping	Sea-Land Service Inc. 6000 Carnegie Blvd. Charlotte, NC 28209 T: 704-571-2000 F: 704-571-4613 Clint Eisenhauer
Sealed Air (Far East) Ltd. 9/F Wing Kwai Ind. Bldg. 2-8 Wang Wo Tsai St., Hong Kong T: 2439-7600 F: 2407-3385 Eric Lau	Packaging Products	Sealed Air Corp. Park 80 E. Saddle Brook, NJ 07663 T: 201-791-7600 F: 201-703-4205 Mary Coventry
Sears Buying Services Inc. 11/F New World Office Bldg. East Wing 24 Salisbury Rd., Kowloon, Hong Kong T: 2733-6233 F: 2723-7197 Jeffrey Macho	Buying Services	Sears, Roebuck & Co. 3333 Beverly Rd. Hoffman Estates, IL 60179 T: 847-286-1933 F: 847-286-5039 John Costello / Douglas Liu
Selectronics Corp. 804 Arion Commercial Centre 2-12 Queen's Rd. W., Hong Kong T: 2366-4207 F: 2723-6722 Ray Kalani	Portable Phone Dialers	Selectronics Inc. 2 Tobay Village Office Park Pittsford, NY 14534 T: 716-248-3875 F: 716-248-3868 Roy Haythorne
Sentrol Life Safety Asia Pacific 2509/11 Paul Y Centre 51 Hung To Rd., Hong Kong T: 2142-5896 F: 2142-5063 Michael Wong	Fire & Burglar Alarms Smoke Detectors	Sentrol Inc. 12345 S. W. Leveton Dr. Tualatin, OR 97062 T: 503-692-4052 F: 503-691-7564 Martha Florez
Sequent Computer Systems Inc. 2301, 23/F, China Resources Bldg. 26 Harbour Rd., Hong Kong T: 2802-3133 F: 2802-1800 David Runacres	Computers	Sequent Computer Systems Inc. 15450 SW Koll Pkwy. Beaverton, OR 97006 T: 503-626-5700 F: 503-578-9890 Jeff Pancottine

China Office	Product/Service	U.S. Head Office
SGS Hong Kong Ltd. Block J, 7/F, Kaiser Estate, Phase 2 51 Man Yue St., Kowloon, Hong Kong T: 2364-2272 F: 2764-3126 John McHale	Testing & Inspection Certification Services	SGS U.S. Testing Co., Inc. 291 Fairfield Ave. Fairfield, NJ 07004 T: 973-575-5252 F: 973-575-7175 Dave Downic
Shakespear (Hong Kong) Ltd. 6/F, Int'l Industrial Bldg. 175 Hoi Bun Rd., Kowloon, Hong Kong T: 2341-1110 F: 2341-9456 Robert Ni	Fishing Tackles Sporting Goods	Anthony Industries Inc. 4900 S. Eastern Ave. Los Angeles, CA 90040 T: 213-724-2800 B I Forester
Shelcore Hong Kong Ltd. 9/F Wah Yiu Industrial Centre 30-32 Au Pui Wan St., Hong Kong T: 2699-9668 F: 2601-1830 Cyril Wong	Toys	Shelcore Inc. 347 Elizabeth Ave. Somerset, NJ 08873 T: 908-777-0700 S Greenberg
Sheraton Asia Pacific Corp. 9/F New World Office Bldg. West Wing Tsim Sha Tsui, Kowloon, Hong Kong T: 2369-6562 F: 2721-7083 Phil Lee	Hotel	ITT Shearton Corp. 60 State St. Boston, MA 02109 T: 617-367-3600 F: 617-367-5543 Dolores Sanchez
Sherwood Medical (HK) Ltd. 2601, 26/F, K Wah Centre 191 Java Rd., North Point, Hong Kong T: 2574-3251 F: 2838-0749 James Lam	Medical Products	Sherwood 1915 Olive St. St. Louis, MO 63103 T: 314-241-7648 F: 314-436-7574 D. G. Thomas
Shipley Chemicals (Hong Kong) Ltd. Unit 1303 New Town Tower 10-18 Pok Hok Ting St., Hong Kong T: 2694-0661 F: 2694-0939 May Lee	Chemicals Electronic Products	Shipley Co. Inc. 455 Forest St. Marborough, MA 01752 T: 508-481-7950 F: 508-229-7607 Michael Foster
Shirtailors Ltd. 6/F Wai Shun Ind. Bldg. 5 Yuk Yat St., To Kwan, Hong Kong T: 2362-0349 F: 2764-5112 Agnes Lai	Apparel	Cardeens Inc. 5128 Valley Blvd. Los Angeles, CA 90032 T: 213-227-1983 F: 213-221-2004 Joy Swift
Signode Hong Kong Ltd. 4/F Din Wai Industrial Bldg. 13 On Chuen St., San Ling, Hong Kong T: 2785-2328 F: 2786-2866 William Yau	Packaging Systems	ITW Signode 3600 W. Lake Ave. Glenview, IL 60025 T: 847-724-6100 F: 847-724-5910 Frank Ptak
Silicon Graphics Ltd. 513/22 Hong Kong Industrial Tech. Centre 72 Tat Chee Ave., Kowloon, Hong Kong T: 2784-3111 F: 2778-9100 Jeff Lam	Computers	Silicon Graphics Inc. 2011 N. Shoreline Blvd., PO Box 7311 Mountain View, CA 94039 T: 415-960-1980 F: 415-961-0595 Teruyasu Sekimoto

China Office	**Product/Service**	**U.S. Head Office**
Simplex Asia Suite 1-6, 20/F, Tower II, Enterprise Square 9 Sheung Rd., Kowloon, Hong Kong T: 2796-6133 F: 2795-3006 Mark Chan	Fire Alarms	Simplex Time Recorder Co. Simplex Plaza Gardner, MA 01441-0001 T: 508-632-2500 F: 508-632-8027 Jim Spicer
Skadden Arps Slate Meagher & Flom Peregrine Tower 89 Queensway, Hong Kong T: 2820-0700 F: 2820-0727 Raymond W Vickers	Law	Skadden Arps Slate Meagher & Flom 919 Third Ave. New York, NY 10022 T: 212-735-3000 F: 212-735-2000 William P. Frank
Smart Shirts Ltd. 55 King Yip St. Kwun Tong, Kowloon, Hong Kong T: 2797-5111 F: 2343-2715 Jesse Zee	Apparel	Kellwood Co. 600 Kellwood Parkway Chesterfield, MO 63017 T: 314-576-3100 F: 314-576-3462 William J McKenna
Sonca Products Ltd. 16/F Kwong Sang Hong Centre 151-153 Hoi Bun Rd., Kowloon, Hong Kong T: 2357-0322 F: 2357-0876 K C Leung	Lighting Equipment	Ralston Purina Int'l Checkerboard Square St. Louis, MO 63164 T: 314-982-3000 F: 314-982-2752 Jim von der Heydt
Southern Electric Int'l 1401 Two Exchange Square 8 Caonnuaght Place, Hong Kong T: 2523-6630 F: 2523-7866 Ray Harris	Electric Utility	The Southern Co. 64 Perimeter Center E. Atlanta, GA 30346 T: 770-393-0650 F: 770-506-0569 Ken Lange / David Retcliffe
Spencer Stuart & Associstes (HK) Ltd. 17/F Bank of East Asia Bldg. 10 Des Voeux St., Central, Hong Kong T: 2521-8373 F: 2810-5246 Martin Y Tang	Executive Search	Spencer Stuart 401 N. Michigan Ave. Chicago, IL 60611 T: 312-822-0088 Dayton Ogden
Sprint Int'l Communications HK Ltd. 1212 Two Pacific Place 88 Queensway, Hong Kong T: 2810-7373 F: 2810-8810 Braham Singh	Telecommunications	Sprint International P. O. Box 11315 Kansas City, MO 64112 T: 800-829-0965 Andres Bande
Standard Motors Products (HK) Ltd. 6/F Keep Mount Centre 9-11 Shing Wan Rd., Shatin, Hong Kong T: 2605-5311 F: 2695-3739 Chirk-Wing Mok	Automotive Products	Standard Motor Products Inc. 37-18 Northern Blvd. Long Island City, NY 11101-1616 T: 718-392-0200 F: 718-472-0122 Luis Cartaya
State Street Asia Ltd. 32/F Two Exchange Square 8 Connaught Place, Central, Hong Kong T: 2840-5388 F: 2845-9020 Thomas E. Lynch	Banking	State Street Boston Corp. 225 Franklin St. Boston, MA 02110 T: 617-786-3000 F: 617-664-6531 Jacques-Philippe Marson

China Office	Product/Service	U.S. Head Office
Steelcase Inc. World Wide House Hong Kong T: 2520-0160 F: 2529-6001 James Holson	Office Furniture Interior Designers	Steelcase Inc. PO Box 1967, 901 44th St. SE Grand Rapids, MI 49508 T: 616-247-2710 Mark Greiner / Jerry K Myers
Stelis Corp. 301/02 Kodak House II 39 Healthy St. E., Hong Kong T: 2858-5485 F: 2857-5720 Dominic Yin	Medical Equipment Surgical Tables Infection Control Equipment	Amsco International 5960 Heisley Rd. Mentor, OH 44060 T: 440-354-2600 F: 440-639-4459 John Snyder
Stepan Co. House 15 61 Deep Water Bay Rd., Hong Kong T: 2592-7116 F: 2592-7872 General Manager	Chemicals	Stepan Co. 22 W. Frontage Rd. Northfield, IL 60093 T: 847-446-7500 F: 847-501-2443 Herman Hoepermans
Stewart & Stevenson Services (HK) 804/10 Austin Tower 22-26 Austin Ave., Kowloon, Hong Kong T: 2739-0063 F: 2739-2631 Jeff McClellan	Diesel & Turbine Systems	Stewart & Stevenson Services Inc. 2707 N Loop W. Houston, TX 77008 T: 713-868-7700 F: 713-868-7692 C. Jim Stewart III
Stratus Computer (HK) Ltd. 801 Central Plaza 18 Harbour Rd., Wanchai, Hong Kong T: 2844-5200 F: 2810-5227 Gary H Okimoto	Computer Vendor	Stratus Computer 55 Fairbanks Blvd. Marlboro, MA 01752-1298 T: 508-460-2000 F: 508-481-8945 Gary Okimoto / Shirley Yee
Sullivan & Cromwell 28/F, 9 Queen's Rd. Central, Hong Kong T: 2826-8688 F: 2522-2280 Donald C Walkovik	Law	Sullivan & Cromwell 125 Broad St. New York, NY 10004 T: 212-558-4000 F: 212-558-3588 Charlie Osborne
Summit Asia Ltd. B502 Seaview Estate 2-8 Watson Rd., North Point, Hong Kong T: 2571-4231 F: 2807-1260 Richard Chan	Pharmaceuticals	Summit Industrial Corp. 600 Third Ave. New York, NY 10016 T: 212-490-1100 Leonard Chan
Sun Microsystems of California Ltd. 22/F Shui On Centre 8 Harbour Rd., Wanchai, Hong Kong T: 2802-4188 F: 2802-8655 Daniel Yu	Computers	Sun Microsystems 2550 Garcia Ave. M/S: UMPK01-16 Mountian View, CA 94043 T: 415-960-1300 F: 415-969-9131 Tim Dwyer / Bob MacRitchie
Sunrider International (HK) Ltd. 5/F Mirror Tower 61 Mody Rd., Kowloon, Hong Kong T: 2368-0141 F: 2368-2490 Man-Tat Tsui	Health Products Nutritional Supplement	Sunrider International 1625 Abalone Ave. Torrance, CA 90501-2860 T: 310-781-3808 F: 310-222-9273 Tei Fu Chen

- - - - - T: Telephone # - - - - - F: Fax # - - - - - Hong Kong Area Code: (852) - - - - -

China Office	**Product/Service**	**U.S. Head Office**
Sybase Hong Kong Ltd. 33/F Nat West Tower, Times Square 1 matheson St., Causeway Bay, Hong Kong T: 2506-6000 F: 2506-6050 Wain Brian Beard	Computers	Sybase, Inc. 6475 Christie Avenue Emeryville, CA 94608 T: 510-596-3500 F: 510-658-9441 Yvonne Van Leeuewen
Tandem Computers Hong Kong Ltd. 3701/05 China Resources Bldg. 26 Harbour d., Wanchai, Hong Kong T: 2802-0288 F: 2802-0025 Sung Wook Khang	Computers	Tandem Computers Inc. 19333 Valco Pkwy. Cupertino, CA 95014 T: 408-725-6000 F: 408-285-4545 Gerald Peterson / Scott Thompson
Tandy Radio Shack Ltd. Blk. B, 9/F, Veristrong Ind. Centre 34-36 Au Pui Wan St., Hong Kong T: 2601-4660 F: 2694-0497 Kenji A Nishikawa	Electronic Products	Tandy Corp. 100 Throckmorton, #1800 Ft. Worth, TX 76102 T: 817-390-3700 F: 817-390-3500 Ronald Parrish
TCL Technology Ltd. 7/F Kingsfield Centre 18 Shell St., North Point, Hong Kong T: 2891-3281 F: 2891-6335 Ting Ming Lam	Electronic Products Data Communications Eqmt	TCL Inc. 41829 Albrae St. Fremont, CA 94538 T: 510-657-3800 F: 510-490-5814 Mabel Yuen
Technomic Consultants FE Ltd. 19/F, 80 Gloucester Rd. Hong Kong T: 2511-2831 F: 2519-9503 Tan Wai Kee	Consultants	Technomic Consultants Int'l 500 Skokie Blvd. Northbrook, IL 60062 T: 847-291-1212 S Rasin
Tektronix China/Hong Kong Ltd. 36/F The Lee Gardens 33 Hysan Ave., Causeway Bay, Hong Kong T: 2585-6688 F: 2598-6260 Daniel Brophy	Electronic Products	Tektronix Inc. 26660 SW Parkway Wilsonville, OR 97070 T: 503-627-7111 F: 503-685-4042 Timothy Thorsteinson / John Vold
Telcom Semiconductor HK Ltd. 1/F, Jing Wah Bldg., 10 Sam Chuk St. San Po Kong, Kowloon, Hong Kong T: 2324-0122 F: 2351-2344 Jerry S H Wang	Semiconductor Products	Telcom Semiconductor Inc. 1300 Terra Bella Ave. Mountain View, CA 94043 T: 415-968-9241 F: 415-967-1590 Gary Pinelli / Jerry Wang
Teledyne Hong Kong Ltd. 918 New World Centre East Wing 24 Salibury Rd., Kowloon, Hong Kong T: 2368-5231 F: 2369-8978 Hau-Tak Kwan	Aerospace/Aviation	Allegheny Ludlum Inc. RIDC Park N., 609 Epsilon Dr. Pittsburgh, PA 15238 T: 412-394-2800 F: 412-252-3164 Robert Ball
Tellabs Hong Kong Ltd. 12/F Asia Orient Tower 33 Lockhart Rd., Hong Kong T: 2866-2983 F: 2866-2965 Peter E. Busch	Voice/Data Transport Devices Networking Access Systems	Tellabs Operations Inc. 4951 Indiana Ave. Lisle, IL 60532 T: 630-378-8800 F: 630-852-7346 Peter A Guglielm

- - - - - T: Telephone # - - - - - F: Fax # - - - - - Hong Kong Area Code: (852) - - - - -

China Office	**Product/Service**	**U.S. Head Office**
Temic Hong Kong Ltd. 1701 South Tower, Harbour City 17 Canton Rd., Kowloon, Hong Kong T: 2378-9789 F: 2375-5733 General Manager	Semiconductor Components	Siliconix Inc. 2201 Laurelwood Dr. Santa Clara, CA 95054 T: 408-988-8000 F: 408-567-8950 Richard Kulle
Templeton/Franklin Investment Services Ltd. 2701 Shui On Centre 6-8 Harbour Rd., Wanchai, Hong Kong T: 2877-7733 F: 2877-5401 Lawrence Murray	Fund Management	Franklin Resources Inc. 777 Mariners Island Blvd. San Mateo, CA 94404 T: 415-312-2000 F: 415-312-3832 Murray Simpson
Teradyne Hong Kong Ltd. 1319 Grand Central Plaza 138 Shatin Rd., Hong Kong T: 2730-3131 F: 2735-1150 Patrick Tong	Electronic Testing Equipment	Teradyne Inc. 321 Harrison Ave. Boston, MA 02118 T: 617-482-2700 F: 617-422-2840 David Sulman
Texaco Hong Kong Ltd. 2005 New World Tower 16-18 Queen's Rd., Hong Kong T: 2526-6451 F: 2736-3026 Peter C W Tong	Oil/Gas Exploration Petrochemicals	Texaco Inc. 2000 West Chester Ave. White Plain, NY 10650 T: 914-253-4000 F: 914-253-7839 S. A. Carlson / James W Kinnear
Texas Instruments Asia Ltd. 1508 Tower II, Grand Century Place 193 Prince Edward Rd. W., Hong Kong T: 2956-7288 F: 2956-2200 Gerald Kuo	Consumer Electronics Business Machines Computers	Texas Instruments Inc. 13500 N Central Expy, PO Box 655474 Dallas, TX 75265 T: 972-995-2011 F: 972-995-4360 Fred Geyer
Therm-O-Disc/Asia 101 King's Rd. North Point, Hong Kong T: 2571-0220 F: 2503-3969 Steven Chan	Thermostats & Controls Sensors & Thermal Cutoffs	Therm-O-Disc Inc. 1320 S. Main St. Mansfield, OH 44907-0538 T: 419-525-8500 F: 419-525-8282 Carl Gigandet
Thermo King Corp. 535/39 Sun Hung Kai Centre 30 Harbour Rd., Wanchai, Hong Kong T: 2507-9100 F: 2827-5159 John Ngai	Air Conditioning Refrigeration Heating	Thermo King Corp. 314 W. 90th St. Bloomington, MN 55420 T: 612-887-2200 F: 612-887-2615 Michael Komar
Tiffany & Co of New York Ltd. 1301 The Hong Kong Club Bldg. 3A Chater Rd., Hong Kong T: 2847-5600 F: 2845-3027 Claire Chao	Fine Jewelry Silverware	Tiffany & Co. 727 Fifth Ave. New York, NY 10022 T: 212-755-8000 F: 212-605-4465 Thomas O'Neil / Schaun Lew
Tillinghast - Towers Perrin 3001 Central Plaza 18 Harbour Rd., Hong Kong T: 2593-4538 F: 2868-1517 Doug Stanton	Management Consultants	Towers Perrin 335 Madison Ave. New York, NY 10017 T: 212-309-3400 F: 212-309-3857 John Kneen

China Office	**Product/Service**	**U.S. Head Office**
Time Inc Asia 34/F Citicorp Centre 18 Whitfield Rd., Causeway Bay, Hong Kong T: 2512-5111 F: 2510-8693 Rudy Chan	Publishing	Time Warner Inc. 75 Rockefeller Plaza, 14/F New York, NY 10019 T: 212-484-8000 F: 212-275-3970 Jeanette Lerman / Anne Pappas
TMX Hong Kong Ltd. 2301/07, 23/F Tower 1 Metroplaza 223 Hing Fong Rd., Kwai Chung, Hong Kong T: 2418-0889 F: 2418-1251 Franklin Wai	Watches & Clocks	Timex Corp. Park Rd. Extension Middlebury, CT 06762 T: 203-573-5000 F: 203-573-5143 Ray Pezzi
TOYS R US Lifung Ltd. 10/F, 868 Cheung Sha Wan Rd. Lai Chi Kok, Hong Kong T: 2742-5188 F: 2741-5956 Kwok King Fung	Toys	Toys R US Inc. 461 From Rd. Paramus, NJ 07652 T: 201-262-7800 F: 201-262-7851 Gregory Staley
Trane Pacific 13-16/F St. John's Bldg. 33 Garden Rd., Central, Hong Kong T: 2594-9700 F: 2530-4722 Roberto Camizares	Air Conditioning	Trane Co. 3600 Pammel Creek Rd. La Crosse, WI 54601 T: 608-787-2000 F: 608-787-4990 William Klug
Trans World Airlines Inc. M/F Sun House 90 Connaught Rd., Central, Hong Kong T: 2851-1411 F: 2851-8069 William Cheng	Airlines	Trans World Airlines One City Center, 515 N. 6th St. St. Louis, MO 63101 T: 314-589-3000 F: 314-589-3302 Joe Vilmain
Transmerica Leasing (HK) Ltd. 2308 Kwong Wai Bldg., Phase II 25 Canton Rd., Kowloon, Hong Kong T: 2956-0882 F: 2956-1689 Fred A Baptista	Transportation	Transamerica Leasing Inc. 100 Mahattanville Rd. Purchase, NY 10577 T: 914-251-9000 F: 914-697-2690 Trevor Smith
Transamerica Occidental Life Insurance Co. 2006/07 NatWest Tower, Times Square 1 Matheson Rd., Causeway Bay, Hong Kong T: 2506-0311 F: 2506-1455 K. Y. To	Insurance	Transamerica Occidental Life Co. 1150 S. Olive St. Los Angeles, CA 90015-2211 T: 213-742-3823 F: 213-741-6985 Stephen W. Pinkham
Tremco Far East Ltd. 303 Hennessy Rd. Hong Kong T: 2880-0082 F: 2880-0774 Ronnie Cheong	Protective Coatings Sealants	Tremco Inc. 3735 Green Rd. Beechwood, OH 44122 T: 216-229-5000 F: 216-229-5134 Les Vinney / Leigh Carter
Tricon Restaurants Int'l 1602 Manulife Plaza, The Lee Gardens 33 Hysan Ave., Causeway Bay, Hong Kong T: 2834-8330 F: 2838-1879 Art Rautio	Restaurants / Catering Food Provision	Pepsico Restaurants Int'l 14841 Dallas Parkway Dallas, TX 75240 T: 214-338-7700 James H O'Neal

China Office	Product/Service	U.S. Head Office
TTC Asia Pacific Units 708/09, Tower II, Grand Central Plaza 138 Shatin Rd., Hong Kong T: 2892-0990 F: 2892-0770 Sidney Tam	Communications Equipment	Dynatech Corp. 3 New England Executive Park Burlington, MA 01803 T: 617-272-6100 F: 617-272-2304 Roger C. Cady
Tupperware Asia Pacific 2001 Manulife Plaza, The Lee Gardens 33 Hysan Ave., Causeway Bay, Hong Kong T: 2832-9303 F: 2873-1899 Bob Williams	Direct Sales of Household Products	**Tupperware Corp.** P. O. Box 2353 Orlando, FL 32802 T: 407-826-5050 F: 407-826-8849 Gaylin Olson
Turner Int'l (Asia Pacific) Ltd. 30/F Entertainment Bldg. 30 Queen's Rd., Central, Hong Kong T: 2826-4500 F: 2804-6415 Mike Byrd	Broadcast Media	Turner Broadcasting System Inc. 190 NW Marietta St., One CNN Center Atlanta, GA 30303-2705 T: 404-827-1700 F: 404-827-2024 Steven J. Heyer
Tuthill Asia Ltd. 909 Kornhill Metro Tower 1 Kornhill Rd., Quarry Bay, Hong Kong T: 2513-7113 F: 2513-7793 Rockne Porter	Pumps Fluid Power Valves	Tuthill Corp. 908 N. Elm St., #100 Hinsdale, IL 60521 T: 630-655-2266 F: 630-655-2297 James Tuthill, Jr.
Tyco Asia Ltd. 12/F New T&T Centre 7 Canton Rd., Kowloon, Hong Kong T: 2378-4100 F: 2317-0618 Bob Rossi	Toys	Tyco Industries Inc. 6000 Midlantic Dr. Mt. Laurel, NJ 08054 T: 609-234-7400 F: 609-722-9343 Karsten Malmos
UL International Ltd. 14/F, Block B, Veristrong Centre 34 Au Pui Wan St., Shatin, Hong Kong T: 2695-9599 F: 2695-8196 Angela Yu	Standards & Testing Quality Controls	Underwriters Laboratories 333 Pfingsten Rd. Northbrook, IL 60062 T: 847-272-8800 F: 847-272-8129 T Castino
Union Carbide Asia Ltd. 15/F Prudential Assurance Tower 79 Chatham Rd. S., Kowloon, Hong Kong T: 2485-6888 F: 2610-2822 Bernard Miu	Chemicals	Union Carbide Corp. 39 Old Ridgebury Rd. Danbury, CT 06817 T: 203-794-2000 F: 203-794-3170 Lou Agnello
Union Special Far East Ltd. 1908 Tower II Metroplaza 223 Hing Fong Rd., Kwai Chung, Hong Kong T: 2494-8868 F: 2423-1206 Edward Tang Shu Wing	Sewing Machines	Union Special Corp. One Union Special Plaza Huntley, IL 60142 T: 708-669-4345 F: 708-669-3534 A Hayakawa
Uniroyal Chemical Co Inc. 3701 Peregrine Tower, Lippo Center 84 Queensway, Hong Kong T: 2526-2355 F: 2868-4226 I R Duthie	Chemicals & Prepolymers Plastic Additives Rubber Additives	Uniroyal Chemical Corp. World Headquarters Middlebury, CT 06749 T: 203-573-2000 F: 203-573-2489 Robert J. Pertrausch

China Office	**Product/Service**	**U.S. Head Office**
Unisys China/Hong Kong Ltd. 12/F World Trade Centre 280 Gloucester Rd., Hong Kong T: 2879-3800 F: 2827-5304 Stephen Kucia	Computers Information Technology	Unisys Corp. P. O. Box 500 Blue Bell, PA 19424 T: 215-986-6990 F: 215-986-2312 Thomas Yan
United Airlines 29/F Gloucester Tower, The Landmark Bldg. 15 Queen's Rd., Central, Hong Kong T: 2810-4888 F: 2810-0877 Henry Ma	Airlines	United Airlines Inc. 1200 E. Algonquin Rd. Elk Grove Village, IL 60007 T: 847-952-4000 MacDonald Curran
United Distribution Services Ltd. 4501/05, 45/F, Tower I, Metroplaza 223 Hing Fong Rd., Hong Kong T: 2480-6133 F: 2480-6226 Dennis Hou	Trucking & Leasing Warehousing	Penske Corp. Rt. 10 Greenhill, PO Box 563 Redding, PA 19603 T: 610-775-6300 F: 610-775-6432 Jim Feenstra
United Press International 1108 Boss Commercial Centre 28 Ferry St., Kowloon, Hong Kong T: 2802-0221 F: 2802-4972 Eric Choi	News Media	United Press Int'l 1400 I St., 9/F Washington, DC 20005 T: 202-898-8000 F: 202-842-3625 Ron Macintyre
United Technologies Pratt & Whitney 1208 Great Eagle Centre 23 Harbour Rd., Wanchai, Hong Kong T: 2567-4411 F: 2827-8288 Alan Cheung	Aerospace/Aviation	United Technologies Corp. United Technologies Bldg. Hartford, CT 06101 T: 860-728-7000 F: 860-728-7901 David C. Manke
Unitrode Electronics Asia Ltd. 526 New World Office Bldg West Wing 20 Salisbury Rd., Kowloon, Hong Kong T: 2722-1101 F: 2369-7596 Edith Chan	Electronic Capacitors Printed Circuit Boards	Unitrode Corp. 7 Continental Blvd. Merrimack, NH 03054 T: 603-424-2410 F: 603-429-8771 K Y Chan
Universal Flavors (HK) Ltd. 10/F Fortei Bldg. 98 Texaco Rd., Hong Kong T: 2408-0511 F: 2408-0428 Derek Ng	Flavors & Fragrances	Universal Flavors Int'l Inc. 5600 W. Raymond St. Indianapolis, IN 46241 T: 317-243-3521 F: 317-248-1753 Jorge Slatter
Universal Instruments (Hong Kong) Corp. 161409, Tower 3, China Hong Kong City 33 Canton Rd., Kowloon, Hong Kong T: 2723-2800 F: 2739-2698 Jimson Lee	Electronic Assembly Eqmt	Universal Instruments Corp. P. O. Box 825, 90 Bevier Ct. Binghamton, NY 13901 T: 607-779-5184 F: 607-779-7312 Chris Hill
Upjohn Co (Hong Kong) Ltd. 18/F Allied Kajima Bldg. 138 Gloucester Rd., Hong Kong T:2861-2801 F: 2861-3937 William Kuo	Pharmaceuticals Industrial Chemicals	Upjohn Co. 7000 Portage Rd. Kalamazoo, MI 49001 T: 616-323-4000 F: 616-323-4077 William N Hubbard

China Office	Product/Service	U.S. Head Office
UPS Parcel Delivery Service Ltd. 602/10 North Tower, World Finance Centre Harbour City, Canton Rd., Hong Kong T: 2735-3535 F: 2738-5070 Perry Chao	Courier Service Package Delivery Service	United Parcel Service of America Inc 55 Glenlake Pkwy Atlanta, GA 30328 T: 404-828-6000 F: 404-828-6593 Edward Schroeder
US Filter Hong Kong Unit 8, 5/F, Block B, New Trade Plaza 6 On Hing St., Shatin, Hong Kong T: 2649-0788 F: 2649-8212 L V Pace	Water Filters	United States Filter Corp. 40-004 Cook St. Palm Desert, CA 92211 T: 619-340-0098 F: 619-341-9368 Larry L. Crabtree
US West International Inc. 1001 Two Exchange Square 8 Connaught Place, Central, Hong Kong T: 2845-4133 F: 2845-1269 Alan Khoo	Telecommunications	US West Inc. 7800 E. Orchard Rd. Englewood, CO 80111 T: 303-793-6500 F: 303-793-6654 A. Gary Ames
US-China Business Council 2802/04 Admiralty Centre, Tower I 18 Harcourt Rd., Hong Kong T: 2527-5397 F: 2527-1516 Pamela Baldinger	Membership Organization	**US-China Business Council** 1818 N St. NW, #200 Washington, DC 20036 T: 202-429-0340 F: 202-775-2476 Robert A Kapp
Valvoline Int'l Inc. 12/F Jubilee Commercial Bldg. 42-46 Gloucester Rd., Wanchai, Hong Kong T: 2527-9133 General Manager	Petroleum Exploration Chemicals Oils & Lubricants	Valvoline 3499 Dabney Dr. Lexington, KY 40509 T: 606-357-7777 F: 606-357-7381 John M. Gordon
Varian Pacific Inc. 1018/20 Tower A, New Mandarin Plaza Tsim Sha Tsui, Kowloon, Hong Kong T: 2724-2836 F: 2369-4280 Colin Shaw	Medical Equipment Microwave Tubes & Devices Analytical Instruments	Varian Associates Inc. 3050 Hansen Way Palo Alto, CA 94304 T: 650-493-4000 F: 415-856-4351 Derrel DePasse
VF Asia Ltd. Rm. B, 10/F, Kader Ind. Bldg. 22 Kai Cheung Rd., Kowloon, Hong Kong T: 2318-1268 F: 2318-1787 Carol Marchetti	Apparel	VF Corp. 1047 N Park Rd. Wyomissing, PA 19610 T: 610-378-1151 F: 610-375-9371 John G Johnson
Vickers Systems Ltd. 629, 18/F, Citimark 28 Yuen Shun Circuit, Hong Kong T: 2637-7803 F: 2637-7212 Steven Y M Chew	Industrial Automation Process Controls	Vickers Inc. 3000 Strayer Maumee, OH 43537 T: 419-867-2200 F: 419-867-2650 Michael L. Teadt
Viva Yachts Hong Kong Ltd. 502/03 Kinwick Centre 32 Hollywood Rd., Central, Hong Kong T: 2810-4300 F: 2810-4510 Paul F Savage	Yacht Brokers	Viva Yachts Int'l Inc. 1900 SE 15th St. Ft. Lauderdale, FL 33316 T: 954-766-6006 Stephen Sadosky

China Office	**Product/Service**	**U.S. Head Office**
W H Brady Co. Hong Kong 1803/04 CRE Centre 889 Cheung Sha Wan Rd., Hong Kong T: 2359-3149 F: 2359-3164 Danny Law	Construction Materials Software & Printing Systems Electronic Products Paper Products Coated Fabrics	W H Brady Co. 6555 W. Good Hope Rd. Milwaukee, WI 53223 T: 414-358-6600 F: 800-292-2289 Laurie Bernardy
W L Gore & Associates (Far East) Ltd. 1041 New World Office Bldg East Wing 18-24 Salisbury Rd., Kowloon, Hong Kong T: 2723-5756 F: 2721-4632 Chee Lung Tham	Coated Fabrics Adhesives & Sealants	W L Gore & Associates Inc. 555 Paper Mill Rd. Newark, DE 19714 T: 302-738-4880 F: 302-738-7710 Robert Gore
W R Grace (Hong Kong) Ltd. 20/F Devon House, Taikoo Place 979 King's Rd., Quarry Bay, Hong Kong T: 2590-2828 F: 2811-2661 Reginald B Lloyd	Chemicals Construction Materials	W R Grace & Co. One Town Center Rd. Boca Raton, FL 33486-1010 T: 561-362-2000 F: 561-362-2193 Bernd A. Schulte
Wackenhut Security (Hong Kong) Ltd. 1404A Argyle Centre 1 688 nathan Rd., Kowloon, Hong Kong T: 2390-3456 F: 2787-4990 George Chow	Security Products	Wackenhut Int'l Inc. 4200 Wackenhut Dr., #100 Palm Beach, FL 33410 T: 561-622-5656 F: 561-691-6721 Fernando Carrizosa
Walt Disney Co. (Asia Pacific) Ltd. 15/F Citibank Tower, Citibank Plaza 3 Garden Rd., Central, Hong Kong T: 2536-2200 F: 2536-2410 John J Feenie	Consumer Products	Walt Disney Co. 500 S. Buena Vista St. Burbank, CA 91521 T: 818-560-1000 John Dreyer
Wandel & Goltermann Ltd. 1501 Fook Lee Commercial Centre 33 Lockhart Rd., Wanchai, Hong Kong T: 2528-6283 F: 2529-5593 Yuk Hon Lam	Electronic Testing Equipment	Wandel & Goltermann Inc. 1030 Swabia Ct. Durham, NC 27703 T: 919-941-5730 F: 919-941-9160 Traugott Goll
Wang Pacific Ltd. 15/F Somerset House, Taikoo Place 979 King's Rd., Quarry bay, Hong Kong T: 2880-4888 F: 2590-9614 Mias van Vuuren	Computers	Wang Laboratories Inc. 600 Technology Park Dr. Billerica, MA 01821-4149 T: 508-967-5000 F: 508-967-6045 James Hogan
Warner-Jenkinson Hong Kong 10/F Fortei Bldg. 98 Texaco d., Hong Kong T: 2409-6580 F: 2409-9719 Richard Lai	Synthetic Colors for Food Natural Colors for Food Pharmaceuticals Cosmetics	Warner-Jenkinson Co Inc. 2526 Baldwin St. St. Louis, MO 63106 T: 314-889-7600 F: 314-658-7318 Mike Wick
Warner-Lambert HK/Int'l Ltd. 36/F, Manulife Tower 169 Electric Rd., North Point, Hong Kong T: 2566-6615 F: 2806-0409 Dennis Fuge	Pharmaceuticals	Warner-Lambert Co. 201 Tabor Road Morris Plains, NJ 07950 T: 201-540-2000 F: 201-540-3761 Philip Gross / Frank Ritt

China Office	Product/Service	U.S. Head Office
Watson Wyatt Co (Hong Kong) Ltd. 27/F Sun Hung Kai Centre 30 Harbour Rd., Wanchai, Hong Kong T: 2820-8200 F: 2827-8899 A Grahame Stott	Executive Search Profit Sharing Plans	Wyatt Co. 1500 NW K St., #800 Washington, DC 20005-1209 T: 202-626-9600 F: 202-626-9700 Paula A DeLisle
Welch Allyn Hong Kong Inc. 1002, 10/F, Tung Sun Commercial Centre 194-200 Lockhart Rd., Hong Kong T: 2511-3050 F: 2511-3557 Toh Hong Keng	Bar Code Data Collection Sys.	Welch Allyn Inc. 4619 Jordan Rd. Skaneateles Falls, NY 13153 T: 315-685-8945 F: 315-685-3172 C N Benoit
Wells Fargo Bank NA 30/F Hong Kong Bank Bldg. 1 Queen's Rd., Central, Hong Kong T: 2822-1417 F: 2845-9128 Ignatius Choong	Banking	Wells Fargo Bank 525 Market St., 25/F San Francisco, CA 94163 T: 415-222-5000 F: 415-788-3039 Jane Hennessy
Western Digital Hong Kong 1603B, Tower 6, China Hong Kong City 33 Canton Rd., Tsim Sha Tsui, Hong kong T: 2736-5123 F: 2736-5070 Eric Lo	Hard Disk Drives Video Graphics Boards	Western Digital Corp. 8105 Irvine Center Dr. Irvine, CA 92718 T: 714-932-5000 F: 714-932-6498 Cathy Scott
Western Union Financial Services (HK) Ltd. 1609, 16/F, Devon House, Taikoo Place 979 King's Rd., Quarry Bay, Hong Kong T: 2590-0988 F: 2565-1003 Ray Paske	Worldwide Money Transfer	Western Union Financial Services Int'l One Mack Center Dr. Paramus, NJ 07652 T: 201-986-5456 F: 201-986-5168 Ray Paske
Westin Hotels & Resorts 3712B Shun Tak Centre 200 Connaught Rd., Central, Hong Kong T: 2803-2008 F: 2547-2525 Andy Yeung	Hotel	Westin Hotels & Resorts 2001 6th Ave. Seattle, WA 98121-2522 T: 206-443-5000 F: 206-443-8997 Mark Pujalet
Westvaco Hong Kong Ltd. 611, One Pacific Place 88 Queensway, Hong Kong T: 2526-5707 F: 2810-6470 William K Smith	Paper & Packaging Products Chemicals	Westvaco Corp. 299 Park Ave. New York, NY 10171 T: 212-688-5000 F: 212-644-9790 James F. Jordan
Weyerhaeuser Far East Ltd. 2409 Harcourt House 39 Gloucester Rd., Wanchai, Hong Kong T: 2865-5922 F: 2865-7652 Tommy Siu Kue-Yuen	Paper Products	Weyerhaeuser Co. 33663 Weyerhaeuser Way S. Federal Way, WA 98003 T: 206-924-3423 F: 206-924-3332 Montye Male
Whirlpool Greater China Inc. 16/F Paliburg Plaza 68 Yee Woo St., Causeway Bay, Hong Kong T: 2881-0882 F: 2881-1018 Roy Armes	Air Conditioning Major Home Appliance	Whirlpool Corp. Administr. Center, 2000 North M-63 Benton Harbor, MI 49022-2692 T: 616-923-5000 F: 616-923-3785 Robert D. Hall

China Office	Product/Service	U.S. Head Office
White & Case 9/F Gloucester Tower 11 Pedder St., Central, Hong Kong T: 2822-8700 F: 2845-9070 Lawrence Yee	Law	White & Case 1155 Ave. of the Americas New York, NY 10036 T: 212-819-8200 F: 212-354-8113 James B Hurlock
Wilbur Smith Associates 18/F Kowloon Bldg. 555 Nathan Rd., Hong Kong T: 2374-4479 F: 2722-0930 Brian Stanley	Consulting Services Project Management	Wilbur Smith Associates 1301 Gervais St., #1600, PO Box 92 Columbia, SC 29202 T: 803-758-4500 F: 803-758-4610 John W Bonniville
William M Mercer Ltd. 3206 NatWest Tower, Times Square 1 Matheson Rd., Hong Kong T: 2506-1288 F: 2506-4161 Mark Baxter	Human Resources Employee Benefits	William M Mercer Co Inc. 2 World Trade Center, 55/F New York, NY 10048 T: 212-345-7884 F: 212-345-8483 Carl Goodman
Wilson Learning Corp. 2105 Harcourt House 39 Gloucester Rd., Wanchai, Hong Kong T: 2865-1191 F: 2865-1406 Francis Lam	Management Consultants Training Programs	Wilson Learning Corp. 7500 Flying Cloud Dr. Eden Prairie, MN 55344 T: 612-944-2880 F: 612-828-8835 Dave Ehlen
Wing Hang Bank Ltd. Wing Hang Bank Bldg. 161 Queen's Rd., Central, Hong Kong T: 2852-5111 F: 2541-0036 Patrick Fung	Banking	Bank of New York 48 Wall St. New York, NY 10286 T: 212-495-3007 F: 212-495-2413 Thomas A. Renyi
Woolkong Ltd. 2315 Tower I, Metroplaza 223 Hing Fong Rd., Hong Kong T: 2418-1777 F: 2418-1615 Orson Cheng	Fabrics & Apparel	Woolrich Inc. 1 Mill St. Woolrich, PA 17779 T: 717-769-6464 F: 717-769-6287 Al Zindel
World Courier Hong Kong Ltd. 2101 C C Wu Bldg. 302 Hennessy Rd., Hong Kong T: 2833-5775 F: 2834-5023 Eric Chan	Courier Service	World Courier Inc. 1313 Fourth Ave. New Hyde Park, NY 11040 T: 516-354-2600 F: 516-354-2679 James R Berger
World Expo (Asia) Ltd. 1016/19 Mount Parker House 1111 King's Rd., Quarry Bay, Hong Kong T: 2527-9338 F: 2529-9956 Gary Fung	Trade Show Organizer Information Technology	International Data Group (IDG) One Exter Plaza Boston, MA 02116 T: 617-534-1200 F: 617-859-8642 Chris McAndrews
Wormald Engineering Services Ltd. 901/02 Kornhill Metro Tower 1 Kornhill Rd., Quarry Bay, Hong Kong T: 2764-2511 F: 2764-1624 Murray Mok	Fire Protection Equipment Pipe & Pipe Fittings	Tyco International Ltd. 1 Tyco Park Exeter, NH 03833 T: 603-778-9700 F: 603-778-7733 Barbara Jacques

China Office	**Product/Service**	**U.S. Head Office**
Wrigley Co (Hong Kong) Ltd. 3113/14 Hong Kong Plaza 186-191 Connaught Rd. W., Hong Kong T: 2858-9202 F: 2858-2722 Peter C K Tsang	Chewing Gum	WM Wrigley Jr. Co. 410 N. Michigan Ave. Chicago, IL 60611 T: 312-644-2121 F: 312-644-0015 Douglas S Barrie / Stefan Pfander
Wyeth (Hong Kong) Ltd. 25/F Shell Tower, Times Square 1 Matheson St., Causeway Bay, Hong Kong T: 2599-8888 F: 2599-8999 Brian Cheung	Pharmaceutical Products Nutritional Products	American Home Products Corp. 5 Giralda Farms Madison, NJ 07940 T: 201-660-5000 F: 201-660-7178 Robert Blount / Fred Hassan
Xilinx Asia Pacific Ltd. 4312 Tower II, Metroplaza Hing Fong Rd., Kwai Fong, Hong Kong T: 2401-5100 F: 2494-7159 Stacy Fender	Semiconductor Memory	Xilinx Inc. 2100 Logic Dr. San Jose, CA 95124 T: 408-559-7778 F: 408-879-4780 R. Scott Brown
Xtra International 801 Crocodile House 50 Connaught Rd., Central, Hong Kong T: 2854-3280 F: 2544-2304 Patrick Li	Container Leasing	Xtra Corp. 60 State St., 11/F Boston, MA 02109 T: 617-367-5000 F: 617-227-3173 Karen McHenry
Yale Security Products (HK) Ltd. Rm. 1502A East Point Centre 555 Hennessy Rd., Causeway Bay, Hong Kong T: 2833-6665 F: 2834-5507 Mark Oliver	Security Products	Yale Security Inc. 3000 E. Highway 74 Monroe, NC 28112 T: 704-233-4011 F: 704-233-5053 Wilson Griffin
York Air Conditioning & Refrigeration Inc. Unit 1008, Tower 2, World Trade Square 121 Hoi Bun Rd., Kwun Tong, Hong Kong T: 2331-9286 F: 2331-9840 David H Hou	Air Conditioning	York International Corp. 631 S. Richland Ave., P. O. Box 1592 York, PA 17405 T: 717-771-7890 F: 717-771-6819 Jeff Cook
Zilog Asia Ltd. 5/F Victoria Heights Bldg. 192-194 Nathan Rd., Hong Kong T: 2723-8979 F: 2721-4329 Andy Yu	Electronic Products Computers	Zilog Inc. 210 E. Hacienda Ave. Campbell, CA 95008-6600 T: 408-370-8000 F: 408-370-8056 Thomas C Carson

China Office	Product/Service	U.S. Head Office
Beijing Trade Exchange 418 Mandarin Garden Hotel 9 Zhang Yuan Jing, Nanjing 210001 T: 223-1120 F: 223-0624 Yang Qin Yuan	Trade	Beijing Trade Exchange 701 E St. SE Washington, DC 20003 T: 202-546-5534 F: 202-543-2488 John Canellakis
ITOCHU Corp. 13/F, Huaxin Bldg. No. 9 Guanjiaqiao, Nanjing T: 452-0613 F: 452-1760 General Manager	Equipment & Machinery Aviation, Chemicals & Energy Textiles & Garment Metals & Raw Materials Grain & Auto Parts	ITOCHU International Inc. 335 Madison Avenue New York, NY 10017 T: 212-818-8477 F: 212-818-8420 Albert Ping
Nanjing Bijur Machinery Products Ltd. 177 Xiaolingwe St. Nanjing 210014 T: 443-9440 F: 443-2724 Robert He	Machinery Lubrication Equipment	Bijur Lubricating Corp. 50 Kocher Dr. Bennington, VT 05201 T: 802-447-2174 F: 802-447-1365 Peter Sweeney
Nanjing Gould Pumps Ltd. Luhe County Nanjing T: 775-8819 F: 775-8621 Elie Melhen	Deep Water Pumps	Gould Pumps Inc. 240 Fall St. Seneca Falls, NY 13148 T: 315-568-7214 F: 315-568-5737 Frank Zonarich
Nanjing Int'l Container Termical Services Nanjing Xin Sheng Wei Xi Xia Dist., Nanjing 200038 T: 556-1200 F: 556-1902 Fu Qizhao	Shipping Containerized Transportation	Encinal Termical USA P. O. Box 2453 Alameda, CA 94501 T: 510-523-8800 F: 510-628-9124 Mary Wang
OOCL (China) Ltd. 21/F, Chang Jiang Bldg. 99 Chang Jiang Rd., Nanjing 210005 T: 451-2317 F: 451-4767 General Manager	Global Transportation	**OOCL (USA) Inc.** 4141 Hacienda Dr. Pleasanton, CA 94588 T: 510-460-1380 F: 510-460-3109 M. K. Wong / Peter Leng
Zen Continental Co., Inc. 22F-A Yang Guang Mansion 98 Shi Gu Rd., Nanjing 210005 T: 470-9796 F: 470-9744 Heavin Ni	Shipping	**Zen Continental Co., Inc.** 18111A S. Santa Fe Ave., #168 Rancho Dominguez, CA 90221 T: 310-631-5155 F: 310-631-5222 Rachel Liu
Schenker (HK) Ltd. 613 Xi Yuan Bldg. 395 Guangqin Rd., Wuxi 214011 T: 244-4888 x 5883 F: 246-8392 General Manager	Freight Forwarding	**Schenker International** 150 Albany Ave. Freeport, NY 11520 T: 516-377-3000 F: 516-377-3100 Mike Bujold
Torrington Wuxi Bearings Co., Ltd. 30-1 Hubin Road Wuxi 214061 T: 580-3667 F: 580-2773 Steve Edmondson	Bearings	**The Torrington Company** 59 Field St. Torrington, CT 06790 T: 860-482-9511 F: 860-496-3642 Al Nixon

China Office	Product/Service	U.S. Head Office
American President Lines Block A, 6/F, Heng Tong Mansion 28 Zhi Gong St., Dalian 116001 T: 280-0088 F: 280-5200 Xu Cheng Meng	Shipping	APL Limited 1111 Broadway Oakland, CA 94607 T: 510-272-8000 F: 510-272-7941 Keith Mackie
Coopers & Lybrand 1705 Gold Name Tower 68 Renmin Rd., dalian 116001 T: 271-4468 F: 271-4498 General Manager	Accounting	Coopers & Lybrand 1530 Wilson Blvd. Arlington, VA 22209-2447 T: 703-908-1500 F: 703-908-1695 Bob Rourke
Dalian Allen Bradley Electronic Service Ctr 801 Southwest Road Dalian T: 664-1199 F: 664-1819 Ran Longming	Industrial Automation	Allen-Bradley Co. 1201 S. Second St., P. O. Box 2086 Milwaukee, WI 53201 T: 414-382-2000 F: 414-382-4444 Richard E. Shelton
Dalian Float Glass Co., Ltd. 3 Nenjiang Rd. Dalian ETDZ, Dalian 116600 T: 761-4190 F: 761-4197 Bryan Arveson / William Tjader	Glass Products	PPG Industries, Inc. 1 PPG Place Pittsburgh, PA 15272 T: 412-434-2049 F: 412-434-2125 Valentino Buttignol
Dalian Pacific Clay Products Co., Ltd. No. 48 Nanshong Rd. Shahekou Dist., Dalian T: 664-1663 F: 664-1081 Pan Baijin	Building Materials	Interkiln Corporation of America 2800 Post Oak Blvd., #5320 Houston, TX 77056 T: 713-961-4044 F: 713-963-0261 Frank Henshall
Dalian Pome Instrument Corp. Room 101, 122 Xicun, Heishijiao Shahekou Dist., Dalian T: 467-1423 F: 467-1389 Zhang Ruiming	Application Eqmt Cables Brewing Technology Alcoholic Beverages	Pacific Link Inc. 11 Airport Blvd., #100 South San Francisco, CA 94080 T: 650-589-5415 K. Lim
Dalian Supertech Electronic Energy 39 Harbin Rd. Dalian ETDZ, Dalian T: 761-2688 F: 761-2690 Li Xiaochan	Electronic Products	Leecoy International 2033 6th Ave., #320 Seattle, WA 98121 T: 206-441-3551 F: 206-441-3558 D. Lee
Deloitte Touche Tohmatsu 3/F Dalian North Accounting Corp. Bldg. Sec. 2, Changchun Rd., Dalian 116600 T: 761-9844/45 F: 761-9846 General Manager	Accounting	Deloitte Touche Tohmatsu Int'l Ten Westport Rd. Wilton, CT 06897 T: 203-761-3000 F: 203-834-2200 Dina A. Elliott
Epoch International Enterprises Inc. 46 Ginma Bldg. Dalian ETDZ, Dalian 116600 T: 761-6657 F: 761-6654 Foad Ghalili	Computers	Epoch Int'l Enterprises Inc. 1411 Standiford Ave., #B Modesto, CA 95350 T: 209-579-1040 F: 209-579-0867 Justine Branlett

- - - - - T: Telephone # - - - - - F: Fax # - - - - - Dalian Area Code: (86)411 - - - - -

China Office	**Product/Service**	**U.S. Head Office**
Goodyear Dalian Tire Co., Ltd. 25 Shiqiao St. Shahekou Dist., Dalian T: 664-2340 F: 666-0608 Jerry C. K. Liang	Rubber Products	Goodyear Tire & Rubber Co. 1144 E. Market St. Akron, OH 44316 T: 216-796-2244 F: 216-796-9112 C Perez / William Sharp
Keystone International Inc. 1118 Bohai Hotel 5 Jiefang St., Dalian 116001 T: 280-6705 F: 280-4947 General Manager	Valves & Actuators	Keystone Int'l Inc. 9600 W. Gulf Bank Rd., PO Box 40010 Houston, TX 77040 T: 713-937-5355 F: 713-895-4044 Paul Woodward
NCH Huayang Ltd. 609 Huaxing Bldg. 38 Shengli Rd., dalian T: 364-1110 F: 364-1110 Christopher Boyett	Chemicals	NCH Corp. 2727 Chemsearch Blvd. Irving, TX 75062 T: 214-438-0211 F: 214-438-0100 I. Levy
OOCL (China) Ltd. 807/09 Furama Hotel 60 Renmin Rd., Dalian 116001 T: 265-1222 F: 264-2028 General Manager	Global Transportation	**OOCL (USA) Inc.** 4141 Hacienda Dr. Pleasanton, CA 94588 T: 510-460-3180 F: 510-460-3109 M. K. Wong / Peter Leng
Pfizer Pharmaceuticals Ltd. 22 Daqing Rd. Dalian ETDZ, Dalian 116600 T: 761-5446 F: 761-5445 Lawrence M. Woo / Dudley Schleier	Pharmaceuticals	Pfizer, Inc. 235 E. 42nd St. New York, NY 10017 T: 212-573-2506 F: 212-309-4344 Mohand Sidi Said
Schenker (H. K.) Ltd. 406 Yin He Garden 5 Ganwan St., Dalian 116001 T: 270-2323 F: 270-2650 General Managwer	Freight Forwarder	**Schenker Int'l Inc.** 150 Albany Ave. Freeport, NY 11520 T: 516-377-3000 F: 516-377-3100 Mike Bujold
Sea-Land Service Inc. 608 dalian Holiday Inn 18 Shengli Square, Dalian T: 280-5673 F: 280-7052 Arthur Leung	Shipping	Sea-Land Service Inc. 6000 Carnegie Blvd. Charlotte, NC 28209 T: 704-571-2000 F: 704-571-4613 Clint Eisenhauer
Vickers Hydraulic Pressure System Co. 1 Xiangzhou Rd. Gan Jingzhi Dist., Dalian T: 664-1118 F: 664-1642 Wang Rui / Otto P. Langosch	Hydraulic Systems	Vickers Inc. 3000 Strayer Maumee, OH 43537 T: 419-867-2200 F: 419-867-2650 Michael L. Teadt
Zen Continental Co., Inc. 503 Friendship Shopping Center No. 1, 71 St., Zhongshan Dist., Dalian 116001 T: 280-8388 F: 264-2298 William Xiao	Shipping Freight Forwarder	**Zen Continental Co., Inc.** 18111A S. Santa Fe Ave., #168 Rancho Dominquez, CA 90221 T: 310-631-5155 F: 310-631-5222 Rachel Liu

China Office	Product/Service	U.S. Head Office
3M China Ltd. 1/F, Liaoning Hotel 97 Zhongshan Rd., Shenyang 110001 T: 383-9166 x 405 F: 383-5058 General Manager	Chemical Products Consumer & Safety Products	**3M Company** 3M Center Bldg. Bldg. 220-14E-02 Saint Paul, MN 55144-1000 T: 612-737-0702 F: 612-733-2095 Tony Gastaldo
ABB China Ltd. Rm. A&B, 20/F, Sankei Torch Mansion 262A Shifu Dalu, Shenyang 110013 T: 279-0012 F: 279-0013 General Manager	Industrial Automation Power	**ABB** 1515 Broad St. Bloomfield, NJ 07003 T: 201-893-2416 F: 201-893-3150 Y J Chen
AST Research Inc. 606 Nanhu Hotel 63 Wenhua Rd., Shenyang 110003 T: 390-2416 F: 390-2416 General Manager	Computers	AST Research Inc. 16215 Alton Parkway Irvine, CA 92619 T: 714-727-4141 F: 714-727-8584 Hoon Choo / Scott Bower
Boeing Co. c/o Shenyang Aircraft Corporation P. o. Box 328, Shenyang 110031 T: 652-6100 F: 652-5905 Gary Jacobs	Aviation	**The Boeing Company** 7755 E. Marginal Way South Seattle, WA 98108 T: 206-655-7300 F: 206-544-2791 Raymond J. Waldmann
China Hewlett-Packard Co., Ltd. 12/F, Sankei Torch Mansion 262A Shifu Rd., Shenyang 110013 T: 279-0169 x 175 F: 279-0232 Dang Yingjian	Computers	Hewlett-Packard Co. 3000 Hanover St. Palo Alto, CA 94304 T: 650-857-1501 F: 650-857-5518 Manuel F. Diaz
Compaq Computer Hong Kong Ltd. 228 Liaoning Hotel 97 Zhongshan Rd., Shenyang 110001 T: 383-9166 x 228 F: 383-9103 x 228 General Manager	Computers	Compaq Computer Corp. 20555 State Highway 249 Houston, TX 77070 T: 281-370-0670 F: 281-514-1740 Michael Heil
Dow Jones Markets (HK) Ltd. 212 Taishan Hotel 22 Taishan Rd., Shenyang 110031 T: 611-2290 F: 611-2291 General Manager	Business Information	Dow Jones & Co., Inc. 200 Liberty St. New York, NY 10281 T: 212-416-2000 F: 212-416-2885 Karen House / James Friedlich
Eli Lilly 238 Liaoning Hotel 97 Zhongshan Rd., Shenyang 110001 T: 340-4484 F: 340-4485 Main Meng	Pharmaceuticals	Eli Lilly & Co. Lilly Corporate Center Indianapolis, IN 46285 T: 317-276-2000 F: 317-276-2095 Gino Santini
Flexible Tiger Metal Bellows Co., Ltd. 61 Twelfth St. Shenhe Dist., Shenyang 110003 T: 282-4310 F: 282-7459 Liang Jingmo / Miao Pengru	Industrial Bellows Pressure Hoses	Flexible Metal Hose Mfg. Co., Ltd. 345 Fisher Costa Mesa, CA 92626 T: 714-751-1000 F: 714-545-6619 F. Berkenkemp

China Office	Product/Service	U.S. Head Office

General Motors Shenyang Rep. Office
No. 1-2, Riverside Garden
Heping Dist., Shenyang 110015
T: 384-3429 F: 384-3423
James Abell

Automotive

General Motors Corp.
482-A39-C08, 100 Renaissance Center
Detroit, MI 48265-1000
T: 313-556-3527 F: 313-556-5083
Louis Hughes

Homestead Fire Resistant Decorating Mat'ls
15 Ningshan Middle Rd.
Huanggu Dist., Shenyang 110031
T: 622-2441 F: 622-2547
T. Paul Shih

Building Materials

┌─────────────────────────────────────┐
│ **1998 Fairs & Exhibitions China** │
│ Details on 260+ fairs & exhibitions in 19 │
│ cities of China. Bilingual.   │
│ Tel: 310-325-0100 Fax: 310-325-2583 │
└─────────────────────────────────────┘

IBM China Co.
25/F Sankei Torch Mansion
262A Shifu Rd., Shenyang 110013
T: 279-0420 F: 279-0421
General Manager

Computers

International Business Machines Corp.
Rockwood Dr.
Sleepy Hallow, NY 10591
T: 914-765-1900 F: 914-332-3753
John Dejoy

Informix Software (China) Co., Ltd.
Sankei Torch Mansion
262A Shifu Rd., Shenyang 110013
T: 279-0356 F: 279-0346
Wang Shen

Software

Informix Software, Inc.
4100 Bohannon Dr.
Menlo Park, CA 94025
T: 650-926-6300 F: 650-926-6593
Kathleen Critchfield

Inter-Seas Exchange, Inc.
406 Huaxing Office Bldg.
58 Culture Rd., Shenyang 110003
T: 389-1122 F: 389-6899 x 406
Michael D. Smith

Trading

Inter-Seas Exchange, Inc.
9350 Harrison St.
Romulus, MI 48174
T: 313-946-9601
J. Wofford

KFC Shenyang Co., Ltd.
No. 152, Wan Shou Si Street
Shenhe Dist., Shenyang 110013
T: 291-5022 F: 291-5916
Jiang Chunxian

Fast Food

KFC Corp.
P. O. Box 32070
Louisville, KY 40232
T: 502-456-8300 F: 502-456-8306
Donald Parkinson / Jean Litterst

Liaoning Meadow Gold Food Co., Ltd.
No. 26-1, Dongwu Xiang, Nujiang St.
Yuhong Dist., Shenyang 110034
T: 611-2956 F: 680-3415
Li Anguo

Ice Cream

Borden, Inc.
180 E. Broad St.
Columbus, OH 43215
T: 614-225-7480 F: 614-225-7602
J. R. Anderson

Liaoning Rank Xerox Office Automation Ltd.
No. 25, Nanshuencheng Rd.
Shenhe Dist., Shenyang 110011
T: 411-6265 F: 480-1154
Jiang Ren

Photocopiers

Xerox Corp.
800 Long Ridge Rd., PO Box 1600
Stamford, CT 06904
T: 203-968-3000 F: 203-968-4458
Allan E. Dugan

Lucent Technologies
25/F, Sankei Torch Mansion
262A Shifu Rd., Shenyang 110013
T: 279-1166 F: 279-1155
Liu Xuelin

Telecommunications

Lucent Technologies
600 Mountain Ave.
Murray Hill, NJ 07974
T: 908-582-8500 F: 908-508-2576
Tom Uhlman / Carl Hsu

China Office	Product/Service	U.S. Head Office
Magement Technologies Int'l, Inc. (MTI) 502 Liaoning Science & Technology Bldg. 44 Wenyi Rd., Shenyang 110015 T: 389-3733 F: 389-1185 Stephen Collins	Market Research	Management Technologies Int'l (MTI) 800 Fifth Ave., #101 Seattle, WA 98104 T: 360-779-4430 F: 360-779-4933 Walter Rogers
McDonnell Douglas China Taoxian Airport Shenyang 110169 T: 939-2736 F: 272-8428 Bill Young	Aircraft	McDonnell Douglas Corp. P. O. Box 516 St. Louis, MO 63166 T: 314-234-7015 F: 314-234-3826 Rita Luddon
Merck Sharp & Dohme (China) Ltd. 2705 Sankei Torch Mansion 262A Shifu Rd., Shenyang 110013 T: 279-1513 F: 279-1514 General Manager	Pharmaceuticals	Merck & co. One Merck Dr. Whitehouse Station, NJ 08889 T: 908-423-1000 F: 908-423-1043 Attn: Japan Administration WS-2B-80
Shenmei Daily Use Products Co., Ltd. 123 Hezuo St. DaDong Dist., Shenyang 110044 T: 889-3987 F: 889-3680 Su Guoquan / Wu Zhipeng	Personal Care Products	The Gillette Co. Prudential Tower Bldg. Boston, MA 02199 T: 617-421-7000 F: 617-421-7123 Peter Kent
Shenyang Coca-Cola Beverage Co., Ltd. Guangdong Street, Shenxin Rd. Shenyang ETDZ, Shenyang 110141 T: 581-8707 F: 581-8480 Ray Kong	Soft Drinks	Coca-Cola Co. One Coca-Cola Plaza Atlanta, GA 30313 T: 404-676-2121 F: 404-676-6792 Douglas N. Daft / Sergio Zyman
Shenyang Scotsman-Xinle Refrigeration Co. Daoyi Development Zone Huanggu Dist., Shenyang 110135 T: 973-1888 F: 973-1889 Jesse R. Ma	Ice Making Machinery	Scotsman Ice Systems 775 Corporate Woods Pkwy. Vernon Hills, IL 60061 T: 847-215-4500 F: 847-913-9844 R. Rossi / Frank E. Hebner
Shenyang Tambrands Co., Ltd. 6, Lane 103, Lingyun St. Dongling Dist., Shenyang 110044 T: 483-1796 F: 483-0159 Lu Shi	Feminine Hygiene Products	Tambrands Inc. 65 Springfield St. Three Rivers, MA 01080 T: 413-283-3431 F: 413-289-3399 J. Gamache / Stephen Hebert
Sybase China Ltd. 2507 Sankei Torch Mansion 262A Shifu Rd., Shenyang 110013 T: 279-1313/14 F: 279-1309 General Manager	Computers	Sybase, Inc. 6475 Christie Avenue Emeryville, CA 94608 T: 510-596-3500 F: 510-658-9441 Yvonne Van Leeuewen
United Technologies Pratt and Whitney Taoxian Airport Shenyang 110169 T: 939-2735 F: 272-9368 James Lee	Aircraft Engines	Pratt & Whitney 400 Main St. East Hartford, CT 06108 T: 203-565-4321 x 5875 James Johnson / A. Anderson

WESTERN TRANSIT EXPRESS, INC. 威士通運

- **Specialized in freight forwarding to China and Far East destinations**
- **Weekly consolidations to Shanghai and other inland cities in China**
- **25,000 sq. ft. warehouse with professional shipping services**
- **Oversize cargo loading including truck/auto loading**
- **FCL & LCL hazardous cargoes handling**

San Francisco Office

2140 W. Winton Ave.
Hayward, CA 94545
Tel: 510-266-0333
Fax: 510-266-0338

Los Angeles Headquarter

1600 Walnut Parkway
Compton, CA 90220
Tel: 310-898-1868
Fax: 310-898-1860

Shanghai Office in China

Rm 704, #3 Building Huban Complex,
1250 N. 1st Zhongshan Rd., Shanghai
Tel: (86-21)-6542-6030
Fax: (86-21)-6544-0037

China Office	Product/Service	U.S. Head Office
3Com Asia Ltd. Shanghai Office Suite 11, 6/F, Central Place 16 Henan South Rd., Shanghai 200002 T: 6374-0220 x 6115 F: 6355-2079 General Manager	Computer Systems Networking Products	3Com Corp. 5400 Bayfront Plaza Santa Clara, CA 95052 T: 408-764-5000 F: 408-764-5001 Matthew Kapp
3M China Ltd. 10/F, New Town Mansion 55 Loushanguan Rd., Shanghai 200355 T: 6275-3535 F: 6275-2343 Michael Threinen	Consumer Products Magnetic Media Products Office Products Telecom Products Safety / Security Products	**3M Company** 3M Center Bldg., Bldg. 220-14E-02 Saint Paul, MN 55144-1000 T: 612-737-0702 F: 612-733-2095 Tony Gastaldo
A C Nielsen SRG China Shanghai Office 5/F Conch Bldg. 1271 Zhongshan West Rd., Shanghai 200051 T: 6270-0933 F: 6270-0939 General Manager	Market Research	A C Nielsen 177 Broad St. Stamford, CT 06901 T: 203-961-3300 F: 203-961-3170 Nicholas Trivisonno
ABB China Ltd. Suite 701, 7/F, Union Bldg. 100 Yanan East Rd. Shanghai 200002 T: 6320-3333 F: 6320-1132 Evelyn Wang	Industrial Automation Petrochemical	**ABB** 1515 Broad St. Bloomfield, NJ 07003-3096 T: 201-893-2416 F: 201-893-3150 Y J Chen
Abbott Int'l Ltd. 12/F, Shanghai Indu-Pharm Mansion 200 Tai Cang Rd., Shanghai 200020 T: 6355-8777 F: 6328-7948 James Tsui	Nutritional Products/Services	Abbott Laboratories 100 Abbott Park Rd. Abbot Park, IL 60064 T: 847-937-6100 F: 847-937-1511 Robert Parkinson
Advance Micro Devices Ltd. (AMD) Rm. 1402 Shanghai Novel Plaza 128 Nanjing West Rd., Shanghai 200003 T: 6350-0837/39 F: 6350-0840 General Manager	Computers	Advanced Micro Devices, Inc. One AMD Pl. Sunnyvale, CA 94085 T: 408-732-2400 F: 408-749-3127 Gerald A. Lynch
Air Products China, Inc. Shanghai Rm. 2201 Shartex Plaza 88 Zunyi South Rd., Shanghai 200335 T: 6219-1819 F: 6209-8024 Mark Modjeska	Chemical Products	**Air Products & Chemicals Inc.** 7201 amilton Blvd. Allentown, PA 18195 T: 610-481-4911 F: 610-481-5900 Joseph J Kaminski
Allen-Bradley Co. Shanghai Shanghai T: 6270-1878 F: 6275-6217 General Manager	Industrial Automation Process Controls	Allen-Bradley Co. 1201 S. Second St., P. O. Box 2086 Milwaukee, WI 53201 T: 414-382-2000 F: 414-382-4444 Richard E. Shelton
Allied Pickfords Ltd. 8501B, Block A, Jiahua Business Center 808 Hongqiao Rd., Shanghai 200030 T: 6486-0833 F: 6486-0831 General Manager	Moving Service Storage & Trucking	Allied International 215 W. Diehl Rd. Naperville, IL 60563 T: 630-717-3500 F: 630-717-3496 Mike Cosnett / Dave Buth

China Office	**Product/Service**	**U.S. Head Office**
Allied Signal China Inc. Shanghai 8 Niudun Rd., Pudong Hi-Tech Zone Shanghai 201203 T: 5855-4020 F: 5855-4030 Brent Mei Tak Lok	Automotive Products	**Allied Signal International Inc.** 101 Columbia Road, P O Box 2245 Morristown, NJ 07962 T: 201-455-2000 F: 201-455-4807 Paul R. Schindler
Alpha Yunnan Tin Solder Co. Rm. 103/06 Xin Xu Hui Business Bldg. #33, 1480 Xie Tu Rd., Shanghai 200032 T: 6418-0300 F: 6418-0230 Xu Ji Yong	Metal Products	Alpha Metals Inc. 600 State Rt. 440 Jersey City, NJ 07304-1059 T: 201-434-6778 F: 201-434-2307 David B. Zerfoss
Alphagraphics Suite 455, Shanghai Center 1376 Nanjing Rd. S., Shanghai 200040 T: 6215-0069 F: 6215-0432 Linda Zhang	Design, Copy & Print	Alphagraphics, Inc. 3760 N. Commerce Dr., #100 Tucson, AZ 85705 T: 520-293-9200 F: 520-887-2850 Allen Daniel
American Bureau of Shipping 3/F, 40 Nandan Rd. Shanghai 200030 T: 6438-9047 F: 6438-9048 C. C. Chang	Marine Products Marine Services	American Bureau of Shipping 2 World Trade Center, 106/F New York, NY 10048 T: 212-839-5000 F: 212-839-5130 Robert D Somerville
American Chamber of Commerce Suite 435, Shanghai Center 1376 Nanjing West Rd., Shanghai 200040 T: 6279-7119 F: 6279-8802 Rebecca Gould	Business Facilitator	**CHINA CD-ROM** More than 150,000 listings under 300 product categories. English version. Tel: 310-325-0100 Fax: 310-325-2583
American Express Bank Rm. 1502, Ruijin Bldg. 205 Maoming South Rd., Shanghai 200020 T: 6472-9390 F: 6472-8400 Lennon Lau	Banking	American Express Co. 200 Vessey St. New York, NY 10285 T: 212-640-2000 F: 212-619-8802 David Beeman
American Express Shanghai Office Suite 206, Retail Plaza, Shanghai Center 1376 Nanjing West Rd., Shanghai 200040 T: 6279-8082 F: 6279-7183 Li Jun	Travel Services	American Express Co. 200 Vessey St. New York, NY 10285 T: 212-640-2000 F: 212-619-8802 Stephen Friedman / John Sutphen
American International Assurance Co Ltd. 7/F, Novel Plaza 128 Nanjing Rd. West, Shanghai 200003 T: 6350-8180 F: 6350-8182/83 Michael Morrison	Insurance	American International Group 70 Pine Street New York, Ny 10270 T: 212-770-7000 F: 212-770-7821 Evan Greenberg / Martin J. Sullivan
American President Lines (China) Ltd. 3/F, 88 Tongren Rd. Shanghai 200040 T: 6247-6789 F: 6279-1231 Frank Chen	Shipping	APL Ltd. 1111 Broadway Oakland, CA 94607 T: 510-272-8000 F: 510-272-7941 Keith Mackie

China Office	Product/Service	U.S. Head Office
American Standard Shanghai Office 11/F, Wanzhong Business Mansion 1303 Yanan West Rd., Shanghai 200050 T: 6210-1699 F: 6212-5811 Gary Brogoch	Sanitary Wares	American Standard Inc. 1 Centennial Plaza Piscataway, NJ 08855 T: 908-980-3000 F: 908-980-3219 Alan Silver
Ametek Shanghai #A6, 18/F, Harvest Bldg. 585 Long Hua West Rd., Shanghai 200232 T: 6469-2979 F: 6469-2973 Ivan Peng / Lizhi Wei	Electric Motors Instruments Engineered Materials	Ametek Inc. Station Square Paoli, PA 19301 T: 610-647-2121 F: 610-296-3412 Doyle Cavin
Ammirati Puris Lintas China 7/F Olive Bldg. 620 Huashan Rd., Shanghai 200040 T: 6248-4826 F: 6248-4808 General Manager	Advertising	Ammirati Puris Lintas 1 Dag Hammerskjold Plaza New York, NY 10017 T: 212-605-8000 F: 212-605-4708 Kenneth L Robbins / Terry Rosenquist
AMP Shanghai Connector Ltd. 668 Guiping Rd. Shanghai 200233 T: 6485-0602 F: 6485-0728 Donald Choi	Electronic Connectors	AMP Inc. 470 Friendship Rd., P. O. Box 3608 Harrisburg, PA 17105 T: 717-564-0100 F: 717-780-6130 Herbert M. Cole / Ted L. Dalrymple
Apple Computer Int'l Ltd. Rm. 1913 Shanghai Int'l Trade Center 2200 Yanan West Rd., Shanghai 200335 T: 6278-0415 F: 6278-0412 General Manager	Computers	Apple Computer Inc. 1 Infinite Loop Cupertino, CA 95014 T: 408-996-1010 F: 408-974-2113 Dave Manovich
Applied Materials Shanghai Shanghai T: 6485-3332 F: 6485-2824 General Manager	Semiconductor Products	Applied Materials 3050 Bowers Ave. Santa Clara, CA 95052 T: 408-727-5555 F: 408-748-9943 David N. K. Wang
ARCO Chemical China Ltd. Suite 718, Shanghai Center West Tower 1376 Nanjing W. Rd., Shanghai 200040 T: 6279-8830 F: 6279-8831 Fung Kwok Yin	Petrochemical Products	**ARCO Chemical Co.** 3801 W. Chester Pike Newton Square, PA 19073 T: 610-359-2000 F: 610-359-2722 Edward V. Zenzola
Armstrong Building Products Co. 7 Bridge, 318 Highway Zhaoxiang, Shanghai 201703 T: 5975-3366 x 103 F: 5975-2250 General Manager	Building Materials	Armstrong World Industries Inc. Liberty & Charlotte Streets Lancaster, PA 17604 T: 717-397-0611 F: 717-346-2126 William W. Adams
Armstrong World Industries (China) Ltd. Rm. 509, Shanghai Bund Center 555 Zhongshan E. 2 Rd., Shanghai 200010 T: 6326-9599 F: 6326-9430 Sydney Chang	Building Materials	Armstrong World Industries Inc. Liberty & Charlotte Streets Lancaster, PA 17604 T: 717-397-0611 F: 717-346-2126 William W. Adams

China Office	**Product/Service**	**U.S. Head Office**
Arthur Andersen & Co. 19/F, Shui On Plaza 333 Huai Hai Zhong Rd., Shanghai 200021 T: 6386-6688 F: 6386-2288 Albert Ng	Accounting Consulting	**Arthur Andersen & Co.** 69 W. Washington St. Chicago, IL 60602 T: 312-580-0069 F: 312-507-6748 Richard Measelle
AST Research Co. Rm. 1010/11, Shanghai Int'l Trade Center 2200 Yanan West Rd., Shanghai 200335 T: 6219-0117/18 F: 6219-2546 Nelson Poon	Computers	AST Research Inc. 16215 Alton Parkway Irvine, CA 92619 T: 714-727-4141 F: 714-72-8584 Hoon Choo / Scott Bower
AT&T China Inc. Suite 2103, Shartex Plaza 88 Zunyi South Rd., Shanghai 200335 T: 6209-1849/51 F: 6209-2959 Jim Bercaw	Telecommunications	AT&T International 295 N. Maple Ave., Rm. I-14 Basking Ridge, NJ 07920 T: 248-262-6646 F: 248-952-5095 Elizabeth Mallek
AT&T Global Information Solution Suite 408, Shanghai Center 1376 Nanjing West Rd., Shanghai 200040 T: 6279-8484 F: 6279-8483 Jimmy Chang	Computers	AT&T Corp. 32 Ave. of the Americas New York, NY 10013 T: 212-387-5400 F: 212-841-4715 Victor A Pelson / Gail J McGovern
AVX/Kyocera HK Ltd. Shanghai Office Rm. 402 Hotel Equatorial Office Complex 65 Yanan West Rd., Shanghai 200040 T: 6249-0316 F: 6249-0313 General Manager	Multilayer Ceramic Capacitors	Avx Corp. 750 Lexington Ave. New York, NY 10019 T: 212-935-6363 Benedict Rosen
Baker Hughes Inc. Rm. 2701, Offshore Oil Tower 583 Lingling Rd., Shanghai 200030 T: 6481-1808 F: 6481-4873 Larry Williams	Petroleum & Mining Eqmt	Baker Hughes Inc. 3900 Essex Ln., #1200 Houston, TX 77027 T: 713-439-8600 F: 713-439-8261 Edwin C. Howell / Ron Bitto
Bank of America NT &SA Rm. 104-107A, Union Bldg. 100 Yanan E. Rd., Shanghai 200002 T: 6329-2828 F: 6320-1297 James Chiou	Banking	BankAmerica Corp. 315 Montgomery St., M/S-10540 San Francisco, CA 94010 T: 415-622-2507 F: 415-622-5719 John Mauney
Bank of Boston Rm. 1110, Union Bldg. 100 Yanan East Rd., Shanghai 200002 T: 6321-2357 F: 6321-2353 Alen Liu	Banking	Bank Boston Corp. 100 Federal St. Boston, MA 02110 T: 617-434-2200 Clark W. Miller
Bank of New York Rm. 503 Dynasty Business Center 457 Wulumuqi North Rd., Shanghai 200040 T: 6249-4110 F: 6249-4112 General Manager	Banking	Bank of New York 48 Wall St. New York, Ny 10286 T: 212-495-3007 F: 212-495-2413 Thomas A. Renyi

China Office	Product/Service	U.S. Head Office
Baxter Healthcare Ltd. Rm. 1202 Novel Plaza 128 Nanjing West Rd., Shanghai 200040 T: 6350-0489 General Manager	Medical Equipment Microorganism Cultures	Baxter International Inc. One Baxter Parkway Deerfield, IL 60015 T: 847-948-2000 F: 847-948-2887 John F. Gaither, Jr.
Bear Stearns & Co. Inc. Rm. 1710, Shanghai Int'l Trade Center 2200 Yanan West Rd., Shanghai 200335 T: 6219-2642 F: 6219-7249 Donald Wei Tang	Investment Consulting	Bear Stearns & Co., Inc. 245 Park Ave. New York, NY 10167 T: 212-272-2000 F: 212-272-5143 Michael Conway
Bellsouth Shanghai Center Ltd. Suite 431/35 Shanghai Center East Tower 1376 Nanjing West Rd., Shanghai 200040 T: 6279-8900 F: 6279-8910 David Livingston	Telecommunications	Bellsouth International 1155 Peachtree St. NE, #2001 Atlanta, GA 30309-3610 T: 404-249-2000 F: 404-249-2866 Charles C Miller, III
Bindicator Shanghai #22A Hai Xing Plaza 1 Ryuhub (S) Road, Shanghai 200023 T: 6258-2582 F: 6472-5588 Zhang Peizhen	Level Controls Sensors	Bindicator Co. 1915 Dove St. Port Huron, MI 48060 T: 810-987-2700 F: 810-987-4476 Norm Marsh
Black & Decker HK Ltd. Shanghai Shanghai T: 6482-7125 F: 6482-7128 General Manager	Hardware Power Tools	Black & Decker Corp. 701 E. Joppa Rd. Towson, MD 21286 T: 410-583-3900 F: 410-583-2923 Don Graber
Black & Veatch Int'l Shanghai Office Unit A, 20/F, Ziyun Bldg. 55-800 Lane, Zhongshan West Rd., Shanghai T: 6234-6658 F: 6234-6658 General Manager	Engineering Service	Black & Veatch International 8400 Ward Pkwy., PO Box 8405 Kansas City, MO 64114 T: 913-458-2000 F: 913-458-7677 Ronald E. Zitterkopf
Booz-Allen & Hamilton (China) Ltd. Suite 510 Shanghai Center 1376 Nanjing West Rd., Shanghai 200040 T: 6279-8500 F: 6279-8501 General Manager	Management Consultants	Booz Allen & Hamilton Inc. 101 California St., #3300 San Francisco, CA 94111-5802 T: 415-595-2700 F: 415-627-4283 G. Salameh
Boyden International Rm. 435 Shanghai Center East Tower 1376 Nanjing West Rd., Shanghai 200040 T: 6279-8246 F: 6279-8802 General Manager	Executive Search	Boyden Consulting Corp. 55 Madison Ave. Morristown, NJ 07960 T: 973-267-0980 F: 973-267-6172 Joseph F. DiPiazza
Branson Ultrasonic Co Ltd. 227 Caobao Rd. Shanghai 200233 T: 6408-7779 F: 6433-3194 Gary Chan	Ultrasonic Cleaning Eqmt	Branson Ultrasonics Corp. 41 Eagle Rd. Dansbury, CT 06813 T: 203-796-0400 F: 203-796-9813 Sylvio Mainolfi

China Office	Product/Service	U.S. Head Office
Briggs & Stratton Corp. Rm. 1109 Hangtian Bldg. 222 Caoxi Rd., Shanghai 200233 T: 6482-1258 F: 6482-1259 General Manager	Air Cooled Engines	Briggs & Stratton Corp. P. O. Box 702 Milwaukee, WI 53201 T: 414-259-5333 F: 414-259-9594 Mike Schoen
Brighton Information Technology Co. 3/F, 519 Xihua Rd. Shanghai 200052 T: 6280-2190 F: 6280-2190 General Manager	Computer Products Software	Brighton Industries Corp. 6 Pearl Court Allendale, NJ 07401 T: 201-818-2889 F: 201-818-0983 K. Kung
Bristol-Myers Squibb Co. Rm. 2302 Shartex Plaza 88 Zunyi South Rd., Shanghai 200335 T: 6219-0483 F: 6219-5223 William Tsui	Pharmaceuticals	Bristol-Myers Squibb Co. 345 Park Ave. New York, Ny 10154 T: 212-546-4000 F: 212-546-9585 Donald J. Hayden, Jr.
Brunswick International (China) Ltd. Suite 1804, Union Bldg. 100 Yanan E. Rd., Shanghai 200002 T: 6326-5800 F: 6320-0203 Michael Q. Qi	Sporting Goods Recreation Products	Brunswick Corp. One N. Field Ct. Lake Forest, IL 60045 T: 847-735-4700 F: 847-735-4765 Jerry Perkins
BSCC/VP 3962 Yun Chuan Rd. Bao Shan Dist., Shanghai T: 5693-1760 F: 5693-0750 William Whatley	Pre-engineered Metal Bldgs	Varco Pruden Buildings 6000 Poplar Ave., #400 Memphis, TN 38119 T: 901-762-6000 F: 901-537-8216 Patrick Kern
Burlington Air Express Rm. 502/03 Lianheng Bldg. No. 8, Lane 394 Yanan West Rd., Shanghai 200040 T: 6249-3093 F: 6249-1578 Jeff S. Ross	Freight Forwarder	**Burlington Air Express** 2005 W. 14th St., Suite 130 Tempe, AZ 85281 T: 602-966-5094 F: 602-921-8111 Larry Manrose
Burson-Marsteller Shanghai 1908 Shanghai Overseas Chinese Mansion 129 Yanan West Rd., Shanghai 200040 T: 6249-1640 F: 6249-1646 General Manager	Public Relations	Burson-Marsteller 230 Park Ave. New York, NY 10003-1566 T: 212-614-4000 F: 212-614-4262 Thomas D. Bell, Jr.
Butler Manufacturing Co. Shanghai Office 6/F, Tianwei Industry City, Yudang Rd. East Part Develpmt Zone, Shanghai 200040 T: 5783-1717 F: 5783-1813 Moufid A. Alossi	Building Material	Butler Manufacturing Co. BMA Tower, 310 S. W. Traffic Way Kansas City, MO 64141 T: 816-968-3293 Pauline Jung
C. Melchers GmbH & Co. 13/F, East Ocean Center 558 Yanan East Rd., Shanghai 200001 T: 6352-8848 F: 6351-3138 Ron Glotzer	General Trading	C. Melchers America 55 New Montgomery St., #888 San Francisco, CA 94105 T: 415-974-6210 F: 415-974-1640 Hellmuth Starnitzky

- - - - - T: Telephone # - - - - - F: Fax # - - - - - Shanghai Area Code: (86)21 - - - - -

China Office	Product/Service	U.S. Head Office
Cabot Chemical Company Ltd. Rm. 1602, 2200 Yanan West Rd. Shanghai 200335 T: 6219-4414 Michael Fowler	Carbon Black	Cabot Corp. 75 State St. Boston, MA 02109 T: 617-345-0100 F: 617-342-6103 Ken Burnes
Caltex Oil Co. Suite B, 6/F, Qihua Tower 1375 Huaihai Middle Rd., Shanghai 200031 T: 6471-1015 F: 6471-1284 Ronald Y. Koo	Petroleum Products	Caltex Petroleum Corp. 125 E John Carpenter Freeway Irving, TX 75602 T: 972-830-1000 F: 972-830-3034 H. S. Nichols
Carrier China Ltd. Rm. 1501, Shanghai Int'l Trade Center 2200 Yanan West Rd., Shanghai 200335 T: 6275-3822/23 F: 6275-3824 Michael Van Scoyk	Air Conditioning	Carrier International Carrier Pkwy., P. O. Box 4808 Syracuse, NY 13221 T: 315-432-3352 F: 315-433-4744 Robert Fiesinger
Casco Signal Ltd. 1150 Qiujiang Rd. Shanghai 200071 T: 5663-7080 F: 5663-9223 Delian Lu	Railway Signal Products	General Railway Signal Co. P. O. Box 20600 Rochester, NY 14602 T: 716-783-2000 F: 716-783-2099 D. F. Donatello
Caterpillar Shanghai Engine Co. Ltd. 2602 Jungong Rd. Shanghai 200432 T: 6538-5180 F: 6533-2180 John Airola	Engines	Caterpillar Inc. 100 N E Adams St. Peoria, IL 61629 T: 309-675-1000 F: 309-675-1717 Siegfried R. Ramseyer
CCI China Suite A3, 7/F, The Harvest Bldg. 585 Long Hua Rd., Shanghai 200232 T: 6469-8935 F: 6469-8945 Sheng Rong Xia	Airconditioning Compressors	Climate Control Inc. 2120 N. 22nd St. Decatur, IL 62526 T: 217-422-0055 F: 217-422-4323 J. Michael Dawson
Chase Manhattan Bank Suite 203A, Shanghai Center 1376 Nanjing West Rd., Shanghai 200040 T: 6279-7022 F: 6279-7023 Lawrence Wong	Banking	Chase Manhattan Corp. 270 Park Ave., #220 New York, NY 10017 T: 212-270-6000 F: 212-270-2613 Donald H. Layton
Chemical Bank Shanghai Rep. Office 700A Shanghai Center 1376 Nanjing W. Rd., Shanghai 200040 T: 6279-7288 F: 6279-8101 General Manager	Banking	Chase Manhattan Corp. 270 Park Ave. New York, NY 10017 T: 212-270-6000 F: 212-270-2613 Donald H. Layton
Chevron Chemical Co. Rm. 1202, Shanghai Int'l Trade Center 2200 Yanan West Rd., Shanghai 200335 T: 6219-4041 F: 6219-7680 Dave Cummins	Petroleum Products	Chevron Corp. 575 Market St. San Francisco, CA 94104 T: 415-894-7700 F: 415-894-6817 Greg J. Matiuk

China Office	**Product/Service**	**U.S. Head Office**
China Business Group 600 Heng Feng Rd., Suite 1027 Shanghai 200070 T: 6317-6992 F: 6317-6992 Zhou Jianding	Consulting	**China Business Group, Inc.** Exchange Place Boston, MA 02109 T: 617-570-8118 F: 617-720-1673 Bryan Batson
Chindex - U.S. China Industrial Exchange Inc. Rm. 1311, Donghu Hotel 167 Xinle Rd., Shanghai 200031 T: 6415-8158 x 1311 F: 6415-8308 Zhiqiang Ren	Medical Equipment	US-China Industrial Exchange Inc. 7201 Wisconsin Ave., 7/F Bethesda, MD 20814 T: 301-215-7777 F: 301-215-7719 Robert C. Goodwin, Jr.
Chubb Insurance Shanghai Office Rm. 2318 Hilton Hotel 250 Huashan Rd., Shanghai 200040 T: 6248-0000 x 2318 F: 6248-2858 Eugene Yu	Insurance	**The Chubb Corp.** 15 Mountain View Rd. Warren, NJ 07059 T: 908-903-2000 F: 908-903-2003 Robert M Lynyak
CIGNA Corp. Shanghai Office 8/F, Dongxin Bldg. 288 Pudong Ave., Pudong, Shanghai 200120 T: 5879-6568 F: 5879-6566 Donald Dong	Insurance	CIGNA Corp. One Liberty Place, 1650 Market St. Philadelphia, PA 19192 T: 215-761-1000 F: 215-761-5505 B. Kingsley Schubert / Ed Loughman
Citibank China Corporate Office 5/F, Union Bldg. 100 Yanan East Rd., Shanghai, 200002 T: 6328-9661 F: 6321-5271/72 Chung Ping Cheng	Banking	**Citicorp** 399 Park Ave. New York, NY 10043 T: 212-559-1000 F: 212-559-5138 Robert Martinsen / Peter Schuring
Coca-Cola China Ltd. 3/F, 175 Xiangyang South Rd. Shanghai 200031 T: 6472-5528 F: 6473-9499 Charles Tang	Soft Drinks	Coca-Cola Co. One Coca-Cola Plaza Atlanta, GA 30313 T: 404-676-2121 F: 404-676-6792 Douglas N. Daft / Sergio Zyman
Compair Compressor Company Ltd. 40 Guangxin Village No. 2 Guangxin Rd., Shanghai 200061 T: 6214-0019 F: 6214-1619 Thomas G. Prebola	Air Compressors	Compair LeRoy 211 E. Russell Rd., P. O. Box 927 Sidney, OH 45365-0927 T: 937-498-2500 F: 937-498-2270 R. Sweaney / Thomas G. Prebola
Compaq Computer Hong Kong Ltd. Rm. 803B Central Place 16 Henan South Rd., Shanghai 200002 T: 6374-8888 x 8031 F: 6373-6936 General Manager	Computers	Compaq Computer Corp. 20555 State Highway 249 Houston, TX 77070 T: 281-370-0670 F: 281-514-1740 Michael Heil
Computer Associates China Co. Rm. 206 Wanbao Int'l Business Center 660 Xinhua Rd., Shanghai 200052 T: 6282-8030 F: 6282-8031 General Manager	Software	Computer Associates Int'l Inc. One Computer Associates Plaza Islandia, NY 11788 T: 516-342-2811 F: 516-342-4864 Kurt Seibert

China Office	Product/Service	U.S. Head Office
Computervision Co. Ltd. Rm. 217/18 North Bldg. injiang Hotel 59 Maoming South Rd., Shanghai 200020 T: 6472-8764 F: 6415-3099 Hanson Suen	Data Management Software	Computervision 100 Crosby Dr., MS 21-17 Bedford, MA 01730 T: 617-275-1800 F: 617-275-2670 Richard Moore
Connell Brothers Co Ltd. Rm. 301, Nanwaitan Building 760 Zhongshan South Rd., Shanghai 200002 T: 6378-1194 F: 6320-3194 Derek P. K. Sze	Consumer Electtronics Foods; Fibers & Textiles Construction Materials Chemicals	Wilbur-Ellis Co. Ltd. 320 California St., #200 San Francisco, CA 94104 T: 415-772-4000 F: 415-772-4011 Frank Brown
Coopers & Lybrand (China) 7/F, Shartex Plaza 88 Zunyi South Rd., Shanghai 200335 T: 6270-9989 F: 6270-9990 John Stuttard	Accounting Consulting	Coopers & Lybrand 1530 Wilson Blvd. Arlington, VA 22209-2447 T: 703-908-1500 F: 703-908-1695 Bob Rourke
Corning Engineering Corp. Ltd. 138 Aomen Rd. Shanghai 200060 T: 6266-4219 F: 6266-4219 David H. Lee	Glass Products	Corning Inc. One Riverfront Plaza Corning, NY 14831 T: 607-974-9000 F: 607-974-8551 Larry Aiello / Ken Kao
Corestates Bank Shanghai #905/06 CSJ Conference Center 388 Zhejiang Middle Rd., Shanghai 200001 T: 6351-9612 F: 6351-9413 Lily Zou	Financial Services	Corestates Financial Corp. 1500 Market St. Philadelphia, PA 19101 T: 215-973-3100 F: 215-973-1761 Michael Heavener
Cosfra Ltd. No. 3, Lane 1231, Beijing Rd. West Shanghai 200040 T: 5693-1088 F: 5693-5815 C. Fred Chueh	Fragrances & Flavors	Florasynth Inc. 300 North St. Teterboro, NJ 07608 T: 201-288-3200 F: 201-288-0843 J. Freidman
Coudert Brothers Shanghai Office Rm. 1804 Union Bldg. 100 Yanan East Rd., Shanghai 200002 T: 6326-5800 F: 6320-0203 General Manager	Law	Coudert Brothers 1114 Avenue of the Americas New York, NY 10036-7794 T: 212-626-4400 F: 212-626-4120 Robert Hornick
Coulter Electronics Rm. 367 Jinjiang Hotel 59 Mao Ming South Rd., Shanghai 200020 T: 6258-2582 x 367 F: 6215-5588 x 367 Matthew Wong	Electronic Products	Coulter Corp. 11800 S. W. 147th St., PO Box 169015 Miami, FL 33116-9015 T: 305-380-3800 F: 305-380-8312 Mike Crochu / James Schepp
Crown Packaging Co. Ltd. Shanghai Lot 28, Suda Rd., Jinqiao Export Zone Pudong, Shanghai 201206 T: 5899-5108 F: 5899-5106 Philip Lo	Packaging Products	Crwon Cork & Seal Co., Inc. 9300 Ashton Rd., PO Box 63290 Philadelphia, PA 19114 T: 215-698-5100 F: 215-676-7245 William Voss / Nigel Gilson

China Office	Product/Service	U.S. Head Office

Crown Worldwide Ltd.
Rm. 6306/07, Ruijin Business Bldg.
Ruijin Er Rd., Shanghai 200020
T: 6472-8761 F: 6472-0225
Jim Ward

Freight Forwarder

Crwon Pacific
5252 Argosy Dr.
Huntington Beach, CA 92649
T: 714-898-0955 F: 714-898-5640
James Thompson

D'Arcy Masius Benton & Bowles Ltd.
Rm. 201 Shanghai Universal Center
175 Xiangyang South Rd., Shanghai 200031
T: 6472-9011 F: 6472-9173
General Manager

Advertising

D'Arcy Masius Benton & Bowles
1675 Broadway
New York, NY 10019
T: 212-468-3622 F: 212-468-4385
Clayton White

Dames & Moore
#06/09 New Caohejing Tower
509 Caoboa Rd., Shanghai 200233
T: 6485-2302 F: 6485-2303
Paul Whincup

Engineering Services
Construction Management

Dames & Moore
911 Wilshire Blvd.
Los Angeles, CA 90017
T: 213-683-1560 F: 213-628-0015
Peter Rowley

Davis, Wright, Termaine
Suite 450 Shanghai Center
1374 Nanjing West Rd., Shanghai 200020
T: 6472-3344 F: 6415-3003
J. H. Jerry Zhu

Law

Davis, Wright, Tremaine
10500 NE 8th St.
Bellevue, WA 98004
T: 206-646-6100 F: 206-646-6179
Beth Haimann

DeLeuw Cather Int'l Ltd.
Rm. 522, 12 Hengshan Rd.
Shanghai 200031
T: 6433-5526 F: 6433-5526
David A Swenson

Consulting Engineers

DeLeuw Cather & Co.
1133 15th St. NW, #800
Washington, DC 20005
T: 202-775-3300 F: 202-775-3244
R. O'Neil

Deloitte Touche Tohmatsu Shanghai
16/F Shanghai Bund Int'l Tower
99 Huangpu Rd., Shanghai 200080
T: 6393-6292 F: 6393-6290/91
Kenny Poon

Accounting

Deloitte Touche Tohmatsu Int'l
Ten Westport Rd.
Wilton, CT 06897
T: 203-761-3000 F: 203-834-2200
Dina A. Elliott

DELPHI Automotive Systems Inc.
4/F, Tomson Int'l Commercial Bldg.
710 Dong Fabg Rd., Pudong, Shanghai
T: 6875-8866 F: 5830-7429
Marcus Chao

Automotive Products

DELPHI Automotive Systems
1000 Lexington Ave.
Rochester, NY 14606
T: 716-747-7000 F: 716-647-4417
C. Gifford

Dentsu, Young & Rubicam Advertising Co.
Rm. 1206, Shanghai Int'l Trade Center
2200 Yanan West Rd., Shanghai, 200335
T: 6275-2949 F: 6275-4202
Wendy Tso

Advertising

Young & Rubicam Inc.
285 Madison Ave.
New York, NY 10017
T: 212-210-3000 F: 212-490-9073
James Hood / Mike Samet

Dexter Co.
Rm. 1305 Astronauts Bldg.
222 Caoxi Rd., Shanghai 200233
T: 6482-2286 F: 6482-1261
Hirst Geldmacher

Nonwoven Materials
Polymer Products

Dexter Corp.
1 Elm St.
Windsor Locks, CT 06096
T: 860-292-7675 F: 860-292-7673
Horst Geldmacher

China Office	Product/Service	U.S. Head Office
Diebold Financial Equipment Co Ltd. Lot 29-30, 485 Ximenzi Rd. Jinqiao Export Zone, Shanghai 201206 T: 5854-5678 F: 5854-4351 Thorpe McConville	Financial Equipment	Diebold Inc. 5995 Mayfair Rd., P. O. Box 8320 Canton, OH 44711 T: 330-489-4000 F: 330-490-4549 Edgar Peterson
Digital Equipment China Inc. 21/F, Jiefang Daily Bldg. 300 Hankou Rd., Shanghai 200001 T: 6351-0389 F: 6351-0772 JohnTang	Computers	Digital Equipment Corp. 111 Powermill Rd. Maynard, MA 01754 T: 508-493-5111 F: 508-497-7374 Ronald Spinek
Donaldson Far East Ltd. Shanghai Shanghai T: 6471-3122 F: 6471-3103 General Manager	Filters	Donaldson Co., Inc. 1400 W.94th St., PO Box 1299 Minneapolis, MN 55440 T: 612-887-3500 F: 612-887-3377 William Cook / Steve Mulder
Dow Chemical (China) Ltd. Suite 628, Shanghai Center 1376 Nanjing West Rd., Shanghai 200040 T: 6279-8867 F: 6279-8869 John Ho	Chemical Products	Dow Chemical Co. 2030 Dow Center Midland, MI 48674 T: 517-636-1000 F: 517-636-3518 Dick Sosville
Dow Corning China Ltd. Suite 709 Dynasty Business Center 457 Wulumuqi North Rd., Shanghai 200040 T: 6249-2316 F: 6249-2317 General Manager	Chemicals	Dow Corning Corp. 2220 W Salzburg Rd., P O Box 1767 Midland, MI 48640 T: 517-496-4000 F: 517-496-4586 G. J. Ziarno
Dow Jones & Co. 18B Jiushi Renaissance Mansion 918 Huaihai Middle Rd., Shanghai 200020 T: 6415-9550 F: 6415-9536/37 General Manager	Business Information	Dow Jones & Co., Inc. 200 Liberty St. New York, NY 10281 T: 212-416-2000 F: 212-416-2885 Karen House / James Friedlich
Du Pont China Ltd. 15/F Shui On Plaza 333 Huaihai Middle Rd., Shanghai 200021 T: 6386-6366 F: 6386-6333 Sulian Yu	Chemical Products	E I DuPont De Nemours & Co. 1007 Market St. Wilmington, DE 19898 T: 302-774-1000 F: 302-774-7321 Charles O. Holliday, Jr.
Dun & Bradstreet Shanghai Int'l Consultant 3/F Champion Bldg. 363 Changping Rd., Shanghai 200041 T: 6218-9402/03 F: 6218-8103 Patrick Lehane	Consulting Information Service	Dun & Bradstreet Co. One Diamond Hill Rd. Murray Hill, NJ 07974 T: 908-665-5000 F: 908-665-5803 Nick Mancini
DuPont Agricultural Chemicals Ltd. 989 Pudong North Road Shanghai 200137 T: 5867-2488 F: 5867-9025 Steven Pao	Herbicide	E I DuPont De Nemours & Co. 1007 Market St. Wilmington, DE 19898 T: 302-774-1000 F: 302-774-7321 Charles O. Holliday, Jr.

China Office	Product/Service	U.S. Head Office
Duracell Asia Ltd. Rm. 1702 Bldg. 2, Sheraton Huating Hotel 1200 Caoxi Rd., Shanghai 200030 T: 6210-5716 F; 6210-5892 Sikai Yeung	Batteries	Duracell Int'l Inc. Berkshire Corporate Park Bethel, CT 06801 T: 203-796-4000 F: 203-796-4516 Bob Giacolone
DZ Trading (China) Ltd. Rm. 721, Shanghai Center 1376 Nanjing West Rd., Shanghai 200040 T: 6279-8654 F: 6279-8656 Michael Duffy	Textile & Garment	DZ Trading 110 E. 9th St., #C701 Los Angeles, CA 90079 T: 213-532-8000 F: 213-532-8088 E. Duffy
E I Freight (HK) Ltd. Rms. 203, 206 & 208, 77 Xian-Xia Rd. Shanghai 200051 T: 6233-1822 F: 6233-5158 General Manager	Freight Forwarder	Expeditors International P. O. Box 69620 Seattle, WA 98168-9620 T: 206-246-3711 F: 206-674-3459 James L. K. Wang
East Balt Bakeries of China Ltd. Shanghai Shanghai T: 5915-9081 F: 5915-9181 General Manager	Food Products	East Balt Bakery - Florida Inc. 1108 Collins Dr. Kissimmee, FL 34741 T: 407-933-2222 F: 407-933-5367 Jim Pimpinella
Eastern American Shanghai Shanghai T: 6473-5357 F: 6473-4354 Clark Friedman	Metal Buildings	Eastern American 77 Oak St., #1 Newton, MA 02164 T: 617-926-4025 Clark Friedman
Eastglen House Electric Apparatus Co Ltd. 958 Beijing West Rd. Shanghai 200040 T: 6253-0169 F: 6253-4750 Zude Zhuang	Electric Products	Westinghouse Electric Corp. 11 Stanwix St. Pittsburgh, PA 15222 T: 412-642-6000 F: 412-642-3266 Gregory Vereschagin / Gary M Clark
Eastman Chemical Ltd. Rm. 1612, Ruijin Bldg. 205 Maoming South Rd., Shanghai 200020 T: 6472-9777 F: 6472-3760 Albert Keptron	Chemical Products	Eastman Chemical Co. P. O. Box 431 Kingsport, TN 37662 T: 615-229-2000 F: 615-229-1525 A. R. Rothwell
Eaton Corp. Shanghai Shanghai T: 6279-8940 F: 6279-8942 General Manager	Vehicle Components	**Eaton Corp.** Eaton Center, 1111 Superior Ave. Cleveland, OH 44114-2584 T: 216-523-5000 F: 216-479-7014 Laurence M. Ivan
Ecolab Chemicals Ltd. Suite 1207, International Trade Center 2200 Yanan West Rd., Shanghai 200335 T: 6275-0888 F: 6275-7466 Alan Du	Chemicals	Ecolab Inc. Ecolab Center, 370 N. Wabasha St. St. Paul, MN 55102 T: 612-293-2185 F: 612-225-3136 Mike Muenstermann

China Office	Product/Service	U.S. Head Office
Edelman Public Relations Worldwide Co. Rm. 4008, 88 Tongren Rd. Shanghai 200040 T: 6279-2117 F: 6279-2560 McLanie Hamilton	Public Relations	Edelman Public Relations Worldwide 200 E. Randolph Dr., #6300 Chicago, IL 60601 T: 312-240-3000 F: 312-240-2900 Diane B. Dalbke
Edison Brothers Apparel Stores Co. Suite 701 Shanghai Center 1376 Nanjing West Rd., Shanghai 200040 T: 6279-8940 F: 6279-8942 Robert Wang	Retail Purchasing	Edison Brothers Stores Inc. 501 N. Broadway St. Louis, MO 63102 T: 314-331-6000 Martin K. Sneider
EDS (Electronic Data Systems) Tianhong Center 80 Xianxia Rd., Shanghai 200335 T: 6208-2288 F: 6209-0444 Fred Croxton	Information Technology Software	EDS 5400 Legacy Dr. Plano, TX 75024 T: 972-605-6000 F: 972-605-6662 John R. Harris
EG&G Reticon Opto-Electronics Co. Ltd. 420 Zhongshan No. 1 Road Shanghai 200083 T: 6542-0850 x 101 F: 6531-1974 Andris Ramans	Optical-Electronic Products	EG&G, Inc. 45 William St. Wellesley, MA 02181 T: 617-237-5100 F: 617-431-4115 Anthony L. Klemner / Donald M Kerr
Electroglas Shanghai 798 Zhao Jia Bang Rd. Chu Hui Dist., Shanghai 200030 T: 6473-9198 F: 6473-9156 Tony Lam	Semiconductor Testing Eqmt	Electroglas Inc. 2901 Coronado Dr. Santa Clara, CA 95054 T: 408-727-6500 F: 408-982-8025 Conor Omahony
Elf Atochem Shanghai Office Rm. 5E Shanghai Universal Center 175 Xiangyang South Rd., Shanghai 200031 T: 6472-7790 F: 6472-7658 General Manager	Chemical Products	Elf Atochem North America, Inc. 2000 Market St. Philadelphia, PA 19103 T: 215-419-7000 Tom Stocker
Eli Lilly Asia inc. Rm. 408 Manpo Int'l Business Center 660 Xinhua Rd., Shanghai 200052 T: 6282-6008 F: 6282-5554 Robert Brown	Pharmaceuticals	Eli Lilly & Co. Lilly Corporate Center Indianapolis, IN 46285 T: 317-276-2000 F: 317-276-2095 Gino Santini
Emerson Electric (China) Holdings Co. Rm. 403/06 Manpo Int'l Business Center 660 Xinhua Rd., Shanghai 200052 T: 6282-6223 F: 6282-6077 General Manager	Electric Products Electronic Products	Emerson Electric Co. 8000 Florissant Ave. St. Louis, MO 63136 T: 314-553-2000 F: 314-553-3527 R W Staley
Engelhard Asia Pacific Inc. Rm. N201 Universal Center Commercial Bldg. 175 Xiangyang South Rd., Shanghai 200031 T: 6473-9501 F: 6473-9502 General Manager	Precious Metals	Engelhard Corp. 101 Wood Ave. South Iselin, NJ 08830 T: 732-205-6888 F: 732-205-5915 George C. Hsu

China Office	**Product/Service**	**U.S. Head Office**
Ernst & Young 12/F Shartex Plaza 88 Zunyi South Rd., Shanghai 200335 T: 6219-1219 F: 6219-3219 Philip Leung	Accounting Consulting	Ernst & Young 787 Seventh Ave., 14/F New York, NY 10019 T: 212-773-3000 F: 212-773-6350 Eli Spielman
Esso China Ltd. Suite 1610, Offshore Oil Tower 583 Lingling Rd., Shanghai 200030 T: 6481-1814 F: 6814-0154 Jon Benesch	Oil Products	Exxon Corp. 225 E. John W Carpenter Freeway Irving, TX 75062 T: 214-444-1000 F: 214-444-1348 R Dahan
Evergreen Int'l Airlines Inc. Rm. 805 Hongqiao Int'l Airport Hotel Hongqiao Rd., Shanghai 200335 T: 6255-6914 F: 6255-6206 Jim Kriksciun	Cargo Freight	Evergreen Int'l Airlines 3850 Three Mile Lane McMinnville, OR 97128 T: 503-472-9361 F: 503-434-4210 Linda Woodbury
Everwealth Paper Industries Co Ltd. 2 Xinjie Rd., Xinqiao Township Industrial park, Shanghai 201612 T: 5764-5009 F: 5764-5118 Jason F. Fang	Paper Products	**S.E.S. International Express, Inc.** 神龍國際運通有限公司 International Freight Forwarder Tel: 310-673-9937 Fax: 310-673-9935
Export Import of East Asia Inc. Rm. 701 Dongyun Int'l Business Center 8864 Renmin Rd., Shanghai 200021 T: 6320-3303 F: 6320-3920 Mardi Mastain	Trading	Export Import East Asia Inc. 1801 E. Edinger Ave., #240 Santa Ana, CA 92705 T: 714-480-8888 F: 714-480-8889 Stan Gailey
Exxon Chemical China Inc. Rm. 1701 Offshore Oil Tower 583 Lingling Rd., Shanghai T: 6468-1117 F: 6468-1135 General Manager	Petroleum Products	Exxon Corp. 225 E. John W Carpenter Freeway Irving, TX 75062 T: 214-444-1000 F: 214-444-1348 R Dahan
Federal Express Rm. 1805 Shartex Plaza 88 Zunyi Rd., Shanghai 200335 T: 6275-0808 F: 6275-7522 Thomas Liu	Courier Service	Federal Express Corp. 2005 Corporate Ave., 3/F Memphis, TN 38132 T: 901-369-3600 F: 901-395-4858 T Michael Glenn / David Cunningham
First National Bank of Boston Rm. 1110 Union Bldg. 100 Yanan East Rd., Shanghai 200002 T: 6321-2357 F: 6321-2353 General Manager	Banking	BankBoston Corp. 100 Federal St. Boston, MA 02110 T: 617-434-2200 Clark W Miller
Fisher-Rosemount China Co Ltd. 20/F Astronautics Bldg. 222 Caoxi Rd., Shanghai 200233 T: 6482-2298 F: 6482-2300 Steven Kao	Process Controls	Rosemount Inc. 12001 Technology Dr. Eden Prairie, MN 55344 T: 612-941-5560 F: 612-828-7795 Ron A Ward

- - - - - T: Telephone # - - - - - F: Fax # - - - - - Shanghai Area Code: (86)21 - - - - -

China Office	Product/Service	U.S. Head Office
Fleetguard Filter Co. Ltd. 2266 Yanggao Rd. Pudong New Area, Shanghai 201208 T: 5865-7949 F: 5865-8066 Hengnan Ma	Automotive Products	Fleetguard, Inc. Rte. 8 Cookeville, TN 38501 T: 615-526-9551 G. J. Arthur
Fluke Corp. Rm. 405 Jinan Guest House 301 Huashan Rd., Shanghai 200040 T:6248-8999 F: 6248-3789 Chew Siong Teck	Electric Measurement Devices	**Fluke Corp.** 6920 Seaway Blvd. Everett, WA 98203 T: 425-347-6100 F: 425-356-5116 Linda Cheever
Fluor Daniel Shanghai Office Unit 522, Manpo Int'l Business Center 660 Xinhua Rd., Shanghai 200052 T: 6282-3009 F: 6282-5548 Peter Han	Engineering Services	**Fluor Corp.** 3353 Michelson Dr. Irvine, CA 92698 T: 714-975-2000 F: 714-975-5976 Jake Easton
FMC Asia-Pacific Inc. Units C, D&E, 9/F, Wanzhong Bldg. 1303 Yanan West Rd., Shanghai 200050 T: 6210-4799 F: 6212-1014 Jesse H. Chen	Chemical Products Metals & Machinery	FMC Corp. 200 E. Randolph Dr. Chicago, IL 60601 T: 312-861-6000 F: 312-861-6176 James A MacLung / William Wheeler
Ford Motor Automotive Components Inc. Suite B, 3/F, Yinhai Bldg. 250 Caoxi Rd., Shanghai 200033 T: 6475-1135 x 1228 F: 6482-2241 Gerald J Kania	Automobiles	**Ford Motor Co.** The American Road Deerborn, MI 48126 T: 313-322-3000 Bob Kramer
Formica (Shanghai) Co. Ltd. Rm. 201/05 Yuandong Hotel 90 Xizang Middle Rd., Shanghai 200001 T: 6322-9308 F: 6351-6157 Li Wan	Fire-Proof Boards Man-Made Stones	Formica Corp. 10155 Reading Rd. Cincinnati, OH 45241-3109 T: 513-786-3400 F: 513-786-3024 Vince Langone
Formica Decorative Material Co Ltd. 2 Shengli Rd. Yinzhong Town, Shanghai 201700 T: 5920-1143 F: 5920-1142 Benson Wang	Fire-Proof Boards	Formica Corp. 10155 Reading Rd. Cincinnati, OH 45241-3024 T: 513-786-3400 F: 513-786-3024 Vince Langone
Fourth Shift Asia Computer Corp. Rm. 302/A Equatorial Hotel 65 Yanan East Rd., Shanghai 200040 T: 6249-0438 F: 6249-0445 General Manager	Manufacturing Software	Fourth Shift Corp. 7900 International Dr. Minneapolis, MN 55425 T: 612-851-1500 F: 612-851-1560 D. J. Bowman
Fox, Fowle, Gluckman, & Liu Rm. 5313, Jinjiang Hotel 59 Maoming South d., Shanghai 200020 T: 6472-8181 F: 6472-9579 Thomas Czarnowski	Architects	Fox & Fowle 22 W. 19th St., 11/F New York, NY 10011 T: 212-627-1700 F: 212-463-8716 Susan Bogaty

China Office	**Product/Service**	**U.S. Head Office**
Foxboro Co. Ltd. 161 Caobao Rd. Shanghai 200233 T: 6436-2380 F: 6470-0447 E. J. Debellis	Process Controls	Foxboro Co. 33 Commercial St. Foxboro, MA 02035 T: 508-543-8750 F: 508-549-6750 Stan Shaffron
Franco Manufacturing Co. Rm. 321, No. 3 Zhong Shan Rd. East. Shanghai T: 6323-8060 x 321 F: 6323-5681 Mike Defrancesco	Towels Wash Cloths	Franco Manufacturing Co. 555 Prospect St. Metuchen, NJ 08840 T: 732-494-0500 F: 732-494-3457 Howard Berstein / Mike Defrancesco
Fritz Air Freight 2/F Yin Yin Bin Rd. 2250 Shanghai Hongqiao Airport, Shanghai T: 6268-1177 F: 6269-5380 Toby Tse	Freight Forwarder	Fritz Companies inc. 706 Mission St., #900 San Francisco, CA 94103 T: 415-904-8360 F: 415-904-8661 John H. Johung
Fuhua Glass Co. Ltd. 700 Yaohua Rd. Pudong, Shanghai 200126 T: 5883-6224 F: 5874-3817 Dennis A Rohne	Glass Products	**Ford Motor Co.** The America Road Deerborn, MI 48126 T: 313-322-3000 Bob Kramer
Gallup Research Co. Ltd. Shanghai Shanghai T: 6433-0443 F: 6433-6923 General Manager	Marketing Research Management Research	The Gallup Organization P. O. Box 82513 Lincoln, NE 68501-9645 T: 800-398-8789 H. Gallup, Jr.
Gaoqiao Caltex Lubricating Oil Co. Ltd. No. 900B Datong Rd. Pudong, Shanghai 200137 T: 5861-1060 x 2080 F: 5861-0163 Ronald Yulin Koo	Lubricating Oil	Caltex Petroleum Corp. 125 E. John Carpenter Freeway Irving, TX 75602 T: 972-830-1000 F: 972-830-3034 H. S. Nichols
General Electric (USA) China Co. 10/F, Shartex Plaza 88 Zunyi South Rd., Shanghai 200335 T: 6270-6789 F: 6270-9976 Alex To	Electrical Equipment	General Electric Co. 3135 Easton Turnpike Fairfield, CT 06431 T: 518-869-5555 F: 518-869-2828 Guy Rabbat
General Electric Jiabao Lighting Co. Ltd. 4727 Zhennan Rd. Jiading Dist., Shanghai 201802 T: 5912-3678 F: 5912-6287 Charles M McIntyre	Lighting	GE Appliance Appliance Park Louisville, KY 50211 T: 502-452-4311 F: 502-452-0644 Steven C Reidel
General Jewelry Machine Co., Ltd. 16 Kunming Rd. Shanghai 200082 T: 6512-7732 F: 6512-7734 Lanyu Zhang	Jewelry Processing Eqmt	Harold Jewelry Group 131 W. 35th St., 8/F New York, NY 10001 T: 212-695-4905 F: 212-629-6817 Harold Ha

China Office	Product/Service	U.S. Head Office
General Motors Overseas Co. Tianhong Center 80 Xianxia Rd., Shanghai 200335 T: 6208-2288 F: 6209-0444 Stephen G. Schell	Automobiles	General Motors Corp. 482-A39-C08, 100 Renaissance Center Detroit, MI 48265-1000 T: 313-556-3527 F: 313-556-5083 Louis Hughes
General Signal (China) Co., Ltd. 1/F, Bldg. 18, No. 485 Guiping Rd. Caohejing Develop. Zone, Shanghai 200233 T: 6485-3018 F: 6485-2438 General Manager	Signal Products	General Signal Corp. One High Ridge Park Stamford, CT 06904 T: 203-329-4100 F: 203-329-4159 Phillip A. Goodrich
Genstar Container Co. Suite 335, Shanghai Center 1376 Nanjing West Rd., Shanghai 200040 T: 6279-8313 F: 6279-8648 Bea Ho	Container Leasing	Genstar Container Co. 2200 Powell St. Emeryville,CA 94608 T: 510-596-2976 F: 510-596-2988 Jim Kachidurian
Gillette (Shanghai) Ltd. 550 Sanlin Rd. Pudong, Shanghai 200124 T: 5841-1030 F: 5841-1724 Tony Au-Yeung	Safety Razor Products	The Gillette Co. Pridential Tower Bldg. Boston, MA 02199 T: 617-421-7000 F: 617-421-7123 Peter Kent
Golden Atom Holdings Ltd. 4/F, No. 401, Fuzhou Rd. Shanghai 200001 T: 6328-8585 x 112 F: 6328-0069 Man-Jiang Zhou	Electronic Dictionary	Golden Mate Inc. 2646 Durfee Ave. El Monte, CA 91732 T: 626-279-9898 F: 626-279-9899 Patrick Chien
Golden State I/E Enterprises Inc. Rm. 514, 1206 Huaihai Middle Rd. Shanghai 200031 T: 6437-4746 F: 6437-4746 General Manager	Trading	Golden State Import & Export 2435 Pine Street Pomona, CA 91767 T: 909-392-1078 F: 909-392-1081 Sheni Y. Shieh
Goldman Sachs (China) Ltd. Co. Suite 505, Shanghai Center 1376 Nanjing West Rd., Shanghai 200040 T: 6279-7261 F: 6279-8331/34 Chingshan Lin	Investment Banking	Goldman Sachs & Co. 85 Broad St. New York, NY 10004 T: 212-902-1000 F: 212-902-3000 Sussan Zuckerman / Mark Evans
Grace China Ltd. 30 Honghe Rd., Economic Development Zone Minhang, Shanghai 200240 T: 6430-0950 F: 6430-0425 Tony Mak	Sealants for Cans/Bottles	W. R. Grace & Co. One Town Center Rd. Boca Raton, FL 33486-1010 T: 407-362-2000 F: 407-362-2193 Bernd A. Schulte
Grace China, Shanghai Office 2/F, Power Building 430 Xujiahui Rd., Shanghai 200025 T: 6472-8259 F: 6472-3783 Will Knorr	Fire-Retardant Products	W. R. Grace & Co. One Town Center Boca Raton, FL 33486-1010 T: 407-362-2000 F: 407-362-2193 Bernd A. Schulte

China Office	**Product/Service**	**U.S. Head Office**
Graco HK Ltd. Rm. 1807 Shanghai Int'l Trade Center 2200 Yanan West Rd., Shanghai 200335 T: 6275-6000 F: 6275-9777 General Manager	Fluid Pumps	Graco Inc. 4050 Olson Memorial Hy, PO Box 1441 Minneapolis, MN 55440-1441 T: 612-623-6000 F: 612-623-6942 Pam Dovenmuehler
Grumman International Fire Equipment Co. 32 Beinei Rd. Songjiang, Shanghai 201600 T: 5783-3768 F: 5783-0472 Zhiyi Liu	Fire Trucks Fire-Prevention Products	Grumman International Inc. 1111 Stewart Ave. Bethpage, NY 11714 T: 516-575-6801 M. Heaslip
Hai Jing Electron Ltd. Shanghai 58 Sida Rd. Shanghai 200081 T: 6521-7875 F: 6521-0282 Chizhi Wu	Liquid Crystal Displays	Hante Inc. 4525 Production Dr. Dallas, TX 75235 T: 214-638-7412 F: 214-638-8887 C. C. Lee
Harris Semiconductor China Ltd. Shanghai Shanghai T: 6247-7923 F: 6247-7926 General Manager	Communications Equipment	Harris Corp. 1025 W. NASA Blvd. Mebourne, FL 32919 T: 407-727-9260 F: 407-727-9644 Larry Smith
Hellmuth, Obata & Kassabaum Inc. (HOK) 19C, Guardian Mansion 651 Nanjing West Rd., Shanghai 200041 T: 6267-9260 F: 6267-9259 Silas Chiow	Architectural Design	Hellmuth, Obata & Kassabaum 71 Stevenson St., #2200 San Francisco, CA 94105 T: 415-243-0555 F: 415-882-7763 Patrick MacLeamy
Hersey Foods Corp. Shanghai Shanghai T: 6210-7674 F: 6210-2625 General Manager	Food Products	Hersey Foods Corp. 100 Mansion Rd. E. Hersey, PA 17033 T: 717-534-4200 Richard M Marcks
Hewitt East Gate Consulting Corp. 2/F Building 9 500 Caobao Rd., Shanghai 200233 T: 6483-7495 F: 6483-6230 Yong Ling Beiman	Consulting	Hewitt Assocaites LLC 100 Half Day Rd. Lincolnshire, IL 60069 T: 847-295-5000 F: 847-295-7634 D. Gifford
Hewlett-Packard (China) Co. Ltd. 281 Gangao Rd., Bldg. 2, Block F-10 Waigaoqiao Free Trade Zone, Shanghai T: 5865-8088 x 8319 F: 5865-8102 Ge Yongji	Computers Electronic Products	Hewlett-Packard Co. 3000 Hanover St. Palo Alto, CA 94304 T: 650-857-1501 F: 650-857-5518 Manuel F. Diaz
Hezhong-Carrier Air Conditioning Eqmt Co. 24 Shuangyangzhi Rd. Shanghai 200090 T: 6543-0952 F: 6543-5404 John Waring	Air Conditioning	Carrier International Carrier Pkwy., P. O. Box 4808 Syracuse, NY 13221 T: 315-432-3352 F: 315-433-4744 Robert Fiesinger

China Office	Product/Service	U.S. Head Office
Hill & Knowlton Asia Ltd. Rm. I, 7/F, Wanzhong Bldg. 303 Yanan Middle Rd., Shanghai 200050 T: 6213-1778 F: 6475-0496 Jason Fu	Public Rrelations	Hill & Knowlton 466 Lexington Ave. New York, NY 10017 T: 212-885-0300 F: 212-885-0540 Thomas Hoog
Holiday Inn Crown Plaza Shanghai 400 Panyu Rd. Shanghai 200052 T: 6280-8888 F: 6280-2788 General Manager	Hotel	Holiday Inns Worldwide 3 Ravina Dr. Atlanta, GA 30346 T: 770-604-2000 Richard L Smith
Honeywell China Inc. 12/F, Hangtian Bldg. 222 Caoxi Rd., Shanghai 200233 T: 6482-8988 F: 6482-8987 Lee Swee Chee	Computers	Honeywell Inc. 2701 4th Ave. S. Minneapolis, MN 55440-0524 T: 612-951-1000 F: 612-951-0075 Larry W. Stranghoener
Hormel Foods Co., Ltd. 30 Nan Da Rd. Shanghai 200436 T: 5668-6445 F: 5668-7086 Rod Kekkonen	Pork Slaughtering Pork Processing	Hormel International Corp. 1 Hormel Place Austin, MN 55912 T: 507-437-5478 F: 507-437-5113 David Dickson / Richard Crane
Huatek Software Engineering Co. 5/F, 470 Guiping Rd. Shanghai 200233 T: 6485-0178 F: 6485-0177 Chining Liu	Software	Hewlett-Packard Co. 3000 Hanover St. Palo Alto, CA 94304 T: 650-857-1501 F: 650-857-5518 Manuel F. Diaz
Hughes Network Systems Co. Ltd. Building 4, Lot 20, Jinqiao Export Zone Pudong, Shanghai 201206 T: 5854-7938 F: 5854-8608 Wilfrid Maillet	Satellite Communications	Hughes Network Systems Inc. 11717 Exploration Lane Germantown, MD 20876 T: 301-428-7159 F: 301-428-5511 K. C. Kup
IBM China-Hong Kong Corp. Suite 507, Shanghai Center 1376 Nanjing West Rd., Shanghai 200040 T: 6279-8806 F: 6279-8807 Charles Wu	Computers	International Business Machines Corp. Rockwood Dr. Sleepy Hallow, NY 10591 T: 914-765-1900 F: 914-332-3753 John Dejoy
IMAG Industries Inc. Rm. 409, Office Block, Int'l Equatorial Hotel 65 Yanan West Rd., Shanghai 200040 T: 6248-8144 F: 6248-8534 Qingguan Wang	CAD Software	IMAG Industries Inc. 3350 Scott Blvd., #54 Santa Clara, CA 95054 T: 408-727-8222 F: 408-727-8438 S Cheung
Inductotherm Co. Shanghai Office Rm. 3321 Jinjiang Hotel 59 Maoming South Rd., Shanghai 200020 T: 6258-2582 x 3321 F: 6472-8402 Junxiong Xu	Induction Melting Equipment	Inductotherm Corp. 10 Indel Ave. Rancocas, NJ 08073 T: 609-267-9000 F: 609-267-3537 B. M. Raffner

China Office	**Product/Service**	**U.S. Head Office**
Ingersoll-Rand Compressors Ltd. 16/F Meike Bldg. 1 Tianyaoqiao Rd., Shanghai 200030 T: 6468-1081/82 F: 6468-1083 Douglas Dawson	Compressors Bearings	Ingersoll-Rand Co. 200 Chestnut Ridge Rd. Woodcliff Lake, NJ 07675 T: 201-573-0123 F: 201-573-3172 Paul L. Bergen
Instron Int'l Ltd. Rm. 80909 Jin Jiang Tower Hotel 161 Changle Rd., Shanghai 200020 T: 6415-1188 x 80909 F: 6415-0045 General Manager	Instruments	Instron Corp. 100 Royal St. Canton, MA 02021 T: 617-828-2500 F: 617-575-5750 Arthur Hindman
Interconex (China) Ltd. Rm. 2128 New Garden Hotel Shanghai 200335 T: 6242-6810 F: 6242-6810 General Manager	Freight Forwarder	**Interconex Inc.** 55 Hunter Lane Elmsford, NY 10523 T: 914-593-4200 F: 914-347-0131 Phil Hamill
International Flavors & Fragrances Ltd. Rm. 1019 North Jinjiang Hotel 59 Maoming South Rd., Sahnghai 200020 T: 6472-3869 F: 6472-0808 General Manager	Chemicals	International Flavors & Fragrances 521 W. 57th St. New York, NY 10019 T: 212-765-5500 F: 212-708-7132 Frans Nijnens
International Paper, Shanghai 9/F, Tseng Chow Commercial Bldg. Yanan West Rd., Shanghai 200052 T: 6280-8280 F: 6280-8281 Carol Cheng	Paper Products Pulp	International Paper Co. 865 John L. Reigel Rd. Riegelwood, NC 28456 T: 910-655-2211 F: 910-655-6199 Susan Clayter
International Power Machines (IPM) Room 8017, Shanghai Hotel 505 Wulumuqi Rd., Shanghai 200040 T: 6248-0088 Keyne Gu	Electrical Apparatus Uninterruptable Power Systems	International Power Machines 10451 Brockwood Rd. Dallas, TX 75238 T: 972-272-8000 F: 972-494-2690 Kevin Iao
Ion Laser Technology Co Ltd. 247 Wenjing Rd. Minhang, Shanghai 200240 T: 6430-4207 F: 6430-4208 Steven Fartey	Ion laser	Ion Laser Technology Inc. 3828 S. Main St. Salt Lake City, UT 84115 T: 801-262-5555 F: 801-262-5770 L. Barney
ITOCHU Corp. 2112, 21/F, Shanghai Int'l Trade Center 2200 Yan An Xi Lu., Shanghai 200335 T: 6219-9203 F: 6219-2071 General Manager	Equipment & Machinery Aviation, Chemicals & Energy Textiles & Garment Metals & Raw Materials Grain & Auto Parts	ITOCHU International Inc. 335 Madison Avenue New York, NY 10017 T: 212-818-8477 F: 212-818-8420 Albert Ping
ITT Shanghai Automotive Electric Systems 2281 Jianchuan Rd. Minhang, Shanghai 200245 T: 6462-6150 F: 6430-7584 General Manager	Automotive Products	ITT Automotive Inc. 3000 University Dr. Auburn Hills, MI 48326 T: 810-340-3000 F: 810-340-3190 D. Soule

China Office	Product/Service	U.S. Head Office
J Walter Thompson Advertising Co. Rm. 309 Main Bldg. 223 Xikang Rd., Shanghai 200040 T: 6247-8280 F: 6247-2122 General Manager	Advertising	J. Walter Thompson Co. 466 Lexington Ave. New York, NY 10017 T: 212-210-7000 F: 212-210-7066 Burt Manning
Jetronics Co. Ltd. Lot 31, Jiaqiao Export Zone Pudong, Shanghai 201206 T: 5899-5470 F: 5899-2966 Robert Lee	Flexible Printed Circuit	Jetronics Co. 204 Franklin St. Redwood City, CA 94063 T: 650-368-8930 M. Vallarino
John Hancock Shanghai Office Rm. 08-01 Laifoshi Business Center 736 Huaian Rd., Shanghai 200041 T: 6276-5326 F: 6276-5326 General Manager	Insurance	John Hancock Mutual Life 200 Clarendon St., PO Box 111 Boston, MA 02117 T: 617-572-6000 F: 617-572-6451 Derek Chilvers
John Portman & Associates Inc. Suite 900, Shanghai Center 1376 1376 Nanjing West Rd., Shanghai 200040 T: 6279-8926 F: 6279-8936 Walter N. Jackson	Architectural Services Engineering Services	Portman Properties 225 Peachtree St. NE Atlanta, GA 30303 T: 404-614-5777 F: 404-614-5400 John Portman, Jr.
Johnson & Johnson China Ltd. 3285 Dongguan Rd. Minhang, Shanghai 200240 T: 6430-2010 F: 6430-4220 Albert Bennett	Health Care Products	Johnson & Johnson One Johnson & Johnson Plaza New Brunswick, NJ 08933 T: 908-524-0400 F: 908-214-0332 Willard D. Nielsen
Johnson & Johnson Ltd. Shanghai 120 Nanya Rd. Minhang, Shanghai 200240 T: 6430-2410 F: 6430-2579 David M. Chan	Adhesive Bandages	Johnson & Johnson One Johnson & Johnson Plaza New Brunswick, NJ 08933 T: 908-524-0400 F: 908-214-0332 Willard D. Nielsen
JP Morgan Shanghai Office Suite 665, Shanghai Center 1376 Nanjing West Rd., Shanghai 200040 T: 6279-7301 F: 6279-7316 Jianshan Wei	Investment Banking Financial Services	J. P. Morgan & Co. 60 Wall St. New York, NY 10260 T: 212-648-9528 F: 212-648-5193 Neil Gluckin
K-Mart Far East Ltd. Rm. 708 Union Bldg. 100 Yanan East Rd., Shanghai 200002 T: 6311-4708 F: 6320-2164 Heidi E. Landry	Consumer Products	KMART Corp. 3100 W. Big Beaver Rd. Troy, MI 48084 T: 313-643-1000 F: 313-643-5249 Thomas Watkins
Kemtech Inc. Rm. 1404 Donghu Hotel 167 Xingle Rd., Shanghai 200031 T: 6437-0050 x 1404 F: 6433-1275 x 1404 Xitan Wang	Medical Instruments	Kemtech 20488 Chalet Lane Saratoga, CA 95070 T: 408-867-0818 F: 408-867-3693 Shauley Cheng

China Office	**Product/Service**	**U.S. Head Office**
Kentucky Fried Chicken Co. 1221 Yanan West Rd. Shanghai 200050 T: 6210-7008 F: 6210-7500 Benjamin Koo	Fast Food	KFC Corp. P. O. Box 32070 Louisville, KY 40232 T: 502-456-8300 F: 502-456-8306 Donald Parkinson / Jean Litterst
Ketchum-Newscan Public Relations Ltd. Rm. 412 Main Bldg., Donglong AIA Bldg. 223 Xikang Rd., Shanghai 200040 T: 6247-3023 F: 6247-3069 Li Yixin	Public Relations	Ketchum Communications Inc. 6 PPG Place Pittsburg, PA 15222 T: 412-456-3500 Daniel Madia / David R Drobis
Kimberly-Clark Corp. Shanghai Shanghai T: 6482-1274 General Manager	Fiber-based Products Lumber & Paper Products	Kimberly-Clark Corp. P. O. Box 619100 Dallas, TX 75261 T: 972-281-1200 F: 972-281-1490 Tina S. Barry
Kodak (China) Ltd. 2-5/F Novel Plaza 128 Nanjing West Rd., Shanghai 200003 T: 6350-0888 x 1687 F: 6372-8866 Jiwen Zhang	Film Products	Eastman Lodak Co. 343 State St. Rochester, NY 14650 T: 716-724-4000 F: 716-724-0663 Willy Shih / Robert Smith
Kohler Co. Shanghai Office Unit A-914 Yin Hai Bldg. 250 Caoxi Rd., Shanghai 200233 T: 6482-1252 F: 6482-1255 General Manager	Sanitary Ware	**Kohler Co.** 444 Highland Dr. Kohler, WI 53044-1500 T: 920-457-1271 F: 920-457-1595 Bernhard H. Langel
KPMG Peat Marwick G/F, Office Bldg., Yangtze New World Hotel 2099 Yanan West Rd., Shanghai 200335 T: 6275-6658 F: 6275-7314 General Manager	Accounting	**KPMG Peat Marwick** 530 Chestnut Ridge Rd. Woodcliff Lake, NJ 07675 T: 201-505-3585 F: 201-505-3411 Timothy Pearson
Kraft General Foods Suite 318 Shanghai Center 1376 Nanjing West Rd., Shanghai 200040 T: 6279-8108 F: 6279-8800 Karl Feng	Food Products	Kraft Foods Int'l Inc. 800 Westchester Ave. Rye Brook, NY 10573 T: 914-335-7831 F: 914-335-1522 James King / James Ko
Kunlun Alloy Materials Co., Ltd. Yuan Town Chongqing County, Shanghai 202162 T: 5943-1628 F: 5945-1854 Suqin He	Alloy Materials for H. V. Resistor	**"American Business in China"** **is** **the leading publication** **on US-China trade.**
Lattice Semiconductor Shanghai Co Ltd. 6/F, No. 10, 471 Guiping Rd. Shanghai 200233 T: 6485-2865 F: 6485-2860 Kaihe Zhang	Semiconductor Products	Lattice Semiconductor Corp. 5555 NE Moore Ct. Hillsboro, OR 97214 T: 503-681-0118 F: 503-681-0347 C. Tsui

China Office	Product/Service	U.S. Head Office
Leo Burnett Shanghai Advertising Co. 325 Changle Rd. Shanghai 200031 T: 6433-5045 F: 6433-1419 General Manager	Advertising	Leo Burnett Co., Inc. 35 West Wacker Dr. Chicago, IL 60601 T: 312-220-5959 F: 312-220-3299 James G. Oates
Lester B Knight Int'l 712 Electric Power Bldg. 430 Xu Jia Hui Rd., Shanghai 200025 T: 6472-9878 F: 6472-4764 Hai-Chao Chen	Architectural Services Engineering Services	Lester B Knight & Associates Inc. 549 W. Randolph St. Chicago, IL 60661 T: 312-577-3000 F: 312-346-9725 S. Mitchell
Liebert Suite 510 Shanghai Center 1376 Nanjing West Rd., Shanghai 200040 T: 6279-8325 F: 6279-8397 Barry Kwok	Computer Support Systems	Liebert Corp. 1050 Dearborn Dr. Columbus, OH 43229 T: 614-888-0246 F: 614-841-6022 Dennis Webb / Joe Filippi
Lighnin (China) Mixers Co. Ltd. 1/F, Building 18, 485 Guiping Rd. Shanghai 200233 T: 6485-3018 F: 6485-2438 S. H. Chung	Industrial Mixers	Lightnin 135 Mt. Read Blvd., PO Box 1370 Rochester, NY 14611 T: 716-436-5550 F: 716-436-5589 W. Owen Li
Linco Color Printing Co. Ltd. No. 150 Zhaoxiang, Weining Rd. Shanghai 200335 T: 6233-2581 F: 6241-0566 You-ou Lin	Computer Printing	Linco Printing Inc. 5022 23rd St. Long Island City, NY 11101 T: 718-729-4450 A. Lin
Liz Claiborne Rm. 2501/05 Union Bldg. 100 Yanan East Rd., Shanghai 200002 T: 6326-5910 F: 6320-1124 Margaret Li	Apparel	Liz Claiborne 1441 Broadway New York, NY 10018 T: 212-354-4900 F: 212-626-1594 Robin Scheer-Ettinger
Loctite (China) Co. Ltd. Rm. B-909, Yin Hai Bldg. 250 Caoxi Rd., Shanghai 200233 T: 6482-4676 F: 6482-4677 General Manager	Industrial Adhesives	Loctite Corp. 10 Columbus Blvd. Hartford, CT 06106 T: 860-520-5000 F: 860-520-5073 David Freeman
Lucent Technologies 704 Yishan Rd. Shanghai 200233 T: 6470-5858 F: 6470-0441 Yeng Paul Wong	Computers	Lucent Technologies 600 Mountain Ave. Murray Hill, NJ 07974 T: 908-582-8500 F: 908-508-2576 Tom Uhlman / Carl Hsu
Mannington Carpets Shanghai Shanghai T: 6255-4135 F: 6255-5133 General Manager	Carpets & Rugs	Mannington Mills Inc. Box 30, Mannington Mills Rd. Salem, NJ 08079 T: 609-935-3000 F: 609-339-5813 G. Anderson

China Office	Product/Service	U.S. Head Office
Mary Kay Cosmetics Inc. Shanghai Shanghai T: 6249-1507 F: 6249-0306 General Manager	Cosmetic Products	Mary Kay Cosmetics Inc. 16251 Dallas Parkway Dallas, TX 75248 T: 972-687-6300 F: 972-638-4755 Tim Wentworth
Maybelline Co. Suite E, 2/F, Apollo Bldg. 1440 Yanan Middle Rd., Shanghai 200040 T: 6248-6263 x 118 F: 6249-3486 General Maanger	Cosmetic Products	Maybelline Co. P. O. Box 3392 N. Little Rocks, AR 72117 T: 501-945-0811 F: 501-945-8503 Jack Bucher
McCann-Erickson Guangming Ltd. 5/F, 277 Wuxing Rd. Shanghai 200030 T: 6433-1233 F: 6433-1286 Bernard Yiu	Advertising	McCann-Erickson Worldwide 750 Third Ave. New York, NY 10017 T: 212-697-6000 F: 212-867-5177 Marcia Moreira
McCormick Seasonings & Foodstuffs Co Ltd. 550 Zhumei Rd. Shanghai 200237 T: 6476-0859 F: 6476-1620 Xiaofang Hou	Food Products Seasonings & Flavorings	McCormick & Co., Inc. 18 Loveton Circle Sparks, MD 21152-6000 T: 410-771-7830 F: 410-527-8195 Gary Zimmerman
McDonald's (China) Co. Ltd. 2/F Matlock Center 890 Chengde Rd., Shanghai 200040 T: 6271-3532 F: 6218-6493 Joseph Lao	Fast Food	McDonald's Corp. One McDonald's Plaza Oak Brook, IL 60521 T: 630-623-3000 F: 630-623-8843 James R. Cantalupo
McDonnell Douglas China Technical Services 3115 Changzhong Rd. Shanghai 200436 T: 5668-1122 F: 5668-4345 Arlen Marsyla	Aircraft	McDonnell Douglas Corp. P. O. Box 516 St. Louis, MO 63134 T: 314-234-7015 F: 314-234-3826 Rita Luddon
McKinsey & Co. Shanghai Shanghai T: 6323-9233 F: 6323-9850 General Maanger	Management Consultants	McKinsey & Co., Inc. 55 E. 52nd St. New York, NY 10022 T: 212-446-7000 F: 212-446-8575 Stewart Flack
Meadow Gold Foods Co Ltd. 1267 Yangshupu Rd. Shanghai 200082 T: 6546-1020 F: 6541-8056 Sam Wang	Ice Cream & Frozen Food	Borden, Inc. 180 E. Broad St. Columbus, OH 43215 T: 614-225-7480 F: 614-225-7602 J. R. Anderson
Mearl Corp. Rm. 207, 30 Si Nan Rd. Shanghai 200020 T: 6473-9501 General Manager	Paerlescent Luster Pigments	Engelhard Corp. 101 Wood Ave. Iselin, NJ 08830 T: 732-205-7125 F: 732-494-9009 Charles Eggert

China Office	Product/Service	U.S. Head Office
Merck Sharp & Dohme (China) Ltd. Rm. 1001 Astronautics Bldg. 222 Caoxi Rd., Shanghai 200233 T: 6472-1992 F: 6472-1980 General Manager	Pharmaceuticals	Merck & Co., Inc. One Merck Dr. Whitehouse Station, NJ 08889 T: 908-423-1000 F: 908-423-1043 Attn: Japan Administration WS-2B-80
Merrill Lynch International Co. Suite 308 Shanghai Center 1376 Nanjing West Rd., Shanghai 200040 T: 6279-7032 F: 6279-7031 Liping Zhang	Investment Banking Financial Services	Merrill Lynch & Co. World Financial Center North Tower New York, NY 10281 T: 212-449-1000 F: 212-449-7357 Winthrop H. Smith, Jr.
Mettler-Toledo Instruments (Shanghai) Ltd. A-4, 471 Guiping Rd. Shanghai 200233 T: 6485-0435 F: 6485-3351 Ted Xia	Laboratory Instruments	Mettler-Toledo, Inc. 350 West Wilson Bridge Rd. Worthington, OH 43085 T: 614-438-4511 F: 614-438-4900 John Robechek
Micro Intelligent Systems Corp. Rm. 58340 Jinjiang Club 58 Maoming South Rd., Shanghai 200070 T: 6431-9047 F: 6431-5670 Zhang Xiao Lu	Software	Auto-Trol Technology Corp. 12500 N. Washington St. Denver, CO 80241 T: 303-452-4919 F: 303-252-2249 R. Eubanks
Micro Max Electronics Co. Ltd. 332 Lingling Rd. Shanghai 200032 T: 6416-7308 F: 6416-7821 John Lee	Monitor Testing Cards Electronic Products	Micro Max 10518 Harwin Dr. Houston, TX 77036 T: 713-772-3888 F: 713-772-3889 John Lee
Milliken China Inc. Suite 302, In-Point Center 266 Xikang Rd., Shanghai 200040 T: 6213-5005 F: 6213-5006 Craig Ackerman	Carpet Fabric Finishing	Milliken & Co. PO Box 29304, 920 Milliken Rd. Spartanburg, SC 29303 T: 864-503-2020 F: 864-503-2100 John Fly / Richard Dillard
Millipore Corp Shanghai Office Rm. 2806 Union Bldg. 100 Yanan East Rd., Shanghai 200002 T: 6373-7256 F: 6320-0236 General Manager	Precision Filters	Millipore Corp. Ashley Rd. Bedford, MA 01730 T: 781-533-6000 F: 781-533-3110 Thomas Anderson
Mobil Asia-Pacific PTE Ltd. Suite 528 Shanghai Center 1376 Nanjing West Rd., Shanghai 200040 T: 6279-8229 F: 6279-8329 P. M. Chua	Chemicals Petrochemicals	Mobil Corp. 3225 Gallows Rd. Fairfax, VA 22037-0001 T: 703-846-3000 F: 703-846-4669 Robert Swanson
Monsanto Far East Ltd. 9/F Novel Plaza 128 Nanjing West Rd., Shanghai 200003 T: 6350-9645 F: 6350-9655 Dennis Wan	Agro-Chemical Products Pharmaceuticals	Monsanto Co. 800 N. Lindbergh Blvd. St. Louis, MO 63167 T: 314-694-3316 F: 314-694-3635 Nha D. Hoang

China Office	**Product/Service**	**U.S. Head Office**
Morgan Stanley Asia Ltd. Suite 700B Shanghai Center 1376 Nanjing West Rd., Shanghai 200040 T: 6279-7150 F: 6279-7157 Ziwang Xu	Investment Banking Consulting	Morgan Stanley & Co. 60 Wall St. New York, NY 10260 T: 212-761-4000 F: 212-762-0094 Jeanmarie McFadden
Motorola China Electronics Ltd. 5/F, Center Plaza 16 Henan South Rd., Shanghai 200002 T: 6374-7668 F: 6374-3788 Kurt Kalwitz	Telecommunications	Motorola Inc. 1303 E. Algonquin Rd. Schaumburg, IL 60196 T: 847-576-5000 F: 847-576-4700 Richard W. Younts
MSL Express Inc. Shanghai Shanghai T: 6406-5563 F: 6406-5611 General Manager	Freight Forwarder	MSL Express Inc. 16019 Rockaway Blvd. Jamaica, NY 11434 T: 718-528-1833 F: 718-528-1507 C Tong
MTS Systems (China) Inc. Rm. 288, New South Bldg., Jingjiang Hotel 59 Maoming Rd., Shanghai 200020 T: 6472-5950 F: 6472-3573 Desmond Choir	Sensors & Controls	MTS Systems Corp. 14000 Technology Dr. den Prairie, MN 55344-2290 T: 612-937-4000 F: 612-937-4515 Karen Odash
National Starch & Chemical Ltd. Rm. 4048 Huating Hotel 1200 Caoxi North Rd., Shanghai 200030 T: 6439-7715 F: 6439-6322 General Manager	Adhesives & Sealants Resins & Chemicals	National Starch & Chemical Co. 10 Finderne Ave. Bridgewater, NJ 08807-3300 T: 908-685-5000 F: 908-685-5005 R. John Forrest
NCR (China) Ltd. Rm. 2504/07, LT Square 500 Chendu North Rd., Shanghai 200003 T: 6360-6863 F: 6360-6864 General Manager	Computers	NCR Corp. 1700 S. Patterson Blvd. Dayton, OH 45479 T: 937-445-2000 F: 937-445-1847 Hideaki Takahashi
Neles Jamesbury Valve Co. Ltd. 1063 Siping Rd. Shanghai 200092 T: 6502-1410 F: 6502-0368 John Lucy	Valves	Neles-Jamesbury Inc. 40 Lincoln St. Worcester, MA 01615 T: 508-852-0200 F: 508-852-8172 Thomas Sturiale
New York Life Worldwide Holding Inc. Rm. 619, Central Place 16 Henan South Rd., Shanghai 200002 T: 6374-0220 F: 6374-8180 Yide Qiao	Insurance	New York Life Insurance Co. 51 Madison Ave. New York, NY 10010 T: 212-576-7000 F: 212-576-8145 Richard Wecker / William F Yelverton
Nordson China Co., Ltd. 828 Xinjinqiao Rd. Pudong, Shanghai 201206 T: 5845-2345 F: 5854-9150 Bai Zhiying	Industrial Coatings Packaging Machinery Sealant Application Eqmt	Nordson Corp. 11475 Lakefield Dr. Duluth, GA 30097 T: 770-497-3400 F: 770-497-3588 Peg Watkins / Daniel Chen

China Office	Product/Service	U.S. Head Office
Northern Telecom Rm. 807 Central Place 16 Henan South Rd., Shanghai 200002 T: 6355-2008 F: 6355-3003 General Manager	Telecommunications Eqmt	Northern Telecom P. O. Box 1222 Minneapolis, MN 55440 T: 612-932-8000 F: 612-932-8235 Flo Graham
Northwest Airlines Suite 207, Shanghai Center 1376 Nanjing West Rd., Shanghai 200040 T: 6279-8100 F: 6279-8007 Herman Wan	Airlines	Northwest Airlines 2700 Lone Oak Pkwy. Egan, MN 55112 T: 612-726-2111 F: 612-726-0343 Michael E. Levine
Norton Abrasives Co. Ltd. 198 Beidou Road Minhang, Shanghai 200240 T: 6430-7002 F: 6430-4614 Jack Bresnahan	Ceramic Wheels	Norton Company 1 New Bond St. Worcester, MA 01605 T: 508-795-5000 F: 508-795-2599 Mae Wang
O'Melveny & Myers LLP Rm. 2011 Shanghai Int'l Trade Center 2200 Yanan West Rd., Shanghai 200335 T: 6219-5363 F: 6275-4949 Howard Chao	Law	O'Melveny & Myers 54/F, Citicorp Center, 153 E. 53rd St. New York, NY 10022-4611 T: 212-326-2000 F: 212-326-2061 Ko-Yung Tung
Occidental Chemical China Ltd. Rm. 2106 Ruijin Bldg. 205 Maoming South Rd., Shanghai 200020 T: 6472-3667 F: 6472-3595 General Manager	Chemicals	Occidental Petroleum Corp. 10889 Wilshire Blvd. Los Angeles, CA 90024 T: 310-208-8800 F: 310-443-6688 John Morgan
Ogilvy & Mather 7/F Yixiang Bldg. 1599 Yanan West Rd., Shanghai 200050 T: 6210-8068 F: 6210-8048 Harrison Dong	Advertising Public Relations	Ogilvy & Mather Worldwide Worldwide Plaza, 309 W. 49th St. New York, NY 10019 T: 212-237-4000 F: 212-237-5515 William Gray
Oracle Systems China Ltd. North Mansion, 999 Zhongshan Nan Yi Rd. Shanghai 200023 T: 6472-9810 F: 6472-9410 James Xu	Software	Oracle Corp. 500 Oracle Parkway Redwood City, CA 94065 T: 415-506-7000 F: 415-506-7200 Raymond Lane / David Roux
Oral-B (Shanghai) Ltd. 550 Sanlin Rd. Pudong, Shanghai 200124 T: 5841-1030 F: 5841-1724 Shaokun Huang	Tooth Brushes	The Gillette Co. Prudential Tower Boston, MA 02199 T: 617-421-7000 F: 617-421-7123 Peter Kent
Otis Elevator Co. Ltd. 9/F, Guanming Mansion 2 Jinling East Rd., Shanghai 200002 T: 6248-8431 F: 6248-5363 Diane Long	Elevators	Otis Elevators Co. 10 Farm Springs Farmington, CT 06032 T: 860-676-6000 F: 860-676-6970 Steve Page

China Office	Product/Service	U.S. Head Office
Pacific Rim Resources Inc. Rm. 406 Huashan Hotel 2004 Nanjing West Rd., Shanghai 200040 T: 6248-8431 F: 6248-5363 Angie Eagan	Consulting	Pacific Rim Resources, Inc. 201 Spear St., #1620 San Francisco, CA 94105 T: 415-986-6715 F: 415-495-1821 Julie Reinganum
Pacific Technology Venture Fund Co. 383 Yongjia Rd. Shanghai 200031 T: 6433-7799 F: 6431-4102 Suyang Zhang	Consulting Venture Capital	PTV-China, Inc. 155 Bovet Road, #650 San Mateo, CA 94402 T: 650-286-2796 F: 650-286-2790 John Breyer
Panduit Shanghai Rm. 803 Gold Field Office Bldg. Lu Jia Bang Rd., Shanghai 200011 T: 6312-3215 F: 6312-1654 Joseph Zhu	Communication Products	**Panduit Corp.** 17301 Ridgeland Ave. Tinley Park, IL 60477 T: 708-532-1800 F: 708-614-0254 John Kwong / William Wholley
Paper Cup Co., Ltd. Rm. 203, Building 11 Lane 536, Xujiahui Rd., Shanghai 200025 T: 6482-1319 F: 6473-9132 Meixia Zhu	Paper Cups Paper Tableware	**"American Business in China"** **is** **the leading publication** **on US-China trade.**
Parheavy Co., Ltd. Rm. 504, Bldg. 17 17 Xhong Shan Rd. E., Shanghai 200002 T: 6321-5770 x 504 F: 6323-5965 Xing Zhichun	Silk Products	Parheavy USA Inc. 111 West 40th St., 19/F New York, NY 10018 T: 212-302-4550 F: 212-302-4592 Fu Kang Huang
Parker Hannifin Singapore Pte Ltd. Rm. 703 Dynasty Business Center 459 North Wulumuqi Rd., Shanghai 200004 T: 6249-0308 General Manager	Motion-control Products	Parker Hannifin Corp. 17325 Euclid Ave. Cleveland, OH 44112 T: 216-531-3000 F: 216-383-9414 Duane E Collins
Parlex Circuit Co. Shanghai Shanghai T: 6436-3464 F: 6470-3128 General Manager	Electronic Products	Parlex Flexible Circuit Products Co. 145 Milk St. Methuen, MA 01844 T: 508-685-4341 H Pollack
Peking Handicrafts Inc. Shanghai Shanghai T: 6406-9166 F: 6406-9186 General Maanger	Arts & Crafts	Peking Handicraft Inc. 1388 San Mateo Ave. S San Francisco, CA 94080 T: 650-871-3788 F: 650-871-3781 Dicky Lo
Pepsi-Cola Beverage Co. Ltd. 288 Wenjing Rd. Minhang, Shanghai 200240 T: 6430-3280 F: 6430-1377 Qiufang Chen	Soft Drinks	PepsiCo International 1 Pepsi Way Somers, NY 10589 T: 914-767-6000 F: 914-767-6553 Keith Hughes

China Office	Product/Service	U.S. Head Office
Pepsico Snacks Co. Ltd. Block 2, Pan Pacific Building 1221 Yanan West Rd., Shanghai 200050 T: 6210-2005 F: 6210-2004 Kelly S. C. Yu	Snacks & Crackers	PepsiCo International 1 Pepsi Way Somers, NY 10589 T: 914-767-6000 F: 914-767-6533 Keith Hughes
Perkin Elmer China Inc. 2/F, Baozhaolong Library 1954 Huashan Rd., Shanghai 200030 T: 6282-4703 F: 6282-4597 Xue Xing Guo	Analytical Instruments	Perkin-Elmer Corp. 761 Main St. Norwalk, CT 06859 T: 203-762-1000 F: 203-762-6000 Leslie O'Carmody
Philip Morris Asia Inc. Rm. 410, Dynasty Business Center 457 Wulumuqi North Rd., Shanghai 200040 T: 6248-8026 F: 6248-8410 John Y. N. Sze	Cigarette Products	Philip Morris Int'l 800 Westchester Ave. Rye Brook, NY 10573 T: 914-335-1120 F: 914-335-1372 Andreas Gembler
Phillips China Inc. Rm. 1513 Shanghai Int'l Trade Center 2200 Yanan West Rd., Shanghai 200335 T: 6270-8438/39 F: 6270-8437 General Manager	Petroleum Products	Phillips Petroleum Co. Plaza Office Bldg. Bartlesville, OK 74004 T: 918-661-6600 F: 918-662-2780 Mike Coffelt
PictureTel Int'l Corp. Rm. 15, 6/F, Central Place Business Center No. 16, Henan Rd. South, Shanghai 200002 T: 6374-0220 x 6155 F: 6374-8180 Jiangong Ma	Video Conferencing Systems Network Bridging Products	PictureTel Corp. 100 Minuteman Rd. Andover, MA 01810 T: 508-292-5000 F: 508-292-3375 Tom Pesut
Pillar Industries Shanghai Ofice Rm. 104 Jian Lan Bldg., Magnolia Garden 50 Puhuitang Rd., Shanghai 200030 T: 6481-1485 F: 6481-3573 General Manager	Heating & Melting Equipment Electronic Components	Pillar Industries N92 W15800 Megal Dr. Menomonee Falls, WI 53051 T: 414-255-6470 F: 414-255-0359 W. Blackmong
Pinkerton (China) Shanghai Office Rm. 6207, Office Tower, Ruijing Hotel 116 Ruijing Er Rd., Shanghai 200020 T: 6467-0539 F: 6467-0541 Ken Mason	Security Services	Pinkerton's Inc. 15910 Ventura Blvd., #900 Encino, CA 91436 T: 818-380-8800 F: 818-380-8997 Mike Sturgin
Polaroid of Shanghai Ltd. Suite 1001, Shanghai Int'l Trade Center 2200 Yanan West Rd., Shanghai 200335 T: 6275-1124 F: 6275-8784 Charles Mo	Electric Circuit Cameras & Instant Film	Polaroid Corp. 549 Technology Square Cambridge, MA 02139 T: 781-386-3284 F: 781-386-9333 Carole Uhrich
Porta Asiatica Trading Ltd. Rm. 301A, Shanghai Equatorial Hotel 65 Yanan West Rd., Shanghai 200040 T: 6248-2598 F: 6248-1834 Robert S. Smith	Trading	A W Chesterton Company 225 Fallon Rd. Stoneham, MA 02180 T: 617-438-7000 F: 617-438-2930 Sue Myers

China Office	Product/Service	U.S. Head Office
Portman Shangri-La 1376 Nanjing West Rd. Shanghai 200040 T: 6279-8888 F: 6279-8800 General Manager	Hotel	Portman Properties 225 Peachtree St. NE Atlanta, GA 30303 T: 404-614-5777 F: 404-614-5400 John Portman, Jr.
Pratt & Whitney Rm. 305, Bldg. #4, Hongqiao Int'l Airport 2550 Hongqiao Rd., Shanghai 200335 T: 6255-8899 x 5322 F: 6255-7210 Ted Kwan	Aircraft Engines	Pratt & Whitney 400 Main St. East Hardford, CT 06108 T: 203-565-4321 x 5875 James Johnson / A. Anderson
Praxair-Baosteel Inc. Shanghai Rm. 8130/31/35 Shanghai Worldfield Hotel 2106 Hongqiao Rd., Shanghai 200335 T: 6270-4552 F: 6270-4551 Charles M. Richbaum	Industrial Gas	Praxair Inc. 39 Old Ridgebury Rd. Danbury, CT 06810 T: 203-837-2000 F: 203-837-2505 Jose L. Travassos
President Int'l Foods Co. Ltd. 580 Laohumin Rd. Shanghai 200237 T: 6482-0280 F: 6482-4882 Shenji Zhang	Food Products	President Global Corp. 6965 Aragon Cir. Buena Park, CA 90620 T: 714-994-2990 F: 714-523-3142 Ping C. Wu
Price Waterhouse 8/F, Hangtian Bldg. 222 Caoxi Rd., Shanghai 200030 T: 6482-8028 F: 6482-0688 Alistir Laband	Accounting Consulting	Price Waterhouse LLP 1177 Ave. of the Americas New York,NY 10020 T: 212-596-7000 F: 212-596-8910 James Daley / Robert Gazzi
Proctor & Gamble Ltd. 1807/08 Rujin Bldg. 205 Maoming Rd., Shanghai 200020 T: 6472-8489 F: 6472-7590 James Yin	Consumer Products	Proctor & Gamble Co. 1 Proctor & Gamble Plaza, PO Box 599 Cincinnati, OH 45201-0599 T: 513-983-1100 F: 513-983-9369 Alan G. Lafley
Project Hope c/o Shanghai Second Medical University 280 Chongqing South Rd., Shanghai 200025 T: 6384-0609 F: 6385-0525 Tom McLean	Health Education	Project Hope 454 N. Pearl St. Albany, NY 12204 T: 518-465-7378 F: 518-465-9672 S. Roberts
Prudential Securities Shanghai Rep. Office Rm. 453 Shanghai Center 1376 Nanjing West Rd., Shanghai 200040 T: 6279-8562 F: 6279-8205 Brewer S. Stone	Fianncial Services	Prudential Securities Inc. 199 Water St. New York, NY 10292 T: 212-214-1000 Michael Madigan
Quaker Chemical Shanghai Unit C, 29/F, Industrial Investment Bldg. 18 Cao Xi Rd. N. , Shanghai 200030 T: 6427-5775 F: 6427-5780 William Wu	Chemicals	Quaker Chemicals Corp. Elm & Lee Streets Conshohocken, PA 19428-0809 T: 610-832-4000 F: 610-832-8682 Daniel S. Ma

China Office	Product/Service	U.S. Head Office
R. R. Donnelly & Sons Corp. Rm. 2506 Shartex Plaza 88 Zunyi South Rd., Shanghai 200335 T: 6219-8888 F: 6219-2288 Mark P. S. Hing	Printing & Publishing	R R Donnelley & Sons Co. 77 W. Wacker Dr. Chicago, IL 60601 T: 312-326-8000 F: 312-326-8543 Steven J. Baumgartner
Rass Blood Products Co. Ltd. 55 Beidou Rd. Minhang, Shanghai 200240 T: 6430-4004 F: 4630-1713 Jihong Zhang	Blood Products	Rare Antibody & Antigens Supply Co. 30423 Canwood St. Agoura Hills, CA 91301 T: 818-991-6117 F: 818-991-1870 Christine Duque
Ray & Berndtson Ltd. Suite 321 Shanghai Int'l Business Center 2004 nanjing West Rd., Shanghai 200040 T: 6248-2282 F: 6248-0489 General Manager	Executive Search	Ray & Berndtson 301 Commerce, #2300 Fort Worth, TX 76102 T: 817-334-0500 F: 817-334-0779 D Radden
Raychem Shanghai Cable Accessories Ltd. 287 Qinjiang Rd. Caohejing Hi-Tech Park, Shanghai 201103 T: 6485-3288x 2308 F: 6485-0361 Robert Lo	Cable Accessories	Raychem Corp. 300 Constitution Dr. Menlo Park, CA 94025 T: 650-361-3333 F: 650-361-7377 Scott Wylie
Rayonier China Ltd. Unit 304, Office Bldg., Hotel Equatorial 65 Yanan West Rd., Shanghai 200040 T: 6248-2510 F: 6248-8929 General Manager	Forestry Pulp	Rayonier Inc. 1177 Summer St. Stamford, CT 06905 T: 203-348-7000 F: 203-348-0005 Kent B. Smith
Raytheon Int'l Inc. Rm. 562 Shanghai Center 1376 Nanjing West Rd., Shanghai 200040 T: 6279-7468 F: 6279-7140 Jon Reynolds	Electronic Products Aviation	Raytheon Co. 141 Spring St. Lexington, MA 02173 T: 617-862-6600 F: 617-860-2172 James E. Drumgool
Rev Power Ltd. Suite 2109 Shanghai Center 1376 Nanjing West Rd., Shangha 200040 T: 6279-8080 F: 6279-8081 Robert R. Aronson	Battery Components	Rev Power Products 268 W. Cluster St. San Bernardino, CA 92408 T: 909-889-5612 K. Jensen
Rhone Poulenc Shanghai Office Rm. 604, Electrical Power Bldg. 430 Xujiahui Rd., Shanghai 200025 T: 6472-8860 F: 6472-8256 General Manager	Pharmaceuticals	Rhone-Poulenc Rorer Inc. 500 Arcola Rd., P. O. Box 1200 Collegeville, PA 19426-0107 T: 215-454-8000 F: 215-454-3812 Alain Audubert
Rich Products Co. Rm. 406, Jingan Commercial House 301 Huashan Rd., Shanghai 200040 T: 6248-8437 F: 6248-8086 Jay Gmerek	Frozen Foods	Rich Products 1 W. Ferry Buffalo, NY 14240 T: 716-878-8000 F: 716-878-8368 J. Gmerek

China Office	**Product/Service**	**U.S. Head Office**
Rockwell Collins International Inc. Suite 1310 New Town Mansion 55 Loushanguan Rd., Shanghai 200335 T: 6219-5507 F: 6219-9152 Martin Lin	Avionics	Rockwell International Corp. 600 Anton Blvd., #700 Costa Mesa, CA 92628-5090 T: 714-424-4320 F: 714-424-4360 Derek Wimmer
Rosemount China, Inc. Suite 730 Shanghai Center 1376 Nanjing West Rd., Shanghai 200040 T: 6279-8198 F: 6279-8218 Steve A. Sonnenberg	Instruments	Rosemount Inc. 12001 Technology Dr. Eden Prairie, MN 55344 T: 612-941-5560 F: 612-828-7795 Ron A. Ward
Rust China Shanghai Shanghai T: 6249-2087 F: 6249-2084 General Manager	Engineering Services	Rust International Inc. 100 Corporate Pkwy. Birmingham, AL 35242 T: 205-995-7878 F: 205-995-7150 R Gilbert
Saatchi & Saatchi Advertising 3/F Hufu Commerce Bldg. 365 Xinhua Rd., Shanghai 200052 T: 6280-0152 F: 6280-1860 General Manager	Advertising	Saatchi & Saatchi Worldwide 375 Hudson St. New York, NY 10014 T: 212-463-2000 F: 212-463-9855 Joe Cronin / Dick O'Brien
Sara Lee East Asia Unit 1012A, Yinhai Commercial Bldg. 250 Caoxi Rd., Shanghai 200233 T: 6482-9700 F: 6482-9701 A. Bennett	Personal Care Products Household Products	Sara Lee Corp. 3 First National Plaza, 70 W Madison Chicago, IL 60602 T: 312-726-2600 F: 312-726-3712 Jeffrey Smith
Sauer Shanghai Hydrostatic Transmission Co Site 76 Jinqiao Export Processing Zone Pudong, Shanghai 201206 T: 5834-5876 x 20 F: 5834-5748 General Manager	Hydrostatic Products	Sauer-Sundstrand 2800 E. 13th St. Ames, IA 50010 T: 515-239-6000 F: 515-239-6318 J. Holtan
Sauer-Sundstrand Co. Rm. 1106 Tower A, Yin Hai Bldg. 250 Caoxi Rd., Shanghai 200233 T: 6482-0569 F: 6482-2229 General Manager	Machinery	Sauer-Sundstrand 2800 E. 13th St. Ames, IA 50010 T: 515-239-6000 F: 515-239-6318 J. Holtan
Schenker (H.K.) Ltd Shanghai Office Unit 304/06 SH Taipan Business Center 20 Donghu Rd., Shanghai 200031 T: 6474-8087 F: 6472-0341 General Manager	Freight Forwarder	**Schenker Int'l Inc.** 150 Albany Ave. Freeport, NY 11520 T: 516-377-3000 F: 516-377-3100 Mike Bujold
Schring-Plough (China) Ltd. 200 Wuwei Rd. Shanghai 200333 T: 6250-2011 F: 6250-2030 Edward Tsang	Pharmaceuticals	Schering-Plough Corp. USA 1 Giralda Farms Madison, NJ 07940 T: 201-822-7000 F: 201-822-7048 Russell Elliott

China Office	Product/Service	U.S. Head Office
Scientific Atlanta of Shanghai Co Ltd. 3/F, Bldg. 18 300 Tian Lin Rd., Shanghai 200233 T: 6485-0770 F: 6485-0132 Robert Fonow	Telecommunications Test & Measurement Instru.	Scientific Atlanta Inc. 1 Technology Pkwy. Norcross, GA 30092 T: 770-903-5000 F: 770-903-4617 John Buckett / Donald Upton
Seacliff Ltd. Suite 568 Shanghai Center 1376 Nanjing West Rd., Shanghai 200040 T: 6279-8600 F: 6279-8610 Bruce Feuer	Hotel & Apartment Exhibition Center Mgmt	Portman Properties 225 Peachtree St. NE Atlanta, GA 30303 T: 404-614-5777 F: 404-614-5400 John Portman, Jr.
Sealand Service (China) Co. Ltd. Rm. 313/15, Art Center 200 Yanan West Rd., Shanghai 200040 T: 6248-1466 F: 6248-7466 Anthony Barnes	Shipping	Sea-Land Service Inc. 6000 Carnegie Blvd. Charlotte, NC 28209 T: 704-571-2000 F: 704-571-4613 Clint Eisenhauer
Sentrol Lifesafety (China) Ltd. 3/F 1399 Hunan Rd. Pudong New Area, Shanghai 201204 T: 5891-9806 F: 5891-5224 Hohnny Gu / David Henderson	Safety Sensors	Sentrol, Inc. 12345 S. E. Levetin Dr. Tualatin, OR 97062 T: 503-692-4052 F: 503-691-7564 Martha Florez
SGS-CSTC Standards and Testing Services No. 50 Qingpu Rd. Hongkou Dist., Shanghai 200080 T: 6356-1500 F: 6356-1510 Elenor Chen	Testing & Inspection Certification	SGS U.S. Testing Co Inc. 291 Fairfield Ave. Fairfield, NJ 07004 T: 973-575-5252 F: 973-575-7175 Dave Downic
Shandwick Asia Pacific Ltd. Suite 302A, Dynasty Business Center 457 Wulumuqi North Rd., Shanghai 200040 T: 6249-1901 F: 6249-0708 General Manager	Advertising	Shandwick USA 111 5th Ave., 3/F New York, NY 10003 T: 212-420-8100 F: 212-505-1397 P. Snyder
Shanghai Blackhawk Machinery Co Ltd. #902 China Record Bldg. 811 Hengshan Rd., Shanghai T: 6469-7502 F: 6469-7502 General Manager	Electrical Tools Vibration Control Products	Applied Power Inc. 13000 W. Silver Spring Dr. Butler, WI 53007 T: 414-781-6600 F: 414-781-5561 Terry Maskel
Shanghai ChiaTai Sifco Forging Co Ltd. 3301 Gonghexin Rd. Shanghai 200072 T: 5665-3100 F: 5665-3134 Yanchang Wang	Closed & Open Die Forging	Sifco Industries Inc. 970 E. 64th St. Cleveland, OH 44103 T: 216-881-8600 F: 216-881-1828 Jeffrey P. Gotschell
Shanghai Dong Fang Xerox Regional Center 12 Songshan Rd. Shanghai 200021 T: 6327-2753 F: 6327-1931 Chen Zhengming	Office Automation Eqmt	Xerox Corp. 800 Long Ridge Rd., PO Box 1600 Stamford, CT 06904 T: 203-968-3000 F: 203-968-4458 Allan E. Dugan

China Office	**Product/Service**	**U.S. Head Office**
Shanghai General Bearing Co., Ltd. 1201 Humin Rd. Minhang, Shanghai 200240 T: 6435-9874 F: 6435-7202 Joseph C. Hoo	Bearings	General Bearing Corp. 44 High St. West Nyack, NY 10994 T: 914-358-6000 David Gussack
Shanghai Hercules Chemicals Co. 9B1 Harvest Bldg. 585 Longhua West Rd., Shanghai 200232 T: 6469-5438 F: 6469-5439 General Manager	Chemicals	Hercules Inc. 1313 North Market St. Wilmington, DE 19894 T: 302-594-6600 F: 302-594-5400 Harry Tucci / Frazer Reid
Shanghai Int'l Medical Research, Inc. 207 Fu-Ter Rd. Free Trade Zone, Pudong, Shanghai T: 5866-8111 F: 5866-8222 Allan Wang	Herbal Medicine	International Medical Research Inc. 2900-B Saturn St. Brea, CA 92821 T: 714-524-5533 F: 714-524-5222 John Chen
Shanghai Int'l Port Engr. Consultants Ltd. 4/F, 110 Huang Pu Rd. Shanghai 200080 T: 6306-0665 F: 6329-0202 Yu Qingeng	Engineering Services	Han-Padron Associates 11 Penn Plaza, #925 New York, NY 10001 T: 212-736-5466 F: 212-629-4406 Edward Han
Shanghai Johnson Ltd. 932 Xinjinqiao Rd. Shanghai 201206 T: 5899-4833 F: 5899-0288 General Manager	Chemical Products	S C Johnson & Son Inc. 1525 Howe St. Racina, WI 53403 T: 414-631-2000 F: 414-260-2632 John R. Buerkle
Shanghai Klemp Metal Products Co., Ltd. 8515 Shanghai Road Pudong Area, Shanghai 201201 T: 5858-5588 F: 5858-5892 Xu Zhi Yuan	Metal Bar Grating	Klemp Corporation 1132 West Blackhawk St. Chicago, IL 60622 T: 312-440-3855 F: 312-440-9139 Kristern Sweat
Shanghai Machine Tool Works (SMTW) 1146 Jungong Rd. Shanghai 200093 T: 6548-3006 F: 6542-6752 General Manager	Machine Tools	Landis Tool Co. 20 E. 6th St. Waynesboro, PA 17268 T: 717-762-2161 F: 717-762-9530 Gary Miller
Shanghai Oakland Timber Co., Ltd. 470 Jun Gong Rd. Shanghai 200093 T: 6519-3507 F: 6539-9265 Wang Changai	Wood Products	SNP America, Inc. 2 World Trade Center, #1556 New York, NY 10048 T: 212-775-0322 F: 212-775-0325 Gui Feng Yong
Shanghai SPS Biao Wu Fasteners Co., Ltd. No. 90 Shiziwan Road, Yi Shan d. Shanghai 200030 T: 6487-7705 F: 6439-0413 Scott Keaton / Qiang Sun	Automotive Fasteners Industrial Fasteners	**SPS Technologies, Inc.** 101 Greenwood Ave., #470 Jenkintown, PA 19046 T: 215-517-2019 F: 215-517-2032 Scott Keaton

China Office	Product/Service	U.S. Head Office
Shanghai Viewsonic Electronics Co Ltd. Shanghai Shanghai T: 6470-8221 F: 6436-0236 General Manager	Computers	Viewsonic Corp. 20480 Business Parkway Walnut, CA 91789 T: 909-444-8800 F: 909-468-3756 James Chu
Shenmei Beverage & Food Co. Ltd. 3/F Universal Center 175 Xiangyang S. Rd., Shanghai 200031 T: 6430-2180 F: 6430-1915 Chengxi Chen	Bottling Coca-Cola	Coca-Cola Co. One Coca-Cola Plaza Atlanta, GA 30313 T: 404-676-2121 F: 404-676-6792 Douglas N. Daft / Sergio Zyman
Sheraton Overseas Management Corp. Sheration Huating Hotel 1200 Caoxi North Rd., Shanghai 200030 T: 6439-1000 F: 6255-0830 Grant Morrison	Hotel Management	ITT Shearton Corp. 60 State St. Boston, MA 02109 T: 617-367-3600 F: 617-367-5543 Dolores Sanchez
Siebe Environmental Controls Co. Ltd. 1599 Yanan West Rd. Shanghai 200050 T: 6210-1091 F: 6210-5848 John Cheng	Environ. Control Products	Siebe Environmental Controls 1354 Clifford Ave., PO Box 2940 Loves Park, IL 61132-2940 T: 815-637-3000 F: 815-637-5300 M. L. Rehwald
Sigma Metals Inc. 2727 Taihe West Rd. Baoshan Dist., Shanghai 201907 T: 5604-1111 F: 5604-1115 Tony Huang	Metal Forging/Smelting	Sigma International 30 Gladstone Dr. E. Brunswick, NJ 08816 T: 732-432-9755 F: 732-432-9759 Jerry Weinberg
Signode Shanghai 6E, 6F, Tseng Chow Group Bldg. 1590 Yan An Rd. W., Shanghai 200052 T: 6282-0584 F: 6280-0897 Ming Xu	Packaging Systems	ITW Signode 3600 W. Lake Ave. Glenview, IL 60025 T: 847-724-6100 F: 847-724-5910 Frank Ptak
Sonoco Hongwen Paper Company Ltd. 243 Xitai Rd. Songjiang County, Shanghai 201600 T: 6436-4431 F: 6470-0332 General Manager	Paper Products	Sonoco Products Co. 13300 Interstate Dr. Maryland Heights, MO 63043 T: 314-344-2200 F: 314-344-2223 G. I. Claes
Spencer Stuart Executive Search Shanghai Rm. 312 Wen Yi Hotel 200 Yanan West Rd., Shanghai 200040 T: 6248-5070 F: 6248-9103 General Manager	Executive Search	Spencer Stuart 401 N. Michigan Ave. Chicago, IL 60611 T: 312-822-0088 Dayton Ogden
Squibb Pharmaceuticals (Shanghai) Ltd. 1315 Jianchuan Rd. Minhang, Shanghai 200024 T: 6430-2740 F: 6430-1498 C. J. Robbins	Pharmaceuticals	Bristol-Myers Squibb Co. 345 Park Ave. New York, NY 10154 T: 212-546-4000 F: 212-546-9585 Donald J. Hayden, Jr.

China Office	**Product/Service**	**U.S. Head Office**
Steelcase Asia Inc. Flat 20, F2, Jiushi Renaissance Mansion 918 uaihai Middle Rd., Shanghai 200020 T: 6415-5363 F: 6415-5364 General Manager	Office Furniture	Steelcase Inc. P. O. Box 1967, 901 44th St. SE Grand Rapids, MI 49508 T: 616-247-2710 Mark Greiner / Jerry K Myers
Stratus Computer Inc. Suite 5C, Jinming Bldg. 8 Zunyi South Rd., Shanghai 200335 T: 6219-4861 F: 6275-7362 Tomuel Yick	Computers	Stratus Computer 55 Fairbanks Blvd. Marboro, MA 01752 T: 508-460-2000 F: 508-481-8945 Gary Okimoto / Shirley Yee
Sun Microsystems China Ltd. 206/07, South Bldg., Donglong AIA Bldg. 233 Xikang Rd., Shanghai 200040 T: 6247-4068 F: 6279-3793 Freeman Nung	Computers	Sun Microsystems 2550 Garcia Ave. M/S: UMPK01-16 Mountain View, CA 94043 T: 650-960-1300 F: 650-969-9131 Tim Dwyer / Bob MacRitchie
Sunrise Furniture Industries Co. Ltd. 3050 Baoyang Rd. Shanghai 201901 T: 5680-3127 F: 5680-3126 Sangzhi Cai	Furniture	Fairmont Designs 3131 E. Main St. Compton, CA 90221 T: 310-604-9974 F: 310-604-9833 George Tsai
Sunstar United Shanghai Office Rm. 216/17 United Bldg. 350 Wu Ning Rd., Shanghai 200063 T: 6257-9690 F: 6257-9691 Sun Rongming	Home Appliance	Sunstar United Corp. 5359 Valley Blvd. Los Angeles, CA 90032 T: 213-225-4080 D. Sun
Sybase China Ltd. Rm. 2008 Shanghai Int'l Trade Center 2200 Yanan West Rd., Shanghai 200335 T: 6275-3802 F: 6275-3120 General Manager	Software	Sybase, Inc. 6475 Christie Avenue Emeryville, CA 94608 T: 510-596-3500 F: 510-658-9441 Yvonne Van Leeuwen
Tandem Software Systems Co. 418 Guilin Rd. Shanghai 200233 T: 6472-2868 F: 6472-8625 Spencer E. Loh	Computers	Tandem Computers Inc. 19333 Valco Pkwy. Cupertino, CA 95014 T: 408-725-6000 F: 408-285-4545 Gerald Peterson / Scott Thompson
Temic Shanghai 3/F, 501 Jiangchang W. Rd. Shanghai 200436 T: 5603-3193 F: 5603-3194 Allen Kwan	Electronics	Siliconix Inc. 2201 Laurelwood Dr. Santa Clara, CA 95054 T: 408-988-8000 F: 408-567-8950 Richard Kulle
Tektronix Electronic Instrument Co. Ltd. 631 Jiangning Rd. Shanghai 200041 T: 6258-0215 F: 6258-7067 Changfeng Xu	Electronic Products	Tektronix Inc. 26660 SW Parkway Wilsonville, OR 97070 T: 503-627-7111 F: 503-685-4038 Timothy Thorsteinson

China Office	Product/Service	U.S. Head Office
Tektronix Inc. Rm. 614/16 Shanghai Convention Center 500 Zhaojiabang Rd., Shanghai 200031 T: 6471-0281 F: 6471-0282 Dehui Ye	Testing/Measurement Instru.	Tektronix Inc. 26660 SW Parkway Wilsonville, OR 97070 T: 503-627-7111 F: 503-685-4038 Timothy Thorsteinson
Texas Instruments (Shanghai) Co. Rm. 1101/03 Novel Plaza 128 Nanjing West Rd., Shanghai 200003 T: 6350-9566 x 221 F: 6350-9583 General Manager	Electronics	Texas Instruments Inc. 13500 N Central Expy, PO Box 655474 Dallas, TX 75265 T: 972-995-2011 F: 972-995-4360 Fred Geyer
Tritek Int'l Co. Daan Square, 9A, Middle Bldg. 829 Yanan Middle Rd., Shanghai 200040 T: 6279-1389 F: 6247-1539 James Zhang	Semiconductor Equipment	Tritek International Co. 5000 North Pkwy Calabasas, #304 Calabasas, CA 91302 T: 818-222-9168 F: 818-225-7168 Albert Chiang
Unison International Rm. 5311 Jinjiang Hotel 58 Maoming South Rd., Shanghai 200020 T: 6472-9579 F: 6472-2551 K. W. Zhang	Trading	Unison International Corp. 651 Gateway Blvd., #880 South San Francisco, CA 94080 T: 650-877-0846 F: 650-742-0828 Deidra Deamer
Unisys China Services, Inc. 9/F, Yixiang Bldg. 1599 Yanan West Rd., Shanghai 200050 T: 6240-6240 F: 6240-6241 Kin Sang Mak	Computers	Unisys Corp. P. O. Box 500 Blue Bell, PA 19424 T: 215-986-6990 F: 215-986-2312 Thomas Yan
United Airlines Suite 204 Shanghai Center 1376 Nanjing West Rd., Shanghai 200040 T: 6279-8010 F: 6279-8853 Robert Barrett	Airlines	United Airlines Inc. 1200 E. Algonquin Rd. Elk Grove Village, IL 60007 T: 847-952-4000 McDonald Curran
United Carrier (Shanghai) Engineering Co. 1576 Nanjing West Rd. Shanghai 200040 T: 6215-4429 F: 6256-9556 Zhaowang Pan	Refrigeration	Carrier International Carrier Pkwy., P. O. Box 4808 Syracuse, NY 13221 T: 315-432-3352 F: 315-432-7216 Robert Fiesinger
United Technologies Automotive Shanghai Rm. 1209 Yinhai Commercial Bldg. 250 Caoxi Rd., Shanghai 200233 T: 6482-9686 F: 6482-9687 General Manager	Automotive Products	United Technologies Corp. United Technologies Bldg. Hartford, CT 06101 T: 860-728-7000 F: 860-728-7901 David C Manke
UOP Ltd. Shanghai 500 Wenjing Rd. Minhang, Shanghai 200245 T: 6215-5218 F: 6215-5934 James D. Yao	Chemical Products Molecular Sieves	UOP Inc. 25 E. Algonquin Rd. Des Plaines, IL 60016 T: 847-391-2000 F: 847-391-2253 M. Winfield

China Office	Product/Service	U.S. Head Office
Upjohn Suzhou Pharmaceuticals Co. 17/F, North Bldg., Vanke Plaza 37-45 Shui Cheng S. Rd., Shanghai 201103 T: 6270-2717 F: 6270-2718 Luk Depotter	Pharmaceuticals	Upjohn Co. 7000 Portage Rd. Kalamazoo, MI 49001 T: 616-323-4000 F: 616-323-4077 William N Hubbard
UPS Parcel Delivery Service Ltd. Unit 304A, Main Bldg., Equitorial Hotel 65 Yanan West Rd., Shanghai 200040 T: 6248-6060 F: 6248-1295 Leo Ng	Parcel Delivery Service	United Parcel Service of America Inc. 55 Glenlake Pkwy. Atlanta, GA 30328 T: 404-828-6000 F: 404-828-6593 Edward Schroeder
Universal Instruments (HK) Ltd. 1911/12, New Caohejing Tower 509 Cao Bao Rd., Shanghai 200233 T: 6485-3409 F: 6485-3608 Jimson Lee	Electronic Assembly Eqmt	Universal Instrument Corp. P. O. Box 825, 90 Bevier Ct. Binghamton, NY 13901 T: 607-779-5184 F: 607-779-7312 Chris Hill
US-China Business Council 2331 Jinjiang Hotel 59 Mao Ming Rd., Shanghai 200020 T: 6415-2579 F: 6415-2584 Sheila Melvin	Membership Organization	**US-China Business Council** 1818 N St. NW, #200 Washington, DC 20036 T: 202-429-0340 F: 202-775-2476 Robert A Kapp
Valmont SST Suite A802, 250 Cao Xi Rd. Shanghai 200233 T: 5760-2760 F: 5760-2345 General Manager	Irrigation Systems Steel Lighting Utility Poles	Valmont Industries One Valmont Pkwy., PO Box 358 Valley, NE 68064 T: 402-359-2201 F: 402-359-2848 M. Bay
Vetco Gray Petroleum Equipment Co. 40 Guangxin Estate (No. 2) Guangxin Rd., Shanghai 200061 T: 6214-6002 F: 6214-9670 S. K. Boey / Nekheng Tan	Oil Drilling Equipment	ABB Vetco Gray Inc. 10777 Northwest Freeway Houston, TX 77092 T: 713-681-4685 F: 713-683-2471 John Rosso
Vickers Systems Ltd. Rm. 1004/06 Shanghai Astronautics Bldg. 222 Caoxi Rd., Shanghai 200233 T: 6482-0680/81 F: 6482-0679 Yayun Li	Hydraulic Products	Vickers Inc. 3000 Strayer Maumee, OH 43537 T: 419-867-2200 F: 419-867-2650 Michael L. Teadt
W R Grace Ltd. Rm. 201/03 Shanghai Electric Power Bldg. 430 Xujiahui Rd., Shanghai 200025 T: 6472-0697 F: 6472-3783 General Manager	Chemicals	W R Grace & Co. One Town Center Rd. Boca Raton, FL 33486-1010 T: 561-362-2000 F: 561-362-2193 Bernd A. Schulte
Watlow China, Inc. Shanghai Shanghai T: 6229-8917 F: 6228-4654 Watson Ng	Temperature Controls	Watlow Electric Manufacturing Co. 12001 Lackland Rd. St. Louis, MO 63146 T: 314-878-4600 F: 314-434-1020 Jeff Melly

China Office	Product/Service	U.S. Head Office
Watson Wyatt Shanghai Office Rm. 4055 Sheraton Hua Ting 1200 Caoxi North Rd., Shanghai 200030 T: 6439-1000 x 4055 F: 6255-0830 x 4055 General Manager	Executive Search	Wyatt Co. 1500 NW K St., #800 Washington, DC 20005-1209 T: 202-626-9600 F: 202-626-9700 Paula A DeLisle
Wescon Control (Shanghai) Inc. Bldg. 6, 471 Guiping Rd. Shanghai 200233 T: 6485-0085 F: 6485-0086 Fred Ma	Ind. Automation Control	**The next edition of "American Business in China" will be published in January, 2000.**
Westinghouse Electric (China) S.A. Rm. 303/06 Dynasty Business Center 457 Wulumuqi North Rd., Shanghai 200040 T: 6249-0185 F: 6249-0702 Jane S. Lee	Power Generation Equipment	Westinghouse Electric Corp. 11 Stanwix St. Pittsburgh, PA 15222 T: 412-642-6000 F: 412-642-3266 Gregory Vereschagin / Gary M Clark
Western Transit Express Rm. 704, #3 Building Huban Complex 1250 N. 1st Zhongshan Rd., Shanghai T: 6542-6030 F: 6544-0037 David Liang	Freight Forwarder	**Western Transit Express** 1600 Walnut Pkwy. Compton, CA 90220 T: 310-898-1868 F: 310-898-1860 Edward Liang
Weyerhaeuser China Ltd. Rm. 8009 Novel Bldg. 887 Huaihai Middle Rd., Shanghai 200020 T: 6474-7606 F: 6467-3701 General Manager	Forest Timber	Weyerhaeuser Company 33663 Weyerhaeuser Way South Federal Way, WA 98003 T: 206-924-3423 F: 206-924-3332 Montye Male
Wheelabrator Shanghai Office Suite 2211, Shenxin Bldg. 200 Ninghai East Rd., Shanghai 200021 T: 6374-5997/98 F: 6374-1463 Lansun Zhang	Environmental Equipment	Wheelabrator Air Pollution Control 441 Smithfield St. Pittsburgh, PA 15222 T: 412-562-7300 F: 412-562-7254 D. Doyle
Whirlpool Greater China Inc. 8/F Novel Plaza 128 Nanjing West Rd., Shanghai 200003 T: 6350-8228 x 208 F: 6350-8239 General Manager	Major Home Appliance	Whirlpool Corp. Administrative Ctr, 2000 North M-63 Benton Harbor, MI 49022-2692 T: 616-923-5000 F: 616-923-3785 Robert D. Hall
Wyeth-Lederle (China) 19/F, Indu-Pharm Mansion 200 Tai cang Rd., Shanghai 200020 T: 6373-0303 F: 6373-0404 Lawrence Woo	Nutritional Products Pharmaceutical Products	Wyeth-Ayerst St Davids Ctr, 150 Radnor-Chester Rd. St. Davids, PA 19087 T: 610-902-1200 Kewen Jin
Xerox Shanghai Ltd. 46 Nangu Rd. Minhang, Shanghai 200240 T: 6430-0480 x 339 F: 6430-2489 Kinkuen Chang	Office Equipment Copy Machines	Xerox Corp. 800 Long Ridge Rd. PO Box 1600 Stamford, CT 06904 T: 203-968-3000 F: 203-968-4458 Allan E. Dugan

China Office	Product/Service	U.S. Head Office
Xtra International 15A, East Ocean Centre 588 Yan An Rd. E., Shanghai 200001 T: 6352-8640/41 F: 6352-8642 William Qin	Container Leasing	Xtra Corp. 60 State St., 11/F Boston, MA 02109 T: 617-367-5000 F: 617-227-3173 Karen McHenry
York Air Conditioning Refrigeration Inc. 1/F, Wanhang Commercial Center 297 Wanhang Rd., Shanghai 200335 T: 6267-5064 F: 6267-5062 Kamwai Lam	Air Conditioning Refrigeration Equipment	York International Corp. 631 S. Richland Ave., P. O. Box 1592 York, PA 17405 T: 717-771-7890 F: 717-771-6819 Jeff Cook
Zen Continental Co. Inc. 6F-A Watanabe Bldg. No. 7 N. Lin Ping Rd., Shanghai 200080 T: 6508-5146 F: 6507-0544 Robert Huang	Freight Forwarder Shipping	**Zen Continental Co., Inc**. 18111A S. Santa Fe Ave. Rancho Dominguez, CA 90221 T: 310-631-5155 F: 310-631-5222 Rachel Liu
Zoom Express Rm. 606, Block B, Yijing Bldg. 188 Zhongshan N. Rd., Shanghai 200083 T: 5671-5812 F: 5666-0810 Jack Wei	Express Courier Services	**Zoom Express** 248-58 Rockaway Blvd. Rosedale, NY 11422 T: 718-527-6222 F: 718-528-2876 Michael Duan

- - - - - T: Telephone # - - - - - F: Fax # - - - - - Shanghai Area Code: (86)21 - - - - -

China Office	Product/Service	U.S. Head Office
3Com Asia Ltd. Rm. 2405 Minshan Hotel Business Bldg. 55, Sec. 2, Renmin S. Rd., Chengdu 610021 T: 558-3333 x 2405 F: 557-3950 Jason Dong	Computer Systems Networking Products	3Com Corp. 5400 Bayfront Plaza Santa Clara, CA 95052 T: 408-764-5000 F: 408-764-5001 Matthew Kapp
3M China Ltd. 7/F, Jinzhu Bldg. 1, Xinkai St., PO Box 39, Chengdu 610016 T: 666-5259 F: 666-7442 Qin Qin	Chemical Products	**3M Company** 3M Center Bldg., Bldg. 220-14E-02 Saint Paul, MN 55144-1000 T: 612-737-0702 F: 612-733-2095 Tony Gastaldo
ADM/Archer Daniels Midland 19/F, Block B, New Times Plaza 42 Wen Wu Road, Chengdu 610017 T: 678-9381 F: 678-8601 Pan Tao	Agricultural Products	Archer-Daniels-Midland Co. P. O. Box 1470 Decatur, IL 62525 T: 217-424-5200 F: 217-424-6196 Roger Kilburn
Allen-Bradley Co. Beisi Lou, Lianda Keji Dasha No. 19, Kehua N. Rd., Chengdu 610061 T: 558-0412 F: 558-9103 Liao Zhongshu	Industrial Automation	Allen-Bradley Co. 1201 S. Second St., P. O. Box 2086 Milwaukee, WI 53201 T: 414-382-2000 F: 414-382-4444 Richard Shelton
American Standard (China) Co., Ltd. 11/F, New Times Plaza 42 Wen Wu Rd., Chengdu 610017 T: 661-3366 x 1101 F: 678-7964 Zhong Junxi	Sanitary Wares	American Standard Inc. 1 Centennial Plaza Piscataway, NJ 08855 T: 908-980-3000 F: 908-980-3219 Alan Silver
AMF Bowling Inc. 551 Jinjiang Hotel Sec. 2, Renmin S. Rd., Chengdu 610012 T: 558-2222 x 551 F: 555-7573 Liu Jiang	Sporting Goods	AMF Bowling Inc. 8100 AMF Dr. Mechanicsville, VA 23111 T: 804-730-4325 F: 804-730-0923 B Morin
AST Research Inc. 318 Tiange Wucheng Bldg. Sec. 2, Yihuan S. Rd., Chengdu 610041 T: 558-5178 F: 558-1087 Bruce Wong	Computers	AST Research Inc. 16215 Alton Parkway Irvine, CA 92619 T: 714-727-4141 F: 714-727-8584 Hoon Choo / Scott Bower
AT&T China Co., Ltd. 13/F, No. 251 Shuanglin Rd. Chengdu 610051 T: 445-6065/69 F: 445-6072 Edward Lee / Philip Shih	Telecommunications	AT&T International 295 N. Maple Ave., Rm. I-14 Basking Ridge, NJ 07920 T: 248-262-6646 F: 248-952-5095 Elizabeth Mallek
Baxter Chengdu Office Rm. 2607 Minshan Hotel Commercial Bldg. 55, Sec. 2. Renmin S. Rd., Chengdu 610021 T: 558-3333 x 2607 Liao Xiang / Sie Hong	Disposable Medical Products	Baxter International Inc. One Baxter Parkway Deerfield, IL 60015 T: 847-948-2000 F: 847-948-2887 John F. Gaither, Jr.

China Office	**Product/Service**	**U.S. Head Office**
Boeing Commercial Airplane Group Shuangliu Airport Chengdu T: 570-4278 F: 518-3799 Ron Webb	Aviation	**The Boeing Company** 7755 E. Marginal Way South Seattle, WA 98108 T: 206-655-7300 F: 206-544-2791 Raymond J. Waldmann
Cadence China Ltd. 16/F, Block B, New Times Plaza Wen Wu Rd., Chengdu 610017 T: 678-9631 F: 678-9633 Zheng Xiaofeng	Software	Cadence Design Systems Inc. 555 River Oaks Pkwy. San Jose, CA 95134 T: 408-943-1234 F: 408-944-0747 J. Costello
Chengdu KV Engine Corp. Waibei Zhaojue S. Rd., Chengdu 610082 T: 351-6591 F: 351-3035 Robert W. Hu		
Chuanshi Christiansen Corp. 3-5 West St. Er Xianqiao Rd. Chengdu 610051 T: 333-4611 F: 333-6402 Al James	Drilling Bits	
Coca-Cola Chengdu 12/F, Pacific Department Store 12 Zongfu Rd., Chengdu 610016 T: 665-3388 x 5226 F: 671-1175 Feng Jian	Soft Drinks	Coca-Cola Co. One Coca-Cola Plaza Atlanta, GA 30313 T: 404-676-2121 F: 404-676-6792 Douglas N. Daft / Sergio Zyman
Compaq Computer Hong Kong Ltd. 401 Tiange Wucheng Bldg. Sec. 2, Yihuan S. Rd., Chengdu 610041 T: 556-2758/59 F: 555-5724 General Manager	Computers	Compaq Computer Corp. 20555 State Highway 249 Houston, TX 77070 T: 281-370-0670 F: 281-514-1740 Michael Heil
Crown Worldwide Group 608 Yiyuan Dasha 8 Shaocheng Rd., Chengdu 610015 T: 663-6614 x 2213 F: 625-2046 Ren Li	Freight Forwarder	Crown Pacific 5252 Argosy Dr. Huntington Beach, CA 92649 T: 714-898-0955 F: 714-898-5640 James Thompson
Digital Equipment Corp. 2304 Minshan Hotel Business Bldg. 55 Renmin S. Rd., Chengdu 610021 T: 558-3333 x 2304 F: 557-6626 Tony Zhan	Computers	Digital Equipment Corp. 111 Powermill Rd. Maynard, MA 01754 T: 508-493-5111 F: 508-497-7374 Ronald Spinek
Dow Jones & Co., Inc. 377 Jinjiang Hotel Sec. 2, Renmin S. Rd., Chengdu 610012 T: 558-2222 F: 554-3851 Laura Luo	Business Information	Dow Jones & Co., nc. 200 Liberty St. New York, NY 10281 T: 212-416-2000 F: 212-416-2885 Karen House / James Friedlih

China Office	Product/Service	U.S. Head Office
ECI-Metro/Caterpillar No. 1, 1/F, Yingmenkou Rural Govt. Bldg. 2nd Ring Rd., W. Sec. III, Chengdu 610036 T: 779-3448 F: 774-8508 Surachai Siriluekopas	Construction Machinery	Caterpillar Inc. 100 NE Adams St. Peoria, IL 61629 T: 309-675-1000 F: 309-675-1717 Siegfried R. Ramseyer
EDS Unigraphics Rm. H-J, 14/F, New Times Plaza 42 Wen Wu Rd., Chengdu 610017 T: 678-9427 F: 662-1126 Zhang Yan	Software	EDS 5400 Legacy Dr. Plano, TX 75024 T: 972-605-6000 F: 972-605-6662 John R. Harris
EG&G Rm. 135 Sunjoy Inn 34, Sec. 4, Renmin S. Rd., Chengdu 610041 T: 556-3388 x 135 F: 557-2632 Zhang Jian	High-Tech Instruments	EG&G, Inc. 45 William St. Wellesley, MA 02181 T: 617-237-5100 F: 617-431-4115 Anthony L. Klemner / Donald M Kerr
Eli Lilly Rm. 2-B, Sunjoy Inn 34, Sec. 4, Renmin S. Rd., Chengdu 610041 T: 558-9599 F: 557-1664 Jia Ying	Pharmaceuticals	Eli Lilly & Co. Lilly Corporate Center Indianapolis, IN 46285 T: 317-276-2000 F: 317-276-2095 Gino Santini
Enron Oil & Gas China 2404 Minshan Hotel Business Bldg. 55, Sec. 2, Renmin S. Rd., Chengdu 610021 T: 558-3333 x 2404 F: 559-0267 Robert Mustard	Petroleum	Enron Corp. 333 Clay St. Houston, TX 77002 T: 713-853-6161 F: 713-646-6190 Jack White
Esso Petroleum China Ltd. Unit B, 11/F, New Times Plaza 42, Wen Wu Rd., Chengdu 610017 T: 678-9800 F: 678-5692 General Manager	Petroleum Products	Exxon Exploration Co. 233 Benmar Houston, TX 77060 T: 713-423-7765 F: 713-423-7799 J. L. Hall, Jr.
Federal Express (FedEx) 1-1 Nan Yi Bldg. Sec. 4, Renmin S. Rd., Chengdu 610041 T: 521-7082/83 F: 521-0235 Chen Jian	Courier Sevice	Federal Express Corp. 2005 Corporate Ave., 3/F Memphis, TN 38132 T: 901-369-3600 F: 901-395-4858 T Michael Glenn / David Cunningham
Fluke Co. C-1, 9/F, New Times Plaza 42 Wen Wu Rd., Chengdu 610017 T: 678-4250 F: 678-4249 Deng Wenyu	Electronic Testing & Measurement Instrument	**Fluke Corp.** 6920 Seaway Blvd. Everett, WA 98203 T: 206-347-6100 F: 206-356-5116 Ronald Wambolt / Linda Cheever
General Electric CFMI Office c/o China SW Airlines Shuangliu Airport, Chengdu 620202 T: 522-8889 x 4279 F: 555-1001 Tong Ruijun	Aircraft Engines	General Electric Co. 3135 Easton Turnpike Fairfield, CT 06431 T: 518-869-5555 F: 518-869-2828 Guy Rabbat

China Office	**Product/Service**	**U.S. Head Office**
Hewlett-Packard 7/F, Dianzi Foreign Trade Bldg. 48 Sec. 2, Yi Huan E. Rd., Chengdu 610051 T: 431-2666 F: 431-2618 He Changjian	Computers	Hewlett-Packard Co. 3000 Hanover St. Palo Alto, CA 94304 T: 650-857-1501 F: 650-857-5518 Manuel F. Diaz
Honeywell (Tianjin) Ltd. Block D, 17/F, New Times Plaza 42 Wen Wu Rd., Chengdu 610017 T: 678-6348 F: 678-7061 Lisa Li	Automatic Control Systems	Honeywell, Inc. P. O. Box 524 Minneapolis, MN 55440-0524 T: 612-951-1000 F: 612-951-0075 Larry W. Stranghoener
Huamei Steel Tubing Engineering Niu Shi Ko, Stainless Steel Tubing Factory Chengdu 610069 T: 445-1820 F: 444-3420 Chen Ganpeng	Steel Tubing	

China Office	**Product/Service**	**U.S. Head Office**
IBM China Company Ltd. 2704 Minshan Hotel 55 Renmin S. Rd., Chengdu 610021 T: 557-3369 F: 557-3364 Liu Moyuan	Computers	International Business Machines Corp. Rockwood Dr. Sleepy Hallow, NY 10591 T: 914-765-1900 F: 914-332-3753 John Dejoys
IMAG Industries inc. Rm. F&G, 18/F, New Times Plaza Wen Wu Rd., Chengdu 610017 T: 678-8584 F: 678-9608 Louis Liu	Software	IMAG Industries Inc. 3350 Scott Blvd., #54 Santa Clara, CA 95054 T: 408-727-8222 F: 408-727-8438 S Cheung
Informix Software Ltd. Unit D&E, 14/F, New Times Plaza 42 Wen Wu Rd., Chengdu 610017 T: 678-6020 F: 678-7806 Zhi Xiaojin	Software	Informix Software, Inc. 4100 Bohannon Dr. Menlo Park, CA 94025 T: 650-926-6300 F: 650-926-6593 Katleen Critchfield
Intel Architecture Development Co., Ltd. 417 Tiange Mansion Sec. 2, Yihuan Rd., Chengdu 610041 T: 558-5493 F: 558-5493 General Manager	Computers	Intel Corp. P. O. Box 58119 Santa Clara, CA 95052-8119 T: 408-765-8080 F: 408-765-5590 Leslie Vadasz / William Howe
ISP (GAF) Chengdu 381, Jinjiang Hotel 36 Renmin S. Rd., Sec. 2, Chengdu 610012 T: 557-1040 F: 557-2313 Allen Xie	Chemicals	ISP Chemicals Inc. Route 95 Calvert City, KY 42029 T: 502-395-4165 F: 502-395-1464 R. Taylor
Johnson & Johnson China Ltd. 6/F, No. 173 Zhengfu Rd. Chengdu 610017 T: 662-4066 x 3068 F: 662-1575 Hong Lei	Health Products	Johnson & Johnson One Johnson & Johnson Plaza New Brunswick, NJ 08933 T: 908-524-0400 F: 908-214-0332 Willard D. Nielsen

China Office	Product/Service	U.S. Head Office
Keystone International 1719/20 Shudu mansion Hotel 20 Shuwa Beisanjie, Chengdu 610016 T: 678-1174 F: 678-1137 General Manager	Valves & Actuators	Keystone International Inc. 9600 W. Gulf Bank Rd., PO Box 40010 Houston, TX 77040 T: 713-937-5355 F: 713-895-4044 Paul Woodward
KFC Chengdu 7/F, No. 2 Department Store 83, Dachi W. Rd., Chengdu 610016 T: 667-3145 F: 666-4618 Xiang Renkuang	Food & Beverage	KFC Corp. P. O. Box 32070 Louisville, KY 40232 T: 502-456-8300 F: 502-456-8306 Donald Parkinson / Jean Litterst
Kennametal Hardpoint, Inc. 2609 Minshan Hotel Business Bldg. 55 rrenmin S. Rd., Sec. 2, Chengdu 610021 T: 557-6510/11 F: 557-6045 Sandy Chen	Metalcutting Products	Kennametal Inc. P. O. Box 30700 Raleigh, NC 27622-0700 T: 919-829-5331 F: 919-829-5148 J. V. Massey
Kodak (China) Ltd. Suite E, 15/F, New Times Plaza 42 Wen Wu Rd., Chengdu 610017 T: 678-3866 F: 678-8308 Steven Cheng	Photographic Supplies	Eastman Kodak co. 343 State St. Rochester, NY 14650 T: 716-724-4000 F: 716-724-0663 Willy Shih / Robert Smith
Liebert Chengdu 553 Kinjiang Hotel 36 Renmin S. Rd., Sec. 2, Chengdu 610012 T: 627-8660 F: 625-9462 Xue Yanqun	Air Conditioning Refrigeration	Liebert Corp. 1050 Dearborn Dr. Columbus, OH 43229 T: 614-888-0246 F: 614-841-6022 Dennis Webb / Joe Filippi
Lucent technologies (China) Ltd. 12/F, New Times Plaza 42 Wen Wu Rd., Chengdu 610017 T: 661-3366 x 1208 Nikkei Nie	Telecommunications	Lucent Technologies 600 Mountain Ave. Murray Hill, NJ 07974 T: 908-582-8500 F: 908-508-2576 Tom Uhlman / Carl Hsu
McDonnell Douglas c/o Chengdu Aircraft Company P. O. Box 800, Chengdu 610092 T: 740-4971 F: 741-5636 Rick Sampson	Aviation	McDonnell Douglas Corp. P. O. Box 516 St. Louis, MO 63166 T: 314-234-7015 F: 314-234-3826 Rita Luddon
Meadow Gold No. 9, Industry District Hi-Tech Devel. Zone, Chengdu T: 518-6637 F: 518-6073 Huang Jiayi	Food Products	Borden, Inc. 180 E. Broad St. Columbus, OH 43215 T: 614-225-7480 F: 614-225-7602 J. R. Anderson
Medtronic China Ltd. 2511 Minshan Hotel Business Bldg. 55 renmin S.Rd., Sec. 2, Chengdu 610021 T: 555-4779 F: 555-2624 Xing Ming	Medical Products	Medtronic Inc. 7000 Central Ave. NE Minneapolis, MN 55432 T: 612-514-4000 F: 612-514-4879 Arthur D. Collins, Jr.

China Office	Product/Service	U.S. Head Office
Mobil Asia Pte. Ltd. 351 Jinjiang Hotel 36 Rrenmin S. Rd., Chengdu 610012 T: 627-4695 F: 663-8805 Victor C. W. Lee	Petroleum Petrochemicals	Mobil Corp. 3225 Gallows Rd. Fairfax, VA 22037 T: 703-846-3000 F: 703-846-4669 Robert Swanson
Motorola (China) Electronics Ltd. 859/61 Jinjiang Hotel 36 Renmin S. Rd., Chengdu 610012 T: 558-2222 x 859 F: 558-1849 Wang Li	Electronics Telecommunications	Motorola Inc. 1303 E. Algonquin Rd. Schaumburg, IL 60196 T: 847-576-5000 F: 847-576-4700 Richard W. Younts
Northrop Grumman Commercial Aircraft Co. Chengdu Aircraft Company, Factory 132 Chengdu 610019 T:741-5816 F: 740-4993 Andy Pao	Aviation	Grumman International Inc. 1111 Stewart Ave. Bethpage, NY 11714 T: 516-575-6801 M. Heaslip
Oracle 9/F, Huanglin dasha 133 Shangdong Dajie, Chengdu 610016 T: 666-2222 F: 666-1893 Li Xiuguo	Software	Oracle Corp. 500 Oracle Parkway Redwood Shores, CA 94065 T: 415-506-7000 F: 415-506-7200 Raymond Lane / David Roux
Parametric Technology Corp. 2303 Minshan Hotel Business Bldg. 55 Renmin S. Rd., Sec. 2, Chengdu 610021 T: 558-3333 x 2303 F: 558-3333 x 2323 Robert Flynn	CAD/CAM Software	Parametric Technology Corp. 128 Technology Dr. Waltham, MA 02154 T: 617-894-7111 L. J. Volpe
Pepsi Co. 8 Hongmen St. Chengdu 610041 T: 555-2540 F: 555-2573 Hu Fengxian	Food & Beverage	PepsiCo International 1 Pepsi Way Somers, NY 10589 T: 914-767-6000 F: 914-767-6553 Keith Hughes
Perkin-Elmer 404 Jincheng Bldg. 1st Sec., Yihuan S. Rd., Chengdu 610021 T: 556-9029/30 F: 556-6912 Wang Tao	Precision Instruments	Perkin-Elmer Corp. 761 Main St. Norwalk, CT 06859 T: 203-762-1000 F: 203-762-6000 Leslie O'Carmody
Philip Morris Asia, Inc. 9/F, Bldg. A, Friendship Plaza 1-37 Shangdong Dajie, Chengdu 610012 T: 671-1731 F: 671-1733 C. F. Cheung	Tobacco Products	Philip Morris Int'l 800 Westchester Ave. Rye Brook, NY 10573 T: 914-335-1120 F: 914-335-1372 Andreas Gembler
Polaroid 501 Waimao Dasha 210 Xiyulong St., Chengdu T: 661-1346 F: 661-1091 He Dexian	Film Products	Polaroid Corp. 549 Technology Square Cambridge, MA 02139 T: 781-386-3284 F: 781-386-9333 Carole Uhrich

China Office	Product/Service	U.S. Head Office
Pratt and Whitney c/o Chengdu Engine Company P.O. Box 613, Chengdu 610067 T: 446-1674 F: 518-1305 Mark Atkenson	Aircraft Engines & Parts	Pratt & Whitney 400 Main St. East Hartford, CT 06108 T: 860-565-4321 James Johnson / A. Anderson
Sun Microsystems China Ltd. Suites F&G, 15/F, New Times Plaza 42 Wen Wu Rd., Chengdu 610017 T: 678-0121 F: 678-0546 Connie ao	Workstation & Server	Sun Microsystems 2550 Garcia Ave. M/S: UMPK01-16 Mountain View, CA 94043 T: 650-960-1300 F: 650-969-9131 Tim Dwyer / Bob MacRitchie
Sybase Chengdu 757 Jinjiang Hotel Sec. 2, Renmin S. Rd., Chengdu 610021 T: 558-2222 x 757 F: 666-7794 Wu Yue	Software	Sybase Inc. 6475 Christie Avenue Emeryville, CA 94608 T: 510-596-3500 F: 510-658-9441 Yvonne Van Leeuwen
Tektronix 411 Tiange Bldg. Sec. 2, Yihuan S. Rd., Chengdu 610041 T: 558-6770 F: 554-4631 Deng Wenyu	Electronic Test Equipment	Tektronix Inc. 26660 S W Parkway Wilsonville, OR 97070 T: 503-627-7111 F: 503-685-4038 Timothy Thorsteinson
Texaco China B.V. 551 Jinjiang Hotel 36 Renmin S. Rd., Sec. 2, Chengdu 610012 T: 518-5500 F: 555-1001 T. H. Hutto, Jr.	Petroleum	Texaco Inc. 2000 Westchester Ave. White Plains, NY 10650 T: 914-253-4000 F: 914-253-7839 S. A. Carlson / James Kinnear
Unocal Corp. 2507 Minshan Hotel Business Bldg. 55 Sec. 2, Renmin S. Rd., Chengdu 610021 T: 558-3333 x 2507 F: 557-3605 Charles Han	Petroleum	Unocal Corp. 1 Sugar Creek Place, 14141 SW Frwy Sugar Land, TX 77478 T: 281-287-5601 F: 281-287-7345 Glen G. Edwards
Watson Industries 2/F, Jincheng Art Palace 61 Renmin E. Rd., Chengdu T: 674-6727 F: 667-4589 Qiao Zhiwei	Office Equipment	Watson Industries 335 Harrison St., PO Box 1028 Jamestown, NY 14702-1028 T: 716-487-1901 F: 716-664-4949 B. Okwumabua
Xerox 13/F Foreign Trade Bldg. 210 Xiyulong St., Chengdu T: 678-4649 F: 662-6711 Zhang Li	Photocopiers	**Xerox Corp.** 800 Long Ridge Rd., PO Box 1600 Stamford, CT 06904 T: 203-968-3000 F: 203-968-4458 Allan E. Dugan
York Chengdu Unit E, 13/F, New Times Plaza 42 Wen Wu Rd., Chengdu 610017 T: 678-9832 F: 678-9834 Song Hongmei	Refrigeration	York International Corp. 631 S. Richland Ave., P. O. Box 1592 York, PA 17405 T: 717-771-7890 F: 717-771-6819 Jeff Cook

China Office	**Product/Service**	**U.S. Head Office**
American Consolidated Service 2001 Tianjin International Bldg. 75 Nanjing Road, Tianjin 300050 T: 2332-1752 F: 2330-3913 General Manager	Freight Forwarding	ACS Ltd. 100 Central Ave., Bldg. 40C S. Kearny, NJ 07032 T: 973-522-3500 F: 973-522-3505 Brigitte Wagner
American President Lines Ltd. 2010 Tianjin International Bldg. 75 Nanjing Road, Tianjin 300050` T: 2332-1752 F: 2330-3913 General Manager	Shipping	APL Limited 1111 Broadway Oakland, CA 94607 T: 510-272-8000 F: 510-272-7941 Keith Mackie
APN Industries, Inc. Rm. 206 Vanshine House 114 Machang Dao, Tianjin 300050 T: 2330-8200 F: 2332-2266 General Manager	Pharmaceuticals	APN Industries, Inc. 251 Park St. Montclair, NJ 07043 T: 973-509-1042 F: 973-509-6958 General Manager
AT&T China Inc. Yibai Road, Canglianzhuang Hebei Dist., Tianjin 300231 T: 2630-8978 F: 2630-6785 General Manager	Telecommunications	AT&T International 295 N. Maple Ave., Rm. I-14 Basking Ridge, NJ 07920 T: 248-262-6646 F: 248-952-5095 Elizabeth Mallek
China Tianjin Otis Elevator Co., Ltd. 443 Jie Fang South Rd. Hexi Dist., Tianjin 300210 T: 2830-7147/49 F: 2830-1256 Huang Xiong	Elevators & Escalators	Otis Elevators Co. 10 Farm Springs Farmington, CT 06032 T: 860-676-6000 F: 860-676-6970 Steve Page
Deloitte Touche Tohmatsu Rm. 807 Tianjin International ldg. 75 Nanjing Road, Tianjin 300050 T: 2332-1671 F: 2332-2840 General Manager	Accounting Consulting	**Deloitte Touche Tohmatsu Int'l** Ten Westport Rd. Wilton, CT 06897 T: 203-761-3000 F: 203-834-2200 Dina A. Elliott
Fourth Shift Asia Headquarters Wan Hai Office Building, No. 1 Section 8, Wei Di Rd., Tianjin 300211 T: 2831-9852 F: 2831-9853 Benjamin Lee	Manufacturing Software	Fourth Shift Corp. 7900 International Dr. Minneapolis, MN 55425 T: 612-851-1500 F: 612-851-1560 D. J. Bowman
Great Lakes Fresh Food & Juice Co., Ltd. Tie Dong Rd., Zhong Huan Xian He Bei Dist., Tianjin 300402 T: 2631-3481 F: 2631-3376 Rod Meachen / Tom Shen	Food Products	
Lincoln Electric Co. 1703, 17/F, Tianjin Int'l Bldg. 75 Nanjing Rd., Tianjin 300050 T: 2330-7407 F: 2330-7417 Bruce Sterling	Electric Motors Welding Machines Power Sources	Lincoln Electric Co., Inc. 22801 St. Clair Ave. Cleveland, OH 44117 T: 216-481-8100 F: 216-486-1751 A Massaro

China Office	Product/Service	U.S. Head Office
Mobil Asia Pacific Pte Ltd. 2102 Tianjin International Bldg. 75 Nanjing Road, Tianjin 300050 T: 2319-1213 F: 2319-1225 General Manager	Petrochemical	Mobil Corp. 3225 Gallows Rd. Fairfax, VA 22037 T: 703-846-3000 F: 703-846-4669 Robert Swanson
Motorala (China) Electronics Ltd. 10, 4th Dajie Tanggu TEDA, Tianjin 300457 T: 2532-5050 F: 2532-5048 C. K. Thong	Telecommunications	Motorola Inc. 1303 E. Algonquin Rd. Schaumburg, IL 60196 T: 847-576-5000 F: 847-576-4700 Richard W. Younts
Nestle Tianjin Ltd. Nanhai Rd., 8th Ave. Tianjin TEDA, Tianjin 300457 T: 2532-6313/15 F: 2532-6314 Trivelli Victor	Food Products	Nestle Inc. 800 N. Brand Blvd. Glendale, CA 91203 T: 818-549-6000 F: 818-543-7897 Guy Dumas
OOCL (HK) Ltd. 2502 Tianjin International Bldg. 75 Nanjing Road, Tianjin 300050 T: 2330-7760 F: 2330-7761 General Manager	Global Transportation	**OOCL (USA) Inc.** 4141 Hacienda Dr. Pleasanton, CA 94588 T: 510-460-3180 F: 510-460-3109 M. K. Wong / Peter Leng
PPG Coatings (Tianjin) Co., Ltd. 192 Huanghai Rd. TEDA, Tianjin 300457 T: 2532-3470 F: 2532-5183 General Manager	Glass Products Automotive Paints Industrial Chemicals Industrial Paints	PPG Industries, Inc. 1 PPG Place Pittsburgh, PA 15272 T: 412-434-3131 F: 412-434-2125 Valentino Buttignol
Smithkline Beecham Cheng Lin Zhuang Ind. Dist. Tianjin T: 2437-1047 F: 2437-5330 Richard Yu	Pharmaceuticals	Smithkline Beecham Pharmaceuticals One Franklin Plaza, PO Box 7929 Philadelphia, PA 19101 T: 215-751-4000 F: 215-751-3233 D. Schuma
Tianjin Tanggu Watts Valve Co., Ltd. 5 Yong Tai Rd. Tanggu Dist., Tianjin 300450 T: 2589-3772 F: 2589-5087 Bob Dexter	Valves	Watts Industries, Inc. 815 Chestnut St. North Andover, MA 01845 T: 978-688-1811 F: 978-794-1848 Kevin Stumm
Tianjin Wix Filter Corp. Ltd. Shi Yan Lou Hou Ce He Dong Dist., Tianjin 300180 T: 2439-0419 F: 2439-4388 Dieter Daniel	Industrial Filters	Wix Corp. 1301 E. Ozark Ave. Gastonia, NC 28052 T: 704-864-6711 F: 704-864-1813 Jan Black
Zen Continental Co., Inc. No. 32 Mu Nan Street He Ping Dist., Tianjin 300050 T: 2332-8665 F: 2332-8664 Tim Zhu	Shipping	**Zen Continental Co., Inc.** 18111A S. Santa Fe Ave., #168 Rancho Dominguez, CA 90221 T: 310-631-5155 F: 310-631-5222 Rachel Liu

China Office	Product/Service	U.S. Head Office
Changzhou Times Fiber Communications Co. Changzhou New & high Tech Develop. Zone Hehai Rd, Changzhou, Jiangsu Province 213000 T: (86-519)-510-6004 F: (86-519)-510-5897 Du Bin	Coaxial Cables	Times Fiber Communications Inc. 358 Hall Avenue Wallingford, CT 06492 T: 203-265-8500 F: 203-265-8749 Gary Williams
Diamond Power Hubei Machine Co., Ltd. 251 Jing Yuan Rd. Jingshan County, Hubei Province T: (86-716)-722-1349 F: (86-716)-722-2924 Fran Liedel	Machinery Sootblowers & Controls Rodding Robots	Diamond Power Specialty Co. P. O. Box 415 Lancaster, OH 43130 T: 614-687-6500 F: 614-687-4304 David Gibbs
Kendall Yantai Medical Products Co., Ltd. 1 Tianchi Rd. Tantai ETDZ, Yantai, Shandong Province T: (86-535)-637-1274 F: (86-535)-637-1681 Li Jian Ming	Medical Disposable Products	Kendall Co. 15 Hamshire St. Mansfield, MA 02048 T: 508-261-8000 F: 508-261-8501 Warren Pezold
Mentholatum (Zhongshan) Pharmaceuticals The Second Industrial Estates Sam Heung, Zhongshan, Guangdong Province T: (86-760)-668-5596 F: (86-760)-668-5433 Shu Wong	Proprietary Medicines Drugs & OTC's	Mentholatum Co., Inc. 1360 Niagara St. Buffalo, NY 14213 T: 716-882-7660 F: 716-677-9528 Cheryl Gondek
Wuhan Larch Wackenhut Security Co. No. 29, Huang Ziao River Rd. Jiangan Dist., Wuhan, Hubei Province T: (86-27)-262-9604 F: (86-27)-262-9564 Hai He Zhang	Security Services & Systems	Wackenhut Int'l Inc . 4200 Wackenhut Rd., #100 Palm Beach Gardens, FL 33410 T: 561-622-5656 F: 561-691-6721 Fernando Carrizosa
Zhuhai Hiwin Boise Cascade Specialty Paper No. 9 Bldg., Nanshan Ind. Area Zhuhai, Guangdong Province 519015 T: (86-756)-335-0611 F: (86-756)-335-0911 Jim Kirby	Paper Products	Boise Cascade Corp. P. O. Box 1414 Portland, OR 97207-1414 T: 503-224-7250 F: 503-790-9457 John Plumberg

***** US-China Trade Associations and Non-Profit Organizations *****

China Chamber of Commerce in USA
2 World Trade Center, #2700
New York, NY 10048
Tel: 212-432-0383
Fax: 212-775-8074

China Institue in America
125 E. 65th Street
New York, NY 10021
Tel: 212-644-8181
Fax: 212-628-3068

Committee of 100
125 E. 65th Street
New York, NY 10021
Tel: 212-249-0016
Fax: 212-249-3068

China Council for Promotion of Int'l Trade
4301 Connecticut Ave. NW, #136
Washington, DC 20008
Tel: 202-244-3244
Fax: 202-244-0478

Hong Kong Trade Development Council
219 E. 46th Street
New York, NY 10017
Tel: 212-838-8688
Fax: 212-838-8941

Nat'l Committee on U.S.-China Relations
71 West 23rd St., #1901
New York, NY 10010
Tel: 212-645-9677
Fax: 212-645-1695

Northwest Regional China Council
P. O. Box 751
Portland, OR 97207
Tel: 503-725-4567
Fax: 503-725-4342

Oregon Economic Development Dept.
Attn: China Trade Officer, Int'l Division
121 S. W. Salmon, #300, Portland, OR 97204
Tel: 503-229-5625
Fax: 503-222-5050

US-China Art Exchange Center
423 W. 118th St., #1E
New York, NY 10027
Tel: 212-280-4648
Fax: 212-662-6346

US-China Business Council
1818 N Street, NW, #500
Washington, DC 20036
Tel: 202-429-0340
Fax: 202-775-2476

US-China Chamber of Commerce
1 World Trade Center, #4635
New York, NY 10048
Tel: 212-912-9100
Fax: 212-912-1006

USA-ROC Economic Council
1726 M St. NW
Washington, DC 20036
Tel: 202-331-8966
Fax: 202-331-8985

Washington State China Relations Council
2601 4th Avenue, #330
Seattle, WA 98121
Tel: 206-441-4419
Fax: 206-443-3828

***** US-China Embassies & Consulate Offices *****

U.S. Embassy & Consulate Offices in China	PRC Embassy & Consulate Offices in U.S.

U.S. Embassy & Consulate Offices in China

American Embassy, Beijing
3 Xiu Shui Bei Jie, Jianguomenwai
Beijing, China 100600
Tel: (86-10)-6532-3831
Fax: (86-10)-6532-6057
Alan Turley

American Consulate General, Chengdu
4 Lingshiguan Lu, Renmin Nan Lu Siduan
Chengdu, China 610041
Tel: (86-28)-558-9642; 558-3992
Fax: (86-28)-558-3520
Rob Tansey

American Consulate General, Guangzhou
China Hotel Office Tower, 12/F
Guangzhou, China 510015
Tel: (86-20)-8188-8911; 8667-4011
Fax: (86-20)-8186-2341; 8666-6409
Robert Strotman

American Consulate General, Hong Kong
26 Garden Road
Hong Kong
Tel: (852-2)-2521-1467
Fax: (852-2)-2845-9800
David Katz

American Consulate General, Shanghai
Shanghai Centre, Suite 631
1376 Nanjing West Road, Shanghai 200040
Tel: (86-21)-6279-7630; 6433-6880
Fax: (86-21)-6279-7639; 6433-4122
Amy Sau Yuen Chang

American Consulate General, Shenyang
52 Shi Si Wei Lu, Heping District
Shenyang, China 110003
Tel: (86-24)-322-1198; 322-0848
Fax: (86-24)-322-2374
Jon Frauenfelder

PRC Embassy & Consulate Offices in U.S.

PRC Embassy, Washington DC
2300 Connecticut Ave., N.W.
Washington, DC 20008
Tel: 202-328-2520; 328-2517
Fax: 202-232-7855

PRC Consulate General, Chicago
100 West Erie Street
Chicago, IL 60606
Tel: 312-803-0115; 803-0097
Fax: 312-803-0114

PRC Consulate General, Houston
3417 Montrose Blvd.
Houston, TX 77006
Tel: 713-524-4064; 524-4311
Fax: 713-524-7656

PRC Consulate General, Los Angeles
443 Shatto Place
Los Angeles, CA 90020
Tel: 213-807-8016; 807-8088
Fax: 213-380-1961; 380-3131

PRC General Consulate, New York
520 12th Avenue
New York, NY 10036
Tel: 212-868-7752; 330-7409
Fax: 212-502-0248

PRC Consulate General, San Francisco
1450 Laguna Street
San Francisco, CA 94115
Tel: 415-563-4857; 563-4858
Fax: 415-563-0494

FREE LISTING!

The new (2000/2001) edition of **"American Business in China" (ABC)** will be published in January, 2000. U.S. firms with representation(s) in China and Hong Kong are eligible to be listed free of charge (up to 3 locations). Please provide us with the following information of your company for accurate listing.

U. S. Head Office

Name of comapny: _____

Address: _____

City: _____ State: _____ Zip Code: _____

Tel #: _____ Fax #: _____

Name of person in charge of China or Asia/Pacific operations: _____

China / Hong Kong Office*

Name of company: _____

Address: _____

_____

Tel #: _____ Fax #: _____

Name of contact person: _____

Nature of business: _____

* Please use additional sheet(s) if you have more than one office in China & Hong Kong.

Please check the following if appropriate:

_____ We are interested in advertsing in **"American Business in China" (ABC)**, please send us a media kit with detailed information.

_____ Please send us a free brochure with order form of **"American Business in China" (ABC)** when the new edition is published.

Please mail or fax this form to:

CARAVEL, INC.
2508 West 225th Place
Torrance, CA 90505 USA

Tel: 310-325-0100
310-325-0331
Fax: 310-325-2583

Speak, Read, and Write Like a Native TODAY! ™

PROFESSIONAL INTERACTIVE CHINESE

▼ Suggested Retail Price: $199.00

◀ **CHINESE LEARNWARE**

Suggested Retail Price: $79.95

The explosive growth of the Pacific Rim has placed China firmly in the center of the global economy. LearnWare offers you comprehensive language learning tools to help you take advantage of rapidly expanding opportunities!

LearnWare's interactive tutorials on CD-ROM actively engage you and simplify the formerly complicated process of learning Mandarin Chinese. Each program incorporates vocabulary, grammar, phonics, and pronunciation, and covers all 1300 basic sounds in Chinese!

Professional Interactive Chinese... is one of the most comprehensive language learning tools I have ever seen.

- Electronic Learning

Professional Interactive Chinese features over 2000 characters and lessons equivalent to 2 years of college-level instruction

Chinese LearnWare features over 1000 characters and lessons equivalent to 1 year of college-level instruction

Other features include:

- **Speech Recognition and Voice Record & Compare**
- **Recorded conversations between native speakers**
- **Voice Animation**
- **Text displayed in traditional or simplified characters, *pinyin* romanization, or *zhuyin* symbols**
- **Exercises and games**
- **Grammar notes**
- **Character Writing**
- **Electronic English to Chinese dictionary**
- **Chinese word processor**

Get WebWare! Additional downloadable lessons available on the World Wide Web

Does business travel take you many different places? Be prepared! Contact your favorite software retailer or catalogue, or call us today for information about all of LearnWare's Asian and European language tutorials.

LEARNWARE ™
A World of Interactive Language Learning ™
A VentureTech Company

228 Krams Avenue Philadelphia, PA 19127
Phone:(215) 509-6100 Fax:(215) 509-6550
www.learnware.net

Phone: (800) 409-8368
E-mail: info@learnware.net

Discover a World of Interactive Language Learning

SPANISH • FRENCH • GERMAN • CHINESE • VIETNAMESE • INDONESIAN • THAI • ASIAN EXPRESS

LW-ABC-1097

CARAVEL, INC.

Worldwide Distribution Offices*

China

Beijing Huimeng Int'l Business Consultants
15 Fuxing Road
Beijing 100038, People's Republic of China
Tel: (86-10)-6852-4501
Fax: (86-10)-6852-4483

Berkeley Marketing Research, Ltd.
2/F, I-Wan Lida Dasha, No. 17A Andelibeijie
Andingmenwai, Beijing 100011, P. R. China
Tel: (86-10)-6424-1538
Fax: (86-10)-6424-1542

Taiwan

China External Trade Development Council
4/F, CETRA Tower, 333 Keelung Road, Sec. 1
Taipei, 110, Taiwan
Tel: (886-2)-2725-5200 ext. 809
Fax: (886-2)-2757-6829

Taiwan Yellow Pages Corp.
2/F, No. 57, Tunhwa S. Rd., Sec. 1
Taipei, Taiwan
Tel: (886-2)-2570-9966; 2577-3069
Fax: (886-2)-2577-8982; 2578-2739

U.S.A.

Baker & Taylor Books
501 South Gladiolus St.
Momence, IL 60954-1799
Tel: 815-472-2444
Fax: 815-472-4141

China Daily Distribution Corp.
One World Trade Center, Suite 3369
New York, NY 10048
Tel: 212-488-9677
Fax: 212-488-9493

Link China Inc.
246 30th St., Suite 101
Oakland, CA 94611
Tel: 510-628-0500
Fax: 510-628-0400

Sino United Publishing Inc.
111 N. Atlantic Blvd., #228
Monterey Park, CA 91754
Tel: 626-293-3386
Fax: 626-293-3385

*Distributor Inquiry Welcome

ORDER FORM ___check for standing order**

Please send _____ copies of **"American Business in China, 1998-1999"** to:

Name of Company: _____

Address: _____

City: _____ State: _____ Zip Code: _____

Attention: _____ Title: _____

****American Business in China (ABC) is published in January of even years
Price: US$93.00 (California residents please add 8.25% sales tax)
S&H charges: US$6.95 per copy (domestic); US$25.00 per copy (overseas)**

___ Payment enclosed   ___ Invoice Me **(Prepayment required for all overseas orders)**

___VISA___M/C__ AmEx Cardholder's Name: _____ Exp. Date: ____

Account No. _____ Signature Required: _____

Mail/Fax to: **Caravel, Inc.** 23545 Crenshaw Blvd., Suite 101E, Torrance, CA 90505 U.S.A.
Tel: 310-325-0100   Fax: 310-325-2583